EQUALITY AND THE FAMILY

RELIGION, MARRIAGE, AND FAMILY

Series Editors

Don S. Browning
John Witte Jr.

EQUALITY AND THE FAMILY

A Fundamental, Practical Theology of
Children, Mothers, and Fathers
in Modern Societies

Don S. Browning

WILLIAM B. EERDMANS PUBLISHING COMPANY
GRAND RAPIDS, MICHIGAN / CAMBRIDGE, U.K.

Published 2007 by
Wm. B. Eerdmans Publishing Co.
2140 Oak Industrial Drive N.E., Grand Rapids, Michigan 49505 /
P.O. Box 163, Cambridge CB3 9PU U.K.

Printed in the United States of America

12 11 10 09 08 07   7 6 5 4 3 2 1

Library of Congress Cataloging-in-Publication Data

Browning, Don S.
Equality and the family: a fundamental, practical theology of children, mothers,
and fathers in modern societies / Don S. Browning.
p.   cm.
ISBN 978-0-8028-0756-4 (pbk.: alk. paper)
1. Theology, Practical. 2. Theology, Practical — Methodology.
3. Family — Religious aspects — Christianity.
4. Equality — Religious aspects — Christianity. I. Title.

BV3.B75 2007
261.8′3585 — dc22

2006029020

www.eerdmans.com

Contents

Preface   vii

I. Practical Theology as a Critical Research Project

1. Toward a Fundamental and Strategic Practical Theology (1991)   3

2. Empirical Considerations in Religious Praxis
   and Reflection (2005)   31

II. Contexts, Descriptions, and Directions: Searching for an Emphatic Center

3. The Family Debate: A Middle Way (1993)   51

4. Is the Family a Conservative Issue? (1994)   61

5. Better Family Values (1995)   75

6. Children, Mothers, and Fathers in the
   Postmodern Family (1995)   84

III. Critical Foundations: An Ecumenical Search

7. Practical Theology and the American Family Debate (1997)   103

8. Altruism, Civic Virtue, and Religion (1995)   131

9. Narrative, Ethics, and Biology in Christian
   Family Theory (1996)   154

10. The Dialectic of Archaeology and Teleology
    in Christian Marriage Symbolism (2001)   194

11. Can Marriage Be Defined? (2002)   207

Part IV: Spheres, Strategies, and Praxis

12. The Task of Religious Institutions in
    Strengthening Families (1999)   223

13. Modernization: Critical Familism and the
    Reconstruction of Marriage (2003)   244

14. Egos without Selves: A Critique of the Family Theory
    of the Chicago School of Economics (1994)   263

15. Families and the Sixty-Hour Workweek: What It Means
    for Church, Society, and Persons (2002)   283

16. The Language of Health versus the Language
    of Religion: Competing Models of Marriage
    in the Twenty-First Century (2002)   297

17. Critical Familism, Civil Society, and the Law (2004) 312

18. The Meaning of the Family in the Universal Declaration
    of Human Rights (2004)   327

19. Adoption and the Moral Significance of
    Kin Altruism (2005)   347

20. Domestic Violence and the Ethic of Equal Regard (2005) 374

V. A Retrospective: Method in Practical Theology and the Family

21. The Relation of Practical Theology to
    Theological Ethics (2005)   391

    Permissions and Acknowledgments   409

    Index   412

Preface

The purpose of this book is to illustrate new developments in the field of practical theology and the subject of its appropriate methods. I hope to do this by discussing a wide range of issues dealing with changes occurring in modern families, especially the issue of equality within and between families. More specifically, I want to show how practical theology can be envisioned as a practical research program, and I use the family as an example of how this works. I hope to demonstrate how my method of doing practical theology, which I call "fundamental practical theology," led to my position on families — what I call "critical familism." Critical familism is pro-family and pro-marriage but in ways that will promote justice and equality within and between families and create a society that will support what I call the equal-regard family.

Over the last fifteen years, there has been considerable international ferment over new ways to think about theology as a practical discipline. I have tried to contribute to these developments. In 1991, the International Academy of Practical Theology was founded. In 1995, the *International Journal of Practical Theology* was established. New national associations of practical theology have been launched in a significant number of countries throughout the world. Closer ties between practical theology and theological ethics have been developed, and the lines that once separated practical theology from systematic theology have become increasingly blurred and flexible.

Practical theology, once considered theological reflection on the acts of the ordained minister or the inner life of the confessing church, now goes beyond these paradigms. It presently also includes theological reflection on the church's witness and action in the public world. The new vitality of practical theology has been stimulated by developments in practical philosophy and the new prestige of the category of practical reason or *phronēsis* in the philosophies of Hans-Georg Gadamer, Paul Ricoeur, Jürgen Habermas, Ludwig Wittgenstein, and American pragmatism. All of these philosophical movements have influenced theology and helped us see how it is a distinctively practical discipline.

At the same time that I was attempting to contribute to the new practical theology, I was, between 1991 and 2003, directing the Religion, Culture, and Family Project at the Divinity School of the University of Chicago, funded by a series of generous grants from the Division of Religion of the Lilly Endowment, Inc. This project produced over twenty published books and a nationally shown PBS documentary titled "Marriage — Just a Piece of Paper?"

From the beginning, I envisioned the Religion, Culture, and Family Project as a practical theological research program. Many people believe that thinking practically from a Christian theological perspective means trying to address momentary crises or challenges that require immediate responses. That is true: for Christians to act faithfully, they often have to think quickly and more or less spontaneously about how to respond to the needs at hand. But there is another task for practical theology. This is the job of addressing truly complex problems that require a great deal of thought and analysis — thought and analysis that give rise to new long-term trajectories of witness and action. This is what I mean by *practical theology as a research program.* The Religion, Culture, and Family Project was a practical theological research program in this sense. It brought biblical studies, theological ethics, sociology, psychology, biology, law, and economics into a practical theological dialogue. It used these perspectives both to describe the situation of contemporary families, marriage, and children and to think constructively about how to support them and help them thrive in the context of the modern and postmodern social and cultural environments impinging upon them.

Practical theology as a research program can be applied to families, as we did in the Religion, Culture, and Family Project. It also can be applied to any number of other issues facing both the inner life of churches and their witness in the public world. Hence, the essays in this book are designed to illustrate practical theology's value for the American and world debate over the future of the family, but they are also designed to be suggestive about how this model of theological research can be applied to other issues.

The essays have been printed for the most part in the form in which they were first published or written. I have provided a brief introduction to each essay to help the reader understand the original context of the piece. There will be some repetition of core arguments. The names of Aristotle, Thomas Aquinas, Luther, and Louis Janssens will appear more than once, but in different contexts, as I try to employ my basic ideas for new issues and slightly different audiences. The essays in Part I introduce my practical theology method and outline its purpose and movements. The essays in Part II locate the social, political, and ecclesial contexts of the family debate when the project began in the early 1990s. Many aspects of this context and debate are still with us. Part III develops the central concepts of what I have called "critical familism" — my basic practical theology for "equal-regard" marriages and families. The essays in Part IV move into a variety of more concrete issues pertaining to families and marriage, such as adoption, human rights, medicine, economics, and law, as these subjects pertain to families. The final chapter in Part V summarizes the practical theological method and illustrates it with reference to the summary book of the first phase of the Religion, Culture, and Family Project — *From Culture Wars to Common Ground: Religion and the American Family Debate* (1997, 2000). That method pretty much holds for all my writings on the family.

Equality and the Family will be published in close association with a second volume that will consist of a number of critical essays examining the Religion, Culture, and Family Project as well as my practical theological method as it worked to address issues on family, marriage, and children.[1] Of course, I am delighted to have the critical attention of such a distinguished group of scholars analyzing and critiquing the essays in this book as well as my other books and writings on the family. But the purpose of these two books is not to honor me but to outline, illustrate, and evaluate a new approach to doing theology as practical theological research. It is hoped that this project will strengthen practical theological research in graduate schools, seminaries, and the churches. Strengthening the work of these institutions is the aim of these two books. If there is some value in the Religion, Culture, and Family Project and the methods used to conceive and execute it, it is hoped that these two books may help make that clearer to a new generation of practical theologians.

That is the hope, as I understand it, of Craig Dykstra, vice president of the Lilly Endowment and head of its Division of Religion. I want to ex-

---

1. Christian Green and John Witte, *The Equal-Regard Family and Its Friendly Critics* (Grand Rapids: Eerdmans, forthcoming).

press my appreciation for his interest in the Religion, Culture, and Family Project, his concern about the future of practical theology, and his willingness to support financially the preparation of these two volumes.

I also want to express my very deep appreciation to my friend and colleague John Witte, Jonas Robitscher Professor of Law and Ethics and director of the Law and Religion Program in the School of Law of Emory University. It was Professor Witte who conceived the idea of these two volumes and approached the Lilly Endowment for the grant that made them possible. John Witte and I have worked closely together for almost ten years, starting with the contribution of his outstanding book *From Sacrament to Contract: Marriage, Religion, and Law in the Western Tradition* (1997) to the first Religion, Culture, and Family Project book series. This association continued when I joined him at Emory to assist with his two projects on Sex, Marriage, and Family in the Religions of the Book (2001-2002) and The Child in Law, Religion, and Society (2003), both funded by The Pew Charitable Trust. One of the great blessings of my life has been to work with John Witte and to come to count him as a colleague and good friend. And I want to thank Christian Green, who, as a legal intern in the Law and Religion Program at Emory and a former assistant in the Religion, Culture, and Family Project while finishing her Ph.D. at Chicago, also helped John Witte conceive the idea of these two books. I also want to give special thanks to Amy Wheeler and Anita Mann for handling a variety of logistic and financial issues supporting this volume and to April Bogle, Elizah Ellison, and Janice Wiggins, who also contribute to any project going forward with the support of the Center for Law and Religion, including this one.

I also want to thank Kevin Jung, who worked with great skill and dedication to scan and format these essays for publication, also giving me wise advice about their content as we went along. Before Kevin, I have worked with and must thank the group of outstanding graduate students at the Divinity School of the University of Chicago who helped with the Religion, Culture, and Family Project and indirectly and directly discussed some of the ideas in these essays. This group includes David Clairmont, Christian Green, Melanie O'Hara, Kelly Brotzman, John Wall, and Ian Evison. Most recently, Sarah Schuurman skillfully helped finalize the volume for publication and prepared the index. Of course, I must also thank my wife, Carol Browning, who has been a helping hand throughout all my projects and was certainly a part of this one as well. I would have done little in my life had she not been at my side.

Some readers may search these essays to see how they address the two hot-button issues of our day — abortion and same-sex marriage. These essays, however, are in keeping with the Religion, Culture, and Family Project, which throughout its twelve years of existence did not take an official stand on either of these two issues. Instead, we addressed a large number of forgotten, if not suppressed, issues such as the state of children, the feminization of family and children, work and family issues, fatherhood issues, law and family issues, economic issues pertaining to families, health issues, and others. In short, we tried to expand the imagination of the present debates. I recently have addressed the issue of same-sex marriage in other contexts, but these essays do not directly deal with either abortion or same-sex marriage. They primarily address the question of theological method and try to illustrate this with a wide range of other practical issues pertaining to families and marriage.

PART I

Practical Theology as a Critical Research Project

Toward a Fundamental and Strategic Practical Theology (1991)

Every book I have written has been preceded by an Ur-article out of which the book was later developed. This essay, published in 1991 but written at least two years earlier, was that Ur-article for the book *A Fundamental Practical Theology*. For those of you who have not read *A Fundamental Practical Theology* and would prefer not to plow through that rather long and complicated book, simply read this much shorter essay. Most of the basic ideas of the book are contained within it.

The article was written for a book co-edited by Barbara Wheeler and the distinguished Protestant theologian Edward Farley and titled *Shifting Boundaries: Contextual Approaches to the Structure of Theological Education.** This book pointed to the many ways in which the boundaries that once separated systematic theology, historical theology, theological ethics, and practical theology were shifting if not breaking down. As a result, these disciplines were becoming more alike and more a part of a single theological fabric.

My essay advanced an interpretation of what was happening. I introduced Gadamer's hermeneutic circle to explain these developments, making a point that was often overlooked: Gadamer envisioned his circle as a practical circle that began with concrete questions and brought them to the historical classics that form our thought in ways we hardly even understand. If we do this process carefully, we get answers from these classics — indeed, practical answers that have implications for concrete action.

---

*Barbara Wheeler and Edward Farley, eds., *Shifting Boundaries: Contextual Approaches to the Structure of Theological Education* (Louisville, Ky.: Westminster John Knox, 1991), pp. 295-328.

In this article, I turned this hermeneutical circle into a full-blown theological method that saw all fresh theological reflection (1) beginning with the description of concrete questions, (2) moving backward to the interpretive concerns of historical theology, (3) moving to systematic theology as ordered reflection on this interpretive process, and (4) then finally moving forward to strategic practical theological reflection about ways to proceed with concrete and faithful action in the future. In this view of theology, systematic theology no longer is at the foundation of theology as its first step; it is located in the middle of a more broadly practical reflective circle.

This article also introduced my multidimensional view of hermeneutic or interpretive reason, or what I more often call practical reason. I claim that all attempts to interpret anything are also exercises in practical reason. Practical reason is thick and always has narrative, obligational, premoral, contextual, and praxis (or rule-role) dimensions. Of course, presented in such brief fashion in this introduction, these terms must come across to the reader as conceptual sledgehammers. I hope, however, that there will be ample opportunity to learn their meaning and how they work in the chapters that follow in this volume. More specifically, they will help convey how the Religion, Culture, and Family Project and the essays in this book present a practical theological research program guided by a fundamental practical theology.

R ecent philosophical investigations have taught us much about the practical nature of human knowledge. The hermeneutical philosophy of Gadamer and Ricoeur, the critical theory of Habermas, the ordinary language philosophy of Wittgenstein, Peters, and Winch, the pragmatism of Peirce, James, and Dewey, the neopragmatism of Bernstein and Rorty, and the philosophy of science of Kuhn all in different ways argue for the priority of practical interests in the formation of our cognitive and moral worlds.[1] Historical reason and practical reason, under the impact of

---

1. The list of books pointing toward this turn to practical philosophy is extensive. Representative titles include Hans-Georg Gadamer, *Truth and Method* (New York: Crossroad, 1982); Paul Ricoeur, *Freud and Philosophy* (New Haven: Yale University Press, 1970); Jürgen Habermas, *Knowledge and Human Interests* (Boston: Beacon, 1971); R. S. Peters, *The Concept of Motivation* (London: Routledge and Kegan Paul, 1958); Peter Winch, *The Idea of a Social Science and Its Relation to Philosophy* (London: Routledge and Kegan Paul, 1958); Richard J. Bernstein,

Heidegger and Gadamer, are now seen by many as intimately related, if not identical. If these views are correct, the way we view the past is largely shaped by our present concerns, as indeed the way we deal with the present involves a reconstruction of the past.

These intellectual currents are influencing theological education and the way we envision the structure and movement of theology. This is especially true in the writings on theological education that have come from Edward Farley. The concern with the historicity of knowledge and the importance of the interpretation of situations for the integrity of theological education has been quite prominent in his writings.[2] The heightened prominence of practical knowledge can also be seen in the proposals of Joseph Hough and John Cobb to make "practical theological thinking" and "practical theology" the center of their reform of theological education.[3]

In addition to this appreciation for the practical in these systematic attempts to reformulate theological education, there is additional scattered evidence of the rebirth of the practical in theological education. New efforts to redefine practical theology can be found in Germany, Holland, England, Canada, and Latin America, as well as the United States.[4] These more recent formulations greatly enlarge the province of practical theology. Rather than envision practical theology as primarily theological reflection on the tasks of the ordained minister or the leadership of the church, as was the view of Schleiermacher,[5] these newer trends define

---

Praxis and Action (Philadelphia: University of Pennsylvania Press, 1971), and *Beyond Objectivism and Relativism: Science, Hermeneutics, and Praxis* (Philadelphia: University of Pennsylvania Press, 1983); Richard Rorty, *Philosophy and the Mirror of Nature* (Princeton, N.J.: Princeton University Press, 1979); and Thomas Kuhn, *The Structure of Scientific Revolutions* (Chicago: University of Chicago Press, 1970).

2. Edward Farley, *Theologia: The Fragmentation and Unity of Theological Education* (Philadelphia: Fortress, 1983), and *The Fragility of Knowledge: Theological Education in the Church and the University* (Philadelphia: Fortress, 1988).

3. Joseph C. Hough Jr. and John B. Cobb Jr., *Christian Identity and Theological Education* (Chico, Calif.: Scholars, 1985), pp. 81-94.

4. The following are examples from the various countries. Germany: Dietrich Rossier, *Grundriss der Praktischen Theologie* (Berlin: Walter de Gruyter, 1986); N. Mette, *Theories der Praxis* (Dusseldorf: Patmos Verlag, 1978). Holland: J. A. van der Ven, "Practical Theology: From Applied to Empirical Theology," *Journal of Empirical Theology* 1, no. 1 (1988): 7-28; J. Firet, *Dynamics in Pastoring* (Grand Rapids: Eerdmans, 1987). England: Paul Ballard, ed., *Foundations of Pastoral Studies and Practical Theology* (Cardiff: Faculty of Theology, 1986). Canada: M. Viau, *Introduction auxitudes pastorales* (Montreal: Editions Paulines, 1987). Uruguay: Juan Luis Segundo, *The Liberation of Theology* (New York: Orbis, 1976).

5. Friedrich Schleiermacher, *Brief Outline on the Study of Theology* (Richmond: John Knox, 1970), p. 92.

practical theology as critical theological reflection on the church's ministry to the world.[6] In the United States, two volumes of essays[7] as well as a number of books dealing explicitly with the reconceptualization of practical theology, by Browning, Fowler, Gerkin, Groome, Schreiter, Winquist, Poling and Miller, and McCann and Strain, all point to the breadth and vigor of this renewed interest in practical theology.[8]

In spite of this new interest in the practical in recent reconceptualizations of theological education and in practical theology, it is my conviction that the radical implications of the turn to "practical philosophy" have still not been comprehended fully in theological education circles. It seems not to be understood that, if this philosophical turn is taken seriously, all humanistic studies, including theological studies, are practical and historical through and through. In this view, all theology becomes practical theology; historical theology, systematic theology, and what I will call "strategic" practical theology all become moments within a more inclusive fundamental practical theology. Furthermore, because much of the turn to practical philosophy is presently characterized by an emphasis on dialogue and conversation, I will define fundamental practical theology as critical reflection on the church's dialogue with Christian sources and other communities with the aim of guiding its action toward social and individual transformation.

The Rebirth of Practical Philosophy

I use the phrase "practical philosophy" to refer to a loosely associated group of philosophical positions that emphasize the importance of

6. An excellent statement of this approach can be found in the early article by Alasdair Campbell, "Is Practical Theology Possible?" *Scottish Journal of Theology* 5, no. 25 (1972): 217-27.

7. The two volumes of essays are Don S. Browning, ed., *Practical Theology — The Emerging Field in Theology, Church and World* (San Francisco: Harper and Row, 1983), and Lewis S. Mudge and James N. Poling, eds., *Formation and Rejection: The Promise of Practical Theology* (Philadelphia: Fortress, 1987).

8. The book-length studies are Don S. Browning, *Religious Ethics and Pastoral Care* (Philadelphia: Fortress, 1983); James Fowler, *Faith Development and Pastoral Care* (Philadelphia: Fortress, 1987); Charles Gerkin, *Widening the Horizons* (Philadelphia: Westminster, 1986); Thomas Groome, *Christian Religious Education* (San Francisco: Harper and Row, 1980); Robert Schreiter, *Constructing Local Theologies* (Maryknoll, N.Y.: Orbis, 1985); Charles Winquist, *Practical Hermeneutics* (Chico, Calif.: Scholars, 1980); James Poling and Donald Miller, *Foundations for a Practical Theology of Ministry* (Nashville: Abingdon, 1985); and Dennis McCann and Charles Strain, *Polity and Praxis* (New York: Winston, 1986).

phronēsis (practical wisdom) in contrast to the modern fascination with *theoria* (theoretical knowledge and thinking) or *techne* (technical knowledge and thinking). Since the Enlightenment, the modern experiment increasingly has been dedicated to the improvement of human life through the increase of objective scientific knowledge that is then applied to the technical solution of human problems. The modern university has built itself on the idea of increasing our cognitive grasp of the universe. Issues pertaining to the goals of human action are generally reduced to the technical solution of perceived problems. The goals of action increasingly are held to be self-evident, are thought to be a matter of individual choice, or are taken over uncritically from the surrounding culture. The rebirth of practical philosophy is designed to question the dominance of theoretical and technical reason, to secure in the university a stronger role for practical reason, and to demonstrate that critical reflection about the goals of human action is both possible and necessary, and that, as a matter of fact, practical reason does indeed function in much wider areas of human life than we realize — even, in fact, in the social and natural sciences. Furthermore, the rise of the practical philosophies has brought into closer relation historical thinking, hermeneutics, and practical reason or ethics. These features of the practical philosophies can best be illustrated by examining certain aspects of the thought of Hans-Georg Gadamer. Many of Gadamer's interpreters have overlooked the strong relation he believes to exist between understanding and what Aristotle called practical wisdom *(phronēsis)*. Gadamer writes, "If we relate Aristotle's description of the ethical phenomenon and especially of the virtue of moral knowledge to our own investigation, we find that Aristotle's analysis is in fact a kind of model of the problems of hermeneutics."[9] Gadamer makes this point in discussing the role of application in both his view of understanding and Aristotle's concept of *phronēsis*. The hermeneutic process aimed at the understanding of a classic text is, for Gadamer, like a moral conversation, when "moral" is understood in the broadest sense. The hermeneutical conversation is like Aristotle's concept of practical wisdom, because neither applies abstract universals to concrete situations. In both hermeneutical conversation and moral judgment, concern with application is there from the beginning.

Hence, understanding or interpretation, whether in law, history, or theology, has for Gadamer from the outset a broadly moral concern with application. As Gadamer writes, "Application is neither a subsequent nor a merely occasional part of the phenomenon of understanding, but co-

---

9. Gadamer, *Truth and Method*, p. 289.

determines it as a whole from the beginning."[10] Understanding is a kind of moral conversation with a text or historic witness shaped throughout by practical concerns about application that emerge from our current situation.

Therefore, more than we sometimes have acknowledged, hermeneutics is a broadly moral conversation with a tradition's classic religio-cultural monuments in which concern with practical application shapes from the beginning the questions we bring to these monuments. When seen from this perspective, understanding and *phronēsis* as practical wisdom interpenetrate and overlap. Richard Bernstein astutely makes this observation when he writes that it is a central thesis of Gadamer's *Truth and Method* that understanding, interpretation, and application are not distinct but intimately related. Bernstein writes:

> They are internally related; every act of understanding involves interpretation, and all interpretation involves application. It is Aristotle's analysis of *phronēsis* that, according to Gadamer, enables us to understand the distinctive way in which application is an essential moment of the hermeneutical experience.[11]

Rather than application to practice being an act that follows understanding, concern with practice, in subtle ways we often overlook, guides the hermeneutic process from the beginning. Gadamer's hermeneutic theory clearly breaks down the theory-to-practice (text-to-application) model of humanistic learning. By analogy, it undercuts this model in theological studies as well. The model it implies is more nearly a radical practice-theory-practice model of understanding that gives the entire theological enterprise a thoroughly practical cast.

The practical nature of the hermeneutical process is even more interesting and complicated when considered from the perspective of Gadamer's theory of "effective history." Gadamer develops the idea that the events of the past shape present historical consciousness. As Gadamer writes, there is a "fusion of the whole of the past with the present."[12] This suggests that when we interpret the classic religious texts of the past, we do not confront them as totally separate and alien entities, even if we consider ourselves unbelievers. Rather, these texts are already part of the believer and unbeliever before they begin their interpretation. Through our cul-

10. Gadamer, *Truth and Method,* p. 289.
11. Bernstein, *Beyond Objectivism and Relativism,* p. 38.
12. Gadamer, *Truth and Method,* p. 273.

tural heritage, these monuments of culture shape the fore-concepts and prejudices that make up the practical questions that we bring to our efforts to interpret the monuments themselves. Finally, the understanding process is depicted by Gadamer as a fusion of horizons between the practical questions and fore-concepts that we bring to our classic texts and the meaning and horizon of these texts and the questions they put to us.[13]

Gadamerian hermeneutic theory has profound implications for the reconceptualization of the full range of university studies. Not only does it have implications for the re-envisionment of the purposes of philosophy, the social sciences, and theology, but Richard Bernstein and Richard Rorty, with different degrees of debt to Gadamer, have carried hermeneutic theory into the philosophy of the natural sciences.[14] Earlier, Thomas Kuhn's own variety of hermeneutic theory helped first alert us to the tradition-laden and historically situated nature of the natural sciences.[15] These contemporary movements all have undercut foundationalist preoccupations with objectivity and have helped us understand how all the cultural sciences *(Geisteswissenschaften),* and perhaps the natural sciences *(Naturwissenschaften)* as well, can best be understood as dialectical movements from theory-laden practice to theory and back to a new theory-laden practice.

A Preliminary Sketch of the Structure of Theological Studies

So far, I have not argued that Gadamer's hermeneutical theory is a correct model for the humanities. Nor have I argued that his view of hermeneutics is more sound than the subjective and idealistic models of hermeneutics of Schleiermacher and Dilthey. My goal has been to present an interpretation of Gadamer that emphasizes a point that is often lost, namely, that there is an intimate relation in his thought between the hermeneutical process and practical wisdom, or *phronēsis.* Hence my argument is addressed to those already attracted by the conversational model of hermeneutics. Guided by Gadamer's view of the practical nature of understanding and the hermeneutic task, I would like to propose a theory of the structure of theological studies.

I recommend that we conceive of theology as primarily fundamental

---

13. Gadamer, *Truth and Method,* pp. 273-74, 337-41.

14. Bernstein, *Beyond Objectivism and Relativism,* pp. 173-74; Rorty, *Philosophy and the Mirror of Nature,* pp. 192-209.

15. Kuhn, *The Structure of Scientific Revolutions,* pp. 41, 53.

practical theology that contains within it four submovements: descriptive theology, historical theology, systematic theology, and what I call strategic practical theology. This view differs from several well-known proposals for the organization of theology. For instance, it differs somewhat from Schleiermacher's organization of theology into philosophical theology, historical theology, and practical theology.[16] Although Schleiermacher saw practical theology as the teleological goal and "crown" of theology, his view of theology still had a theory-to-practice structure; he understood theology as a movement from philosophical and historical theology to application in practical theology.[17] It is true that this structure is somewhat mitigated by the fact that Schleiermacher understood the whole of theology as a "positive" science in contrast to a "pure" or theoretical science. By positive science, Schleiermacher meant "an assemblage of scientific elements which belong together not because they form a constituent part of the organization of the sciences, as though by some necessity arising out of the notion of science itself, but only insofar as they are requisite for carrying out a practical task."[18] Such a view of theology clearly emphasizes the practical, conditioned, and historically located nature of all theology, and goes far toward making all of theology a basically practical task. Nonetheless, Schleiermacher saw theology as moving from historical knowledge to practical application and, in addition, had little idea about how the practices of the contemporary church play back onto the way we bring our questions to the historical sources.

My proposal also can be distinguished from other current understandings of the structure of theology. Paul Tillich divided theology into historical theology, systematic theology, and practical theology.[19] In the end, this too was a theory-to-practice model, even though Tillich granted that practical theology has a role in formulating the questions that systematic theology answers.[20] Regardless of this minor admission, the weight of his perspective clearly emphasized the theory-practice dichotomy. In his systematic theology, he wrote: "It is the technical point of view that distinguishes practical from theoretical theology. As occurs in every cognitive approach to reality, a bifurcation between pure and applied

16. Schleiermacher, *Brief Outline*, pp. 25-27; John Burkhart, "Schleiermacher's Vision for Theology," in *Practical Theology*, ed. Browning, pp. 42-60.

17. Schleiermacher, *Brief Outline*, pp. 91-126.

18. Schleiermacher, *Brief Outline*, p. 19.

19. Paul Tillich, *Systematic Theology*, vol. 1 (Chicago: University of Chicago Press, 1951), p. 29.

20. Tillich, *Systematic Theology*, vol. 1, p. 33.

knowledge takes place in theology."[21] This statement is softened somewhat by the fact that Tillich saw the entire theological task as an existential enterprise, but even here "meaning" rather than the reconstruction of
practice was the central thrust of his existential view of theology.

Both Schubert Ogden and David Tracy give heightened visibility to
practical theology in their respective proposals for the organization of theology. Ogden indicates in a number of ways that he believes that practical
theology is the application to practice of the truth of norms discovered by
historical and systematic theology. He proposes a division of theology into
historical, systematic, and practical. He gives a strongly cognitive definition of theology proper (systematic theology) as the task of "understanding the meaning of the Christian witness and assessing its truth." And he
believes that theology as critical reflection on the truth of the Christian
faith should be distinguished from what he calls "witness."[22]

A Revised Correlational Fundamental Practical Theology

My proposal takes its point of departure from the revisionist view of theology found in the work of David Tracy. But whereas Tracy divides theology
into fundamental theology, systematic theology, and practical theology, I
reverse his pattern by proposing a revised correlational fundamental practical theology that has within it the subspecialties of descriptive theology,
historical theology, systematic theology, and strategic practical theology.

The strength of Tracy's proposal is that it is a revised or critical correlational approach to theology. Its weakness is that his vision of fundamental theology is concerned primarily with the conditions for cognitive
and metaphysical verification. The principal criteria for the verification
of the truth of fundamental theological claims are thought by Tracy to be
"Transcendental."[23] Although even in his fundamental theology Tracy

---

21. Tillich, *Systematic Theology,* vol. 1, p. 33.

22. For discussions of Ogden's view of the organization of theology, see his *On Theology*
(San Francisco: Harper and Row, 1986), pp. 7-16, and "The Concept of a Theology of Liberation: Must a Christian Theology Today Be So Conceived?" in *The Challenge of Liberation Theology: A First World Response,* ed. Brian Mahan and Dale Richesin (Maryknoll, N.Y.: Orbis, 1981).
To be fair to Ogden, he does say that theology as a whole should be conceived as practical
"in a broad sense." But if this is so, Ogden should come up with a different flow to the
structure of theology and also come to understand the importance of questions coming
from practice as animating the theological task.

23. David Tracy, *Blessed Rage for Order: The New Pluralism for Theology* (New York: Seabury, 1975), pp. 52-56.

builds significantly on the hermeneutical theory of Gadamer and Ricoeur, he seems not to acknowledge that it is a fundamental practical theology that philosophical hermeneutics suggests rather than a fundamental theology concerned primarily with questions of cognitive and transcendental verification.[24]

The strength of Tracy's view of theology is, however, easily applicable to a fundamental practical theology. But because of Tracy's revisionist correlational commitments, it would be a critical correlational fundamental practical theology. Fundamental theology, according to Tracy, determines the conditions for the possibility of the theological enterprise. If the conditions are strongly influenced by the close association between hermeneutics and *phronēsis*, as I outlined above, then fundamental theology determines the conditions for the possibility of a theology that would be seen first of all as an enterprise that deals with the normative and critical grounds of our religious praxis. Questions of the truth of Christian belief and conviction would be addressed as issues that are embedded in issues pertaining to practice.

Tracy's revised correlational theology is a critical correlational program. The meaning of this can be stated with reference to his understanding of Tillich's correlational approach to theology. Tillich believed that theology is a correlation of existential questions that emerge from cultural experience with answers from the Christian message.[25] Tracy's revised or critical correlational method goes beyond Tillich in envisioning theology as a mutually critical dialogue between the Christian message and contemporary cultural experience. Christian theology becomes a critical dialogue between the questions and answers of the Christian faith and the questions and answers of cultural experience. In fact, according to Tracy, the Christian theologian is obliged to have this critical conversation in principle with "all other 'answers.'"[26]

When Tracy applies the revised correlational model to practical theology, the following definition emerges: "Practical theology is the mutually critical correlation of the interpreted theory and praxis of the Christian faith with the interpreted theory and praxis of the contemporary situation."[27] I propose that this excellent definition of practical theology be extended to become the definition of a fundamental practical theol-

24. Tracy, *Blessed Rage for Order*, pp. 49-52.
25. Tillich, *Systematic Theology*, p. 36.
26. Tracy, *Blessed Rage for Order*, p. 46.
27. David Tracy, "The Foundations of Practical Theology," in *Practical Theology*, ed. Browning, p. 76.

ogy. Furthermore, this fundamental practical theology should be the most inclusive definition of theology, making descriptive, historical, systematic, and strategic practical theology submovements within the larger framework.

This view insists that the description of situated and theory-laden religious and cultural practices is the first movement of both theology and theological education. That is why I suggest that we call this first movement descriptive theology. Questions of the following kind guide this movement of theological reflection: What, within a particular arena of practice, are we actually doing? What reasons, ideals, and symbols do we use to interpret what we are doing? What do we consider to be the sources of authority and legitimation for what we do? The description of these practices engenders questions about what we really should be doing and about the accuracy and consistency of our use of our preferred sources of authority and legitimation. For those who claim to be Christians, this process inevitably leads to a fresh confrontation with the normative texts and monuments of the Christian faith — the source of the norms of practice. Historical theology becomes the heart of the hermeneutical process, but it is now understood as a matter of putting the questions emerging from theory-laden practice to the central texts and monuments of the Christian faith.

Historical theology, then, is the second movement within theology and theological education. The question that guides historical theology is, What do the normative texts that are already a part of our effective history *really* imply for our praxis when they are confronted as carefully and honestly as possible?[28] This is the place where the traditional disciplines of biblical studies, church history, and the history of Christian thought are to be located. But in this scheme, these disciplines and all of their technical literary-historical, textual, and social-scientific explanatory interests would be understood as basically practical hermeneutical enterprises. Their technical, explanatory, and distancing maneuvers would be temporary procedures designed to gain clarity within a larger hermeneutic effort to achieve understanding about our praxis and the theory behind it.[29]

The third movement is the turn to systematic theology. Systematic theology, when seen from the perspective of Gadamer's hermeneutics, is

---

28. Gadamer, *Truth and Method*, p. 273.

29. Tracy, *Blessed Rage for Order*, pp. 75-76; Paul Ricoeur, *Critical Hermeneutics and the Human Sciences: Essays of Language, Action, and Interpretation* (Cambridge: Cambridge University Press, 1981), pp. 149-64.

the fusion of horizons between the vision implicit in contemporary practices and the vision entailed in the practices of the normative Christian texts. This process of fusion between the present and the past is much different from a simple application of the past to the present. Systematic theology tries to gain as comprehensive a view of the present as possible. It tries to examine large encompassing themes about our present practices and the theory and vision latent in them. The systematic character of this movement of theology comes from the effort to investigate general themes of the gospel that respond to the most generic questions that characterize the situations of the present. This may entail questions that emerge out of the theory-laden practices of such general trends as modernity, liberal democracy, or technical rationality. There is a role for systematic theology within a fundamental practical theology, but it is a submovement or specific movement within a larger practical framework.

Two fundamental questions guide systematic theology. The first is, What new horizon of meaning is fused when the questions coming from our present practice are brought to the central Christian witness? The second is, What reasons can be advanced to support the validity claims of the new horizon of meaning that come from the fusion of present and past? This last question points to the additional obligation of systematic theology to introduce a critical and philosophical component into the theological process. There is, for instance, a role for transcendental judgments in critically testing the metaphysical claims of the Christian faith. But of even more importance, practical claims of the Christian faith need to be tested philosophically. And in the order of things suggested here, transcendental questions are the last rather than the first validity claims to be defended. This is true because many areas of collaboration between Christians and non-Christians are frequently developed without the resolution of transcendental claims. Furthermore, many reflective Christians themselves justify their faith on primarily practical grounds, even though they are quite unclear about the validity of its metaphysical claims. This is not to say that transcendental judgments in defense of metaphysical claims have no place in theology; rather, it is to say that we come to them gradually and even then develop only good reasons for these claims rather than definitive and universally convincing arguments.

My emphasis on the importance to hermeneutics of defending validity claims implicit in these new horizons places me in tension with Gadamer at one significant point. Habermas and Bernstein have severely criticized Gadamer for being a traditionalist and for having no method to test the adequacy of the horizons that emerge out of the hermeneutic conversations between the questions of the present and the witness of the classic texts and monuments.[30] To develop the general criteria for testing the practical validity claims of the Christian faith is the task of theological ethics. Theological ethics should be seen as a dimension of systematic theology.

This, in fact, is the way it generally has been conceived in the history of Protestant attempts to organize the theological disciplines (the so-called Protestant encyclopedia).[31] Without developing a foundationalist view of justifying validity claims that would be incompatible with the hermeneutical and pragmatic view of theology developed here, I will give below some suggestions for how systematic theology can advance what Bernstein calls "the best possible reasons and arguments that are appropriate to our hermeneutical situation in order to validate claims to truth."[32] Such reasons will not satisfy the foundational aspirations for absolute validity and total certainty typical of Cartesianism in science and philosophy or Kantianism in morals. They should, however, constitute reasons that can advance conversations between competing perspectives.

And finally, the fourth movement of theology and of theological education is what I am calling "strategic practical theology." I have chosen the word *strategic* to distinguish this form of practical theology from fundamental practical theology, which is, I am proposing, the most inclusive term for the theological task. There are four basic questions of strategic practical theology. First, how do we understand this concrete situation in which we must act? (The concern with the concrete features of situations in contrast to their general features is what distinguishes strategic practical theology from systematic theology.) Second, what should be our praxis in this concrete situation? Third, what means, strategies, and rhetorics should we use in this situation? And fourth, how do we critically defend the norms of our praxis in this concrete situation? By praxis, I do not just mean ethical practice in any narrow sense of that word, although I certainly mean that in part. Praxis here refers to all the realms of strategic practical theology — ethical, educational, homiletic, liturgics, and poimenic (care). For all these areas, questions of norms, rhetorics, and strategies are relevant. At the same time, the ethical component does have

---

30. Bernstein, *Beyond Objectivism and Relativism,* pp. 42-44; Habermas, *Knowledge and Human Interests,* pp. 301-17, and *Communication and the Evolution of Society* (Boston: Beacon, 1979), pp. 201-3.

31. Wolfhart Pannenberg, *Theology and the Philosophy of Science* (Philadelphia: Westminster, 1976), p. 410.

32. Bernstein, *Beyond Objectivism and Relativism,* p. 153.

a unique relevance to all of these realms. But in this fourth movement, ethics has to do with the concrete situations rather than the general features of situations typical of the ethical interests of systematic theology. The range of questions that guides strategic practical theology helps us understand the complexity of both this movement of theology and this aspect of theological education.

This is the place in theology where the interpretation of present situations comes together with both the hermeneutical process and our final critical efforts to advance justifications for the relative adequacy of the new horizons of meaning that hermeneutics has brought into existence. It is indeed the crown, as Schleiermacher said, of the theological task. But strategic practical theology is no longer the application to practice of the theoretical yield of Bible, church history, and systematic theology as it was in the old Protestant quadrivium. Concern with questions of practice and application, as Gadamer has argued, has been present from the beginning. Strategic practical theology is more the culmination of an inquiry that has been practical throughout than it is the application of theory to the specifics of praxis.

The traditional fields associated with practical theology will still be present. These might include liturgics, homiletics, education, and care. But in keeping with the move to go beyond yet include the clerical paradigm, strategic practical theology is concerned with areas of praxis that relate to the church's activity in the world as well as its ministries within its own walls. Therefore, a practical theology of care is not just pastoral care; it has to do with the church's strategy to create and influence the structures of care in society, most of which are allegedly secular. The same is true with education; it entails not only concern with the religious education of the faithful but concern with the goals and purposes of all education in modern societies. Similarly, liturgics and homiletics would be concerned not only with the church's internal worship and preaching but also with the public liturgies and public rhetoric in both the church and the rest of society. As I indicated above, theological ethics as concerned with the concrete contexts of action would be an abiding concern touching all of these traditional regions of practical theology.

The fourth question of a strategic practical theology — the question of the critical validation of the norms of praxis — I will bring up again toward the end of this essay. Let me conclude this section on strategic practical theology by pointing to how this movement of theology plays back on the entire hermeneutic circle. At the beginning of this discussion, I pointed out how descriptions of present religious and secular practices

16

form the questions that we bring to the hermeneutical process. The practices that emerge from the judgments of strategic practical theology will themselves soon engender new questions that start the hermeneutical circle again. Within the flux and turns of history, our present practices only seem secure for a period before they meet a crisis and pose new questions that take us through the hermeneutical circle once again.

Implications for the Movements of Theological Education

The reader will notice that I have spoken simultaneously about the *structure* and *movements* of both *theology* and *theological education*. If one is somewhat convinced by this suggested outline for the structure of theology, what would it imply for theological education? It implies that theological education would be organized around four movements: (1) descriptive theology understood as a "thick description" (to use a phrase of Clifford Geertz) of present religious and cultural practices (and the theories-symbols, myths, and ethics that ground them); (2) historical theology (guided by questions that emerge from movement one); (3) systematic theology (a search for generic features of the Christian message in relation to generic features of the present situation); and (4) strategic practical theology (studies about the norms and strategies of the concrete practices of the church — first for the laity in the world and then for clergy as leaders of both the mission and the cultic life of the church). One can imagine these movements being organized serially over a period of three or four years. One can also imagine them being taught simultaneously in a spiral built around successive exercises in the description and normative address of practice-theory-practice situations. But whether they are organized serially or taught simultaneously is less important than that they be recognized as movements of the total fundamental practical theological task. The main point is that both faculty and students would need to understand and agree that something like these four movements constitutes the practical habitus of theological education, and approach their studies with some variation of this practical hermeneutical model in mind.[33]

In this view of things, the distinction between university theological education and seminary education for clergy would be modest; the only difference between the two would be that seminary education for the professional clergy would give additional attention to descriptions of the

33. Farley, *Theologia*, p. 35.

practices of ordained ministers and would work in its strategic practical theology on the specific leadership practices of ordained ministers. The fact that strategic practical theology serves the church would not mean, in principle, that it would have no place in the university. Just as leaders for the fields of law, medicine, business, and social work are educated in the university, the university can — as it does in Europe, Great Britain, and Canada — provide for critical theological studies relevant to the education of the leadership of those religious institutions that have been central to the life of that society. This is a point that Schleiermacher saw well and argued for in his own view of theology as a positive science.

Fundamental Practical Theology and the CPE Model

Possibly the most novel aspect of my proposal is the suggestion to incorporate into the movements of theological education some of the purposes of clinical pastoral education (CPE). Although I have criticized CPE, I also acknowledge important insights to be gained from this model. The clinical pastoral education method goes back to Anton Boisen's suggestion that ministers should learn to study the "human document" as well as the literary text.[34] This developed into a widely popular supplement to ministerial education. Ministry students would spend a ten- to twelve-week period ministering, under the guidance of an accredited supervisor, to the patients of a general or mental hospital. Although the patient as human document was the main focus of reflection early in the movement, gradually the person of the ministerial student and his or her relation to the patient became the center of attention. The methodology of the CPE movement varies from center to center and frequently degenerates into subjectivism and specialization. Too frequently the interior perceptions and psychological history of the student are central. Also, visions and models of ministry often are restricted to the specialized functions of the modern hospital. This leaves students with narrow understandings of ministry to bring back into the life of the congregation and other nonmedical contexts.

In spite of these criticisms, most students have felt that they received something from their CPE experience. I suggest that the CPE model actually hit upon a rather unsystematic practical hermeneutical model and gained its power from its rough approximation of the first of the four

---

34. See Allison Stokes, *Ministry After Freud* (New York: Pilgrim, 1985), pp. 51-62.

movements of theological education outlined above. It enacted rather well the descriptions of present theory-laden practices, and did so at the same time that the Protestant quadrivium was functioning deductively (from theory to practice) in its movement from Bible, church history, and systematic theology to practical theology. Its main weakness can be found in the unsteady and uncareful progression that the CPE methodology took through the last three steps of the practical hermeneutical process — the movements through historical and systematic theology to strategic practical theology. It also was unable to replicate itself in other than hospital settings; with few exceptions, the CPE model has not been implemented successfully in nonmedical settings like the congregation or other public ministries. Because of this, the CPE model has often produced overly specialized views of ministry that do not serve students well after they leave the hospital.

But in spite of these shortcomings, the CPE model has planted a seed that now needs to be carefully nurtured by a more adequate practical hermeneutical model. In addition, the insights of the CPE model need to be moved out of the medical setting and into theological studies in the university and seminary. This can happen if we understand the full implications of beginning the hermeneutical circle with a careful and multidimensional description of present practices, both religious and secular, and both individual and corporate.

This can be done if we broaden the revised correlational model presented by Tracy. For Tracy, a theology operates on a genuinely revised correlational model if, as he says in his book on fundamental theology, it critically correlates its investigation into the two sources of theology. The two sources are, for him, "Christian Texts and Common Human Experience and Language."[35] As we already have seen, when this formulation is transferred to the arena of praxis, practical theology becomes "the mutually critical correlation of the interpreted theory and praxis of the Christian fact and the interpreted theory and praxis of the contemporary situation."[36] Although one pole of the correlative task actually involves "interpretations" of common experience, Tracy, in effect, elects common cultural experience and practices as one of the poles of the correlative process.

35. Tracy, *Blessed Rage for Order,* p. 43.

36. Tracy, "The Foundations of Practical Theology," in *Practical Theology,* ed. Browning, p. 76. For an adaptation of Tracy's model to a practical theology of care, see my "Mapping the Terrain of Pastoral Theology: Toward a Practical Theology of Care," *Pastoral Psychology* 36, no. 1 (Fall 1987): 20.

In order to make contact between Tracy's revised correlational model and the CPE approach, one needs to refine Tracy's concept of "common human experience" and his more practical reformulation of it into "interpreted theory and praxis of the contemporary situation." Evelyn and James Whitehead, in their *Method in Ministry*, recommend differentiating Tracy's "'common human experience' . . . into two separable poles of reflection."[37] The Whiteheads divide common experience into "personal" experience and the "corporate" experience of the community. Transferred to the arena of praxis, this division would entail (1) personal interpretations of the practices (religious and secular) of individual agents, (2) interpretations of the practices of their communities and institutions, and (3) interpretations of religio-cultural self-interpretations, symbols, and narratives. CPE has its power, I believe, because it takes personal interpretations of individual practices into its systematic reflections. It also allows into reflection interpretations of the practices of the hospital community. And occasionally it relates these two interpretative perspectives to larger interpretations of common cultural experience — for example, the general cultural fear of death and aging, the cultural idolatry of youth, or the cultural reverence for technical reason and medical heroism. The power of CPE does not derive from its concern with general or common experience, however, but from its concern with interpretations of "my experience and practice" and "my community's experience and practice." I propose that something like the full range of the description of experiences and practices (from the personal, to the person's immediate communities, and then to broader religio-cultural symbols and stories) be more systematically included in the first movement of theological education in any of its settings.

This first movement, of course, would not be an end in itself; to stop the theological education process with the first step would be subjectivism. But if this first movement is used to refine the questions (the practical prejudices of Gadamer's hermeneutics) that lead back to historical theology, systematic theology, and then finally to the complexities of strategic practical theology, then the spirit and impulse of CPE can have a healthy influence indeed on theological education in all contexts, the university as well as the seminary dedicated to the education of ordained ministers.

Various disciplines can help describe the theory-laden practices of

37. James Whitehead and Evelyn Whitehead, *Method in Ministry* (New York: Seabury, 1980), p. 12.

concrete people in their specific communities within the context of larger cultural symbols and narratives. Clearly, psychology and psychoanalysis can uncover aspects of the interpreted practices of individuals. These psychological disciplines, however, should not function as natural sciences, exhaustively explaining individual subjective experience. Rather, they should function more as hermeneutic disciplines that permit a unique retrospective glance at the developmental history of the interpretations that the individual brings to his or her social and religious practices.[38] Object relations theory in the writings of Guntrip, Winnicott, Kohut, and others helps us understand ways in which individual experience is actually composed of internalized social experience.[39] A nuanced analysis of individual experience does not necessarily lead to subjectivism and individualism; our inner world leads back to the social world of history, culture, and public issues. When rightly seen, even the interpreted practices of individuals can lead directly to the larger hermeneutical process.

Furthermore, the psychological and psychoanalytic disciplines may help uncover discontinuities between a person's ideals and his or her actual practices. Sociology can function similarly to uncover the unconscious or suppressed interpretations and practices for the communities of the theological student. Also, as Habermas has suggested, psychoanalysis and Marxist social thought can constitute a kind of critical theory uncovering systematic distortions in the communicative practices of individual theological students and their communities.[40] These disciplines, within the context of historical and systematic theology, can also help uncover ideological distortions within the normative religious texts. Furthermore, psychoanalysis and sociology can be used to uncover the depth, or "archeology," to use a phrase of Paul Ricoeur, of broader cultural trends, as Freud, Weber, Rieff, and many others have shown.[41]

There is a role for these secular disciplines in the description of individual, communal, and cultural practices. It must be emphasized, how-

---

38. This is the basic meaning of Paul Ricoeur's view that psychoanalysis helps us uncover the "archeology of the subject." See his *Freud and Philosophy* (New Haven: Yale University Press, 1970), pp. 419-58.

39. For a review of the object-relations school of psychoanalysis, see Jay Greenberg and Stephen Mitchell, *Object Relations in Psychoanalytic Theory* (Cambridge: Harvard University Press, 1983).

40. Habermas, *Knowledge and Human Interests,* pp. 274-300.

41. For the best review of how both psychoanalysis and Weberian sociology can be used to uncover cultural trends, see Philip Rieff, *Freud: The Mind of the Moralist* (New York: Doubleday, 1961), and *Triumph of the Therapeutic* (New York: Harper and Row, 1966).

ever, that the role for the social sciences is partial; they should not be seen as reductively or exhaustively explanatory. These disciplines help us uncover trends that restrict and shape but do not necessarily eliminate human freedom.

Yet the description of situated individual, communal, and general cultural practices is never accomplished by the social sciences alone. These practices are also interpreted by the ideals and norms implicit in the theory of these practices. And, insofar as the practices gain their norms from Christian sources, these meanings too play back on them and constitute one perspective on their interpretation. But this raises the following questions: Does the practice in question really conform to Christian norms? Is the practice humanly authentic when measured from the perspective of Christian meanings? Such questions move the theological student backward through the practical hermeneutical circle that I described above. Theological education can profit from these depth perspectives on the description of practices, some of which were used with reasonable success in the CPE movement.

I offer a brief illustration of what this approach to theological education might mean, not so much for the details of a theological curriculum, but for a teaching ethos that might permeate the entire process of theological education. For example, what might this point of view mean for teaching an introductory course in practical theology? In addition to assigning students a variety of theoretical readings, I made an assignment for a writing project that necessitated the students' making use of these four movements. I did this by asking them to choose a contemporary issue in religious life in our society that was of vital importance to them. It was to be an issue so vital that it served as a basic motivation behind their interest in theological education. In order to aid them in their thick description of the respective issues they chose (the first movement of a fundamental practical theology), I held a long evening meeting when the nine students of this class told the history of their interest in the issue. One student chose the tension between New Age religion and Christianity. Another chose the way psychiatry relates to the religion of its patients. Another was interested in the status and theological understanding of the newly emerging profession of lay ministers in the Roman Catholic Church. Another student chose homosexuality. Another chose the phenomenon of community organizations and the way various churches are using them as extensions of their public ministry. In every case, the students had a significant history of existential concern with their chosen issue. Their initial task was to describe this history at several levels: their personal involvements and motivations, the institutional context of the issue as they saw it, and the religio-cultural meanings that surrounded the issue, especially as they experienced them.

This first step of what we are calling descriptive theology was to be carried over into a major paper to be written for the course. But the paper was actually to center on an interview the student was to have with another person who was, in some way, dealing with the student's chosen issue. The students were to begin the paper with a thick description of their own practices and attitudes as they related to the respective issues. More specifically, each student was to record her or his preunderstanding of the issue. For instance, the student who was concerned with homosexuality recorded his own prejudgments about it. The student concerned about the relation of New Age religion to Christianity recorded his preunderstanding of that issue. But then the students were to describe, as best they could, the personal, institutional, and religio-cultural situation of the interviewee as this related to the selected issue. The student interested in New Age religion interviewed a manager of a New Age bookstore. The student interested in psychiatry's handling of religion interviewed a psychiatrist. The student interested in cults interviewed an acquaintance who had converted to the Jehovah's Witnesses. The student interested in homosexuality interviewed a gay graduate student. The papers summarized these interviews and provided thick descriptions of the situations of both the student and the person being interviewed.

Questions about practice (about what good practice would really be) emerged from these thick descriptions of both interviewer and interviewee. This led to the second movement, that is, historical theology. In the midst of this limited project, however, this movement was addressed by asking the student to present the argument of two serious books that could serve as guides to the Christian witness on the issue he or she was investigating. The point here was to investigate the historical sources from the angle of vision of the student's description of contemporary practices, the theories implicit within them, and the questions they pose. The student investigating homosexuality, for instance, used Helmut Thielicke's *The Ethics of Sex* and James Nelson's *Embodiment*.

The next task, which captured some of the features of systematic theology, was not only to lay out the general themes of these guides to the classic Christian sources but to begin a critical dialogue between these guides in an attempt to determine their relative adequacy. In the case of some projects, this task of isolating basic general themes and beginning the process of critically testing their adequacy was enriched by analytic insights from moral philosophy. The task, here, was to give the student an introductory exercise in making critical judgments about the relative adequacy of different interpretive theological perspectives and advancing reasons as to why one view might be better than another. This, of course, is a large task that involves much more than either I can discuss here or the students could adequately address within the context of an introductory course. Nonetheless, they were introduced to the task of critically testing theological arguments.

The fourth movement, however, gave the project its distinctively practical cast and made it a unique assignment in comparison to the students' other theological studies. Here the task was to write the conclusion of their paper for their interviewee rather than for me, the professor. They were to attempt to communicate their preferred position on the issue at hand to the person they had interviewed. They were to communicate this position with sensitivity to the views and situation of this person as well as their own situation and preunderstandings of the issue. The students were to look for identities, nonidentities, and analogies between their preferred view and the situated views of their interviewee. The students also were to advance critical reasons for the more adequate position, but to do so in such a way as to make contact with the situation and preunderstandings of the person they had interviewed. In most cases, the students actually went back to their interviewees and shared their papers with them. Hence, the entire project was a dialogue between the students and their subjects around an issue that the classics of the Christian faith also in some fashion address. In virtually all cases, the students reported a change — sometimes quite revolutionary — between their initial preunderstanding and their understanding of the issue at the conclusion of their dialogue. Because they were sensitive to the changes in themselves, they were also more sensitive to the changes that this dialogue invoked in their subjects — changes that were sometimes modest and sometimes profound.

Space does not permit a full commentary on this project. I will add only this: I explained to the students that not all classes in their theological education should be structured in this manner. But I suggested that they might better keep track of the various twists and turns of their theological education if they saw it in its entirety as entailing various deeper investigations of each of these four movements, often considered more discretely and deeply than was the case in this rather large practical synthetic assignment. Theological education should provide an opportunity to both see and practice this process as a whole as well as to delve deeply into the various movements and submovements considered relatively discretely but also, once again, in relation to the entire fundamental practical theological task.

Further Comparisons

There are several recent proposals pertaining to the structure of theology that have either influenced or are similar to the view presented here. If space permitted, I would discuss at length the contributions of Juan Luis Segundo, Joseph Hough and John Cobb, and Charles Wood, in addition to those of Johann Baptist Metz, whose views I will discuss more thoroughly. Segundo's view of the hermeneutic circle is very close to mine, but I am somewhat uncomfortable with his rather rigid precommitments.[42] For instance, I agree that "partiality to the poor" is in some way part of the central witness of the Christian faith, but there are other surprises in the Scriptures that these precommitments may lead us to miss.[43] Furthermore, Segundo's own interpretation of this precommitment may obscure other profound elements of biblical justice.

The proposal to make the capacity for "practical theological thinking" the goal of theology and the central task of theological education in Hough and Cobb's *Christian Identity and Theological Education* is extremely appealing. I have said so elsewhere in print.[44] Yet in many ways, their excellent proposals are still caught in a theory-to-practice model; their justifiable concern with Christian identity still leads them to move from historical theology to practical theology, almost leaving out systematic theology altogether.[45]

And finally, I am deeply impressed with Charles Wood's definition of theology in *Vision and Discernment* as "critical inquiry into the validity of the Christian witness."[46] Wood's view of theology as critical reflection on both Christian belief and activity is clearly congruent with my proposals. But Wood comes dangerously close to a theory-to-practice model in his organization of the structure of theology into the five subdisciplines of

---

42. Segundo, *The Liberation of Theology*, p. 9.

43. Segundo, *The Liberation of Theology*, p. 33.

44. Hough and Cobb, *Christian Identity and Theological Education*, p. 104. For my positive response to their proposals, see Don S. Browning, "Globalization and the Task of Theological Education," *Theological Education* 23, no. 1 (Autumn 1986): 43-59.

45. Hough and Cobb, *Christian Identity and Theological Education*, pp. 29-30.

46. Charles M. Wood, *Vision and Discernment: An Orientation in Theological Study* (Atlanta: Scholars, 1985), p. 20.

historical theology, philosophical theology, practical theology, systematic theology, and moral theology.[47] In Wood's beginning with historical theology and moving to practical theology, one detects the older applicational model. Wood tries to correct this by making systematic and moral theology follow and gain from practical theology. Hence, his model becomes something like a theory-practice-theory model. I believe, however, that it is both theologically and philosophically justifiable to use a more thoroughly practical and hermeneutical model from the beginning, a model more consistent with the full implications of the contemporary turn to practical philosophy.

My concept of "fundamental practical theology" is close to Johann Baptist Metz's concept of "practical fundamental theology."[48] Metz as a fundamental theologian is trying to make fundamental theology practical. In contrast, as a practical theologian, I am trying to expand the idea of practical theology and, at the same time, to make it a fundamental and critical discipline. The result is very much the same. Metz and I agree that all theology is practical and that the Christian message is primarily practical in nature.[49] He too emphasizes the "primacy of praxis" over theory and explicitly repudiates the traditional model of practice as the application of theory.[50] He also believes in the importance of beginning theology with a description of contemporary practices, both religious and secular. This leads him to characterize contemporary secular practices as dominated by privatization and the "exchange" principle, and bourgeois religion as primarily in service to these trends.[51]

The differences between Metz's views and mine are few but substantial. I will mention only two. First, Metz is interested in beginning with the description of the contemporary situation, but he does this at the most general level and describes the central dominating global trend, that is, the domination of the exchange principle. In contrast to this, I have suggested beginning theology, and especially theological education, with a more differentiated description of contemporary practices, that is, a description of personal institutional practices and the religio-cultural symbols that give them meaning. There is much that Metz's highly molar analysis misses. For instance, even if the exchange principle and privatism

47. Wood, *Vision and Discernment*, pp. 39-55.
48. Johann Baptist Metz, *Faith in History and Society*, trans. David Smith (New York: Seabury, 1980), pp. 5-8.
49. Metz, *Faith in History*, pp. 50-70.
50. Metz, *Faith in History*, p. 50.
51. Metz, *Faith in History*, pp. 34-36.

dominate much of contemporary social practice, there are still reactions to these trends, some defensible and some less so, that greatly complexify the range of contemporary practices. At this level, Metz's concern with the most generic features of the contemporary situation places his practical fundamental theology closer to what I have called systematic theology. That is, he is searching out, in a significant and creative way, the most general features of the contemporary situation and correlating them with some general themes and categories of the Christian enterprise. Although important, such an approach limits the range of practical issues that could stimulate the theological task.

Second, Metz's model of practical fundamental theology is less dialogical and mutually critical than my vision of a fundamental practical theology. For instance, Metz, in addition to having an extremely molar and generic interpretation of the contemporary situation, has little interest in describing the self-interpretations of contemporary trends, situations, and practices. Hence, Metz shares little of the interest that revised correlational practical theology has in a critical conversation between interpretations (including self-interpretations) of contemporary practices and interpretations of the Christian message. A revised correlational practical theology is interested in the identities, nonidentities, and analogies between interpretations of contemporary practices and interpretations of the praxis implications of the normative Christian events. Metz sees primarily nonidentity and discontinuity between contemporary practices and normative Christian practices. The fact that nonidentity and discontinuity dominate Metz's methodology precludes the possibility, I believe, of hearing and seeing the identities and analogies that may sometimes exist between the Christian message and the self-interpretations of various contemporary secular and religious practices.

There is also little interest, in Metz's view, in allowing a fully critical conversation between the Christian faith and interpretations of contemporary practices. The praxis implications of the *memoria passionis, martis et resurrectionis Jesu Christi* seem to need no test for their validity claims.[52] Indeed, Metz does claim that his practical fundamental theology is apologetic. He works to demonstrate that secular programs of justice require at their meta-ethical level assumptions entailing a Christian doctrine of a just God suffering with and redeeming both the living and the dead. Yet his apologetic stance stops with showing how other self-interpretations require Christian assumptions. Although this is fair enough, the Chris-

---

52. Metz, *Faith in History,* p. III.

tian practical theologian should also go further and enter into a public and critical discourse about the "validity claims" supporting his or her own praxis, especially with regard to more concrete courses of action. Metz has little to say about this issue, and this omission distinguishes his proposals from mine.

Introducing the phrase "validity claims" and the need for a fundamental practical theology to support the claims it makes introduces for our consideration the critical theory project of Jürgen Habermas. Yet one need not be tied to Habermas's particular version of these validity claims (for instance, his division of them into "comprehensibility, truth, rightness, and truthfulness") to appreciate his insistence that communicative competence entails a willingness to advance reasons for our actions, even to those who do not agree with us and who do not seem to share our faith.[53] It is true that Habermas has been accused by various commentators, especially Bernstein and Rorty, of developing a foundationalist drive for certainty in our social discourse.[54] Of course, such a foundationalism would be in tension with the hermeneutical and historical rationale I have advanced here for the centrality of a fundamental practical theology. But one need not lapse into the relativism of a Richard Rorty to avoid foundationalism. Bernstein's counsel is more appropriate when he writes the following with reference to Gadamer's avoidance of the question of validation.

> I have argued Gadamer is really committed to a communicative understanding of truth, believing that "claims to truth" always implicitly demand argumentation to warrant them, but he has failed to make this view fully explicit. . . . For although all claims to truth are fallible and open to criticism, they still require validation — validation that can be realized only through offering the best reasons and arguments that can be given in support of them — reasons and arguments that are themselves embedded in the practices that have been developed in the course of history. We never escape from the obligation of seeking to validate claims to truth through argumentation and opening ourselves to the criticism of others.[55]

53. Habermas, *Communication and the Evolution of Society*, p. 58, and *Theory of Communicative Action*, trans. Thomas McCarthy, 2 vols. (Boston: Beacon, 1984), vol. 1, pp. 325-29.

54. Richard Rorty, *Consequences of Pragmatism* (Minneapolis: University of Minnesota Press, 1982), pp. 173-74; Bernstein, *Beyond Objectivism and Relativism*, pp. 197-207.

55. Bernstein, *Beyond Objectivism and Relativism*, p. 168.

In my own work, I differentiate the validity claims of a fundamental practical theology into five types rather than Habermas's four. I argue that these five validity claims reflect the five dimensions of all forms of practical thinking, whether they be explicitly religious or avowedly secular. I call these dimensions (1) the visional or metaphorical dimension (which inevitably raises metaphysical validity claims), (2) the obligational dimension (which raises normative ethical claims), (3) the tendency-need dimension (which raises claims about the fundamental needs of human nature and the kinds of nonmoral goods that meet them), (4) the contextual dimension (claims about the social-systemic and ecological integrity of situations), and (5) the rule-role dimension (claims about what should be our most concrete behaviors and actions).[56] In fact, I use these five dimensions (I sometimes call them levels) both to describe the theory-laden practices of contemporary situations and to guide the description of the thickness of the Christian witness. Hence, the model is useful to guide description and interpretation at both poles of the revised correlational conversation — the pole of contemporary experience and the pole of the central Christian message.

There is no room here to amplify and justify this division of the validity claims that a fundamental practical theology should address. My goal, rather, is to assert that a critical or revised correlational practical theology must be willing to support its implicit validity claims if it is to take part in the discourse of a free society aimed at shaping the common good. Here I agree with Bernstein. The arguments that a critical practical theology advances cannot be foundational arguments assuring absolute authority. But its arguments can have the status of good reasons that, although not absolutely certain, can advance discourse about the action we should take.

The critical testing of a fundamental practical theology must come at a variety of points in the hermeneutical circle. Sketching out formally the types of validity claims that a critical practical theology might face, however, would be the special province of both systematic theology and strategic practical theology. Furthermore, the actual defense of the validity claims for the purpose of concrete praxis would occur most profoundly at the movement of strategic practical theology.

---

56. Browning, *Religious Ethics and Pastoral Care,* pp. 53-71, and "Practical Theology and Political Theology," *Theology Today* 42 (April 1985): 207-12. For a fuller discussion of these issues, see my *A Fundamental Practical Theology: With Descriptive and Strategic Proposals* (Minneapolis: Fortress, 1991).

But it is important to note that when this structure of theology is translated into the rhythms of theological education, one would still begin theology with a thick description of contemporary practices (personal, institutional, and religio-cultural) and then only gradually move back to historical theology. One would then move through a systematic consideration of the themes of the faith (considered from the perspective of the questions engendered by present practice), to an ideology critique of these themes and the critical examination of the validity claims of the faith, and finally to the critical and strategic consideration of proposals for the alteration of our present practices. The task of supporting the validity claims of the faith is difficult and challenging but important. Yet it is not the first order of business in theological education. To understand our own present practices in their various situations and the questions these practices evoke is the first task of theological education. How these movements might be organized into a course of study in different situations — the seminary, the graduate department of religion, or even the church — would doubtless vary to some extent. But if the position outlined above has some plausibility, these differences would be matters of degree and matters of emphasis rather than matters of categorical distinction.

Chapter 2

Empirical Considerations in Religious Praxis and Reflection (2005)

In April of 2004, I was invited to address the International Society for Empirical Research in Theology at its biennial meeting held at Bielefeld, Germany. The topic assigned to me was "Empirical Considerations in a Practical Theology of Families."

Practical theologians are often asked to address the specific context and interests of particular audiences. This invitation gave me the opportunity to summarize the place of empirical research in practical theology as both teaching and research. I chose to develop my points with reference to the Religion, Culture, and Family Project, which I had directed for twelve years. I argued that this project was, in fact, an elaborate practical theological research program. This research program — its many scholarly books, using a considerable number of scholars, addressing several different audiences, and lasting over a decade — exhibited the structure of practical theological reflection and action.

I further claimed that this large research project was also analogous to how I taught at least one of my introductory courses for first-year ministerial students. Both contexts — the long-term research project and the classroom teaching situation — followed the structure of what I had termed a fundamental practical theology. This entailed the four steps of descriptive theology, historical theology, systematic theology, and strategic practical theology that I outlined in the preceding chapter. At each of these steps of practical theology, the empirical social and psychological sciences have a role to play. But their contribution does not involve providing objective knowledge upon which to erect normative theological and ethical systems. Rather, these empirical disciplines provide clarifying "distance" from the theologian's interpretive beginning points and hermeneutic circle. The reader will be relieved to know that I will try to define the concepts of "distance" and "distanciation" in the chapter that follows. I hope that I succeed to your satisfaction.

My lecture has a complex agenda, perhaps too complex. I first want to describe an exercise I have used with first-year ministry students in a course called Practical Theology and Public Ministry. I also will set forth the hermeneutical theory behind this exercise and what it implies about the relation of practical theology to the so-called empirical social sciences. Second, I will describe the continuity between that classroom exercise and the twelve-year-long Religion, Culture, and Family research project that I administered at the University of Chicago. It too was a practical-theological project that both generated and freely used social-science data. Finally, I will summarize what I have gleaned from these teaching and research situations for our main topic — the role of the empirical in practical theology. In short, I will try to show how our practical-theological teaching and our practical-theological research can fruitfully influence each other. Because of the size of the agenda and the complexity of the issues, what I say on some of these topics will be necessarily brief and condensed.

A Teaching Exercise

In my book *A Fundamental Practical Theology*, I briefly describe an exercise that I have used for twelve years in a class for first-year ministry students.[1] In many ways, the entirety of that rather thick book was designed to amplify the theory behind this relatively simple exercise. The class was on practical theology and what it offers for clarifying the public role of Christian ministry.

Here is the exercise. In the first week, students were asked to do the following: (1) Choose a practical issue pertaining to the church's ministry to the world that had motivated the student to seek academic preparation for ministry. As a part of this first step, the student also was asked to con-

---

1. Don Browning, *A Fundamental Practical Theology* (Minneapolis: Fortress, 1991), p. 7.

vert that issue into a researchable practical-theological question and make a preliminary account of his or her "preunderstanding" of both the description of the issue and its possible answers or resolutions. (2) Interview a leader representing a sector of church or society also struggling with that same question. This was to help the student deal with the issue as a public matter as well as a personal concern. (3) Select two major scholarly theological books or biblical texts (plus commentaries) that also addressed this practical-theological question. (4) Advance a comparative critical analysis of both the description and the answer to the question advanced by each of the two major sources and by your interviewee. Indicate which of the three positions is the strongest, both on description and on normative answer. (5) Write a twenty- to twenty-five-page paper covering all of these steps and concluding with several paragraphs written not to the professor but to the interviewee about which position best describes and addresses your practical-theological issue. (6) Provide a sufficiently rich description of the thickness of the interviewee's world — his or her practices, analysis of contexts, view of relevant goods, moral principles, and narrative vision — to be able to convey your emerging point of view persuasively with an eye toward inspiring change. (7) Finally, the student was asked to recall his or her original "preunderstanding" (in Gadamer's sense of the term) of the issue and assess how this exercise had changed it. I am pleased to report that I would invariably get outstanding papers from highly motivated students.

In connection with this project, these first-year students did a light reading of the rather challenging *A Fundamental Practical Theology;* they did this primarily to give themselves confidence that there was a rather elaborate theoretical basis for what might, at first glance, appear to be a trivial, nuts-and-bolts exercise. You will easily recognize the theoretical frameworks behind this exercise. It draws heavily on the hermeneutic philosophy of Hans-Georg Gadamer, Paul Ricoeur, and the use of this perspective in the hermeneutic sociology of the widely read book by Robert Bellah and his colleagues titled *Habits of the Heart.*[2] Gadamer's hermeneutically oriented understanding of Aristotelian *phronēsis* framed the entire exercise.[3] His view of "effective history"[4] and "preunderstanding"[5] was behind my asking the students to choose a practical-theological question that

---

2. Robert Bellah, Richard Madsen, William Sullivan, Ann Swidler, and Steven Tipton, *Habits of the Heart* (Berkeley, Calif.: University of California Press, 1985), pp. 301-6.

3. Hans-Georg Gadamer, *Truth and Method* (New York: Crossroad, 1982), pp. 278-80.

4. Gadamer, *Truth and Method,* pp. 267-68.

5. Gadamer, *Truth and Method,* pp. 235-37.

emerged out of their own history and to advance a tentative description of their preliminary hunches about how to describe and answer that question. Gadamer's rejection of the separation of application from understanding also was implicit in the assignment; we read and discussed his brilliant argument claiming that understanding should not add application at the end but should be driven by an interest in application from the very beginning.[6] His view of the "classic" as formative of history and thereby latent in our effective histories was behind the request that students use two different scholarly texts that might function as guides to these classics.[7] This was a manageable way to help them gain critical understanding of how their present interpretive praxis gains normative orientation from the monuments of the past.

We used Ricoeur's view of knowing as a dialectic of understanding-explanation-understanding.[8] In close connection with this, we also discussed his brilliant concept of distanciation, which relativizes social-science objectivity by placing it within a larger framework of historically embedded and conditioned understanding. To demonstrate the role of social-science distanciation, students were encouraged to use the explanatory perspectives of the social sciences in analyzing their chosen issue, but always as a subordinate part of a wider framework of understanding and *phronēsis* as these concepts are developed by Gadamer and Ricoeur. We demonstrated the link between a hermeneutically oriented practical theology and the hermeneutical-social sciences as illustrated by Bellah's *Habits of the Heart*. I emphasized that to describe a problem meant to interpret it first from the perspective of one's effective history and only secondarily from the viewpoint of the explanatory interests of economic, social systemic, class, educational, or psychological variables. Of course, describing from the perspective of one's naive first grasp of one's effective history needed correction by the second and more critical grasp that comes from serious historical-critical and hermeneutical retrieval of that history, especially the normative classics of that history.

Although the papers were of unusually high quality for first-year ministry students, the students did have difficulties with two features of this assignment. First, they found it challenging to convert their selected issue into a focused practical-theological question that was sufficiently limited

---

6. Gadamer, *Truth and Method*, p. 289.

7. Gadamer, *Truth and Method*, p. 255.

8. Paul Ricoeur, *Hermeneutics and the Human Sciences* (Cambridge: Cambridge University Press, 1982), pp. 87-90.

to be researchable. I would often have to meet with each student several times before the question could be formulated into a written research proposal. Second, students had difficulty writing the last sections of the paper to the interviewee rather than to the professor. Getting into another person's symbolic world and crafting a rhetorically attractive argument that would be convincing was a challenge for students socialized into the live-and-let-live culture of American society. It is much easier to write upward to the authoritative professor than laterally and convincingly to the neighbor at your side.

Of course, this is not only a problem for our students; it is a fundamental deficiency of contemporary theological scholarship. Theologians write for their academic superiors and not for the social and cultural person on the street. Practical theology as a discipline, however, should do better than this. But in order to write for people in various sectors of common life, we should both describe their effective histories and use scientific distanciation to identify the social and cultural forces that shape their lives. In other words, we need to know how to use the empirical in both its hermeneutic-descriptive and its explanatory forms.

I conclude my description of this exercise by pointing out that this same methodology was followed by many of these students three years later when writing their senior ministry papers. In other words, many did this exercise twice — their first year and their last. The second time, it generally would be on another topic — some issue that grew out of their ministry experiences while a student. The second time, their paper would benefit from the historical, ethical, and theological work done in the intervening time. But the paper would still have the same practical-theological structure.

Students were asked to think of their papers as a scaled-down version of a fundamental practical theology. Those of you who are familiar with my book by that name know that there I systematized the Gadamer-Ricoeur view of understanding and *phronēsis* into a view of theological reflection that sees it as moving through the four steps of *descriptive theology, historical theology, systematic theology,* and *strategic-practical theology.* The two manifestations of the empirical — namely, the empirical as hermeneutic-descriptive and the empirical as distanciated explanation — have roles to play in each of these four movements.

First, fresh theological reflection begins with a rupture in traditional practices; descriptive theology begins theological reflection by advancing an initial, and probably relatively naive, hermeneutic-descriptive and explanatory analysis of that rupture, namely, the problem or issue.

Second, historical theology is an act of self-understanding whereby we move back in history to examine our inherited norms, ideals, or classics. Once again, hermeneutic-description is the primary mode of inquiry governing historical theology. Even then, we cannot fully understand the meaning of the text, monument, or event — what Ricoeur and André LaCoque call the "trajectory" or meaning "in front" of the text — unless historical-critical explanation is employed to grasp its conditioned background.[9] On the other hand, although discovering the historical-critical background may help clarify this meaning or trajectory, it does not itself determine that meaning.

Third, the step of systematic and critical reflection, often associated with the tasks of systematic and moral theology, needs to hold together the dialectic of understanding-explanation-understanding much better than it has in the past. Even these systematic moments of theology need to comprehend the sociocultural contexts from which theological visions are generated as well as the contemporary situations that these scholars are addressing. They also need to grasp the way theological ideas shape, for both good and ill, actual unfolding economic, social-systemic, and psychological processes.

Finally, the fourth step of strategic-practical theology requires the understanding-explanation-understanding dialectic with all the more power and precision. This is the place where practical theologians must finally show what they have to offer, but without renouncing full responsibility for the earlier three steps. Unless the practical theologian moves into the strategic moment by taking responsibility for the earlier three steps, she will fall into the trap of taking the theories of systematic and moral theology and applying them to the situations at hand — the error of the older theory-application model. As Ottmar Fuchs suggests,[10] the strategic-theological moment must critically compare the trajectories of meaning gained when the understanding-explanation dialectic is applied to the classic texts with the trajectories discovered when it is applied to the situations of contemporary church and society. This is a monumentally complex process and probably requires the efforts of finely tuned research teams.

Students also were invited to use the five dimensions of practical rea-

9. André LaCocque and Paul Ricoeur, *Thinking Biblically: Exegetical and Hermeneutical Studies* (Chicago: University of Chicago Press, 1998), pp. xi, xii.

10. Ottmar Fuchs, "Relationship between Practical Theology and Empirical Research," *Journal of Empirical Theology* 14, no. 2 (2001): 7.

son or *phronēsis* that I outlined in *A Fundamental Practical Theology*. Without boring you with how I first derived and named the dimensions or levels, I will say that I have been happy to find them implicit in Paul Ricoeur's recent analysis of praxis.[11] Ricoeur distinguishes his theory of praxis from all behaviorist, functionalist, and communicative models of action that fail to grasp the full multidimensionality of praxis.

Take, for example, the simple descriptive statement, "The farmer is plowing his field." A full analysis of this praxis can be subdivided into roughly five dimensions: (1) a technical means-end practice referring to the moving of dirt in order to plant some seeds; (2) the goods aspired to in the practice of plowing — for example, food, health, and wealth for self and loved ones; (3) the ideals and narratives about the purposes of life that make plowing and the teleological pursuit of these goods a meaningful action; (4) some higher-order principle that solves conflict (for example, by what principle does the farmer act if his neighbor steals his seeds or diverts water needed to fertilize them?); and, finally, (5) a hermeneutic-descriptive *and* explanatory analysis of the original context of the farmer as well as a return to that same context after the first four dimensions are submitted to more critical reflection. This multidimensional view of our practices reveals the full fact of praxis as really a form of *phronēsis;* it demonstrates that a horizon of practical wisdom, adequate or inadequate as it may be, surrounds our various actions. This is an insight that Johannes van der Ven has perceptively used to order the entire field of moral education in his outstanding *Formation of the Moral Self.*[12]

Because Ricoeur sees narrative as an unavoidable aspect of praxis, religion itself can easily fit into his model. There is a narrative fringe to all praxis, and this fringe invariably has implications for the ultimate context of experience. Time and time again, while reading the corpus of great theologians as diverse as Thomas Aquinas or the rabbinic Nachmanides, especially on issues pertaining to marriage and family, I have seen these five dimensions of praxis leap out with startling clarity, with the narrative level playing a distinctly defining and framing role. I will give illustrations of this later in the lecture.

Students would use these five dimensions both descriptively and normatively. They would use them to analyze descriptively and

---

11. Paul Ricoeur, "The Teleological and Deontological Structures of Action: Aristotle and/or Kant?" in *Contemporary French Philosophy* (Cambridge: Cambridge University Press, 1987), pp. 99-103.

12. Johannes van der Ven, *Formation of the Moral Self* (Grand Rapids: Eerdmans, 1998).

explanatorily the situation of their issue or question. Then they would later often frame their own critically achieved normative arguments in terms of these levels as well, although that was sometimes too complex to adequately accomplish in a single brief seminar paper. A simple descriptive or normative narrative theology, such as that associated with the thought of Stanley Hauerwas, is from my perspective inadequate for the task of practical theology. Because Hauerwas and his followers do not chart how the narrative dimension interacts with the other four dimensions of praxis, their views have little lasting value for any of the tasks of practical theology — its confessional, correlative, transformative, apologetic, or public roles.[13] In what follows, I will say more to illustrate what the empirical understood as distanciating explanation has to offer to the clarification of these five dimensions.

The Religion, Culture, and Family Project

There are significant similarities between this classroom exercise and the practical-theological research venture called the Religion, Culture, and Family Project that I led from 1991 to the end of 2003. This project has generated twenty volumes either presently in print or soon to be published as well as a major documentary film shown nationally on our Public Broadcast Station (PBS).[14] The project was funded by a series of generous grants from the Lilly Endowment, one of the few major private endowments that supports research on religious issues.

Like every practical-theological research project, this one started with a question, but not, I confess, a very adequate one. We asked, is it possible to form an alternative liberal and critical Christian theology of families to counter the dominant perspective proffered by the American religious right? But, as was often the case with my students in the classroom, the first formulation of the question was neither adequate nor final. As we began to look more carefully at the social and cultural contexts of modern families, the question became this: *In light of the rapid changes besetting modern families (more divorce, more childbirth outside of marriage, more non-marriage, more cohabitation), what is an adequate practical Christian assessment*

13. See Stanley Hauerwas, *A Community of Character* (Notre Dame, Ind.: Notre Dame University, 1982).

14. The title of the documentary was "Marriage — Just a Piece of Paper?" and was accompanied by a book of the transcripts edited by Kathy Anderson, Don Browning, and Brian Boyer, *Marriage — Just a Piece of Paper?* (Grand Rapids: Eerdmans, 2002).

of and response to these trends? This formulation put more weight on describing and explaining the trends and provided more openness in our critical-hermeneutical retrieval of the various strands of Christian marriage and family thinking.

The first moment of practical theology — the moment of descriptive theology — is always naive and uncritical but still very important. It was difficult to avoid the initial impression that Christianity throughout its history has been skeptical of divorce, discouraged nonmarital births, and frowned on cohabitation. From Augustine to Aquinas to Luther and Calvin, the goods of marriage were seen to be so vital that all family formations should occur within it. The integrations that occurred within marriage were then given the reinforcements of a theology of sacrament or covenant, both modeled on Christ's unbreakable love for the church. The question became, however, whether this preliminary horizon of interpretation should hold up in light of a more serious critical-hermeneutic retrieval of the classics of Christian marriage and family.

Bringing an empirical-explanatory perspective into the first movement quickly complicated this essential step of naive description. We found that many of the specific social-science studies could be nicely ordered by the Weberian-Habermasian theory of how the technical rationality of the systems world was colonizing, and thereby disrupting, the lifeworld of face-to-face relations in family, marriage, neighborhoods, and communities.[15] As Robert Bellah has argued, this impingement into the dependencies of intimate life by the systems world was also further energized by the rise of cultural individualism since the Enlightenment.[16] Many family social scientists such as Larry Bumpass,[17] William Goode,[18] and Anthony Giddens[19] believe that this process is inevitable and that family disruption and the decline of marriage are irresistible features of modern and postmodern life. Rational-choice theorists such as Gary Becker and Richard Posner supplement these predictions with additional theories. They claim that as the technical rationality of free-

---

15. Jürgen Habermas, *The Theory of Communicative Action,* trans. Thomas McCarthy, vol. 2 (Boston: Beacon, 1987), p. 333.

16. Bellah, *Habits of the Heart,* p. 35.

17. Larry Bumpass, "What's Happening to the Family? Interactions between Demographic and Institutional Change," *Demography* 27, no. 4 (November 1990): 493.

18. William Goode, *World Changes in Divorce Patterns* (New Haven, Conn.: Yale University Press, 1993).

19. Anthony Giddens, *The Transformation of Intimacy* (Stanford, Calif.: Stanford University Press, 1992).

market economies spreads into the lifeworld, it increasingly reduces intimate relations to cost-benefit calculations and shifts economic dependencies away from the husband-wife relationship toward job, government,
and welfare transfers.[20]

Frederick Engels in his *The Origin of the Family, Private Property, and the
State* predicted that market rationality would undermine families.[21] But
his hope that socialist countries would do better on family has not proved
to be the case. Once again, Habermas, along with sociologist Alan Wolfe,
shows how technical rationality can take the form of government bureaucracy and welfare interventions that, if not accurately administered, also
undermine the dependencies of civil society and families. We should not
be surprised to learn that the family disruption rates of the United States,
which Wolfe calls the leading example of the market family, and more socialist Sweden, which he dubs the leading example of the state family, are
surprisingly parallel.[22] Furthermore, a recent exhaustive Swedish study of
a million children demonstrates that, in spite of the excellent welfare and
government support of families present in that country, the children of
disrupted families have significantly higher rates of morbidity, addiction,
injury, suicide, and psychiatric problems than do those raised in intact
families.[23] This research parallels the mounting evidence in the United
States that the health of both children and adults is negatively affected in
significant ways by increased rates of divorce and out-of-wedlock births.
Sara McLanahan and Gary Sandefur's research probably has gotten the
most attention. They demonstrated that children not raised by their own
biological parents are, on average and when all relevant variables are controlled, two to three times more likely to drop out of school, have children
out of wedlock, and have difficulties attaching to the job market.[24] In
short, the effects of increased reliance on technical rationality in modern

20. Gary Becker, *A Treatise on the Family* (Cambridge: Harvard University Press, 1991);
Richard Posner, *Sex and Reason* (Cambridge: Harvard University Press, 1992).

21. Frederick Engels, *The Origin of the Family, Private Property, and the State* (New York: International Publications, 1972).

22. Alan Wolfe, *Whose Keeper? Social Science and Moral Obligation* (Berkeley, Calif.: University of California Press, 1989), pp. 52, 133.

23. Gunilla Ringback Weitoft, Anders Hjern, Bengt Haglund, and Mans Rosen, "Mortality, Severe Morbidity and Injury in Children Living with Single Parents in Sweden: A
Population-Based Study," *The Lancet* 361 (January 25): 289-95.

24. Sara McLanahan and Gary Sandefur, *Growing Up with a Single Parent* (Princeton,
N.J.: Princeton University Press, 1994), pp. 32-38. Loss of income is a contributing factor but
accounts for only half of the differential between children raised in intact and disrupted
families.

societies have been ambiguous, with some deleterious consequences for families and the institution of marriage, and this in both market and more socialist countries.

Sharpening the Question

Hence, the explanatory perspectives on the descriptive theological moment were both significant and limited in their meaning. Without the normative horizon of Western theology and a legal tradition significantly influenced by that theology, both the sociological facts and the wider theories would have little meaning. But deepening our first naive descriptions of the situation of families in modern societies did lead us to reformulate our initial question once again. We gradually began to ask this question: *In view of the almost inevitable increase of technical rationality in modern society, with all of its ambiguous effects on families, should the church, in both its ecclesial and public ministries, try to (1) resist these family changes, (2) support the increasingly fragmented families that are the product of these changes, or (3) carry out some combination of resistance and support?* Framed this way, the issue was not just a question about families; it was a question about the church's attitude toward modernity itself.

In order to deal with this emerging question, our research traveled the hermeneutic circle from descriptive theology, to historical theology, to systematic and moral theology, to strategic-practical theology. I will mention only a few of the many books that came from the project and how they tended to specialize on one or another of these steps around the practical-hermeneutical circle. Two biblical books were commissioned that proved to be path-breaking: Carolyn Osiek and David Balch wrote the seminal *Families in the New Testament World*, which helped open the growing field of family biblical research;[25] a team led by Leo Perdue wrote *Families in Ancient Israel* and demonstrated how central families were for mediating the covenant between God and Israel.[26] Legal historian John Witte helped round out our critical retrieval of the Christian classics on marriage and family in his outstanding review of the interaction between Christianity and the law in the formation of Western marriage and family

25. Carolyn Osiek and David Balch, *Families in the New Testament World: Households and House Churches* (Louisville, Ky.: Westminster John Knox, 1997).

26. Leo Perdue, Joseph Blenkinsopp, John J. Collins, and Carol Myers, *Families in Ancient Israel* (Louisville, Ky.: Westminster John Knox, 1997).

institutions — a history, by the way, which very few people, religious or secular, understand. In short, Western society is relatively ignorant about its effective history — that which already has formed it — on marriage and family matters.

The third step in the practical hermeneutical circle is exemplified by the summary book called *From Culture Wars to Common Ground: Religion and the American Family Debate*, which I co-authored with Bonnie Miller-McLemore, Pamela Couture, Bernie Lyon, and Robert Franklin.[27] This book follows the full circle of the practical-theological project but specializes in a group of descriptive and normative arguments about family, children, and marriage. In the last chapters, it advances sixteen strategic-practical theological proposals aimed at both the inner life of the ecclesia and the public worlds of politics, government, and business. Other books in our series move into the strategic area as well.

Of the three alternative strategies mentioned above — to resist the family changes wrought by modernity, to support and include them, or to both critically resist and selectively support, we chose the last. This is the view I have developed in *From Culture Wars to Common Ground* and in two subsequent books, *Reweaving the Social Tapestry: Toward a Public Philosophy and Policy for Families*[28] and *Marriage and Modernization: How Globalization Threatens Marriage and What to Do about It.*[29]

To resist these changes is, in effect, a countercultural stance on the mission of the church to families. It says that the conspiracy between cultural individualism and technical rationality is neither entirely good nor inevitable. A prophetic ministry must critique these trends. On the other hand, my colleagues and I have taken the stance that there are some features of modernity that are indeed good for families and worth preserving — for example, more equality for women, better and more universal education, and generally higher standards of living and health care, at least for those who do not have these benefits jeopardized by family disruption. Hence, our response of resistance was not totalistic; it was selective and not without supportive elements. It followed from the reconstructive and critical hermeneutic retrieval of the marvelous and multidimensional

27. Don Browning, Bonnie Miller-McLemore, Pamela Couture, Bernie Lyon, and Robert Franklin, *From Culture Wars to Common Ground: Religion and the American Family Debate* (Louisville, Ky.: Westminster John Knox, 1997, 2000).

28. Don Browning and Gloria Rodriguez, *Reweaving the Social Tapestry: Toward a Public Philosophy and Policy for Families* (New York: Norton, 2002).

29. Don Browning, *Marriage and Modernization: How Globalization Threatens Marriage and What to Do about It* (Grand Rapids: Eerdmans, 2003).

marriage and family tradition of Christianity. In the remaining portions of this lecture, I will try to illustrate a few points about how our reconstruction and critique came about.

I will illustrate this reconstructive interpretive process by discussing two important and interrelated issues — the role of patriarchy in Christian marriage and the nature of an adequate theology of love for families in the twenty-first century.

Patriarchy

We soon discovered new research on the honor-shame cultural background that surrounded early Christianity. It threw light on the role of patriarchy in early Christianity and helped us understand the emerging new trajectory on the nature of love and marital commitment that was opening in the nascent days of the Jesus movement. New Testament scholars Bruce Malina,[30] Halvor Moxnes,[31] and Karl Sandnes[32] have all employed in their studies the anthropological scholarship on honor-shame cultures developed by J. G. Peristiany, Julian Pitt-Rivers,[33] David Gilmore,[34] and others. This view sees marital relations in ancient Hellenistic culture, including the Roman-Hellenism in the urban centers of Israel, as defined by a popular ethic that associated male honor with dominance and agency. If a free Greek male's wife, mother, sister, or daughter were assaulted or insulted, a dominant and honorable Greek male would respond with riposte — with an aggressive defense that might lead to a duel. If he failed to do this, he would be shamed — rendered weak, submissive, and without agency. On the other hand, in this culture it was honorable for women to have or exhibit shame.[35] This meant restricting their lives as much as possible to the domestic sphere and submitting to the protection and guidance of husband, father, brother, or uncle.

30. Bruce Malina, *The New Testament World: Insights from Cultural Anthropology* (Louisville, Ky.: Westminster John Knox, 1993).

31. Halvor Moxnes, "Honor and Shame," *Biblical Theology Bulletin* 23 (1993): 167-75.

32. Karl Sandnes, *A New Family: Conversion and Ecclesiology in the Early Church with Cross-Comparisons* (New York: Peter Lang, 1994).

33. J. G. Peristiany and Julian Pitt-Rivers, eds., *Honor-Shame: The Values of Mediterranean Society* (London: Weidenfeld and Nicholson, 1966).

34. David Gilmore, *Manhood in the Making: Cultural Concepts of Masculinity* (New Haven: Yale University Press, 1990).

35. Osiek and Balch, *Families in the New Testament World,* pp. 38-41.

This ethic was pervasive in the civic culture of the Mediterranean world, including the urban centers penetrated by the earlier Christians. There is little doubt that disciples of Jesus and the apostle Paul were to some extent influenced by the surrounding honor-shame culture. But there is also evidence that early Christianity resisted it and fractured it to some extent. The model of servant husband and father found in Ephesians 5:25 reverses the image of the dominant and agentive male. The injunction for husbands to love their wives "as they do their own bodies" (Eph. 5:28) brings the principle of neighbor love into the very interior of marital and family relationships and flies in the face of the aristocratic understanding of husband-wife relations found in Aristotle. The Christian symbols of sacrament and covenant gradually began to develop around the model of the servant husband and father.

By the time of Thomas Aquinas, these symbols were used to solidify the virtues of kin altruism, paternal recognition, and paternal care in contrast to males' inclination to be tentative about bonding with and caring for the children they bring into the world.[36] In reviewing the history of the Christian theology of marriage, time and again one notices that the theologies of sacrament and covenant were used to counter such male tentativeness. The collapse of these theologies may have something to do with the emerging worldwide increase in the absence of fathers from the lives of their children, probably the major international family problematic of our time.[37] The central theological and cultural task of an adequate practical theology of families may entail finding ways to maintain the image of the committed servant father without carrying with it the patriarchy that frequently hovered around it in the past.

A New Love Ethic

In *Culture Wars to Common Ground* and my other family writings, I have argued that a love ethic of equal regard was the emerging trajectory — the emerging meaning in front of the text — of family and marriage theology in early Christian families. This could be seen in countless little ways — in women's participation in the love feast in the house church,[38] in the emer-

---

36. Thomas Aquinas, *Summa Contra Gentiles*, vol. 3, pt. 2 (London: Burns, Oates, Washbourne, 1928), pp. 114, 118; Browning, *Marriage and Modernization*, pp. 84-94.

37. Browning, *Marriage and Modernization*, pp. 75-76.

38. Steven Barton, "Paul's Sense of Place: An Anthropological Approach to Community Formation in Corinth," *New Testament Studies* 32 (1986): 74.

gence of women evangelists, and even in the denials of 1 Peter that Christians were upsetting the civic culture by giving their wives more freedom, a denial that would have been unnecessary had it not in fact been happening.[39] The honor-shame literature helps illustrate the useful role of the historical-critical method for providing explanatory insights into the background of the mode of "being-in-the world" that opened in front of the normative New Testament texts.

My colleagues and I developed a normative ethic for marriage around the ideal of love as equal regard. This concept was elaborated more with the neo-Thomistic insights of Louis Jansssens than with the neo-Kantian insights of Gene Outka, the scholar who first coined the term for love as "equal regard."[40] This view requires a strenuous equal regard for the dignity of both husband and wife and equal efforts to open for each the teleological goods of life.[41] This view sees the self-sacrificial love required by the cross as a means to the renewal of love as equal regard rather than as an end in itself.

This ethic provided us with a critique of the impact of modernity on families and marriage as well as an appreciation for some of modernity's value. Insofar as modernity has helped open the public world of politics and paid employment to women, we saw it as a good. But insofar as modernity absorbs marriage and family into the cost-benefit logic of the market or the control mechanisms of the state, we mounted a critique and resistance. We did not recommend a withdrawal of the church from modernity, but advocated introducing a whole range of curtailments to its expanding cultural logics. For instance, we recommended that a sixty-hour workweek should be provided in the paid economy for couples with children; these sixty hours would be divided flexibly between them as a way of relieving the pressures of the market economy on parenting.[42] We advocated a bill of rights for parents who temporarily leave paid employment to care for children that would guarantee tax supports and reentry into the market.[43] We promoted a variety of marriage education programs, supported by both civil society and the state, that would take mar-

39. David Balch, *Let Wives Be Submissive: The Domestic Code in 1 Peter* (Chico, Calif.: Scholars, 1981).

40. Louis Janssens, "Norms and Priorities of a Love Ethics," *Louvain Studies* 6 (Spring 1977): 207-37; Gene Outka, *Agape: An Ethical Analysis* (New Haven: Yale University Press, 1972).

41. Browning et al., *From Culture Wars to Common Ground*, pp. 276-79.

42. Browning et al., *From Culture Wars to Common Ground*, pp. 316-18.

43. Browning et al., *From Culture Wars to Common Ground*, p. 331.

ital preparation as seriously as — or even more seriously than — learning to drive an automobile.[44]

Our strategic practical theology, however, did not place all of its constructive emphasis upon curtailing the dynamics of modernization and the systems world. Even more important is the renewal of the marriage and family cultures of Western societies. This, we grew to believe, must be primarily the task of the institutions of civil society, especially its religious institutions. More than anything, the renewal of family and marriage in Western societies must be accomplished through a critical retrieval of our marriage and family traditions, both religious and legal. For the most part, that history and tradition has been lost to consciousness, even though it still continues silently to function in our effective institutional and personal histories.

There is little doubt that Judaism and Christianity have vigorously interacted with Greek, Roman, and German law as well as Aristotelian philosophy to significantly shape the marriage and family traditions of Western cultures. The fact that mutual consent by the couple, in contrast to arranged marriages by coercive families, became the mark of marriage in late medieval Roman Catholic canon law is an example of an influence most of us would value. The fact that Christian missionaries discouraged polygyny amongst the royal families of northern Europe, and hence the hoarding of women by powerful men, had much to do, as historian David Herlihy has pointed out, with the democratization of marriage in Western societies; poor men left out of the marriage market gradually had access to women, married, and established families.[45] Most of us would value that accomplishment as well. The historical story of Christian marriage and family is not always a pretty one, but principles for internal critique and reconstruction can be found within the tradition itself.

Furthermore, as I point out in my recent *Marriage and Modernization,* the critical retrieval of the Christian marriage tradition must now go hand-in-hand with the critical retrieval of the other major religious traditions — Judaism, Islam, Buddhism, Hinduism, and Confucianism. This should, in my view, be a critical-correlational and comparative scholarly endeavor. This conversation is essential both to highlight the distinctive and possible lasting contributions of the Christian tradition and to protect these religions from the public marginalization of their influence

44. Browning et al., *From Culture Wars to Common Ground,* pp. 328-29; Browning, *Marriage and Modernization,* pp. 191-210.

45. David Herlihy, *Medieval Households* (Cambridge: Harvard University Press, 1985).

during a time when economic, health, and legal perspectives increasingly are taking over the field of public discourse about marriage and family.

Rightly understood, practical theology in conversation with the empirical sciences should inform our classroom teaching. This conversation should also help us form our practical-theological research projects. In this lecture, I have tried to argue for and illustrate these two points and their interrelation.

PART II

Contexts, Descriptions, and Directions: Searching for an Emphatic Center

Chapter 3

The Family Debate: A Middle Way (1993)

(WITH IAN EVISON)

This chapter was published in the *Christian Century* shortly after Bill Clinton was elected to his first term as president of the United States. The Republican Party had determined through their polling organizations that young couples with children composed a huge bloc of citizens who vote in national elections, and that they have more conservative values than either single or elderly individuals.

Although the Republicans actually handled the "family-values" issue poorly during that election season, they were correct, I argued, in understanding that American families were under great stress and that many people were genuinely worried and with some justification. Co-author Ian Evison and I suggested that mainline Protestant Christians — the likely readers of the *Christian Century* — should take family-values issues seriously, both in politics and in the mission of the church. We outlined three possible pro-family strategies for mainline Protestant churches: (1) the new family pluralism that sees all family forms and patterns as equally good for raising children and meeting adult needs; (2) the pro-family strategy of the Christian right with its emphasis on traditional gender roles, paternal authority, and fear of government welfare programs; and (3) a third approach that proposed reconstructing the church's ethics of family toward more egalitarian values while also pushing for selected governmental and market supports for families.

In the book *From Culture Wars to Common Ground*, my colleagues and I advanced the third position and called it "critical familism." It was pro-family and pro-marriage but also critical of all obstacles to what we called the "equal regard" marriage and family. Hence, we developed a long list of social-systemic reforms that were also needed to support a pro-family vision guided by an ethic of equal regard.

A great debate is taking place over the condition and prospects of the American family. This debate reflects the fact that Americans are worried about the family. Republicans had hard evidence during the 1992 presidential campaign of the extent of this concern. The Wirthlin Group, which does most of the national polling for the Republicans, published an article in *Reader's Digest* (May 1992) which in effect outlined the Republican campaign strategy. It demonstrated that one of the largest and most cohesive voting blocs is married couples with children. According to this article, they are "a political powerhouse, a voting block of about 92 million people, 57 percent of all Americans over 25." They are surprisingly conservative on cultural values and family issues, more conservative than either singles or older couples whose children have left the nest — a point which the church should note.

The Republicans tried to win the election by appealing to this group, but they overplayed their hand. They used the family issue to single out scapegoats (single mothers and inner-city residents), they avoided talking about the economy, and they failed to develop meaningful and practical family programs.

Although the Republicans were wrong in how they used the family issue, they were right in recognizing that it is vitally important. The family debate is far from over. Note the countless articles and op-ed pieces on single parenthood, the pros and cons of professional day care, the state of children's health, family-friendly industry, parental leaves, and the sins of absent fathers. Consider the tremendous response to the *Atlantic* article (April 1993) in which Barbara Dafoe Whitehead argued that the two-parent family is better on the whole for child-rearing than are single parents or stepfamilies. This was followed by sociologist James Q. Wilson's almost identical argument in his *Commentary* article (April 1993), "The Family-Values Debate."

Voices from the mainline Protestant churches have been strangely absent from this debate. As James Davison Hunter suggests in his 1991 book *Culture Wars,* churches have been paralyzed by a division between orthodox and progressive parties that see the family issue — as they see abortion, homosexuality, education, and popular culture — in vastly different ways. Mainline churches need to say something relevant to the family debate. Before speaking up, however, they need to face squarely the disturbing trends in family life that are fueling the debate.

1. *Families are in crisis.* The central evidence is the deterioration of the physical and emotional well-being of children. Economists Victor Fuchs and Diane Reklis say bluntly, "American children are in trouble. Not all children, to be sure, but many observers consider today's children to be worse off than their parents' generation in several important dimensions of physical, mental, and emotional well-being." From 1960 to 1988, standardized test scores fell significantly, teenage suicide and homicide rates more than doubled, and obesity increased by 50 percent. In 1970, 15 percent of children were in poverty, but by the late 1980s nearly 20 percent were on or below the poverty line. An authoritative report prepared for the U.S. Department of Health and Human Services by Nicholas Zill and Charlotte Schoenborn provides more discouraging statistics. Twenty percent of children ages 3 to 17 have a developmental, learning, or behavioral disorder. By ages 12 to 17, one in four adolescents suffers from at least one of these disorders. One in three teenage boys has one of these problems.

2. *Changes in cultural values as well as changes in the economy have contributed to the crisis in families.* Changes in values may even be the key factor. Fuchs and Reklis demonstrate that children's well-being began to worsen before the economy turned sour:

> Between 1960 and 1970 the fall in test scores, the doubling of teenage suicide and homicide rates, and the doubling share of births to unwed mothers cannot be attributed to economic adversity. During that decade purchases of goods and services for children by government rose very rapidly, as did real household income per child, and the poverty rate of children plummeted. Thus, we must seek explanations for the rising problems of that period in the cultural realm.[1]

The cultural changes that Fuchs and Reklis have in mind are increasing individualism, growing preoccupation with individual fulfillment, wider tolerance for divorce as a solution to marital problems, and more general acceptance at all social levels of the high rates of out-of-wedlock births and single parenthood. These shifts in values preceded and now interact with worsening economic conditions.

3. *Changing values have interacted with worsening economic conditions to create increasing numbers of poor women and children.* Much of this poverty is as-

1. Victor Fuchs and Diane Reklis, "America's Children: Economic Perspectives and Policy Options," *Science* 255 (Jan. 3, 1992): 42.

sociated with single parents, most of whom are women, and is produced by divorce and out-of-wedlock births. The divorce rate has been increasing for a century. It rose from 7 percent in 1860 to over 50 percent today. Furthermore, demographer Larry Bumpass says that "life table estimates suggest that 17 percent of white women and 70 percent of black women will have a child while unmarried if recent levels persist." According to the Census Bureau the proportion of children born to unmarried women has doubled since 1970 to 28 percent in 1990. Bumpass estimates that 44 percent of all children born between 1970 and 1984 will spend some of their youth in a single-parent home. Frank Furstenberg and Andrew Cherlin say in *Divided Familes* (1991) that if present trends continue, that "figure could reach 60 percent." It is now more frequently admitted that single parenthood, on the whole, is a disadvantage for raising children. This is true even when single-parent families are not poor, although they frequently are. We have been slow to acknowledge this because we do not want to stigmatize single mothers who are often heroic, frequently quite successful as parents, and may be single for a wide variety of reasons. But in avoiding moralism we should not neglect the truth of the situation. Whitehead and Wilson, in the articles mentioned earlier, summarize well the social science data on this point. Children of single-parent families are far more likely even when they are not poor to do badly in school, get in trouble with the law, have poor mental and physical health, and have marital difficulties later in life.

4. *The single most important trend in American families today is the increasing absence of fathers and the feminization of kinship.* By feminization of kinship we mean that the families of children are increasingly composed of women — mothers, grandmothers, and aunts — who do the child care. Men are increasingly absent from families and their children. Social scientists report that fathers of out-of-wedlock children and divorced fathers give surprisingly little economic or emotional support to their biological children. There are exceptions. There are the good fathers who do everything they can to give financial and relational support to their children born from former unions. But a large number of these fathers gradually give less and less of either. Furstenberg and Cherlin report that a recent national survey found that after divorce "only one child in six saw his or her father as often as once a week on average. Close to half had not visited with their fathers in the 12 months preceding the survey. Another sixth had seen them less often than once a month."[2] Monetary payments by di-

---

2. Frank F. Furstenberg Jr. and Andrew J. Cherlin, *Divided Familes: What Happens to Children When Parents Part* (Cambridge, Mass.: Harvard University Press, 1991), p. 11.

vorced fathers to their children are low. Fathers of children born out of wedlock visit and pay even less.

5. *Families in our society are simultaneously undergoing both deinstitutionalization and coercive reinstitutionalization.* Marriage is losing its normative status. By deinstitutionalization we mean not only that fewer couples ask the church to bless their unions but that many are not even asking the state to make their families official. The proportion of first marriages that were preceded by cohabitation increased from 8 percent in the late 1960s to 49 percent by the mid 1980s. The average duration of cohabitation is short — a median of 1.5 years. Forty percent of these unions split before marriage.

Our point is not to moralize about cohabitation but to raise a more complex issue. The deinstitutionalization of marriage and family has led to a new brand of coercive, state-enforced regulation of the family. For example, the state of California requires fathers of out-of-wedlock births to pay the same rate of support as divorced fathers. But such a requirement tremendously expands government control over private lives. Most young men have not awakened to this. One thoughtless sexual adventure can lead to a lifetime responsibility — enforced by the strong arm of the state. A man can avoid marriage, but he is less likely to avoid the courts and their collection agencies. Even the newly developing category of "domestic partnerships" invites coercive state intrusion. Determining the validity of domestic partnerships will entail some investigation by employers and the state into the private lives of couples. Nothing comes free; red tape and public declarations of one kind or another may be required for all those who want government protections and benefits.

6. *Family law is diverging sharply from the inherited traditions of the church.* For centuries family law in Western industrial societies either reflected or was highly consistent with church teachings. Historian James Brundage and legal historian John Witte have described how Catholic canon law of the Middle Ages was used to a significant extent by both the Protestant Reformation and much of secular family law in Western society. It was for this reason that the law, until the 1960s, resisted or delayed divorce, gave a privileged status to monogamous marriage, and upheld the need for public commitments of a mutually consenting man and woman as the ground for the formation of legal families. Now most if not all of these traditional commitments of secular family law are up for grabs. We are likely to hear talk soon of legalizing polygamy, extending marriage privileges to the unmarried, and possibly even abolishing marriage, as the

moderator of a conference on "Law and Nature" at Brown University recently proposed.

Family issues will be the dominant ones facing the churches in the 1990s and possibly into the next century. They will be hotter than issues of race, or of investment in South Africa, or of involvement in Central America. Family issues hit people in their innermost beings.

After several decades of ignoring or neglecting families, mainline churches will have to decide which of three pro-family strategies to adopt. The first strategy, the most popular in many liberal churches and denominations, will be simply to accept the new pluralism of the family. According to this view, churches must accept openly and without prejudice the full range of single families, stepfamilies, cohabiting families, and same-sex families that modern societies are evolving. This position believes that churches also should pressure the government to extend the range of economic and social supports so that these changing families and their children will not become poor. The church in this view should aim in its ministry to provide the psychological and communal supports that help families maintain their dignity and self-esteem.

The second pro-family strategy, that of resisting family pluralism, is advocated by the Christian right. Some of the mainline churches will move in this direction for want of a better strategy. In emphasizing the centrality of the intact two-parent family, the conservative strategy probably will continue to emphasize traditional gender roles (even if gently) and to advocate aggressive anti-homosexual policies. This approach regards the problems of families as primarily cultural, the result of a decline in values, and it distrusts most governmental and legal intrusions. It would cure the problems of families with a triumphalist spread of Christian values into the lives of Christians and non-Christians alike and into all corners of public policy.

The third pro-family strategy, the one we advocate, is to try to reconstruct the church's ethics of families while advocating selected governmental and market supports for families. This approach recognizes that the family crisis is caused both by cultural changes and by social-systematic developments in areas of work, economics, child care, and gender inequality. This view recognizes, along with the conservative voices, that unfettered individualism and its drive for adult fulfillment at the expense of children present a real threat to the family. But this third strategy sees the drive toward individualism as partially good. It supports, for example, the push toward more equality for women. Aspects of individualism can be included with integrity in those interpretations of Christian love which see it as commanding a strenuous equal regard for both self and other. This view tries to hold individual fulfillment and regard for the other, be it spouse or children or both, in rigorous balance. Although the Jesus movement and Pauline Christianity never completely freed themselves from the patriarchy of the ancient world, they went far in replacing Greco-Roman male honor-shame patterns and related aristocratic forms of masculine dominance with servanthood models of male responsibility. Furthermore, they pushed the rule of neighbor love and the egalitarianism of the Galatians 3:28 baptismal formula ("there is neither male nor female; for you are all one in Christ Jesus") to the point of threatening patriarchal patterns both within and outside the early Christian ecclesia. This third pro-family approach affirms gender equality even as it both affirms and criticizes aspects of modern individualism.

Mainline churches must recapture their interest in children. For thirty years mainline denominations have tended to see the problems of children and families as private issues. They have held that if the church could help society establish economic and racial justice, the welfare of families and children would automatically follow. The above analysis shows how inadequate this view has proved to be. It failed to anticipate the tremendous shifts in cultural values that have preoccupied adults and undermined the well-being of children and youth. Today, support for family programs, for developing family theory and family theology, and for local initiatives on behalf of families should be top denominational priorities.

Churches should be skeptical, however, of programs that treat children as if they were not a part of families, thereby undermining family solidarity and parental responsibility. Furthermore, they should resist becoming a tool or agent of government programs that have no interest in the unique values and mission of the church. Churches should attempt to find their own voice, their own style, their own message, and their own programs, making all other necessary collaborations, even with the state, fit with integrity into their unique identities.

To put children first, mainline churches need to resist easy talk about the new family pluralism. Without becoming moralistic, they need to recognize that not all family forms are equal for the task of raising children. Intact families have, on the whole, more emotional and material resources for this task. We need to recognize that family pluralism has too often meant exempting men from their responsibilities in raising children, leaving women to do the job. Some people do not believe that fathers are very important for families. For instance, Judge Richard Posner in *Sex and Reason* (1991) argues that, other things being equal, there is no convincing evidence that outside of their procreative functions fathers are necessary for the well-being of their children. In contrast to this view, we believe that the Christian tradition, common sense, and the recent social-science evidence summarized by Whitehead, Wilson, and others make a strong case for the importance of the educative and moral role of fathers with children, in addition to their procreative and financial contributions. Even if it were possible to replace fathers with government supports, better-paying jobs for single mothers, day care, and elaborate social and extended-family networks, it would be unhealthy for both men and society to have increasing numbers of single men adrift without connections to families.

While the church should promote the egalitarian, intact mother-father partnership as the center of its family ethic, it also must recognize that a pluralism of family forms is a part of modern life, including church life. There is much that churches can do to ease the burden of single parents and stepfamilies and to help them do better jobs of raising children. Some churches — mainly large evangelical churches and some black churches — have outstanding programs for a wide range of family types. They give special emphasis to the two-parent family and at the same time deal realistically, nonjudgmentally, and helpfully with all families. Some of these churches have strong programs in marriage preparation and marriage and family enrichment, as well as strong support groups for single parents, divorced people, and stepfamilies. They preach and teach regularly about family issues. Some run day-care programs, after-school programs, parental training groups, and sometimes even home visitation programs which assist families with their daily interactions. Some have special programs for men and young boys. Many black churches have programs designed to prepare young men for responsible marriage and parenting. Many conservative churches are able to maintain the tension between their ideals about families and realistic support for where families actually are. But many otherwise excellent programs in conservative and fundamentalist churches are marred by rigid gender distinctions and oppressive male authority. The liberal, mainline churches would do well to imitate the energy of some of the conservative churches on family matters, while finding a new language and new ethic to guide their programs.

If liberal churches are to help reverse the trends toward family decline, their youth programs should emphasize preparation for life in the egalitarian, postmodern family. This family will be "postmodern" because it will not idealize the rigid distinctions between public and private, work and home, breadwinner father and domestic mother that characterized the family that adapted to early industrial society. Since one of the major trends of family life in America is the absence of fathers and the feminization of kinship, boys and young men should be a major target for the church's family programs. If all family forms were equal for raising children, then young men could be ignored. They would not be needed. But if intact mother-father teams are generally better for children, then serious work with young men about parenting ideals and skills should be part of the church's mission.

With regard to trends in family law, mainline churches must live with ambivalence. They must realize that family law may continue to diverge from inherited Christian morality on family matters. The law may grant legal status to more forms of domestic partnership. It may continue to ease divorce proceedings through no-fault settlements. It may protect the rights of youth to make moral decisions about abortion and contraception without the knowledge, and against the moral guidance, of their parents.

But mainline churches would be wise not to adopt these legal developments as their basic morality. Churches should forge their own unique position on family and sexual ethics and help their members live by it. At the same time, churches must realize that some of the new trends in family law may make some sense; it is the primary function of law to regulate behavior, not necessarily to project the moral ideal. Projecting the ideal is the task of culture-making institutions such as the church. This does not mean that churches should be entirely passive before the law. They have the right to influence the law, just like any other group in our society. One part of the law worth influencing, for instance, is divorce laws. Here the task may not be to make divorce more difficult to obtain; rather, the task may be to require divorcing parents to make better long-term financial plans for their children, plans which the courts could enforce.

Finally, the church must understand that there is a place for government family supports in complex postindustrial societies. But they should not petition government to solve those problems that only churches and other voluntary organizations can successfully address. Since the days of their successes in the civil rights movement, mainline churches have tended to think they are fulfilling their mission when they lobby government for worthwhile programs. The first obligation of the churches is to discern their own message, their own values, their own programs; only after these are established should they work to influence government policy.

Nevertheless, government policies are important. Some government programs build families; others tear them down. Some undermine family authority and put control in the hands of experts outside the family. Others build family coherence and deliver real assistance. One such proposal, which has gained support from political right and left, is to increase personal federal income tax exemptions for dependent children. It was first proposed by the Progressive Policy Institute. It recommends increasing the exemption that parents can claim for dependent children from $2,300 to $6,000 or $7,000 for each child. This would make exemptions for dependents equal in value to the original $600 per child that families received in 1948, the year the IRS first allowed the exemptions. The Rockefeller Report titled *Beyond Rhetoric* (1991) went in a slightly different direction; it recommended a $1,000 tax credit for each child. These kinds of legislation help families without causing dependency and without putting family functions into the hands of government. They expand the income of parents and make it possible, for instance, to purchase day care or provide the child care themselves.

Our aim has not been to offer a comprehensive pro-family strategy, but to suggest what a coherent strategy might look like. If nothing more, we have tried to show that a middle road exists and that in the long run it may offer the best course to follow both for the church and for society.

Chapter 4

Is the Family a Conservative Issue? (1994)

This chapter was first given as the Rerum Novarum Lecture in Melboune, Australia, in June of 1994. The Roman Catholic archdiocese of Melbourne was my host, and the larger context was the United Nation's First International Year of the Family, which the archdiocese was celebrating. My goal was to communicate to my Australian audience how in the United States the family was moving from a conservative political and religious topic to one that liberals — at least political liberals — also had begun to champion. Actually, I made a distinction between political liberals and a new group of neo-liberals. Neo-liberals were politically engaged persons who interpreted the crisis of families as caused by both social-systemic injustice *and* changing cultural values. Neo-liberals tended to believe that to address constructively family issues required reconstructing cultural values pertaining to marriage and family as well as remedying social-structural injustice. Neo-liberals differed from political conservatives who both advocated and politically exploited family values but tended to ignore remedying social-systemic factors that were undermining families. They also differed from political liberals who tended to address family disruption with social-systemic reform in welfare and employment yet often omitted taking value issues seriously.

In my lecture, I identified with the new political neo-liberals who addressed family values as well as social reforms needed to support families. This was one of the early ways I spoke about critical familism as a practical-theological position on marriage and family issues. The actual concept of critical familism was not fully introduced until the publication of *From Culture Wars to Common Ground* three years later.

I lamented in this essay my failure at that time to find in the main-line Protestant churches anything analogous to the neo-liberal sensibilities that I found among political liberals who debated family matters in the U.S. Congress — a lack which I am afraid exists even today as I pen these words. Hence, a middle and more balanced way on family issues is still hard to find in the churches.

For years, in the political culture of the United States, the family was seen as a conservative issue. Ronald Reagan and George Bush, both Republicans, were elected to the presidency by championing the rhetoric of family values. They successfully appealed to political conservatives, Christian evangelicals, fundamentalists, and conservative Catholics. Their family rhetoric helped them capture the highest office of the land.

In 1992, this strategy failed when Dan Quayle, in his famous *Murphy Brown* address, attempted to implement it once again. Murphy Brown, a sitcom television newswoman played by actress Candice Bergen, decided to have a baby out of wedlock. Dan Quayle attacked the *Murphy Brown* show, and the television and movie industry in general, for undermining family values and undercutting the importance of the two-parent family. This time the Republican appeal to values backfired. Bill Clinton and Al Gore successfully depicted the family-values rhetoric as a ploy to avoid serious issues pertaining to the economy, health care, and welfare reform. Bush lost the election, and, for a brief time, it seemed that the family issue would vanish from the American political, cultural, and religious agenda.

This impression soon proved wrong. What really happened was that the family issue became a liberal issue. It might be more accurate to call it a "neo-liberal" issue. For the last two years, the political culture of the United States has undergone a significant realignment, and the family issue is now at the core of a new set of conversations and a new set of alliances. Why has this happened?

Before I answer this question, let me confess my caution about telling this story. I do not assume that the political, cultural, or religious life of the United States has any direct or immediate relevance to Australia. But comparison is generally useful even if it is not immediately applicable. I assume I can learn something from the Australian experience that will be instructive for issues we face in the United States. It is likely that both the United States and Australia, in spite of important differences, are confronting similar social, cultural, and political trends, as are most of the countries of the advanced industrial world. To learn from one another, we must tell each other something about our national and cultural experiences. With this aim in mind, let me begin the dialogue by telling you something of the shifting cultural, political, and religious climate in the United States insofar as it touches the family debate.

Family as a Conservative Issue

The family was thought to be a conservative issue in the 1970s and 1980s for a wide range of reasons. First, the family in both church and political culture began to be seen as a private issue. The victory of the civil rights movement set the stage for both the religious and political climate. Institutional racial discrimination was largely ended in the United States through Supreme Court rulings, legislative enactments, and state enforcement of the law. The demise of legalized racism did not come about by converting individuals one at a time. Because of this, it suddenly seemed logical to effect social change of all kinds from the top down — at the level of large-scale change in social systems rather than at the level of individuals and families. This emphasis on the importance of large-scale social change also corresponded with Marxism and its stress on class revolution and radical alteration in the means of production. One can find a similar point in liberation theology, which has had a decided impact on the leadership of the liberal American churches. At least a full decade before the Republican Party picked up "family values" as a campaign theme, the leadership of liberal religion and liberal politics believed that family problems were primarily social-systemic problems — the result of discrimination, inadequate distribution of wealth, and lack of access to the educational and occupational goods of society. If family problems existed (and many doubted that they did), then government policies, welfare, and universal education would gradually eradicate them. From one perspective, the conservative emphasis on the values that produce family cohesion was an antithesis to a prior liberal thesis that social conditions, not individual or family values, were the important variables affecting children.

The Neo-Liberal, Neo-Conservative Conversation

There is much more to this story that should be told. But my brief discussion here should be sufficient to illustrate how the conversation about families has changed. The sociologist James Davison Hunter in his 1990 book *Culture Wars* classified the parties in the family debate as orthodox or conservatives on the one side, and liberals or progressives on the other. Today, there is a conversation developing between an emerging group of mediating political, cultural, and religious leaders. This is a conversation between a new group of "neo-liberals" and a new group of "neo-conservatives." Neo-liberals are liberals who still believe that government intervention and support in the areas of families, education, and welfare are necessary to overcome poverty, discrimination, and injustice, but who have now begun to believe that cultural values are also important and that the values men and women hold about family formation, family preservation, and the importance of children are crucial to the common good. Neo-liberals include the Democratic Leadership Council, the Communitarian Movement (led by Amitai Etzioni, Mary Ann Glendon, and Jean Bethke Elshtain), the leadership of the Institute for American Values, William Galston (deputy domestic adviser to President Clinton), and Bill Clinton himself. It is more difficult to find organizations from the mainline churches who hold explicitly neo-liberal views, but there are individuals who do. Although we all eschew labels, especially for ourselves, if I were to be located anywhere, it would be somewhere in this neo-liberal camp — in case you are interested in knowing my position. And I have at least a few friends in religious circles.

In some instances it is difficult to distinguish neo-liberals from neo-conservatives on the family issue. Sometimes their differences are primarily their respective histories. Neo-conservatives are more likely to emphasize deteriorating cultural values in their diagnosis of the problems with families. They are also more skeptical of government solutions than are neo-liberals. But this is precisely where the change has come about. There exists today a group of formerly conservative individuals and institutions now proposing a variety of governmental supports for families — some of which are both expensive and extensive.

The conservative Family Research Council — at one time but no longer the policy wing of Christian psychologist James Dobson's Focus on the Family — is a good example. This conservative think tank has proposed a number of tax measures to support families with children, encourage family formation, and support poor two-parent families. This research group is less interested in direct welfare payments and more interested in tax measures for families that encourage welfare independence and employment. The twist in the contemporary discussion is that many liberals and neo-liberals now believe that tax measures, enlarged

64

child exemptions, earned income tax credits, negative income tax measures, and tax breaks for poor two-income families may be preferable to direct welfare payments and similar cash transfers as means of helping families.

Neo-conservatives are still conservatives; they still believe that changes in cultural values such as increased individualism and careerism, less interest in and commitment to marriage, more readiness to divorce, and greater acceptance of out-of-wedlock births are the deeper causes of family decline. They hold that these value changes need to be addressed by both the cultural institutions of the voluntary sector and the moral influence of government. What is genuinely surprising is that both neo-liberals and neo-conservatives now hold that government needs to go beyond moral neutrality on family issues and state a basic public ethic for families. Hence, we hear in the political talk of both neo-liberals, such as Clinton and Galston, and neo-conservatives, such as the Family Research Council, a new moral language about the importance of the intact two-parent family, the importance of putting children first, the importance of fathers for families, the importance of paternal accountability, and the moral and practical need to discourage teen pregnancies and out-of-wedlock births. We also hear in both groups of a struggle to re-envision more creative, less dependency-producing government assistance to all kinds of families in which the welfare of children is at stake.

Why Liberals Became Interested in the Values Issue

Why did some political liberals suddenly become interested in family formation, family preservation, the renewal of marriage, and the moderation of divorce? The reasons are at least twofold: first, the growing evidence documenting the deteriorating health and economic condition of children and single mothers, and, second, the growing violence among children of broken families and single parents. The facts are sobering and more extreme than those depicting the situation of families in Australia. But I understand that Australia may be catching up with the United States, which is, as you will soon see, the world leader in depressing family statistics.

Evidence for growing poverty of single mothers and the deteriorating mental and physical health of children is the weightiest factor influencing this change of mind. Increases in divorce and out-of-wedlock-births seem to be the proximate causes behind these trends. Take divorce. The 1970s and 1980s saw a tremendous rise in the divorce rate; it now stands at around 50 percent and is predicted to go higher. The Australian divorce rate is around 38 percent. It was not until the mid 1980s, with the research of Lenore Weitzman and Greg Duncan, that we began to understand that divorce corresponded to a precipitous decline in the economic well-being of mothers and their children — about a 30 percent drop during the first year after divorce in contrast to a 15 percent increase in economic well-being for divorcing men. According to one study about 10 percent of white children and 14 percent of black children whose parents separated fell into poverty the following year.

If one combines the consequences of divorce with those of out-of-wedlock births, the facts look darker. Forty-five percent of female-headed families with children under eighteen are poor in contrast to only 7 percent of families with children headed by a married couple. In the United States, fathers of divorce do not, on the whole, support their children very well, either financially or emotionally. Child-support payments amount to only 10 percent of the income of separated and single mothers and 13 percent of the income of divorced mothers. In addition, divorced fathers spend little time with their children. According to one national study conducted in 1981, only one child in six saw his or her father as often as once a week, and close to half had not visited with their fathers in the twelve months preceding the study.

Declining economic well-being, declining attention from fathers, and mounting stress on poor and overworked mothers — all of these factors have resulted in deteriorating mental and physical health of children in the United States. A 1988 national survey conducted by the Department of Health and Human Services showed that 20 percent of children between the ages of three and seventeen had a developmental, learning, or behavioral disorder. Between the ages of twelve and seventeen, one in four had one of these difficulties, and, among boys, the rate was one in three. The report credited the decline of the stable two-parent family as a major factor behind these trends. Other indices of child well-being are discouraging. Economists Victor Fuchs and Diane Reklis report that between 1960 and 1980 teenage suicide rates tripled, standardized academic test scores fell, and obesity rates (and associated symptoms of hypertension, psychosocial problems, respiratory disease, and diabetes) climbed. The correlation between teenage crime and broken homes became clearer. Louis Sullivan, former secretary of the U.S. Department of Health and Human Services, reports that over 70 percent of young males in prison come from homes where the father is absent.

The Great Shift in the Liberal Consensus

These facts began to weigh on the conscience of most everyone interested in the national good. They also weighed on the conscience of many liberals deeply committed to social justice. What did they mean? Were they true? Were they a result of a changing, indeed corrupt, new set of individualistic and self-indulgent values? Or were they the result of changing economic conditions and unjust social practices? Or were both sets of factors involved? Declining economic conditions and inadequate governmental programs are clearly a factor, but there is new information suggesting that their importance can be exaggerated. Changing values and declining commitment to marriage, family, and children explain more than we once thought. For instance, economists Fuchs and Reklis in a 1992 article published in the prestigious *Science* magazine demonstrate how the decline in the physical and emotional well-being of children began in the 1970s when there was less child poverty, higher family incomes, and more government investment in children than ever before. Fuchs and Reklis conclude:

> Both cultural and material changes have probably contributed to the problems of America's children; the relative importance of the different explanations, however, varies over time. Between 1960 and 1970 the fall in test scores, the doubling of teenage suicide and homicide rates, and the doubling share of birth to unwed mothers cannot be attributed to economic adversity. During that decade purchases of goods and services for children by government rose very rapidly, as did real household income per child, and the poverty rate of children plummeted. Thus, we must seek explanations for the rising problems of that period in the cultural realm.

In the decade of the 1980s, Fuchs and Reklis point out, economic conditions in the United States for families and children did grow worse. But their interpretation goes something like this: declining economic conditions further aggravated deteriorations in childhood emotional and physical health — deteriorations caused first by the cultural shifts of the preceding decade of the 1970s. By shifts in the cultural realm, they mean increased individualism, careerism, and the growing tendency to resolve conflicts of interest between adults and children in favor of the interests of adults.

One measure of this cultural shift was the decrease in the amount of

1. Victor Fuchs and Diane Reklis, "America's Children: Economic Perspectives and Policy Options," *Science* 255 (Jan. 3, 1992): 42.

time adults spent with children. During the 1970s the birthrate fell. The result was that there were more adults to take care of fewer children. There should have been more time available for children. But a 1985 study by a University of Maryland sociologist reported that parents spent seventeen hours a week with their children in contrast to thirty hours in 1965. A very recent report shows that it is the middle- and upper-middle-class suburbanites, in contrast to the inner-city poor, who are more likely to leave their children alone and unsupervised. A recent Census Bureau report states, "children mostly to be left unsupervised lived in suburbs, where the rate was 9.3 percent, as opposed to 6.8 percent in cities and 5.3 percent in rural areas." One news account reports that "high-income individuals and those with some college education were more likely than others to leave children unattended." Thus, the declining amount of time spent with children is not a matter of economic necessity alone.

The economic explanation of family decline has been further qualified by the work of my University of Chicago colleagues Mark Testa and William Julius Wilson. Wilson's 1987 book entitled *The Truly Disadvantaged* advanced the thesis that the problems of poor, inner-city families were due to the flight of industry and jobs from the inner city. Inner-city men, most of whom were black, could not form families because they could not afford to support them — hence the explosion of out-of-wedlock births and absent fathers. There is no question that Wilson's thesis is largely true, but it is now being revised. His colleague Mark Testa found that the values of inner-city black males have changed since the 1940s, reflecting changes in the wider society. Even when black males do get jobs and move into the middle class, they are more reluctant to marry, even to marry the women who gave birth to their children. Wilson's next book is expected to emphasize the importance of both cultural values and economic conditions and will begin to explore the importance of culture-making institutions, such as inner-city churches, in reconstructing the value commitments of black men. No one can visit the black churches surrounding the University of Chicago where I teach without learning that it is precisely this agenda to reconstitute the black family by reordering the values of black males that is central to these churches.

The growing recognition of the importance of family stability and family form was reflected in a recent address given by moral philosopher and policy analyst William Galston, presently deputy assistant on domestic affairs to President Clinton. Family structure, he argues, affects the well-being of children more than race. His favorite statistic comes from the *Kids Count* report of the Casey Foundation. The children of single-parent teenagers were ten times more likely to be in poverty than the children of young married couples who finished high school and waited until age twenty to have their first child. Furthermore, Galston reports Census Bureau statistics to the effect that "the children of white single-parent families are two-and-a-half times more likely to be living in poverty [than] are the children in black two-parent families."

Such reports explain why Charles Murray's October 1993 editorial in the *Wall Street Journal* received such a positive hearing, even among neoliberals who do not agree with everything that he says. Murray, a fellow at the American Enterprise Institute and author of the 1984 *Losing Ground,* argued in that editorial that the trend toward out-of-wedlock births, now at 68 percent in the black community, is spreading to the white community and promises to create a new white underclass. The out-of-wedlock birthrate in the white community is now at 22 percent, the rate that existed in the black community in the early 1960s when the rate in the white community was only 5 percent. (The out-of-wedlock birthrate in Australia is 24 percent, only 4 percentage points lower than the national rate of 28 percent in the United States.) Murray argues that social attitudes toward family formation and out-of-wedlock births are changing rapidly and are far more permissive, even among working- and middle-class whites. As a result of these value changes, there now exists the possibility of an explosion of out-of-wedlock births in the white community, with a potential drastic downward spiral in the standard of living by single-parent families that get trapped in this spreading trend. Murray, as is well known, would correct this trend by taking all government support or welfare away from mothers giving birth out-of-wedlock. This is a radical cure that, I would say, might not cure at all. What is new, in the United States, is that many liberals, deeply concerned with social justice and the needs of poor women and children, are now willing to take more seriously Murray's diagnosis even though they reject his solutions.

These recognitions have led much of American liberal political culture to reject the thinking advanced by sociologists such as Jesse Barnard or the 1977 Carnegie report, which claimed that diversity of family form was a benign inevitability and that the effects of family break-up need not be serious. It is not surprising that in the 1991 report of the bipartisan National Commission on Children chaired by Senator John Rockefeller, the following words were written:

Children do best when they have the personal involvement and material support of a father and mother and when both parents fulfill their responsibility to be loving providers. . . . Rising rates of divorce, out-of-wedlock childbearing and absent parents are not just manifestations of alternative lifestyles, they are patterns of adult behavior that increase children's risk of negative consequences.[2]

Similar conclusions stated in even stronger terms were reached by a more recent report submitted to President Bush entitled "Families First." The report argues that "The trend of family fragmentation drives the nation's most pressing social problems: crime, educational failure, declining mental health, drug abuse, and poverty. These in turn further fragment families."

The Role of Religion in the Family Debate

Where are American religious institutions in this new interest in the moral and value dimension of the family discussion? The answer goes something like this. Most Protestant denominations are split between conservative and progressive wings. The bureaucratic leadership of these denominations tends to be old-style liberals who are, for the most part, slow to understand the present dimensions of the family crisis in the United States. When they do address family issues, they are likely to combine a message of social justice with an economic analysis of the reasons for the declining well-being of children and mothers. These denominations have little to say about how churches can help in reconstructing the values supporting a post-industrial, egalitarian, mother-father team dedicated to the flourishing of children. Much of the leadership of the mainstream Protestant denominations assumes the analysis of the older liberalism and seems not to have taken the turn represented in the new conversations between neo-liberals and neo-conservatives in the arena of political culture.

Protestant evangelicals, along with Protestant fundamentalists, have always seen family problems in terms of declining values. This is moderating somewhat as both religious and political neo-conservatives struggle to find new forms of governmental and economic supports for families. The Catholic Church in the United States is very much in the middle. When it looks at family issues from the perspective of the task of the worshipping

2. United States National Commission on Children, *Beyond Rhetoric: A New American Agenda for Children and Families* (Washington, D.C.: National Commission on Children, 1991), p. xix.

and confessing church, it is concerned to implement among the faithful the family ethics of the Catholic Church. The Catholic Church resists the entrance of the state into matters of birth control and sex education, but it generally supports a liberal to neo-liberal agenda on welfare supports and tax breaks for families.

A remarkable twist in contemporary alliances can be found in the fact that, when neo-liberals at the political level look for religious allies, they are more likely to turn to evangelicals and Catholics than they are to liberal Protestants. This is primarily because the new neo-liberals want the church to be the church. What do I mean? They want religious bodies to be a place where a powerful family ethic — and its supporting narratives, rituals, and institutional patterns — is proclaimed and powerfully implemented in the religious socialization of their members. This could be seen in the December 1993 speech by Galston on the emerging family policy of the Clinton administration. After summarizing a vast array of administration's economic and welfare initiatives to help families, he added that government "must do this work in cooperation with perhaps the most important institutions in American civil society: namely, religious institutions. We cannot pretend that government can get the job done . . . unless we learn how to cooperate more fully and more effectively with religious institutions." Galston characterized this new governmental alliance with religious institutions in helping families as "maximum feasible accommodation" between church and state.

Galston is a distinguished moral philosopher on leave to the White House from the University of Maryland. In his 1991 book titled *Liberal Purposes,* he outlines, with great force, the role of religion in creating the cultural and moral prerequisites for a just and democratic state. Galston develops a theory of Aristotelian democracy in contrast to the model of juridical liberalism dominating ideas of democracy in recent liberal theory. Galston's Aristotelian democracy assumes citizens must have a high degree of moral virtue and character. His theory envisions a democracy with quality, culture, taste, and tradition. It is not a minimal juridical democracy that works only to implement a rigorously conceived minimal standard of justice, with no concern to maximize standards of character, virtue, and democratic citizenship. Galston believes that a just democracy requires virtuous citizens. Virtuous citizens by definition will be committed to family responsibilities and the care of children. In turn, strong families are required for the education of virtuous citizens. And finally, Galston believes religion is essential for the creation of the ethics, motivations, and powerful socializing institutions required to form strong families and

71

strong citizens. Galston, along with other neo-liberals, wants churches to be interested in productive and just government programs for families. But he also wants churches to clarify and implement their own ethical vision of families. This is the unique contribution of churches to the total economy of the common good.

Christianity and the Family

Recent research on the development of the family in the West is suggesting Christianity had a powerful and largely efficacious role. Churches made a crucial contribution to the development of strong families in the West, and they have an important role to play in the future. Although Christianity was implicated in the patriarchal institutions of the Greco-Roman world of antiquity, it exerted a discernible transformative influence on the status of women and the well-being of children. In this way, early Christianity laid foundations for the emergence of the companionate family so important for democratic, postindustrial societies. Harvard biblical scholar Elisabeth Schüssler Fiorenza has shown how the pre-Pauline church developed a new discipleship of equals between males and females quite different from male-female relations dominated by the honor-shame codes of Roman Hellenism. The Ephesians 5 passages that identify the husband's relation to his family with Christ's sacrificial relation to the church are now being seen as having fractured the emphasis on male domination, the ethic of the double standard, and the consignment of women to private space characteristic of the Greco-Roman family. The early Christian house church, with its heightened role for female equality and leadership, became the model for the Christian household, literally shaping the family into the more egalitarian patterns of the early Christian ecclesia.

Jack Goody in his *Development of Family and Marriage in Europe* (1983) argues that wherever Christianity spread, the Oriental family structure with its powerful male-headed clans and lineages that served as governments as well as kinship systems seems to have declined. Robert Shaffern argues that the emphasis on monogamy found in both early Christianity and Roman law transformed the family patterns of Germany and Ireland (hence, of Northern Europe), where a variety of family patterns existed. One of the most popular patterns in pre-Christian Irish and German territories was polygyny. Polygyny attracted women into the wealthier households and left wandering bands of brigands, somewhat like the male gangs of modern cities, to live in forests, destroy and steal property, and abduct and rape women. Historian David Herlihy argues that wherever Christian morality spread, buttressed with remnants of Roman family law, the monogamous family grew, poor men found wives, and fathers began taking responsibility for their children. Catholic canon law was the great systematizer of these trends, and, with its strong emphasis on mutual consent between husband and wife as a condition for valid marriage, may have set the stage, as James Q. Wilson argues, for the rise of the concept of universal civil rights — a concept so important for the theories of modern liberal societies.

Thomas Aquinas may have worked out the strongest theoretical rationales for the emerging family theory of the West. With remarkable consistency with modern theories of biology, Aquinas saw marriage and the family as meeting the needs of highly dependent human infants for stable parental care by incorporating males into the nurture of their children. He was aware that humans were nearly unique among mammals in their practice of male involvement with the raising of their children. He also built a strong case for what fathers contribute to their children. Even though Aquinas recognized that polygyny provided the possibility of paternal investment in children, he rejected it as a servile institution for women that made it impossible for marriage to become genuine friendship between husband and wife. When seen in context, Aquinas's sacramental view of marriage must be viewed as an argument for the necessity of males' lifelong commitment to their families, especially their children. Aquinas himself presented this emphasis as a kind of antidote to the archaic mammalian male tendency (which contemporary human ecologists are now describing in detail) to procreate but not become involved with their children. Catholic marital theory must be seen as an intricate and multi-layered effort to domesticate and restructure this archaic male reproductive strategy.

Some historians have even gone so far as to say that the emphasis on the intact, companionate family that Christianity helped establish in Western Europe may have contributed to the emergence of capitalism and modernity. This family form, it is thought, developed the intense socializing procedures (based on deep affections between children and their parents) required to produce disciplined, hardworking, rational capitalists and democratic citizens. We need not determine the truth of this provocative claim in order to entertain a more modest one — that Christianity contributed significantly to the development of the companionate family and that this family has had a productive fit with liberal democratic and liberal economic institutions. For these reasons, Christians should be alert to their continuing responsibilities to study and debate the ethics of families and the values guiding their formation and preservation.

In the great debate over the future of families now sweeping over most Western democracies, the churches must put their eggs in two baskets. This is to say, they must have two equally balanced strategies — one pertaining to the values that should govern family life and another pertaining to just social and economic policies supporting families in their task of raising children. But there is no possibility of the churches finding their way on issues of social policy if they are not clear about their theory of family ethics. And for this, they must understand their heritage, both what they have contributed to the formation of families in the past and how this must be restructured for the present.

Chapter 5

Better Family Values (1995)

(WITH CAROL BROWNING)

This essay was co-authored with my wife Carol and was published in *Christianity Today,* an evangelical magazine of news and opinion. The essay tried to show how evangelicals and mainline (increasingly called old-line) Protestant churches had their respective strengths and weaknesses on the disputed topics of marriage and family. For instance, we acknowledged that evangelicals had a better grasp than mainliners of how absent fatherhood was contributing to the poverty of children and their mothers, but showed how they often resorted to a form of soft patriarchy to address this trend — a solution that the mainline churches officially resisted. Other strengths, weaknesses, and potential creative syntheses were discussed as well. The thrust of the essay was to get beyond the "us against them" mentality on family issues so often seen between liberal and conservative Protestants. This discussion has implications for the relation between Protestants and Catholics on family matters as well.

The American family debate will continue to heat up and take new forms now that Republican majorities have taken over the Senate and House of Representatives. In the months before the midterm elections, the Clinton administration tried to regain the middle ground on family issues: both President Clinton and Health and Human Services Secretary Donna Shalala admitted that Dan Quayle was right about the importance of the two-parent family. And after the Democrats' crushing

November defeat, the Clinton administration tried even harder to firm up its unsteady move toward the center on family issues.

The post-election conservative majorities have two options in the family debate: They, too, could drive toward the center, push Democrats out of the way, and claim the middle for themselves. Or they could move to the extreme right in hopes that the conservative momentum would pull the rest of the nation along. We urge the first strategy, not only for what it means politically, but for what it might contribute to the health of our religious life.

Before the heat of the recent elections, new lines of communication were developing between liberals and conservatives. The political discussion on the family was for a while more flexible, more open, and more experimental. New breeds of neo-conservatives and neo-liberals emerged who could talk to each other and sometimes agree. Examples of neo-liberals were White House Deputy Director of Domestic Policy William Galston, Senator Daniel Moynihan, the Democratic Leadership Conference, and, at times, the president himself. Neo-conservatives on family issues included William Bennett, William Matrox of the Family Research Council, and Representative Henry Hyde of Illinois.

These held some values in common. The neo-liberals were willing to admit that there is a values dimension to the family crisis. They acknowledged, as conservatives had been arguing, that increased individualism, changes in sexual mores, and declining parental responsibility explained some of the mounting problems families face. These factors, they agreed, helped account for such trends as the growing out-of-wedlock birthrate, the growing poverty of divorced and never-married mothers, and the declining mental and physical health of the children of single parents and stepfamilies. On the other hand, neo-conservatives were more willing to admit the partial truth of the standard liberal diagnosis: that the declining economy, fewer jobs, the ravages of market forces, and poorly functioning welfare programs also contribute to family woes. Neo-conservatives were more willing than their old-style counterparts to acknowledge a role for government in helping poor families.

Neo-conservatives were still conservative, placing their primary emphasis on changing cultural values. Neo-liberals were still liberals, seeing a role for government programs that support poor families. The meeting ground between neo-conservatives and neo-liberals on the role of government was the increasing tendency of both groups to turn to tax induce-ments rather than direct welfare payments.

This new political alliance is fragile and may collapse. But the fact that this convergence has been happening in our political culture raises important questions: Is it possible for something similar to happen in the churches? Can new breeds of religious neo-conservatives and neo-liberals emerge and cooperate in addressing the family issues that divide the churches? What would such a new alliance look like? What would be its substance and strategy? What central themes would inform a more productive middle ground in the churches?

A Program for Cooperation

Here are some substantive and strategic approaches we think are important. If cooperation could develop on the following points, good things might happen for American churches, families, and public life.

1. *Religious liberals and conservatives should reconsider, at least for the moment, the narrowly defined sexual issues that have preoccupied them for the last two decades: abortion and homosexuality.* We do not mean that these issues should be dropped, but that they be set within a broader analysis of what is happening to families and children and what the church can do to help. The family viewed as a major social issue — some think the major issue of our time — has had difficulty gaining the attention of churches because of their preoccupation with abortion and homosexuality.

Few church people are well informed about the plunge into poverty of large numbers of mothers and their children following divorce or out-of-wedlock births. Forty-seven percent of all families headed by single mothers live in poverty. Few church people take seriously how these conditions correlate with the declining well-being of children. Princeton University sociologist Sarah McLanahan, who has done definitive research on single parenthood, has written thus:

> Half of all children born in the 1980s will live with a single mother before reaching the age of 18. Half of these children will be poor. As compared with children from the same social class who live with both parents, children of single mothers are twice as likely to drop out of high school and become single parents themselves, and half again as likely to have trouble finding and keeping a steady job.[1]

1. Sarah McLanahan, *Growing Up with a Single Parent* (Cambridge, Mass.: Harvard University Press, 1994), pp. 1-2.

Why aren't churches paying more attention to these trends? Mainline churches for over two decades have viewed family problems as private issues and have allowed their ministries to families and youth to languish, especially at the national level. Conservatives have been far more interested in families but have often failed to understand the complexity of family problems. Both have been so preoccupied with abortion and homosexuality that they have glossed over the less sensational stresses of people trying to raise children to healthy adulthood. It is now time to reconfigure these two divisive issues in a larger context. If this were to happen, new light might shine forth on both issues.

2. *On family matters, both religious conservatives and liberals need to use the Bible with a greater wisdom of context.* Christian liberals get their family theory more from egalitarian contractual theory than they do from biblical texts. They neglect such texts as Matthew 5:32 on divorce, 1 Corinthians 7 on the burdens of marriage, or Ephesians 5:22-33 on the analogy between a husband's love and Christ's sacrificial love. Liberals are attuned to passages suggesting the equality of the sexes, such as Matthew 22:39, which sets forth the principle of neighbor love, and Galatians 3:28, which says that in Christ there is "neither male nor female." To liberals, these passages suggest equality in marital and family relations. This is as far as they are inclined to go with the Bible.

Liberals avoid Ephesians 5 for fear it can be used to justify "patriarchal" teachings. Christian conservatives gravitate toward the Ephesians passage and others like it (e.g., Col. 3:18 and 1 Peter 3:1). Many conservatives, though not all, see in these passages a divinely sanctioned family plan — a benevolent-love paternalism — that husbands and fathers should exercise with faithful responsibility, and wives and children should accept in loving obedience. But this understanding of God's plan for families often gets mixed with the separated-spheres doctrine of the nineteenth-century industrial family, with its breadwinner father and domestic mother. When this happens, such passages are used to give divine justification to this form of family that existed in the United States from roughly 1830 to 1960. Whatever virtues this family form had, it cannot be called "the Christian form of the family" as such.

Both conservative and liberal church members miss the various contexts of these so-called headship passages. Many conservatives overlook the egalitarianism of the early church. Some also miss the way male leadership passages are qualified by the obligations of sacrificial love — a self-giving love that follows the love of Christ for the church. Although these passages — as liberals and feminists charge — reflect a modified patriar-

78

chy, all parties miss how these passages challenge the models of male authority typical of the Greco-Roman world, which was the social and cultural context of early Christianity. In that world, male agency, freedom, and domination were celebrated virtues. Wives were confined primarily to the home with servants and with family. Men enjoyed a range of sexual freedom that was denied to women. To call fathers and husbands to a life of sacrificial love in which wives are treated "as their own bodies" (Eph. 5:28) was revolutionary and seditious in this novel situation.

Religious conservatives should make less out of the male spiritual authority that these passages seem to grant and more out of their direction toward male servanthood and mutuality — "submitting yourselves one to another" (Eph. 5:21). Many Christian conservatives have already taken this step. Religious liberals, on the other hand, need to acknowledge the revolutionary character of these Scriptures and how they set the stage for the subversion of patriarchy.

3. *Christian liberals need to pay less attention to the social sciences on family matters; Christian conservatives need to pay more.* Actually, both religious conservatives and liberals have been deeply influenced by psychology. How can we explain the colossal popularity of James Dobson without pointing to his particular way of synthesizing interpretations of modern psychology with interpretations of Christianity? But conservatives and liberals put their use of psychology into different value contexts. Conservatives place psychological insights into the framework of a community that has a place for biblical and ecclesial authority. Liberals use psychological insights in the framework of a community that supports individualism and personal liberation. Both groups use the *language* of community, but their *concepts* of community are very different.

Liberals tend to use psychology and the social sciences to adapt to changing family trends. They are likely to believe that these changes cannot be stopped and that the right combination of governmental and therapeutic interventions can at least cut their losses. Religious liberals, under the influence of the social sciences, see family ministries as helping individuals adapt to family disruption rather than finding ways to prevent it. They emphasize a supportive and nonjudgmental ministry to the divorced, to single parents, to lonely children, and to tension-filled stepfamilies so that they can all do a little better. Their instincts are more than half right. They have little to say, however, to young people, premarital couples, and young married couples about how to prepare concretely for enduring marriage and parenthood in our challenging world. Conservatives, on the other hand, tend to be heroic in their goals to reverse family decline. They seem to believe that if young Christians have the right values, have the right commitments, and understand the true meaning of marriage and the family, they can successfully withstand the pressures of work, declining economy, divided spheres, seditious cultural values, mounting tax burdens, and the growing intrusions into families of both market values and bureaucratic control. Conservatives need to use the social sciences to be more realistic, but they need to do this in ways that will not undermine their faith that they can reverse the more damaging features of present family trends.

4. *Liberals tend to look too much to government for solving family problems; conservatives too rapidly dismiss the government as a useful resource.* Liberals should look to government less; conservatives should look to government more.

Since their 1960s successes in using government to make racial discrimination illegal, religious liberals have too often thought they were fulfilling the church's mission if they could persuade the government to do what they believed was just and good. In the process, liberal churches, especially at the leadership level, have often been more concerned about what the state should do than what churches should do. As evidence, note that during the 1970s and 1980s the national family programs of most mainline Protestant denominations were severely cut, while lobbying efforts for various federal programs received continued support.

Christian conservatives have a reputation — not always justified — for being against family-support programs such as Aid to Families with Dependent Children, food stamps, and Medicaid. Many religious conservatives believe that these programs undermine family values, function as welfare traps, support out-of-wedlock births, and encourage dependency; and they believe that if everyone followed Christian family ideals, welfare programs would not be needed.

On this point — the attitude of the church toward government — religious conservatives and liberals have the most to learn from each other. This is also the point on which conservatives and liberals in the church can learn something from the pre-election dialogue between political neo-conservatives and neo-liberals. Although tensions continued, both groups agreed that some forms of short-term welfare are needed, that welfare recipients have responsibilities as well as rights, that welfare should not become a trap, and that welfare should not encourage teenage pregnancy and out-of-wedlock births. Furthermore, the consensus held that government assistance should not contradict generally held moral standards. Hence, government should resist merely expedient remedies and communicate moral expectations consistent with settled moral traditions. It is important for that emerging consensus to hold in the new Republican order.

This new consensus is important, not just for what it implies for government family programs but for what it suggests for a wider cultural synthesis on family matters. Since Charles Murray's October 1993 editorial in the *Wall Street Journal* in which he predicted the rise of a new "white underclass," there has been a deeper concern among liberal elites about the health of American families. Murray, in his less inflammatory pre-*Bell Curve* days, wrote that the out-of-wedlock birthrate in the white population, now at 22 percent, is the same as it was for the black community in the early 1960s. The out-of-wedlock birthrate in the black community has now risen to 68 percent. Murray argued that whites are now becoming familiar with the same consequences blacks experienced — deepening poverty for mothers and declining well-being for children. He held that the family issue is the biggest public issue of our time, and he succeeded in convincing leading liberals and conservatives he was right.

But Murray would enlist the help of conservatives, in politics and in the church, to support the withdrawal of all government supports for single mothers, with the exception of medical insurance for their children. If this happens, he believes, couples will take marriage more seriously, confine procreation to marriage, divorce less frequently, or turn to extended family, church, or community organizations if divorce or out-of-wedlock birth throw them into poverty.

If an unfeeling conservatism replaces the fragile consensus that existed before the election, Murray's radical approach is much more likely to be tried. And we think this goes too far. Families need government supports for a wide variety of reasons. The neo-liberal/neo-conservative proposal to preserve family assistance, make it temporary, and connect it with basic moral expectations is worth refining and trying.

Even if this consensus were to endure and mature, neither Christian conservatives nor liberals should invest all of their attention in government programs and public policy initiatives. This message is especially important for liberals. Religious liberals need to attend once again to their theology of marriage and the family. They need to do historical work of the kind they have neglected. They need new programs with youth that start very young and help them to replace current individualistic cultural scripts about sexuality and the family with the classic perspectives of the Christian synthesis. Religious conservatives, on the other hand, need to continue their present energy on family issues, but with a more accurate sense of context in handling ancient texts.

5. Religious conservatives and liberals should be alert to the subversive effects of market forces. Both groups should be more sophisticated in relating family issues to market dynamics. Religious liberals often pride themselves on being critical of capitalism and its excesses. Some mainline religious leaders have been socialist or even somewhat Marxist in their anti-market attitudes. Conservatives are often seen as pro-market, occasionally as ideological defenders of its injustices.

But the family issue shows the positions of both sides to be more complex. Liberals have encouraged wives and mothers to work outside the home, while religious conservatives have had less relish for women joining the labor market. From one angle, the conservatives look patriarchal and appear to confine women to domestic life, while liberals seem to be progressivist, pro-feminist, and egalitarian.

There is, however, another angle of vision. Religious conservatives may inadvertently be the true resisters of competitive market values and of the spread into private life of cost-benefit modes of thinking. By preferring that mothers stay at home and by granting dignity to full-time homemaking, they block the spread of market values into the inner life of families. Religious liberals may have unwittingly sold out to the growing dominance of cost-benefit and rational-choice ways of thinking, even in the home. Religious liberals are far more likely to celebrate the dual-income, ninety-hour-a-week working family. Yet, when both parents work full-time, both are fully absorbed in the world of market values, demands, efficiencies, and logics. The small children of dual-income families do not easily conform to the pressures of market forces.

We believe both Christian conservatives and liberals should affirm the market as an effective method for generating wealth while, at the same time, being vigilant against the ways it can undermine families. The market hurts families by taking too much of their time, by engendering individualistic and cost-benefit mentalities even in intimate affairs, and by promoting consumerism and hedonism in both children and their parents.

Christian men and women alike should resist the spread of market forces by spending less time at paid work. We will not solve this problem by preserving the two-sphere ideology of the industrial family that religious conservatives baptized for decades. We join with Harvard social scientist Jacqueline Olds and her team in their 1992 paper entitled "Part-Time Employment and Marital Well-Being." Their research shows that the families with the most marital, parental, and child satisfaction are those that work one-and-a-half jobs or approximately sixty hours a week between them. Although this may not be financially possible for many couples, we believe it is an ideal toward which society should aim. (This does not necessarily mean that mothers and wives should be the ones with the half-time employment, although that may be best in many cases.)

There are several ways the market can be attuned to the needs of families. Employers might experiment with some thirty-hour-a-week positions. Job sharing could be used more frequently. More half-time employment with partial benefit packages might be offered. These positions could become full-time after children grow older.

There are many other ways Christian conservatives and liberals can cooperate to create healthier families. Religious liberals should study the men's programs of conservative churches. Conservative churches are better than most liberal churches in teaching that male responsibility is crucial in the current cultural climate. Religious liberals will want to soften the notes of male headship that sometimes pervade these programs, but liberals should acknowledge that male responsibility, not authority, is often the deeper theme of these programs. Both liberals and conservatives should work to restore the viability of the two-parent family. Today, however, this family should be an equal mother-father team with flexible role definitions and permeable boundaries between domestic and public life.

Conservative and liberal churches should help their sons and daughters at a young age begin preparing for equal-regard marital partnerships. They should work together to chasten the excesses of the market and force it to adapt to family needs. They should work together to fine-tune government programs. They should, as did the early church, develop leadership patterns in the churches that model egalitarian relations between the sexes. They should work together to protect their children from the demonic values of a materialistic age. They should eliminate all of their inflammatory rhetoric on family issues and search for commonalities before accentuating differences. Finally, they should go beyond the labels of conservative and liberal to find common ground in a faithful interpretation of the Christian tradition that informs them both.

Chapter 6

Children, Mothers, and Fathers in the Postmodern Family (1995)

This chapter reflects both my emerging mid 1990s diagnosis of the crisis of families as well as the outlines of a direction or solution. That direction would be developed much more fully in *From Culture Wars to Common Ground* (1997), *Reweaving the Social Tapestry: Toward a Public Philosophy and Policy for Families* (2002), and *Marriage and Modernization* (2003). By "postmodern family," I meant the emerging new family pluralism — marked by increases in divorce, nonmarital births, and cohabitation, as well as a decline in the marriage rate — that was beginning to be evident in the late 1980s and the early 1990s. The rise of the matrifocal family, the feminization of kinship and poverty, and the rise of fatherless children were new topics of heated discussion and evaluation.

Rather than simplistically blaming either men or women — mothers or fathers — for this new family reality, I began to use the analysis of modernity framed in Jürgen Habermas, David Popenoe, and Alan Wolfe with the hope that it would throw light on the forces causing family difficulties. According to this theory, the spread of technical rationality expressed in both market and government bureaucracy was increasingly undermining the strength and authority of married parents by realigning dependencies between individuals within the family. In this essay, I affirmed these influences from market and bureaucracy yet recommended ways to limit them.

For Christians, one way of doing this is to develop a new model of family authority based on a life-cycle ethic of Christian love. My view of Christian love builds on the theories of Gene Outka, who defines *agape* around the concept of equal regard. I also use even more the neo-Thomistic refinements of love as equal regard introduced by the Roman Catholic moral theologian Louis Janssens. Modernity, love as equal regard, and a life-cycle view of equal regard — these are the major concepts developed in the practical-theological reflections of this essay.

Throughout the period in which pastoral care has been in dialogue with the modern psychologies, there has been a tension between empathy and moral guidance. We have generally felt the need to empathize with people needing the church's care. We have also, however, increasingly tried to inquire into and in some way uphold the church's ethical standards, no matter how difficult it may be to know them with certainty. The relation of ethics to pastoral care has been the subject of a friendly dialogue between Charles Gerkin and me for more than a decade. I use this occasion to further that conversation.

The relation of empathy and care has been concretely and vividly raised by sociologist Judith Stacey's recent book, *Brave New Families: Stories of Domestic Upheaval in Late Twentieth Century America.*[1] Stacey's book asks how the church's care should respond to the growing trend toward matrifocal families in Western industrial societies. Her book is a study of two women and their families, their early marriages to workaholic husbands, their divorces and separations, their troubled children, and their slide to the edge of poverty. At the end of the story, these two women, Pam and Dotty, are the effective heads of matrifocal families. Although Pam is remarried to Al, a working-class and fundamentalist recovering alcoholic, she is the center of a diffuse family network, which entails some shared parenting with her former husband and his mistress, who now live next door to Pam. Dotty, whose semi-estranged husband has died, now lives with her daughter, Kristina, and Kristina's children. Together they are raising the children of Dotty's other daughter, who has recently died. These women, mother and daughter, live together raising their children and grandchildren by themselves.

Stacey, a social scientist and leading feminist theorist, does not hide her empathy for these women. She is correct, I believe, in celebrating their humanity and heroism and that of their families. But Stacey goes beyond

---

1. Judith Stacey, *Brave New Families: Stories of Domestic Upheaval in Late Twentieth Century America* (New York: Basic, 1990).

this; she moves from empathy to full approval, indeed a stance of norma-tive legitimation. She joins thinkers as diverse as Barbara Ehrenreich and Judge Richard Posner in seeing these new matrifocal families as both inev-itable and worthy of emulation.[2] She sees Pam and Dotty as ushering into social reality, and eventually into the middle classes, what Andrew Cherlin calls "the feminization of kinship."[3] It is clear that, in spite of the difficul-ties of these new matrifocal families, Stacey believes that they are the wave of the future and represent an improvement over the traditional or mod-ern family forms, forms that dominated the early marriages of Pam and Dotty. Stacey's book raises the age-old question: Where is the line between empathy and idealization?

Stacey presents us with a forced choice between the traditional family with its bread-winning father and domestic, child-rearing mother and the new fatherless, matrifocal network she finds in the families of Pam and Dotty. But there may be a third perspective that would extend empathy, offer practical help, and rally social and economic resources on their be-half, but define the moral context differently from these two extremes. It is my view that a proper reading of the Judeo-Christian tradition will help establish this third perspective — a perspective that has, on the whole, tried to balance the good of children with a covenant of equal regard be-tween husband and wife, father and mother.[4]

2. Stacey, *Brave New Families,* pp. 251-78; cf. Barbara Ehrenreich, *The Heart of Men* (Gar-den City, N.Y.: Doubleday, 1983); Richard Posner, *Sex and Reason* (Cambridge: Harvard Uni-versity Press, 1992).

3. Stacey, *Brave New Families,* p. 268.

4. Dan Quayle helped establish the lines of debate during the 1992 presidential elec-tion. Those who agree on the limited point of the importance of the two-parent family, but not on the larger political agenda, were David Blankenhorn of the Institute for American Values, William Galston of the University of Maryland and the Progressive Policy Institute and advisor to Democratic presidential candidates including William Clinton, and the manifesto of the journal called *The Responsive Community.* A strong policy statement on be-half of the two-parent family can be found in the final report of the National Commission on Children titled *Beyond Rhetoric* (1991). They write, "Children do best when they have the personal involvement and material support of a father and a mother and when both par-ents fulfill their responsibility to be loving providers" (p. xix). This statement is noteworthy since it differs from more diffuse endorsements of various family forms in several earlier National Commission statements. On the other hand, Betty Friedan, in an exchange with Blankenhorn, made a strong statement on the dangers of stigmatizing alternative families by elevating the importance of the two-parent, mother-father partnership. Joan Beck con-tributed to the debate by pointing out that men may need integration in a family even more than mothers and children need husbands and fathers. She writes, "Children need the civi-lizing, role-modeling influences of an on-the-scene father. But men also benefit and pros-

For some years I have insisted that care and counseling, both secular and religious, are never neutral, that they always proceed in some moral context, and that within the church they achieve their norms through a correlational dialogue between its classics and various voices from its surrounding culture. I propose to take this general point of view into the present family debate that James Davison Hunter in his celebrated *Culture Wars* claims is dividing orthodox and conservatives in contemporary religious faiths and denominations.[5]

On the whole, the orthodox position has tried to give a Christian defense of the modern, industrial, bourgeois family — the breadwinner husband and domestic wife. These groups do not understand that this particular family form was the product of the radical differentiation between home and paid work that emerged with the industrial revolution. This organization of the family, most historians and sociologists agree, is not the divinely sanctioned family form of the New Testament. Mainline churches have, on the whole, been silent on these divisive tensions, probably because they are themselves embedded in the same individualistic cultural trends that have been the principal causes of family fragmentation in the wider culture.[6]

Descriptive Theology and the Situation of Families

Before outlining this third position, I will offer a brief description of the situation of children, mothers, and fathers in American society today.

Description is never easy and is always embedded in certain normative commitments or preunderstandings (as Gadamer calls them), no matter how strenuous our attempts to gain distance and objectivity.[7] I have my precommitments on issues pertaining to children and families that I will develop now and then test later in this essay. They come from the synthesis of New Testament Christianity and Aristotelian philosophy found in the thought of Thomas Aquinas. In these sources one finds a vi-

---

per from the civilizing, mutually nurturing effects of family life. Statistics show they are healthier, live longer, and are much less likely to be homeless or adrift in old age." See her "Maintaining the Father Connection," *Chicago Tribune* (June 18, 1992).

5. James Davison Hunter, *Culture Wars: The Struggle to Define America* (New York: Basic, 1991), p. 43.

6. William D'Antonio, "Family Life, Religion, and Social Values," in *Families and Religions,* ed. William V. D'Antonio and Joan Aldous (Beverly Hills: Sage, 1983), pp. 81-98, 113-40.

7. See Hans-Georg Gadamer, *Truth and Method* (New York: Crossroad, 1982).

sion of the family that sees it as a relative good needed for the raising of children and the mutual benefit and enrichment of parents as they proceed with that task. It is a relative good because the family must be subject to the rule of the kingdom of God and finally measured by its contribution to the realization of that kingdom. In this tradition, Aristotle was joined with interpretations of both Old and New Testaments to give strong, although not idolatrous, support to the importance of men and women becoming one flesh for the purpose of raising highly dependent human infants who would themselves develop into servants of the kingdom of God. Historical research is now making it clear that Christian family theory is not a product, in any simple way, of the New Testament. It is a synthesis of New Testament and Aristotelian teaching that was achieved in Thomism and from there, with some amendments, in the Protestant Reformation.[8]

Aquinas followed Aristotle in basing his theory of the family in part on empirical observations about the long period of nurture and education required by the highly dependent human infant. Aquinas argued that this condition requires "certain and definite parents," by which he meant "a man and a definite woman" committed over time to the nurture and education of their children.[9] The background of Thomas's position is best understood if traced to Aristotle's rejection of Plato's belief that the children of philosopher-kings should be raised by the state rather than by their own parents.[10] Such a social arrangement, Plato believed, would extend the philosopher-kings' sympathy for and identification with their own offspring to all children since they would have no way of knowing which specific child was theirs.[11]

Aristotle objected. He believed that sympathy spreads outward from particular, embodied, and special family relations. What is everyone's responsibility easily becomes, according to Aristotle, no one's responsibility.[12] Empathy and a sense of social solidarity, for Aristotle, are generalized outward from particular investments in our own progeny to identifi-

8. Cf. John Witte Jr., "The Transformation of Marriage Law in the Lutheran Reformation," in *The Weightier Matters of the Law: Essays on Law and Religion; A Tribute to Harold J. Berman,* ed. John Witte Jr. and Frank S. Alexander (Atlanta: Scholars, 1988).

9. Thomas Aquinas, *Summa Theologica,* Supplement to the Third Part, q. 41 (New York: Benziger, 1948).

10. Plato, *The Republic of Plato,* ed. Alan Bloom (New York: Basic, 1968), bk. 5.

11. Plato, *The Republic,* bk. 5:462c.

12. Aristotle, *Politics,* in *The Basic Works of Aristotle,* ed. Richard McKeon (New York: Random House, 1941), bk. 2, 1261b, 30.

cation with the wider community. Aristotle was not saying that local communities and the state should not support families. Nor was he making a plea for family autonomy and isolation. He was simply arguing that we acknowledge the generally higher level of investment that most natural parents have in their children and what this does to provide these children with a base upon which to make later identifications with the wider community.

In spite of Jesus' seeming antipathy to the family in Matthew 10, most of modern Christianity has followed Aquinas's Aristotelian interpretation of such texts. In a section of the *Summa* titled "Of the Order of Charity," Aquinas argues for our special obligations to our own children and other close kin. In commenting on Jesus' alleged antagonism to the family, Aquinas writes, "We are commanded to hate, in our kindred, not their kinship, but only the fact of their being an obstacle between us and God."[13] We must remember that Aquinas saw these parental obligations falling on the shoulders of men as well as women, although perhaps not as equally as we would insist on today.[14]

I will use this classical strand of Christian history to give heuristic guidance to my interpretation of the sociological facts that follow. There is a thunderous debate in our society over whether the family is simply changing or actually in decline. The facts that follow and the horizon of values I have just set forth lead me to affirm that the family is both changing and declining; it is, in fact, in crisis. Of special importance for describing this crisis is the present-day situation of children and youth.

The 10 percent decline in the marriage rate since 1975 and the approximately 1.5 million abortions that occur in the United States each year suggest, some believe, a culture-wide decline of interest in marriage and children.[15] More directly relevant to the thesis of family crisis is the colossal increase in out-of-wedlock births — an increase from 5 percent in 1960 to around 30 percent of all births today.[16] In the black community, out-of-wedlock births have risen from 20 percent in 1960 to roughly 68 percent today.[17] But this rise is not just among minority communities. Twenty-two percent of all births in the white community are now to single women, the same rate that existed in the black community thirty years

---

13. Thomas Aquinas, *Summa Theologica*, II, 2, q. (London: R.&T. Washbourne, 1917).

14. Aquinas, *Summa Theologica Supplement.*

15. David Popenoe, "The Family Transformed," *Family Affairs* 2, nos. 2-3 (Summer 1989): 1-5.

16. Popenoe, "Family Transformed," pp. 1-5.

17. Paul Taylor, "Life without Father," *Washington Post* (June 7, 1992).

ago when the overall out-of-wedlock birth rate was, as you recall, only 5 percent. Single mothers, their mothers and sisters, and other female friends often end up caring for the children of these births. But it is not only out-of-wedlock births that help create the feminization of kinship. The increase of divorce contributes as well. In addition, both divorce and nonmarital births help create another phenomenon called the "feminization of poverty." In fact, the two feminizations — of kinship and poverty — are closely related phenomena. Take divorce. Lenore Weitzman in her ground-breaking *The Divorce Revolution*[18] states that within one year after divorce, women and their children experience a 73 percent drop in disposable income while their ex-husbands enjoy a 42 percent increase. Although these figures are probably exaggerated, even corrections have supported their general validity.[19]

It is now becoming clear that the feminization of kinship and poverty is not particularly good for children. This is where Thomas's argument that the highly dependent human infant needs a definite father and mother rings true. Of course, this dependent human child and its parents need a variety of supportive human communities and networks as well. But this truth should not obscure the fact that these networks work best when they support a fully involved mother-father partnership. A recent federally sponsored study for the National Center for Health Statistics shows that one in five children under age eighteen has a learning, emotional, behavioral, or developmental problem. By the time they are teenagers, one in four suffers from one or more of these problems. For male teenagers, the rate is nearly one in three. What is this study's explanation of these trends? These researchers hold that a leading factor is the continuing dissolution of the two-parent family.[20] There is other highly suggestive although less than conclusive evidence that is often cited for the unfavorable overall effects of the decline of the two-parent family. Louis Sullivan reports that 70 percent of young men in prisons grew up without fathers in their home, that the children of single parents are five times more likely to be poor and two times more likely to drop out of school.[21] Eighty percent of adolescents in psychiatric hospitals come from broken

18. Lenore Weitzman, *The Divorce Revolution: The Unexpected Social and Economic Consequences for Women and Children in America* (New York: Free Press, 1985).

19. Cf. Herbert Jacob, *The Silent Revolution* (Chicago: University of Chicago Press, 1988).

20. N. Zill and C. A. Shoenborn, "Developmental, Learning, and Emotional Problems: Health of Our Nation's Children, United States, 1988," *Advance Data* (U.S. Department of Health and Human Services, 1990), p. 190.

21. Louis Sullivan, "Fatherless Families," *Television and Families* (Summer 1992): 34-36.

homes; three out of four teenage suicides occur in households where a parent (generally the father) has been absent; and children living apart from a biological parent are 20 to 40 percent more vulnerable to illness.[22]

The trends suggested by these facts cannot be blamed solely on the deteriorating financial state of most families, although this is clearly important. Economists Victor Fuchs and Diane Reklis demonstrate that since 1960 almost all indices of teenage well-being have declined. SAT scores have fallen, suicide rates have tripled, homicide and obesity rates have risen sharply, and poverty rates, although declining between 1960 and 1970, have risen for children while staying basically stable for adults. Fuchs and Reklis give a startling interpretation to these facts, especially for economists. Although the deteriorating economic base of children has contributed to these trends, they show that these trends began prior to the economic decline, and they credit cultural shifts — individualism, divorce, changing sexual mores — with most of the decline in the overall health of children.[23] The rise of single-parent families is an important expression of these cultural trends. To summarize these trends is not to denigrate single parents, many of whom are unbelievably heroic and doing a fantastic job. It is rather to speak frankly about a cultural and social trend brought about by a host of systemic social and cultural changes powerfully affecting the lives of individuals — a trend which, taken as a whole, is not good for children of Western societies and should not be idealized.

Social Systems and the Family Crisis

These facts require a deeper interpretation. The decline of the two-parent family is itself a symptom of more profound social patterns. Without displacing my biblical and Thomistic angle of vision, I will review some supplementary social science frameworks. Three factors require attention — the spreading impact of capitalistic market systems, the penetration of governmental bureaucracies in the intimate matters of the family, and the deepening trend toward individualism in all advanced societies, marked in part by a diminishment of parental authority and family cohesion.

---

22. Joe Klein, "Whose Values?" *Newsweek* (June 8, 1992).

23. Victor Fuchs and Diane Reklis, "American Children and Economic Perspectives and Policy Options," *Science* 255 (January 3, 1992): 41.

Capitalism

Both Marxists and Durkheimians place the blame for family decline on the social patterns of capitalistic, market-driven, industrial society. It was competitive industrial society that took men away from domestic farm life and the family-centered small businesses and pushed them into wage labor far removed from wife and children. Industrialization gave men a new kind of economic power over their families and relegated women and children into the so-called nonproductive confines of private domestic existence. Interpreters all the way from Marx and Engels,[24] to religious-socialist feminists such as Rosemary Ruether,[25] to Stacey herself put the blame squarely on modern industrial capitalism. Although feminists have been more articulate about the shortcomings of the modern industrial family, in many ways this family form put far more pressure on men than it did on women. In this sense, modernity may be proving to have been a risky gamble for both sexes. Segregating paid work, as it did, from the rhythms of home life broke formal and informal initiation rites between fathers and their sons. Women were indeed discriminated against in industrial society, but men may have lost their way entirely. This is the message of the mythopoetic men's movement led by Robert Bly,[26] Robert Moore,[27] and others. Erik Erikson and Kenneth Keniston[28] investigated such themes long before but in less dramatic terms.[29] It is perspectives such as these that throw light on the remote, detached, and shadowy men and former husbands in the matrifocal families of Pam and Dotty.

Government Bureaucracies

Marxist analysis can be equally critical of the bureaucratic machinery of the welfare state. Although I personally see a large role for a variety of

24. Frederick Engels, *The Origin of the Family, Private Property, and the State* (New York: International, 1985).

25. Rosemary Radford Ruether, *New Woman, New Earth* (Nashville: Abingdon, 1975).

26. Robert Bly, *Iron John* (New York: Addison-Wesley, 1990).

27. Robert Moore and Douglas Gillette, *King, Warrior, Magician, Love* (San Francisco: Harper, 1990).

28. Kenneth Keniston, *The Uncommitted* (New York: Harcourt, Brace, and World, 1965).

29. Much of Erikson's commentary on generativity has to do with the crisis of being a father in modern societies. For an interpretation of Erikson from this perspective, see my *Generative Man* (1973).

state-supported family programs, it is important to confront how these welfare bureaucracies, whether in socialist or capitalist societies, sometimes contribute to the decline of families and the feminization of kinship. Jürgen Habermas in his *Theory of Communicative Action* shows how the patterns of what he calls the "systems world" of welfare bureaucracies create a growing dependency as government increasingly takes over family functions.[30]

Alan Wolfe in his *Whose Keeper?* makes a distinction between the "private" or market family and the "public" or state family.[31] The United States is the example par excellence of the private family, that is, the family driven and shaped by the market forces of American life. But this family is anything but private. Increasingly, the private space of this family is being penetrated by the calculating and cost-effectiveness logic of modern market forces.

Wolfe shows how the indices of family decline in the United States are effectively matched by the indices of family decline in Sweden. Sweden is Wolfe's best example of the so-called public family. Sweden's cradle-to-grave welfare policies were designed to support families. Instead, according to Wolfe, they have encouraged patterns of divorce, nonmarriage, and state familism.[32] In ways somewhat parallel to those in the United States, children in Sweden are increasingly being cared for by single women. Ironically, it is also women who are staffing the state-run child-care centers and public schools. In both countries, women are increasingly raising the children, albeit with better government subsidies in Sweden than are available in the United States. There is less feminization of poverty in Sweden, but there may be no less feminization of kinship.

Parental Authority and Individualism

The public family of Sweden is a less radical expression of Plato's vision of the relation of the family and the state. Although parents do not completely disappear from the lives of children as they did in Plato's republic, in Sweden's welfare state, according to Wolfe, they become progressively more ephemeral, detached, and unauthoritative. But this is true for mod-

---

30. Jürgen Habermas, *The Theory of Communicative Action*, vol. 2 (Boston: Beacon, 1987), pp. 153-97.

31. Alan Wolfe, *Whose Keeper? Social Science and Moral Obligation* (Berkeley: University of California Press, 1989), pp. 52, 133.

32. Wolfe, *Whose Keeper?* pp. 142-58.

ern societies in general. Both parents and children get more and more of their moral sensibilities from the logics and patterns of state and market.

State and market forces not only combine to inject an alternating dependency and rational choice mentality in families, they also function to undermine the authority of parents in the socialization of their children. At least this is the argument of Christopher Lasch in his *Haven in a Heartless World: The Family Besieged*.[33] As the state and its schools, welfare organizations, and mental health experts more and more insert themselves into family life, parents appear more inept and the center of competence and authority passes to those outside the home. Market values, amplified by the seductive voices of television and other media of communication, also undermine the authority of parents. The market's consumer logic undermines so-called traditional family values. The market's appeal to sex, power, prestige, and the immediate fulfillment of desires through uncontrolled advertising undercuts the parents' capacity to instill values of discipline, focused attention, and long-term commitments.[34]

Lasch uncovers the consequences of the multifarious forces undermining the authority of parents in the lives of their children. The declining authority of parents, according to Lasch, produces a split between love and discipline in modern families.[35] Under the impact of advice from the psychiatric and psychotherapeutic professions, friendship in the twentieth century became the new model for family relations — friendship between husband and wife and increasingly friendship between parent and child. More and more parents could be warm and supportive, but they could not give authoritative guidance. Lasch argues that it is precisely this split between love and discipline that leads young people in modern societies to be so easily manipulated by outside forces, whether they be the forces of the market, the peer group, the video, the television, or the demagogue. Superegos are not deeply internalized in postindustrial society, according to Lasch. Children may love their parents, but they may not deeply internalize their parents' values. And on the whole, Lasch contends, they certainly do not hold their parents in deep respect.

33. Christopher Lasch, *Haven in a Heartless World: The Family Besieged* (New York: Basic, 1977).

34. This truth points to the myopia of the Bush-Quayle attack on the media elite during the 1992 election for undermining family values. They were right in placing blame on television, movies, and advertising elites. But they were wrong in failing to see how these elites simply give voice to market enticements, which the Reagan-Bush years had not only failed to restrain but encouraged.

35. Lasch, *Haven in a Heartless World*, pp. 174-83.

For fear that the reader may believe that Lasch and I have undercut the credibility of all psychologically oriented helping professions, whether religious or secular, let me say this: It should be possible for all counselors to discover and publicly articulate the centers of authority and value out of which they make their interventions. If they were to do this, the parents' authority would not be subtly undermined. Parents would know more clearly when the values of experts vary from their own and be able to confront this directly. *It is the distinct advantage of pastoral counseling, I will argue, that it can more easily work out of a publicly articulate and testable tradition of values.* This testable tradition should be carried by the church. It is the pastoral counselors' relation to the values and authority of the church which may help them escape Lasch's criticism that the mental health professions, along with the market and the state, tend to undercut family cohesion and promote anomic individualism.

The Family Crisis and Religion

Lasch's views are important, but they have limitations. His analysis of the loss of family authority is convincing. It is disappointing, however, that he has no constructive proposals about how family authority can be reconstituted. Furthermore, although Lasch is fully aware of the role that the Protestant Reformation had in elevating families and parenting over the medieval idealization of celibacy, he makes no suggestion about how religion might play a role today.[36] It is my conviction, however, that the church and its pastoral care can play a significant role in giving authoritative grounding to a family form that stands between the male-dominated family of the industrial revolution and the female-dominated family of Stacey's postmodern vision.

The crux is the church's capacity to elaborate a new authoritative love ethic. In recent papers, I have elaborated a love ethic of equal regard as the grounds of a family ethic that provides an alternative to the ethic of the passing "modern" family or the ethic of the feminized kinship patterns that Stacey idealizes. It is an ethic that can provide a new structure of authority that will help the family resist the undermining influences of state and market. It can be an ethic both for the dyadic relation of husband and wife and for the relation of parents to their children.

I rely on the idea of Christian love as equal regard advanced by

36. Lasch, *Haven in a Heartless World,* pp. 183-89.

Protestant ethicist Gene Outka of Yale but enriched by the teleological interests of the Catholic moral theologian Louis Janssens. When considering the command "To love your neighbor as yourself," these theologians interpret this to mean that we are to love our neighbor, be it friend or spouse, with the same seriousness as we naturally love ourselves.[37] To love the other with equal seriousness as ourselves is a strenuous ethic, far more strenuous than either ethical-egoist or utilitarian perspectives. But to love or regard the other as ourselves also means we are entitled to love or regard ourselves equally to the other. This ethic does not allow us to regard ourselves more, but neither does it permit us to take the masochistic stance of regarding ourselves less. This is a rigorous and highly demanding ethic of mutuality.

Interpretations of Christian love as an ethic of mutuality have much to contribute to an ethics of family. They can help open the ethical space between the modern family where the husband still had most of the power and the alternative matrifocal family in which women have the power but also the burden of loneliness and full responsibility. The ethics of mutuality balances largely Protestant, self-sacrificial models of Christian love associated in the modern period with Anders Nygren,[38] Rudolf Bultmann,[39] and, to a lesser degree, Reinhold Niebuhr.[40] Appeals to Christian doctrines of self-sacrificial love *(agape)* were used, in fact, by Paul, the author of 1 Peter, and even Luther to legitimate the patience, long-suffering, and obedience required of women in the Christian family.

Mutuality models of love have been of special interest to feminist theologians such as Mary Stewart Van Leeuwen,[41] Christine Gudorf,[42] and others. To say that love as equal regard rather than love as perpetual self-sacrifice is the goal of the Christian life seems to women less susceptible to the manipulation of powerful agents, mainly men, who may use appeals to self-sacrifice to circumscribe and exploit them. Furthermore, mu-

---

37. Louis Janssens, "Norms and Priorities of a Love Ethics," *Louvain Studies* 6 (Spring 1977): 220.

38. Anders Nygren, *Agape and Eros* (Philadelphia: Westminster, 1953).

39. Garth Hallett, *Christian Neighbor-Love* (Washington, D.C.: Georgetown University Press, 1989), pp. 5-6.

40. Reinhold Niebuhr, *The Nature and Destiny of Man,* vol. 1 (New York: Scribner's Sons, 1941), p. 84.

41. Mary Stewart Van Leeuwen, *Gender and Grace: Love, Work, and Parenting in a Changing World* (Downers Grove, Ill.: InterVarsity, 1990).

42. Barbara H. Andolsen, Christine E. Gudorf, and Mary D. Pellauer, eds., *Women's Conscience, Women's Consciousness: A Reader in Feminist Ethics* (San Francisco: Harper and Row, 1985), pp. 175-91.

tuality models of love provide the ground for resisting the broad trends in our society which, despite the complaints of feminism, are increasingly releasing men from their family obligations and producing the growing feminization of kinship we have discussed. It may be noted that mutuality models of Christian love are significantly informed by *caritas* models of love associated more with the Catholic than the Protestant theological tradition, and that the New Testament scholarship of Victor Furnish[43] and Luise Schottroff[44] lends support to this interpretation of Christian love.

There is biblical support for a love ethic of equal regard. Although it is quite clear that much of biblical literature reflects the patriarchal character of the ancient Jewish, Greek, and Roman families, this is not the whole story. Walter Brueggemann argues that "there is a counter theme which suggests that the marriage relationship in both the Old and New Testament is understood as a covenantal relation which reflects mutual respect, concern and love."[45] Elisabeth Schüssler Fiorenza has found in the early pre-Markan material evidence for an ethics of mutuality between the sexes in what she calls a "discipleship of equals."[46] This continues in a modified way into the letters of Paul, especially the baptismal formula of Galatians 3:28, which proclaims that in Christ there is neither "Jew nor Greek . . . slave nor free . . . male nor female." Furthermore, David Balch in his *Let Wives Be Submissive* detects in the return to the doctrine of female submission in 1 Peter evidence of the early church's apologetic attempt to hide before its Greek patriarchal detractors evidence for a heightened equality between husband and wife within the Christian house church.[47] Is it possible that the seeds of an egalitarian family ethic of covenanted mutuality were sown in early Christianity and, although not fully realized then, have continued to work out their logic in human history?

This view of Christian love as equal regard does not eliminate the symbol of the cross and what it implies about the place of self-sacrificial

43. Victor Furnish, "Neighbor Love in the New Testament," *The Journal of Religious Studies* 10 (Fall 1982): 332.

44. Luise Schottroff, "Non-Violence and the Love of One's Enemies," in *Essays on the Love Commandment*, ed. Reginald Fuller (Philadelphia: Fortress, 1975), p. 23.

45. Walter Brueggemann, "The Covenanted Family: A Zone for Humanness," *Journal of Current Social Issues* 14 (Winter 1977): 19.

46. Elisabeth Schüssler Fiorenza, *In Memory of Her: A Feminist Theological Reconstruction of Christian Origins* (New York: Crossroad, 1983).

47. David Balch, *Let Wives Be Submissive: The Domestic Code in 1 Peter* (Chico, Calif.: Scholars, 1981).

love. Self-sacrifice is still very much a part of the Christian life in this ethic. But according to this view, self-sacrifice is not an end in itself but a transitional ethic in the service of mutuality and equal regard. Self-sacrificial love, in human relations or in the family, refers to the second mile we must often travel in a finite and sinful world in order to restore human relations once again to a situation of mutuality and equal regard.

The Church, Mutuality, and the Centrality of Children

The church's pastoral care must be guided by an ethic consistent with its theological tradition. I believe that an equal-regard love ethic is able to provide such guidance. The church's care should surround this ethic with the ironic values of the doctrines of sin, grace, forgiveness, and redemption. The ironic character of these religious themes helps Christian ethics handle the tension between its demanding ideals and the realities of human frailty. Theology and the social sciences may show that some family forms are better than others for raising children. In fact, this is what I was arguing when I reviewed how certain aspects of the Aristotelian and Christian tradition mesh with certain aspects of the social sciences to support the importance of the mother-father partnership. This tradition provided a theory of the "order of the good" (the *ordo bonorum*), which the love ethic of equal regard further orders and enhances. But Christian irony suggests that all families, even the ostensibly equal-regard, mother-father partnership, can be corrupted under the conditions of finitude and sin.

In addition to the distinctly Christian element of irony, I want to introduce a life-cycle perspective into our understanding of love as equal regard. For instance, I want to ask, What does Christian love as mutuality or equal regard mean for the raising of children? How can the ethic of mutuality be adjusted with viable concepts of parental authority? It is my belief that for the love ethic of mutuality and equal regard to guide the raising of children, it must be supplemented with a theory of the human life cycle. This is the difference between an ethic serving the purposes of moral theology and an ethic serving pastoral care. It is in their knowledge of the dynamics of the life cycle that modern psychology and psychotherapy can make their most profound contribution to an equal-regard ethic relevant to the concrete circumstances of care. They help us understand that mutuality must take different forms at different points in the life cycle. Mutuality constitutes the ideal center of an ethic toward which everything in the life cycle points, even though this norm is not always fully expressed at any one moment along the way.

A few illustrations are in order. For instance, mutuality between parent and infant occurs in anticipatory and preparatory ways. Although the human infant is highly dependent and often makes overwhelming demands, mutuality can still take the form of face-to-face and eye-to-eye contact in parents' interactions with their newly born children. In later phases of childhood, parents who live by an ethic of mutuality need not relinquish parental guidance and good judgment. Instead, they can treat their children with respect and permit ranges of freedom and responsibility appropriate to their ages. When an ethic of mutuality is at the center of a family ethic, parents raise children to grow gradually toward genuine mutuality. Attaining mutuality may not be accomplished fully until adulthood, but if this central value is firmly in place, children sense that patterns of equal regard are progressively being realized.

If mutuality in the sense of equal regard is central to a family ethic, elderly parents can more graciously accept the encroaching physical, and sometimes financial, dependency on their children that old age frequently brings. They can accept this partly because they know that a deeper equal regard and respect has been present in the family process from the beginning and undergirds their life together even in their decline.

Obviously, within such a life-cycle theory of equal regard, there will be many moments of costly self-sacrifice, especially on the part of parents during the early years of their children's infancy and youth. But even here, self-sacrifice is that second mile required to empower children to move toward an ethic of equal regard and mutuality, even with their own parents. This is the ethic that should empower both men and women, husbands and wives, and the supporting structures of extended family, government, the mental health profession, and the church. This is the family ethic that should fill the growing vacuum between the traditional family and the "feminization of kinship" that Stacey's fascinating book failed to explore. This is the family ethic, nuanced by irony and a life-cycle perspective, that should answer Lasch's concern with the declining authority of families.

I believe that such an ethic is possible. Socialization patterns for children and youth should be guided by it. Religious and cultural institutions should accept it and find powerful ways of promoting it. Psychotherapy within a Christian context should uncover the developmental and value lacunae that prevent families from growing toward an equal-regard ethic between spouses and between them and their children. Pastoral psychotherapy should attempt to develop the insight and relational resources needed to help families move toward that goal. Although pastoral care and counseling should never use even the ethic of gentle equal regard rigidly and moralistically, it should still constitute the gently held and judiciously applied moral center of all of the church's care of families.

My argument has been that there are strong ideological and social trends working to create matrifocal families. This unrealistically releases men from the obligations of families and works to the disadvantage of both women and children, creating the feminization of kinship and poverty. Although the women who head these families are both heroic and worthy of empathy and support by church and state, as a general societal trend the drift toward the matrifocal family should not be idealized. Theological strands stemming from the interplay of Aristotelian philosophy with Christian thought provide resources for cherishing as an important proximate good the mother-father partnership. And a love ethic of equal regard can provide a new ethic for the reordering of gender relations in this mother-father team. A life-cycle ethic of equal regard should guide the church's care with families and help restore their moral authority. In addition, an ethic of equal regard should guide the church's socialization of youth and its more specialized pastoral counseling of troubled families.

PART III

Critical Foundations:
An Ecumenical Search

Chapter 7

Practical Theology and the American Family Debate (1997)

This chapter was written for publication in the *International Journal of Practical Theology*. It addressed an international audience of mainly professors of practical theology and their students. It provides a fairly detailed summary of the American debate over the family as the United States was moving into the 1996 presidential campaign between Bill Clinton and Robert Dole.

This essay introduces the concept of "critical hermeneutics," perhaps for the first time in my writings on family issues. This model of hermeneutics or interpretation affirms the importance of tradition as a beginning point for practical theology, indeed for all human knowledge, whether theological or not. Hence, I affirm the importance of Reformation theology's use of the theological orders of creation and covenant in its theology of marriage and family. I locate my use of a revised Roman Catholic natural law perspective as an important submoment within the larger theological doctrines of creation and covenant. A revised model of natural law argument using the resources of philosophy, evolutionary psychology, and the social sciences should be seen, I contend, as a naturalistic moment that helps to identify, clarify, and give additional authority to the common human goods organized and enhanced by faith affirmations grounded in creation and covenant. Although I make considerable use of a flexible version of Catholic natural law thinking, I believe that I do so in a Protestant way.

In what follows, I will give an overview of the American family debate, outline some practical theological responses to this debate, show how these responses relate to political culture, and sketch a brief description of family trends. I will conclude by offering some hints as to how our theological sources should be reconstructed to become more faithful, more convincing to the church, and more articulate in public discourse. Since this essay is an overview, none of these topics will receive the full attention it deserves.

The current family debate in the United States should be understood in relation to the optimism about family change in the social sciences during the 1960s and 1970s. For over two decades, social scientists from Talcott Parsons to Jessie Bernard had argued that these changes — more divorce, out-of-wedlock births, stepfamilies, single parents, both parents in the work force — did *not* mean that families were in crisis.[1]

Many social science texts argued that these changes meant increased freedom from the oppressive weight of traditional families.[2] Jessie Bernard concluded in her book *The Future of Marriage* that marriage as an institution was good for men but produced bad mental and physical health for women. Her solution was more radical than her diagnosis seemed to imply. She did not propose a reform of marriage to make it equal and mutually fulfilling for both husband and wife. Instead, her solution envisioned a "future of options" — a social situation in which the institution of marriage was one of many options ranging from celibacy, trial marriage, open marriage, group marriage, nonsexual marriage, cohabitation, and singleness with an active sexual life.[3] Some social scientists held that family changes were harmful only when they ended in poverty. A wider welfare net and a healthy economy, they argued, could prevent these negative consequences. Even the prestigious Carnegie Council's *All Our Children* played down the importance of the intact, two-parent family for child well-being.[4]

---

1. Talcott Parsons and Robert F. Bales, *Family, Socialization and Interaction* (Glencoe, Ill.: Free Press, 1955), and Jessie Bernard, *The Future of Marriage* (New York: World, 1972).

2. See Barbara Dafoe Whitehead, "The Experts' Story of Marriage," An Institute for American Values Working Paper for the Marriage in America Symposium (New York: Institute for American Values, 1992).

3. Bernard, *The Future of Marriage,* pp. 270-72.

4. Kenneth Keniston and the Carnegie Council on Children, *All Our Children: The American Family under Pressure* (New York: Harcourt Brace Jovanovich, 1977).

The Liberal Response: Relationality and Justice-Love

Three practical theological responses to these trends from American churches can be identified — a liberal Protestant, a Catholic, and a conservative Protestant response. Liberal religious communities tended to agree with the dominant social science analysis. Theological liberals, fresh from battles of the 1960s over civil rights for African-Americans, analogized a relation between equality for minorities and equality for a variety of family forms. Single-parent families, stepfamilies, nonmarried cohabiting families, and gay and lesbian families were seen as equally good for both children and adults if only the onus of prejudice could be removed.

The close approximation of liberal theological views of marriage and family to the growing contractualism of legal theories of marriage should not be overlooked. With the advent of no-fault divorce in the 1960s and 1970s, marriage agreements increasingly were seen as analogous to business contracts.[5] Unliteral divorce — divorce based on the will of one partner even if the other resisted — made marriage contracts among the weakest in American society.

Liberal churches never accepted the secular contractual view as exhaustive of the religious significance of marriage. Their theology of marriage, however, had analogies to the contractual concept. Rather than contract as such, the liberal view talked of marital-type "relationships." These were spoken of as "committed relationships." Their religious meaning was found in the affective quality, justice, and nonexploitative character of these relationships. Although seldom spoken of as "contracts," these ideal relations nonetheless possessed features of contracts because of the voluntary way they were thought to be established and dissolved. Gradually, the classic religious models of marriage — marriage as both legal contract and covenant or legal contract and sacrament — gave way to the idea of a marital-type relationship that was essentially privately contracted and only incidentally legally witnessed or religiously sanctioned.

The concept of "justice love" between consenting adults — a concept found in the Presbyterian *Keeping Body and Soul Together* — is an example of this style of practical theological thinking. A kind of "Kantian relationalism" (to coin a term) became widespread in liberal circles, both religious and secular. This view blurred distinctions between nonsexual friendships, sexual friendships, cohabiting couples, legally contracted

---

5. John Witte Jr., "From Sacrament to Contract: The Legal Transformations of the Western Family," *Criterion* 34, no. 3 (Autumn 1995): 3-11.

marital couples, and couples both legally contracted and covenantally or sacramentally sanctioned. A new democracy of loving and just intimate relationships began replacing older understandings of covenant, sacrament, and contract applied to the sphere of marriage and family.

Those holding this view of marriage and family were not alarmed by the family trends of the 1970s and 1980s, and they saw little reason to either halt or alter these trends. The task of theology and the church, in fact, was to create a new situation of acceptance, justice, and normalization of these emerging family arrangements.

Advocates of this view tended to believe that lobbying for state support of new family forms, especially single-parent households with small children, was a fundamental obligation of the Christian community.

The Catholic Response: The Principle of Subsidiarity

A second response came from American Catholicism. This view was grounded on the shadows of Catholic natural law thinking about families and its associated principle of subsidiarity. In spite of the personalism of some Catholic theologians (even Pope John Paul II),[6] the Catholic view assumed as foundational to families the natural bonding of one man and one woman for the purposes of procreation and education of children, the payment of the marital debt, mutual assistance between spouses, and supernatural grace.[7] The principle of subsidiarity — a view of the family-state relation inspired by Aristotle but explicitly stated by Popes Leo XIII and Pius XI — has its own natural law backing. This view believed that the family, because of the energies of kin preference, has a prima facie competence and right to care for its members, especially young children. Government should not intrude on this capacity. Nonetheless, government has a crucial role in protecting families from the avarice of the market and assuring families of the social conditions needed for a family wage.[8]

6. For evidence of the personalism of Pope John Paul II that still conforms to the classic Catholic natural law position on the family, see his early book, Karol Wojtyla, *Love and Responsibility*, trans. H. T. Willetts (New York: Farrar, Strauss, Giroux, 1994).

7. Thomas Aquinas, *Summa Theologica*, III, q. 41; Augustine, "The Good of Marriage," in *Treatises on Marriage and Other Subjects*, trans. Charles T. Wilcox et al., ed. Roy J. Deferrari, vol. 15 of The Writings of Saint Augustine (New York: Fathers of the Church, 1955).

8. For key documents on the Catholic concept of subsidiarity, see the following: Pope Leo XIII, "Rerum Novarum"; Pope Pius XI, "Quadragesimo Anno"; and Pope John Paul II, "Centesimus Annus"; all in *Proclaiming Justice and Peace: Papal Documents from Rerum*

The Catholic response was conservative on family ethics and relatively progressive on social policy. It resisted the trends toward divorce, out-of-wedlock births, cohabitation, the deinstitutionalization of marriage, and abortion. It continued to champion marriage as grounded in natural law and empowered by supernatural grace. The principle of subsidiarity, however, led Catholic social theory to support state-financed welfare for needy families and children, whatever the cause of their vulnerability. Although Catholics believed government should not intrude on families — especially the family's right to be instructed by the church on family ethics — they believed that the state should protect the family's resources, be this through the guarantee of fair wages, the right through labor unions to bargain with companies, or the right to an adequate education for children.[9]

The Conservative Religious Response: The Orders and Spheres of Creation

Conservative religious and political forces did not share the social scientific optimism about family change. Religious conservatives resisted these family changes, affirming the traditional family roles of wage-earning father and domestic mother. Furthermore, they resisted government intrusion into family life through welfare, progressive values in public schools, and sex education in the schools. Some Christian conservatives justified this thinking by fundamentalist uses of Scriptures that appear to sanction male headship (Eph. 5:23; Col. 3:18; 1 Peter 3:1), forbid divorce (Matt. 19:6-9), or command women to silence in the church (1 Cor. 14:34-36). This group tended to believe that the nineteenth-century family with its working husband and stay-at-home wife was derived directly from the biblical plan for families. They seemed unaware that the family of the 1950s reflected the contingent character of a specific economic organization of domestic life which had its roots in the Industrial Revolution rather than the New Testament.

Although conservatives of this type were skeptical of government intrusion on family life, they seemed less troubled by the intrusions of the

---

Novarum through Centesimus Annus, ed. Michael Walsh and Brian Davies (Mystic, Conn.: Twenty-Third Publications, 1991).

9. Pope John Paul II reiterated both sides of Catholic teachings on the family — conservative personal family ethics and liberal social philosophy on the active but limited role of government — when he visited the United States during the Autumn of 1995. See Gustav Niebuhr, "Homily at Aqueduct Race Track," *New York Times* (October 7, 1995), p. 12.

market. There were exceptions to this rule, however. The conservative mind was often skeptical of market influences that promoted the subversive values of popular culture — hence the interest in developing an alternative popular religious music.

Other Christian conservatives grounded their thinking on more sophisticated theological models. Those working out of Reformed theological traditions were likely to invoke the idea of "orders" or "spheres" of creation to justify their religious sanction for intact married families as well as their theory of the limited rights of government in family life. Genesis 2:24 ("Therefore a man leaves his father and his mother and cleaves to his wife, and they become one flesh") was used to argue that God's intention for covenanted and permanent marriage was that it be an "order of creation." More complicated covenant theologies stemming from Luther, Calvin, Barth, Brunner, and the Dutch educator-statesman Abraham Kuyper developed an idea that the spheres of family, government, and market are differentiated orders under the will of God.[10] Kuyper, whose influence is growing on the American scene, taught that each order or sphere should be governed by the sovereign rule of God. This view theoretically does not end in theocracy, since no specific manifestation of government is concretely sanctioned, just the general idea that Christians operating in the spheres of life, including government, must be attentive to their covenant responsibilities.

This more sophisticated view — argued by such thinkers as Mary Stewart Van Leeuwen, Max Stackhouse, and legal theorist John Witte — affirms the intact, mother-father partnership, but it does not condone male headship or the public-private split of the nineteenth-century family.[11] Although it is cautious about the role of government in family life, this view is likely to see a role for the state in protecting families from destructive market intrusions. Proponents of such a view generally see a place for state welfare as long as it does not undermine the prerogatives of families and their covenants with their religious communities. The Christian Coalition is a powerful but unsophisticated version of elements of

10. Karl Barth, *Church Dogmatics* III.4 (Edinburgh: T.& T. Clark, 1961), pp. 116-29; Emil Brunner, *The Divine Imperative* (Philadelphia: Westminster, 1957), pp. 330-39; Abraham Kuyper, *The Problem of Poverty*, ed. James Skillen (Grand Rapids: Baker, 1991), pp. 29f.

11. Max Stackhouse, *For Richer, For Poorer; For Better, for Worse: Social Teachings of the Churches on Family and Economic Life* (Louisville, Ky.: Westminster John Knox, 1997); Mary Stewart Van Leeuwen, *Gender and Grace: Love, Work, and Parenting in a Changing World* (Downers Grove, Ill.: InterVarsity, 1990); John Witte Jr., *Law, Religion, and Family in the West* (Louisville, Ky.: Westminster John Knox, 1997).

both Catholic subsidiarity and the Reformed doctrine of the spheres. A careful reading of leader Ralph Reed's *Politically Incorrect* shows that he is struggling to articulate the autonomy of family from state in ways which reflect aspects of each of these classic formulations.[12]

Religion, Family, and Political Culture

These three practical theological responses to family trends have interacted with political culture in interesting ways. Theological liberals have tended to be liberal Democrats, even to the point that mainline denominational hierarchies are referred to in some circles as "the Democratic Party at prayer." Since most social scientists are known to be political liberals, they have joined with Democratic liberals and the liberal churches in both accepting and supporting the new private contractualism. It would be unfair to suggest that liberal political culture does not value permanent marriage, but it is correct to say that it increasingly sees marriage as one among many options for the organization of human intimacy, sexuality, and reproduction.[13] Liberal thinkers tend to believe that neither private institutions nor public policy can do much to bring marriage back as *the* socially sanctioned institution for the organization of sexuality and reproduction.[14] They argue, therefore, that government increasingly must function as a surrogate family or substitute "father" for mothers and children who have either lost husbands and fathers or never had them in the first place.[15]

---

12. Ralph Reed, *Politically Incorrect* (Dallas: Ward, 1994), p. 256.

13. Norval Glenn, "A Plea for Objective Assessment of the Notion of Family Decline," *The Journal of Marriage and the Family* 55, no. 3 (August 1993): 543. Glenn writes that in a recent sample of members of the American Sociological Association, "only 6% identified themselves as conservatives or reactionaries while 87% said that they were liberals or radicals."

14. An example of the kind of social science thinking that sees marriage as a declining institution that cannot be brought back can be found in a recent statement by James Levine and Edward Pitt in *New Expectations: Community Strategies for Responsible Fatherhood* (New York: Work and Family Institute, 1995), p. 35. These authors hope to produce more responsible care for children by nonresident fathers. Encouraging marriage, discouraging out-of-wedlock births, and discouraging divorce are not a part of their strategy for producing responsible fatherhood. They write, "But we do not know how to produce more marriages. Nor do any of the experts we cite who argue so passionately for marriage as the only way to socialize men into continuing relationships with their children."

15. Jan Dizard and Howard Gadlin, *The Minimal Family* (Amherst, Mass.: University of Massachusetts Press, 1990).

Many Christian fundamentalists or conservatives, on the other hand, have gravitated to the Republican Party. The Christian Coalition, and the Moral Majority before it, has functioned to organize a large percentage of conservative and evangelical Christians to support the "pro-family" political and cultural agenda of the Republican Party. Conservative Christians working out of the Reformed "spheres" or Catholic "subsidiarity" models are more unpredictable in their orientations to political culture. If they are conservative on abortion, they may go Republican. If they see positive but limited roles for government (as both spheres theory and subsidiarity can sometimes hold), they are likely to go Democratic, or at least "new Democrat" of the kind espoused by Clinton and the Democratic Leadership Conference.

In the late 1970s, the Republican Party, sensing the fears about family fragmentation among conservative Christians, exploited these anxieties for political purposes. Eventually, this strategy resulted in the stunning 1994 Republican congressional victories. Since the 1992 presidential election of William Clinton, however, concern over the condition of families has become a liberal (or at least a neo-liberal) as well as a conservative political issue. The welfare debate in the United States has come to symbolize a wider cultural conflict over the condition and future of American families. Political liberals such as David Ellwood, Mary Jo Bane, William Galston, and President Clinton himself began to express concern about the negative effects of divorce, teenage pregnancy, and the emerging culture of nonmarriage.[16]

In effect, these political liberals became "neo-liberals." Before the November 1994 elections, a new consensus was emerging between neo-liberals such as Ellwood, Galston, and Moynihan and a new brand of neo-conservatives such as William Bennett, Henry Hyde, and the conservative Family Research Council. Neo-liberals and neo-conservatives shared the conviction that government should take an explicit moral stand and encourage family formation, discourage out-of-wedlock births, and reduce the divorce rate.

Neo-liberals on the American scene can be defined as pro-family liberals who repudiate the older liberal optimism about family trends. They want to reverse these trends but also retain an active role for government in supporting needy families. The leadership of the mainline religious denominations, with few exceptions, have continued their alliance with the

16. For an example of this trend, see Mary Jo Bane and David Ellwood, *Welfare Realities: From Rhetoric to Reform* (Cambridge: Harvard University Press, 1994).

older political liberalism and have appeared confused by the steps toward a somewhat more conservative stance by neo-liberals.

Neo-conservatives can be defined as political conservatives who believe family problems are a result of declining cultural values rather than worsening economic conditions. Yet they are neo-conservative precisely because they, in contrast to hard conservatives, believe that there is a place for government supports for needy and disrupted families. Neo-liberals and neo-conservatives could dialogue and cooperate before the 1994 conservative landslide. Although they varied on the details, both saw family problems as simultaneously matters of changing cultural values *and unfortunate economic downturns.* They tended to agree that solutions to family problems needed to involve both cultural and economic proposals.

As we move toward the 1996 presidential elections, this old alliance is once again visible. Now, however, neo-liberals and neo-conservatives are fighting over a viable middle ground — one that emphasizes cultural values and economic solutions. Since the elections are near, they are fighting to take credit for a new government "familism" that encourages family commitment (by discouraging out-of-wedlock births and enforcing child-care payments) yet supports families economically (through tax reductions, tax credits for children, and tax reductions for college tuition). What is striking is how similar the political parties look on family issues even though they struggle to look different.

Christian voices have been in conflict over the family debate. The three voices — the liberal, Protestant conservative, and Catholic — have been unable to develop a dialogue analogous to the neo-liberal–neo-conservative political alliance.[17] This cannot happen unless more fundamental theological dialogue occurs between these groups. Here are some issues they must face.

Liberalism's ethic of relationality and equality has difficulty distinguishing marriages and families from other types of friendship. On the other hand, Reformation and Catholic perspectives are often charged with patriarchy and injustice in their family theologies. Recently, however, Reformation and Catholic perspectives have moved toward formulations of Christian love which de-emphasize paternalism, emphasize Christian

---

17. An example of this can be seen in reviewing the responses of Interfaith Impact, the Washington, D.C., voice of the liberal denominations, to the Contract with the American Family issued by the Christian Coalition during May of 1995. The response was one of total rejection rather than a couching of criticisms within efforts to find points of common ground. See "They Don't Speak for Us: The Religious Community Responds to the Christian Coalition" (Press Conference, May 17, 1995).

love as mutuality,[18] find biblical support for these positions,[19] and place self-sacrificial love in service to mutuality. Hence, these traditions are now absorbing some of the liberal sensibility. But in order for Catholicism and Reformed thinking to speak effectively on the centrality of marriage for sexual intimacy, procreation, and the education of children, the naturalism in Catholic family theory and the "naturalistic moment" in some forms of Reformation thinking need to be strengthened. This is what should happen if a neo-liberal–neo-conservative alliance is to develop at the level of religious culture.

Family Concern among Political and Social-Science Liberals

Family disruption has now become a concern of political liberals in the United States as it was formerly only for political conservatives. There are two reasons why liberals have become concerned about this issue: (1) the changing interpretation of research on the family in the social sciences, and (2) the growing public costs of family difficulties.

The first point is the more dramatic. Distinguished family sociologist Norval Glenn, who describes himself as a political liberal, points out that over 87 percent of sociologists are also liberals.[20] Liberals, he argues, are future-oriented and open to change. For this reason, liberal social scientists were inclined to give a positive interpretation to the family changes of the 1960s and 1970s. Beginning in the 1980s, however, social science studies by Wallerstein, Hetherington, Bumpass, Popenoe, Weitzmann, McLanahan, and Sandefur began to support the idea that divorce and single parenthood had, on average, negative consequences for both children and women.[21]

18. For a statement about the centrality of mutuality in families, see John Paul II, *Familiaris Consortio* (Chicago, Ill.: Archdiocese of Chicago, 1981); for a Reformation emphasis on mutuality, see Van Leeuwen, *Gender and Grace*, p. 243.

19. Elisabeth Schüssler Fiorenza, *In Memory of Her: A Feminist Theological Reconstruction of Christian Origins* (New York: Crossroad, 1983); Warren Carter, *Households and Discipleship: A Study of Matthew* (Sheffield, England: Sheffield Academic, 1994); Stephen Barton, "Paul's Sense of Place: An Anthropological Approach to Community Formation in Corinth," *New Testament Studies* 32 (1986): 74.

20. Glenn, "A Plea for Objective Assessment," pp. 542-45.

21. Judith S. Wallerstein and Sandra Blakeslee, *Second Chances: Men, Women, and Children a Decade after Divorce* (New York: Ticknor and Fields, 1989); K. Mavis Hetherington, Martha Cox, and Roger Cox, "The Aftermath of Divorce," in *Mother-Child, Father-Child Relations,* ed. Joseph H. Stevens and Marilyn Matthews (Washington, D.C.: National Association

Family structure, seen in the 1960s and 1970s as a neutral factor for family well-being, was viewed by the early 1990s as highly relevant to the flourishing of children. During the spring of 1993, Barbara Dafoe White-head published a popular essay for *The Atlantic Monthly* summarizing much of this new research.[22] Charles Murray, in his more balanced pre–*Bell Curve* days, created a sensation when he predicted in the *Wall Street Journal* that out-of-wedlock births would spread and establish a new white under-class.[23] Within months, liberal journalists such as Joan Beck, David Broder, William Raspberry, and Clarence Page began acknowledging the serious-ness of the family crisis in their columns.[24] Reports of government-appointed groups such as the National Commission on Children and the National Commission on America's Urban Families reversed the thinking of the Carnegie Council by re-emphasizing the importance of intact fami-lies for child well-being.[25]

The most definitive research was reported by Sara McLanahan and Gary Sandefur in their *Growing Up with a Single Parent*. Using sophisticated statistical tools to analyze the data of four national surveys, McLanahan and Sandefur concluded that children growing up outside of biological, two-parent families were twice as likely to do poorly in school, twice as likely to be single parents themselves, and one-and-a-half times more likely to have difficulties becoming permanently attached to the labor

---

for the Education of Young Children, 1978); Larry Bumpass, "What's Happening to the Family? Interaction between Demographics and Institutional Change," *Demography* 27, no. 4 (November 1990): 483-98; David Popenoe, "American Family Decline, 1960-1990: A Review and Appraisal," *Journal of Marriage and the Family* 55, no. 3 (August 1993): 527-41; Lenore J. Weitzman, *The Divorce Revolution: The Unexpected Social and Economic Consequences for Women and Children in America* (New York: Free Press, 1985); Sara McLanahan and Gary Sandefur, *Growing Up with a Single Parent* (Cambridge: Harvard University Press, 1994).

22. Barbara Dafoe Whitehead, "Dan Quayle Was Right," *The Atlantic Monthly* (April 1993), pp. 47-84.

23. Charles Murray, "The Coming White Underclass," *The Wall Street Journal* (October 29, 1993), p. 16A.

24. Joan Beck, "Teenage Pregnancy Is an Issue That Crosses Party Lines," *Chicago Tri-bune* (March 27, 1994), sec. 4, p. 3; David Broder, "Family Values: Stop Arguing about Them and Start Changing Them," *Chicago Tribune* (February 16, 1993), sec. 1, p. 17; William Rasp-berry, "That Disturbing Charles Murray," *The Washington Post National Weekly Edition* (De-cember 6-12, 1993); Clarence Page, "Wrong Target for Welfare Reform," *Chicago Tribune* (May 11, 1994).

25. *Beyond Rhetoric: A New American Agenda for Children and Families* (Washington, D.C.: United States Government Printing Office, 1991); *Families First: Report of the National Commis-sion on America's Urban Families* (Washington, D.C.: United States Government Printing Of-fice, 1993).

market.[26] This was true when the data was controlled for the race, education, age, and place of residence of parents. Income reduced these disadvantages, but only by one-half. Furthermore, this study showed that stepfamilies had no advantage over single parents; both were less successful in raising children than intact, biologically related families.[27] This is so even though the average income of stepfamilies is higher than that of intact families, thereby challenging the idea that income rather than family structure is the chief predictor of child well-being.

With the publication of the McLanahan-Sandefur volume, the casualness of the 1960s and 1970s about family structure seems to be coming to an end. McLanahan, herself once a single mother, is surprised with what her own data suggests. She and Sandefur write,

> If we were asked to design a system for making sure that children's basic needs were met, we would probably come up with something quite similar to the two-parent family ideal. Such a design, in theory, would not only ensure that children had access to the time and money of two adults, it also would provide a system of checks and balances that promoted quality parenting. The fact that both adults have a biological connection to the child would increase the likelihood that the parents would identify with the child and be willing to sacrifice for that child, and it would reduce the likelihood that either parent would abuse the child.[28]

Some political liberals have begun to hear this changed message of the social sciences. It is precisely this kind of information which has turned some of them into neo-liberals. On the other hand, there is little evidence that a similar shift is occurring in the liberal religious culture. Although Protestant evangelicals and Catholics are inclined to believe these reports, they differ considerably in how they make use of such information within their practical theological positions.

The Family Crisis and the "Male Problematic"

Social science research is pointing to a level of analysis that only recently has become clear. It has to do with the new understanding of the importance of

26. McLanahan and Sandefur, *Growing Up with a Single Parent,* pp. 1-12.
27. McLanahan and Sandefur, *Growing Up with a Single Parent,* pp. 70f.
28. McLanahan and Sandefur, *Growing Up with a Single Parent,* p. 38.

fathers. Some interpreters believe that the single most important family trend in the United States — and indeed throughout the world — is the growing absence of fathers from their children.[29] I call this trend the "male problematic." This trend is a common factor behind most of the data on family change. Nearly 30 percent of children in the United States under the age of eighteen do not live with their fathers, and nearly 50 percent of children under eighteen will spend several years without their father's presence in the home. Furthermore, divorced fathers, on average, do poorly in financially supporting and visiting their children. The fathers of children born out of wedlock are even worse. As Andrew Cherlin and Frank Furstenberg say in their *Divided Families,* American men see marriage and parenting as a package; when the marriage breaks up, parenting deteriorates as well.[30]

Trends toward father absence are not limited to the United States. Aaron Sachs reports that in a recent study of low-income couples in Chile, 42 percent of the fathers were providing no child support to their first-born child after its sixth birthday.[31] According to a recent study in Barbados, of 333 fathers with eight-year-old children, only 22 percent were still living with their child. Furthermore, the children of the fathers who continued to live with their children were performing significantly better in school.[32] The Population Council's *Families in Focus* reports that the number of female-headed households has risen significantly in almost every country in the world since the mid 1970s. Marital dissolution runs from 40 to 60 percent for women in their forties in poor countries such as the Dominican Republic, Ghana, Indonesia, and Senegal. Divorce rates were 55 per 100 in the United States in 1990 and have doubled since 1970 in Canada, France, Greece, the Netherlands, the United Kingdom, and former West Germany.[33] Out-of-wedlock births were 1.0 percent in Japan, 33.3 percent in Northern Europe, 70 percent in Botswana, and 27 to 28 percent in Kenya.[34] The decline of fathers' financial and social support has had disastrous consequences for both mothers and children throughout the

29. For a summary of this point of view, see David Blankenhorn, *Fatherless America* (New York: Basic, 1995).

30. Frank F. Furstenberg Jr. and Andrew Cherlin, *Divided Families: What Happens to Children When Parents Part* (Cambridge: Harvard University Press, 1991), pp. 34-39.

31. Aaron Sachs, "Men, Sex, and Parenthood," *World Watch* 7, no. 2 (March-April 1994): 13.

32. Sachs, "Men, Sex, and Parenthood," p. 14.

33. J. Bruce, C. B. Lloyd, and A. Leonard, *Families in Focus: New Perspectives on Mothers, Fathers, and Children* (New York: Population Council, 1995), pp. 14-20.

34. Bruce et al., *Families in Focus,* p. 73.

world, even in wealthy countries. Its consequences are especially devastating in poor and undeveloped countries. Poverty both contributes to and is further aggravated by fatherlessness.

Yet, as John Snarey, David Blankenhorn, David Popenoe, and McLanahan and Sandefur show, fathers contribute not only financially but also cognitively and emotionally to the well-being of their children.[35] Furthermore, their contribution is not easily replaced. Although biological relatedness does not guarantee good parenting by either mother or father, it seems to be a premoral condition (a premoral good) that on average correlates positively with moral qualities such as commitment, presence, steadfastness, and positive regard — qualities which are directly related to child flourishing. This raises a question which I will address later — how should information about average premoral conditions for good parenting be used in a more properly ethical argument?

The case for the two-parent, biologically related family can be overstated. Not all biological fathers and mothers are competent parents. Not all two-parent families are just and life-enhancing; some are tyrannical to wives and abusive to children. The facts seem to indicate, however, that alternatives are on average worse. Single mothers are more likely to abuse their children physically than parents in intact families, and children are many times more likely to be physically and sexually abused in stepfamilies and cohabiting arrangements than they are in intact families.[36] There should be, as a matter of ecclesial and public policy, a presumption toward encouraging the formation and maintenance of intact families. This rule has exceptions, but they do not undercut its importance as a cultural and religious guide.

Reasons for the Family Crisis

There are competing explanations for the family crisis in the United States. Different solutions in the family debate can be distinguished par-

---

35. John Snarey, *How Fathers Care for the Next Generation: A Four-Decade Study* (Cambridge: Harvard University Press, 1993); David Popenoe, "The Evolution of Marriage and the Problem of Stepfamilies: A Biosocial Perspective," in *Stepfamilies: Who Benefits? Who Does Not?* ed. Alan Booth and Judy Dunn (Hillsdale, N.J.: Lawrence Erlbaum Associates, 1994), pp. 3-27; McLanahan and Sandefur, *Growing Up with a Single Parent*, pp. 37, 56, 72.

36. One of the most definitive analyses of the risk of abuse in non–biologically related family structures can be found in Martin Daly and Margo Wilson, *Homicide* (New York: Aldine de Gruyter, 1988), pp. 86-90.

tially by their differing analysis of the problem. As we have seen, conservatives, neo-conservatives, and some neo-liberals emphasize the importance of cultural values. Values have changed, they claim, and largely for the worse. Less nuanced conservatives such as James Dobson claim modern society is basically immoral and does not honor family, marital, and parental commitments as it once did.[37] Neo-conservatives such as Christopher Lasch emphasize a new narcissism or, as does William Bennett, a breakdown in virtue.[38] Neo-liberals such as Robert Bellah and David Popenoe, as well as historians such as Edward Shorter and Lawrence Stone, place importance on the rise of Enlightenment individualism.[39] Even demographers such as Larry Bumpass and Ron Lesthaeghe invoke Enlightenment individualism to explain growing family fragmentation.[40]

On the other hand, liberal, progressive, Marxist, and many liberal feminist analyses blame deteriorating economic conditions and decreased welfare support for the family crises. Frederick Engels held that capitalism itself is the problem.[41] Jürgen Habermas and Alan Wolfe follow Max Weber in emphasizing the spread of technical reason as a causative factor. They show, however, that this can take two forms.[42] Technical reason can express itself in market logics that spread into private life, replacing family loyalties with cost-benefit and ethical-egoist modes of moral thinking. Or technical reason can be expressed through state bureaucracies which take over family functions and reduce them to dependent client populations.

Neither cultural nor social-economic analyses are sufficient in themselves. Some combination of both seems required to orient us to the prob-

37. James Dobson, *Dr. Dobson Answers Your Questions about Marriage and Sexuality* (Wheaton, Ill.: Tyndale, 1979), and *Dr. Dobson Answers Your Questions about Confident Healthy Families* (Wheaton, Ill.: Tyndale, 1979).

38. Christopher Lasch, *Haven in a Heartless World* (New York: Basic, 1975); William Bennett, *The Index of Leading Cultural Indicators* (New York: Simon and Schuster, 1994), pp. 5-12.

39. Robert Bellah et al., *Habits of the Heart* (Berkeley: University of California Press, 1985); David Popenoe, "The Family Transformed," *Family Affairs* 2, nos. 2-3 (Summer 1989): 3; Edward Shorter, *The Making of the Modern Family* (New York: Basic, 1977); Lawrence Stone, *The Road to Divorce: England 1530-1987* (Oxford: Oxford University Press, 1990).

40. Bumpass, "What's Happening to the Family?" pp. 492f.; Ron Lesthaeghe, "A Century of Demographic and Cultural Change in Western Europe: An Exploration of Underlying Dimensions," *Population and Development Review* 9, no. 3 (September 1983): 411-32.

41. Frederick Engels, *The Origins of the Family, Private Property, and the State* (New York: International Publications, 1972).

42. Jürgen Habermas, *The Theory of Communicative Action*, trans. Thomas McCarthy, vol. 2 (Boston: Beacon, 1987), pp. 153-78; Alan Wolfe, *Whose Keeper? Social Science and Moral Obligation* (Berkeley: University of California Press, 1989), pp. 54-73.

lems of families in the United States and, for that matter, most Western nations. Progressives and liberals should acknowledge that there has been a significant value shift toward more individualistic values. Many former progressives and liberals have accepted the reality of this shift toward individualism, hence the birth of neo-liberal organizations in the United States such as the Democratic Leadership Conference, the Progressive Policy Institute, the Institute for American Values, the Council on Families in America, and the Communitarian Network. These groups are calling for a cultural conversion — a new balance of individual rights and communal responsibilities and a new marital and parental commitment.[43]

The economic view is also important, but it cannot stand alone any more than the cultural analysis can. Economists Victor Fuchs and Diane Reklis admit that the American economy has slowed during the 1980s and 1990s and that this has hurt families. But they point out that the downturn in the well-being of children in America began in the 1970s when income and government expenditures for families were at their peak. Hence, changes in cultural values — the new individualism and its expressions in divorce, out-of-wedlock births, single-parenting, and careerism — must be invoked, they contend, to supplement the economic explanation.[44]

Cultural shifts can sometimes follow economic decline and then become institutionalized. William Julius Wilson's explanation for the colossal increase in out-of-wedlock births in the African-American community (from 22 percent in the 1960s to 68 percent today) is that declining job opportunities for men in inner cities make family formation nearly impossible.[45] But University of Chicago's Mark Testa has shown that *even when* black men begin earning middle-class incomes they are now less likely to marry than they were a few decades ago.[46] Their commitments to marriage as an institution have declined.

Psychological factors constitute a third set of factors influencing family disruption. Susan Moller Okin believes the family has not sufficiently socialized children for gender justice, hence producing the interpersonal

43. For an example of the kind of thinking that runs through these organizations, see Amitai Etzioni, *The Spirit of Community: Rights, Responsibilities, and the Communitarian Agenda* (New York: Crown, 1993).

44. Victor Fuchs and Diane Reklis, "America's Children: Economic Perspectives and Policy Options," *Science* 255 (January 3, 1992): 41-46.

45. William Julius Wilson, *The Truly Disadvantaged* (Chicago: University of Chicago Press, 1987).

46. Mark Testa, "Male Joblessness, Nonmarital Parenthood, and Marriage" (Chicago: Paper prepared for the Irving B. Harris Graduate School of Public Policy Studies, 1991).

strains which lead to divorce or, in many cases, no marriage at all.[47] Nancy Chodorow and Jessica Benjamin believe that the different ways boys and girls are raised by mothers in our society work against gender justice in the home.[48] Linda Waite and Frances Goldscheider believe the family crisis follows from the fact that men's commitment to housework and child care has not kept pace with women's entry into the wage economy.[49]

The view that couples' psychological and communicative skills are not equal to the demands of modern marriage has some merit. It is at least part of the reason for marital disruption. There clearly are fewer religious, cultural, economic, and extended family supports for enduring marriages in the United States and most post-industrial countries. Interpersonal and communicative skills must be excellent for couples to endure conflict in societies with fewer social and economic reinforcements for family formation and enduring marriage. Along with the cultural and economic causes of the family crisis, there are genuine psychological factors as well.

Evolutionary psychologists have gone deeper and introduced an important new dimension to the psychological level of analysis. They point to the asymmetrical reproductive strategies of males and females in all mammalian species, including Homo sapiens. They point out that males of most mammalian species procreate as widely as possible with a variety of females but do not become involved in the care of their offspring.[50] This raises the question, what were the conditions which led Homo sapiens males long ago to become attached to mates and involved in the care and socialization of their children?

Robert Trivers and other evolutionary theorists have discovered a range of naturalistic conditions which may have brought monogamy and male parental investment into existence for humans.[51] These conditions

47. Susan Moller Okin, *Gender, Justice, and the Family* (New York: Basic, 1989).

48. Nancy Chodorow, *Feminism and Psychoanalytic Theory* (New Haven: Yale University Press, 1989); Jessica Benjamin, *The Bonds of Love* (New York: Pantheon, 1988).

49. Linda Waite and Frances Goldscheider, *New Families, No Families? The Transformation of the American Home* (Berkeley: University of California Press, 1991).

50. Summaries of evolutionary theory on family formation, kin altruism, and inclusive fitness can be found in the following: Pierre van der Berghe, *Human Family Systems: An Evolutionary View* (New York: Elsevier, 1979); Martin Daly and Margo Wilson, *Sex, Evolution, and Behavior* (Belmont, Calif.: Wadsworth, 1983); Don Symons, *The Evolution of Human Sexuality* (New York: Oxford University Press, 1979).

51. Robert Trivers, "Parental Investment and Sexual Selection," in *Sexual Selection and the Descent of Man, 1871-1971*, ed. Bernard Campbell (Chicago: Aldine, 1972); Barry S. Hewlett, *Father-Child Relations: Cultural and Biosocial Contexts* (New York: Aldine de Gruyter, 1992).

are worth reviewing, since it may be precisely these conditions which modern societies are losing. The growing absence of these conditions may constitute the deep reasons for family disruption.

These evolutionary psychological perspectives have relevance for contemporary practical theological responses to the family crisis. They offer a way of reconstructing Catholic natural law theory on the family. In turn, this reconstructed Catholic naturalism can offer what Paul Ricoeur calls a "diagnostic" to the naturalistic depth of the classical Protestant orders of creation. By diagnostic, I mean an indication that the orders of creation actually refer to certain realities and regularities of human existence even though the idea of "orders" means precisely that God shapes these regularities toward God's ends. Finally, the theories of evolutionary psychology and current data about the effects of family disruption on children constitute a critique of the naive justice-love perspectives of liberal Protestantism.

Naturalistic Reasons for Family Formation

To understand these claims, we must review recent theories in evolutionary psychology about how family formation occurred for Homo sapiens. The work of W. D. Hamilton provided the framework for a theory of kin altruism which in turn had important implications for the theory of family formation. Hamilton's theory of kin altruism states that individuals are not concerned only with the survival of their own specific genes; they are also concerned with the survival of those who carry their genes — offspring and siblings first and then cousins, aunts and uncles, and second cousins in descending order. Kin altruism explains why creatures are willing under some circumstances to sacrifice their own well-being or fitness for the well-being or fitness of their children, siblings, or other extended family members.

The idea of kin altruism does not exhaust the idea of love. It certainly should not be used to reduce the meaning of Christian love. The idea of kin altruism should be seen as a dimension of human love — one with powerful implications for family theory. Kin altruism tells us much about why male Homo sapiens joined families and began helping their mates raise their children. It also explains why it is difficult as a general rule to find substitutes for natural parents and extended family for the successful raising of children, although highly motivated adoptive parents often do well. There are very specific reasons why natural parents, on average, care more for their children than do other people.

Evolutionary psychologists are now showing how thousands of years ago the emergence of the following conditions helped integrate human males into families. Four conditions appear to have made this possible: (1) "paternal recognition," or a father's certainty that a particular child was his; (2) the long period of human infant dependency, which required mothers to look for assistance from male consorts; (3) ongoing sexual exchange between mates; and (4) reciprocal altruism (mutual helpfulness) between father and mother.[52] When Robert Trivers in 1972 first introduced the idea that paternal certainty and recognition led Homo sapiens males to invest in the care of their offspring as a way of extending their own lives, it was thought that this condition alone was sufficient to account for male bonding with mate and child. It is now believed that the other conditions are needed as well.[53]

These conditions together constitute a naturalistic theory of the institution of matrimony — a theory similar, as we will soon see, to the naturalistic components of Thomas Aquinas's theology of marriage and the family. These four conditions should be thought of as important premoral goods that should be integrated into any more fully ethical theory of marriage and family.

These evolutionary theorists make a crucial, even though limited, contribution to the contemporary family debate. Kin altruism theory gives a partial account as to why the children of intact biological parents seem, on average, to do better in school, jobs, and their own later marital relations. Biological parents are more inclined to identify with and become invested in their offspring. They sense that in caring for the "other" that is their child they are caring partially for themselves. They sense further that to neglect or abandon one of their own would be to disinvest in part of their own life. This does not explain good parenting in the full sense of that concept. But it does illuminate a significant premoral motivation or condition for why families were formed, why intact families have more success with children, and why passive acceptance of family disruption should be resisted.

---

52. W. D. Hamilton, "The Genetical Evolution of Social Behavior, II," *Journal of Theoretical Biology* 7 (1964): 17-52.

53. Hewlett, ed., *Father-Child Relations,* pp. xi-xix.

Thomism, Natural Law, and Evolutionary Biology

Christian family theory in the work of Thomas Aquinas, without the benefit of modern evolutionary theory, recognized most of the naturalistic conditions for family formation summarized above.[54] But Thomas added the theological belief that the "natural" offspring of parents are also gifts of God and made in God's image.[55] In Thomistic theory, which deserves critical reappropriation, the natural and supernatural reinforce each other. Like Aristotle before him, Aquinas saw children as the semblance or partial image of their parents; this, he thought, was part of the reason parents care for their children. Aquinas added, however, that children are also made in the image of God; therefore, we should love in our children the divine good that is in them.

Children have in Thomistic family theory a double valuation. They are made in part in the image of their parents and in this sense naturally belong to and are valued by them. But more fundamentally, children are made in the image of God and even more radically belong to and are valued by God. Since God's image and goodness spills over into all children, adults — especially adult Christians — should cherish all children whether they are directly their own or not. The power of the Thomistic formulation is this: Although it emphasizes the obligation to show a general benevolence toward all children based on God's love for them and God's goodness in them, it does not obscure the importance of inclinations in parents to exert special energy on behalf of their own offspring.

Thomism also offers a powerful response to the male problematic — the tendency of mammalian males to procreate but not to care for their offspring. Aquinas used the Ephesians analogy between fathers and the sacrificial love of Christ to address his version of the male problematic. The key texts are *Summa Theologica* III, questions 42-50; *Summa Theologica*

---

54. For Aquinas's analogs to the four conditions listed in the text, see his *Summa Theologica* III, qq. 41-46 (New York: Benziger Brothers, 1948), and his *Summa Contra Gentiles,* III.ii (London: Burns, Oates and Washbourne, 1928), pp. 112-23. (In future references *Summa Theologica* will be abbreviated as ST and *Summa Contra Gentiles* as SCG.) See Don Browning, "Biology, Ethics, and Narrative in Christian Family Theory," in *Promises to Keep: Decline and Renewal of Marriage in America,* ed. David Popenoe, Jean Bethke Elshtain, and David Blankenhorn (Lanham, Md.: Rowman and Littlefield, 1996). See also Stephen J. Pope, *The Evolution of Altruism and the Ordering of Love* (Washington, D.C.: Georgetown University Press, 1994). Pope's work on the relation of evolutionary biology and Thomistic theories of love and the family has been groundbreaking.

55. ST, II.ii, q. 26.

II.ii, question 26; and *Summa Contra Gentiles* III.ii, chapters 122-25.[56] Aquinas portrays Christ's self-sacrificial love for the church as an analogy to and reinforcement for the male's commitment to his children and friendship with his wife. Aquinas ties this theological statement about the basis of marital commitment to a naturalistic and ethical analysis of the foundations of matrimony and the family.

I will briefly list a small portion of the total evidence showing that Aquinas had his own version of the naturalistic elements of family formation presently discussed by evolutionary ecologists. First, he was aware that long-term human infant dependency beckons for the male to assist his consort in child care. He believed that since the human infant "needs the parents' care for a long time, there is a very great tie between male and female" Homo sapiens, in contrast to other species.[57] Second, he recognized the role of paternal recognition in binding males to offspring and mate, and how this is disrupted in a system of sexual promiscuity. "Man naturally desires to be assured of his offspring," he wrote, "and this assurance would be altogether nullified in the case of promiscuous copulation."[58] Third, he believed that one of the purposes of matrimony "is the mutual services which married persons render one another in household matters."[59] And fourth, he understood in a distinctively medieval way the role of sexual exchange in integrating marital partners. As had Paul and Augustine before him, he advised the payment of the "marital debt," acknowledging that although it was a venial sin, it was excused by the marriage blessing.[60]

Hence, the naturalistic grounds for matrimony were well recognized by Aquinas, even though the biology that supported them was crude and at points inaccurate. But Aquinas did not remain at the naturalistic level in his theory of matrimony. His vision of matrimony entailed distinctively ethical and theological levels as well. The ethical level is found in his refutation of polyandry and polygyny. His criticism of polyandry was still at the premoral level; one woman with several husbands would lower male interest in offspring since it would work against paternal certainty and recognition. It would, for this reason, achieve a lower order of good for father and child and should therefore be rejected. His critique of polygyny was more directly ethical. He admitted that polygyny can exist with rela-

---

56. ST, II.ii, q. 26 (London: R. & T. Washbourne, 1917).
57. ST, III, q. 41, i.
58. SCG, III.ii, p. 118.
59. ST, III, q. 41, i.
60. ST, III, q. 41, iv.

tively high degrees of paternal certainty and interest in offspring. He also observed, however, that wherever men "have several wives, the friendship of a wife for her husband would not be freely bestowed, but servile as it were. And this argument is confirmed by experience; since where men have several wives, the wives are treated as servants."[61]

A theological argument, however, is the capstone that completes his naturalistic and ethical arguments. Aquinas is all too aware of the fragility and vulnerability of human natural inclinations and moral capacities. For him, human commitment to marital permanence must be reinforced with the grace of God which flows from Christ's love for the church. Although this grace is interpreted as supernatural, Aquinas's *sacramentum* (Eph. 5:32) is more properly translated as a mystery *(mysterion)*.[62] When this is done, the narrative analogy of Christ and church to husband and family comes forth (Eph. 5:21-33). The husband is to model his commitment to wife and children after Christ's sacrificial love for the church. The male's recapitulation of Christ's sacrificial love does not cancel or replace the naturalistic or ethical arguments for matrimony. Instead, it stabilizes and deepens these natural and ethical dimensions. Nature and ethical reason push humans toward matrimony; Christ's love and our participation in it takes us the rest of the way by consolidating these natural and ethical tendencies into stable and permanent marital commitments.

Neo-Thomism and a Critique of the Liberal and Reformed Perspectives

Although I write as a liberal Protestant practical theologian, there are clearly problems with both the liberal and conservative perspectives. Catholic theological naturalism has its difficulties as well, even though it has important contributions to make. Catholic naturalism must be cleansed of those aspects of the Aristotelian biology which depicted women as deficient in rationality. It also must be washed of those features of the Thomistic theology which render women as less completely made in the image of God than men.[63]

Once these corrections are made, Thomism has several advantages. It

61. SCG, III.ii, p. 118.
62. ST, III, q. 42, a. 2.
63. ST, I.i, q. 92.

has the virtue of depicting the sacrificial love of the cross as working to restore the mutual friendship of husband and wife rather than being an end in itself. In the Thomistic view, as various contemporary neo-Thomists have argued, love as mutuality or equal regard (Catholic *caritas*) rather than love as self-sacrifice (Protestant *agape*) has the more central place, even in the relation of husband and wife.[64]

Furthermore, Catholic naturalism exposes the shallowness of Protestant liberalism on marriage and family. The relational contractualism of this perspective has no way of determining why one family form actualizes, on average, more premoral good than another. It cannot absorb recent turns in the social sciences; nor can it appreciate naturalism positioned within a theological context as it was in Aquinas. Since it repudiates as well the classical Protestant orders or spheres of creation, it has no way of discerning the central regularities of life that love should nurture and justice should organize.

Finally, a reconstructed Catholic naturalism can supplement classic Protestant perspectives on the orders of creation. The classic Protestant perspective, with few exceptions, understands these orders as attested to by Scripture. They are generally presented as "ordinances" or "commands" of God and accepted by faith.[65] In a day when hermeneutic perspectives on knowledge have firmly established the importance of tradition for all knowing, neither the eyes of faith nor the counsels of philosophy can object to beginning with the witness of a community of faith. On this score, the traditions of orders or spheres of creation are on solid ground. But beginning with the witness of Scripture, tradition, or faith need not mean that naturalistic perspectives have nothing to contribute to heightening the plausibility of the attestations of faith. Especially is that true when they pertain to faith's perspectives on such human arrangements as marriage and the family. So far I have found two examples of Reformed thinkers who contain a naturalistic moment within their broader use of orders-of-creation thinking — Emil Brunner and the

---

64. See Louis Janssens, "Norms and Priorities of a Love Ethics," *Louvain Studies* 6 (Spring 1977): 207-38; Barbara Hilkert Andolsen, "Agape in Feminist Ethics," *Journal of Religious Ethics* 9, no. 1 (Spring 1981): 68-83; Christine Gudorf, "Parenting, Mutual Love, and Sacrifice," in *Women's Consciousness, Women's Conscience: A Reader in Feminist Ethics,* ed. Barbara Hilkert Andolsen, Christine E. Gudorf, and Mary D. Pellauer (Minneapolis: Winston, 1985), pp. 175-91.

65. Luther uses the language of "ordinance" in "The Estate of Marriage," in *Luther's Works*, vol. 45 (Philadelphia: Muhlenberg, 1962), pp. 13-48. Barth and Brunner use the metaphor "command."

feminist evangelical Mary Stewart Van Leeuwen.[66] Their views should be studied and refined.

The naturalism recommended here is not a scientistic one that wipes tradition away and builds an ethic on the basis of the accumulation of discrete natural facts. The naturalism advocated here uses insights gained from the relatively distanciated epistemological stances of the social and evolutionary sciences to add a dimension of realism to the attestations of faith. In the parlance of contemporary hermeneutical debates, this is a "critical hermeneutics" of the kind advocated by Ricoeur or a "hermeneutical realism" as promoted by my colleague William Schweiker.[67]

Liberal Protestantism, for the most part, has been blind to the worldwide trends and consequences of father absence. Conservative Protestantism has resisted family change but has seldom framed the issue in this way and has, for the most part, been unconvincing in public debate. Some of Catholicism's conservative stand on population issues actually has the male problematic in mind. The Vatican's resistance to some liberal and feminist solutions to the population explosion is based on the fear that widespread abortion and birth control can lead to the worldwide collapse of the institution of marriage and further impoverishment of poor women and children.

I will not debate the merits of this fear. My point, rather, is this: neither its older, scholastic natural law arguments nor its more recent personalism has placed the Catholic Church in a favorable position to make its arguments clear in public debate. I believe that the reconstruction of Catholic naturalism along the lines advanced above has much to offer for a more robust participation of the church in the American and emerging international debate over family issues.

---

66. Brunner has an interesting and somewhat complicated way of combining naturalistic observations and "orders" thinking. He believes that reason through an analysis of human action reveals the spheres of work, family, and government. Within the order of the family, he makes a wide range of natural observations very similar to those of Aquinas. But revelation reveals the proper purpose and direction of the orders, including the order of the family. See *The Divine Imperative*, pp. 330-38. Van Leeuwen uses psychology, specifically object relations theory, within her broader "orders" and "spheres" theology.

67. Paul Ricoeur, *Hermeneutics and the Human Sciences* (Cambridge: Cambridge University Press, 1981), p. 60; William Schweiker, *Responsibility and Christian Ethics* (Cambridge: Cambridge University Press, 1995), pp. 4, 113-17.

Religious, Economic, and Psychological Resources

I have argued that the causes of the contemporary family crisis are multiple. To isolate the cultural, socioeconomic, and psychological factors behind the crisis is not to overlook the pervasive reality of human sin. It is, rather, to suggest that human sin also feeds and cooperates with other causal factors. For this reason, solutions and strategies also must be multiple even if always and everywhere the church primarily addresses the reality of human sin.

Cultural factors — for instance, the rise of modern individualism — are central causes of the family crisis. Excessive individualism may be the modern expression of human sin. If a cultural expression of this kind is central to the family crisis, then a cultural — indeed, religio-cultural — answer must be at the forefront. Antidotes to modern individualism, however, must be advanced without undermining the rights of women, as well as men, to participate in vocations outside the home. Furthermore, religio-cultural resources for halting the male drift from families and parenthood must also be found.

Christianity, when properly interpreted, addresses these issues. First, as I have suggested, recent reinterpretations of Christian love are relevant to rebuilding norms governing family life and the relation of families to work and public. As we have seen, neo-Thomistic ethicists such as Janssens and feminists such as Gudorf and Andolsen advance interpretations of Christian love which more nearly balance self-fulfillment and self-sacrifice. I find Louis Janssens's formulation of neighbor love a particularly useful reinterpretation of much that can be found in Aquinas. Janssens joins Gene Outka in interpreting "you shall love your neighbor as yourself" to mean that valuing "the self as well as others remains a manifest obligation."[68] This is the meaning of Christian love as equal regard. The "other" must be loved equally to the self, but the self should be regarded equally to the other. This formulation of the meaning of Christian love is both faithful to the tradition, sensitive to the self-affirmations of women and minorities, and more adequate to the need of postmodern families for more flexibility between public and private realms.

This understanding of love is especially important for women and wives who have carried disproportionately the burden of enacting self-sacrificial models of Christian love. In love as equal regard, wives are to love their husbands as themselves. They are also obligated, however, to

---

68. Ricoeur, *Hermeneutics and the Human Sciences,* p. 220.

love themselves equally to their husbands. There is a role for self-sacrifice in Janssens's understanding of Christian love, but it is not love's end or goal. Janssens writes, "Self-sacrifice is not the quintessence of love. . . . Self-sacrifice is justified derivatively from other regard."[69] Love as equal regard and mutuality, not self-sacrifice, is the goal of Christian love. Self-sacrifice is designed to reinstitute equal regard and mutuality when they are threatened. It is not the goal or purpose of love.

This view of love preserves a strong sense of communal obligation, thereby inhibiting the excesses of modern individualism. At the same time, love as equal regard finds a place for self-regard, thereby sanctioning the ordinate individual concern for self needed for women and minorities to assert their rightful place in the public world. Love as equal regard mediates between modern individualism and older ethics of extreme duty and self-sacrifice. It honors yet recontextualizes modern values of individual self-fulfillment.

Second, Janssens's view of love as equal regard, in contrast to Outka's more Kantian view, builds a strong place for teleological judgments about the premoral good. Equal regard for him entails both the *ordo caritatis* (the order of equal concern for other and self) and the *ordo bonorum* (the order of the premoral good).[70] Love as equal regard means equal respect for dignity of self and other but also equal concern to actualize the good for the parties involved. The premoral conditions for flourishing become very important in this view of love. Hence, the premoral conditions for child well-being and parental commitment (including paternal commitment) are important goods that love as equal regard attempts to promote. It follows that the premoral goods entailed in the four conditions of family formation should be seen as central values to be promoted by a love ethic of equal regard.

But love as equal regard applies to the wider society as well as the conjugal unit. Families as well as individuals should be objects of equal regard. Here is where the economic analysis comes back to supplement the cultural view calling for a rebirth of marital and family commitment. Jobs needed to support families, tax relief for parents with small children, flextime for working parents, parental leave provisions, adequate health care — all of these proposals may help provide premoral social conditions necessary to support family formation, just relations between families, the care of children, and a more equitable place for women in modern societies.

69. Janssens, "Norms and Priorities of a Love Ethics," p. 228.
70. Janssens, "Norms and Priorities of a Love Ethics," p. 213.

Although addressing the religio-cultural and economic strategies listed above is central to any viable practical theological strategy, the psychological dimensions of the contemporary family crisis should not be neglected. Couples and families need to acquire the skills to implement *intersubjectively* a love ethic of equal regard. It is one thing to subscribe intellectually to an ethic of equal regard; it is another thing to live through the intricacies of equal regard in intersubjective communication.

By the intersubjective communication of equal regard or the love command, I mean the capacity of both partners to affirm the selfhood of the other, to treat that selfhood as always an end in itself, to communicate one's needs to the other, to listen deeply to the other's perceived needs, to communicate one's understanding of the other's communications, to listen to the other communicate the other's understanding of one's own needs, and to do all this in such a way as to continue to affirm and positively regard the selfhood of the other and self. A distinctively Christian perspective on such intersubjective equal regard entails the capacity to sacrifice and endure in listening to and affirming the other *even when the other does not fully reciprocate.* This endurance must be active and transformative as one continues to love so that the other will someday love, not for your sake but for his or for hers.

The intersubjectivity required in distortion-free public communication of the kind discussed by Habermas and the intersubjectivity required for enduring marriages are now seen as highly analogous.[71] Both patterns of intersubjectivity are simultaneously ethical, psychological, and communicative processes. The conditions for such communication can be learned. But the commitment to learn these skills is a religio-cultural preunderstanding — a gift of the effective history of a specific tradition, especially the Christian tradition, that has shaped our cultural resources.

Marital therapy and education have learned much about this intersubjective communicative process. Rather than being expressions of the individualism of a "therapeutic" culture, recent work in these disciplines is increasingly guided by an intersubjective understanding of the ethic of neighbor love — the ethic of equal regard as we have stated it.

For marriage and the family to be renewed, these institutions must receive a new religio-cultural commitment. They must be understood to meet real and very deep human needs. They must be supported by power-

---

71. References to Habermas's theory of intersubjectivity can now be found in the therapeutic literature. See Jessica Benjamin, *The Bonds of Love* (New York: Pantheon, 1988), pp. 19f.

ful social and economic programs. And couples must acquire new communicative skills intentionally imparted and conscientiously learned. This is true even though, in Christianity, families must be seen as very important relative goods which themselves are always subordinate to the more inclusive claims of the kingdom of God.[72]

72. For the best statement of how early Christianity valued families yet subordinated them to the kingdom, see Stephen Barton, *Discipleship and Family Ties in Mark and Matthew* (Cambridge: Cambridge University Press, 1994).

Chapter 8

Altruism, Civic Virtue, and Religion (1995)

This essay was written for a conference held at Harvard Law School on the role of the family and civil society in forming virtue. The conference asked, what are the seedbeds of virtue?

My point of departure in answering this question was to enter into an appreciative yet critical review of some writings by the well-known sociologist Alan Wolfe. Wolfe locates the formation of moral virtue in the institutions of civil society, especially the family. In fact, Wolfe, I claim, is a modern-day version of Aristotle and Thomas Aquinas in seeing virtue as first formed in families and then spreading analogically outward to neighbors and strangers. But, he claims, families and the civil society that nurtures them are being undermined by the spread of technical rationality into the face-to-face interactions of intimate life. Technical rationality tends to reduce the free interactions and deliberations of life in families, neighborhoods, and voluntary organizations to the means-end efficiencies of both the marketplace and government bureaucracy, hence undermining our capacity to treat each other as ends only and never as means. In the language of this book, technical rationality tends to undercut the ends of love as equal regard.

Even though Wolfe's analysis of the decline of the virtue-producing power of the family and civil society is insightful, I claim his argument can be improved. I try to show how Wolfe's point of view can be strengthened by taking more seriously both the dynamics of kin altruism and the power of religion, two features of human life that Wolfe tends to ignore.

The point of departure for this essay is the argument set forth in Alan Wolfe's important *Whose Keeper? Social Science and Moral Obligation*.[1] In this book, Wolfe puts forward a variety of arguments designed both to document the decline of civic virtue and to outline a remedy. He builds on the thought of Jürgen Habermas to show how the two great manifestations of the systems world, the state and the market, are impinging upon everyday life. The diverse logics of these systems, according to Wolfe, undercut our sense of obligation in both intimate family relations and distant relations in the world of public citizenship. His cure for these trends is to reinvigorate what he calls "civil society." Civil society, when it is strong, limits the spread of both state and market and functions as a support to the family, the real crucible of civic virtue. The discipline of sociology, he believes, has special insight into how moral virtue develops in modern societies and will have a major role to play in the revitalization of both civil society and civic virtue.

The general contours of Wolfe's position seem quite valid. Although I will offer an appreciative reading of Wolfe, I also will present four criticisms which, if taken to heart, would make his contribution even stronger. My concerns are systematic. I am not interested so much in focusing on Wolfe as I am in using his engaging perspective to advance a more systematic position. My criticisms have to do with (1) his thin view of culture, (2) his disconnection of the family from its biological basis, (3) his too complete rejection of the kind of deontological liberalism associated with the social philosophy of John Rawls, and (4) his belief that religion, and indeed tradition, can no longer play a significant role in the renewal of civil society. These four points are interconnected, do not necessarily undercut the essence of his argument, and constitute a point of departure for elaborating a constructive position relevant to the rejuvenation of civic virtue.

As a theologian with practical interests, I am concerned to show why Western religious traditions, specifically Christian theology, have something to contribute to this discussion. But practical theology strengthens its case if it can both incorporate and show the limitations of powerful social science perspectives such as Wolfe's.

---

1. Alan Wolfe, *Whose Keeper? Social Science and Moral Obligation* (Berkeley: University of California Press, 1989).

Civic Virtue and the Systems World

Although the phrase "civic virtue" does not appear in Wolfe's book, he is clearly interested in what this concept represents. He is concerned with the deterioration of a strong sense of obligation and care for what he calls "distant relations."[2] By this he means individuals for whom we have some responsibility because they are members of the same nation or state but who are outside of our intimate relations in families, friendship circles, churches, and other voluntary organizations. Wolfe's explanation for the decline of civic virtue in this sense is complex. It entails a theory of how basic human altruism arises in families and becomes analogically extended to distant or nonfamilial relations. It is a theory that he shares with Aristotle, who developed it in his *Nicomachean Ethics* in reaction to Plato's theory of citizenship in *The Republic*. There are three parts to Wolfe's argument.

First, Wolfe's core explanation for the decline of civic virtue is the social trend that he calls "colonization." Colonization is a metaphor for the extension of the logics of the systems world into the intimate relations of civil society — family, friendships, neighborhoods, and voluntary organizations. The concept of colonization comes from the writings of Frankfurt School critical theorist Jürgen Habermas, especially his two-volume *Theory of Communicative Action*.[3] Colonization theory assumes that prior to the rise of modernity, the interaction of these spheres involved face-to-face relations, where mutual recognition and free moral reconstruction were dominant over either market utility or state coercion. The formal theory of civil society was developed by Enlightenment thinkers such as Adam Smith, David Hittite, and Adam Ferguson.[4] They saw this social sphere as a major source of protection against remnants of the monarchical or feudal state and as a presupposition of the necessary constraints of an acquisitive market economy.

Habermas's theory of colonization says that with the rise of modernization, these spheres of face-to-face interaction have become corrupted by the spreading influence of both time- and cost-benefit efficiencies of markets in capitalist systems and the responsibility suppressing, externally imposed rules and regulations of state bureaucracies. These two sys-

2. Wolfe, *Whose Keeper?* pp. 19-23.
3. Jürgen Habermas, *Theory of Communicative Action,* trans. Thomas McCarthy, 2 vols. (Boston: Beacon, 1984-87).
4. Wolfe, *Whose Keeper?* pp. 13-19.

tems are especially disruptive to families, the birthplace of elemental altruism. State bureaucracies are more powerful in socialist countries such as Sweden; market systems are more powerful in capitalist countries such as the United States. In both places, these systems spill over their native boundaries and, as Michael Walzer has described, shape the logics of areas of life, such as the intimate sphere of families, which formerly had been protected from their influence.[5]

Wolfe gives detailed explanation and documentation of how state bureaucracies undermine what he calls the "public family" in countries such as Sweden and how market economies have much the same effect, but for very different reasons, on what he calls the "private family" in the United States.[6] Wolfe tries to document trends in both societies toward weakened charity, declining interest in having children (signaled by lower birthrates), lessening involvement in the care of children and aging parents, dwindling concern for strangers and the homeless, and more concern with the demands of present generations at the expense of generations of the future. All of these humane qualities decline in the public family when these customary family functions are more and more given to the state to perform. On the other hand, they decline just as dramatically in the private family when it increasingly uses market-inspired cost-benefit calculations to measure the value of intimate relations.

The Chicago School of economics, specifically some of my academic neighbors such as Gary Becker and Judge Richard Posner, are directly indicted by Wolfe for systematically extending the rational-choice thinking of neoclassical economics to social arenas traditionally handled in noneconomic ways. This serves to give theoretical legitimation in countries with market economies for what is in fact happening anyway, that is, the increased use of the moral logic of self-interested rational calculation in "such areas as family size, arrangements for child care, patterns of marriage and divorce, and relations among grandparents, children, and grandchildren. . . ."[7]

Wolfe's second main point is this: When a sense of care and obligation declines between family members, these qualities necessarily deteriorate in more distant relations as well. This is a point recently put forth by Mary Ann Glendon and Alice and Peter Rossi as well.[8] Traditionally, mo-

---

5. Michael Walzer, *Spheres of Justice* (New York: Basic, 1983), pp. 12-13, 227-42.
6. Wolfe, *Whose Keeper?* pp. 52-60, 133-41.
7. Wolfe, *Whose Keeper?* p. 54.
8. Glendon refers to the Rossis' research on this issue in her "Virtues, Families, and

rality has been thought to move analogically from the affectional commitments of family members to the larger society. Wolfe believes that this
must continue to be true in modern societies even though accomplishing
this is an uphill battle.

> Being modern will always require some way of linking both inti-
> mate and distant obligations. Although in theory that balance
> could just as easily be found by engendering outward obligations
> inward, the proper balance will more realistically be found by ex-
> tending inward obligations outward. . . . We need civil society —
> families, communities, friendship networks, solidaristic workplace
> ties, voluntarism, spontaneous groups and movements — not to re-
> ject, but to complete the project of modernity.[9]

Wolfe is clearly Aristotelian in seeing civic virtue as a matter of generalizing family and neighborhood affections to the wider community.
Plato, in *The Republic*, argued that if the ruling class were to have sympathy
for the entire community and not just its own families and children, couples should mate but have their children raised by the state. The fact that
children and parents would not know each other, Plato imagined, would
lead his philosopher-kings to extend their altruistic sentiments to include
all children and thus the entire state, rather than just their own offspring
and relatives.[10]

Aristotle in his *Politics* did not respond kindly to Plato's thought experiment. Aristotle believed, as does Wolfe, that human sympathy spreads
outward from special and embodied family relations. "That which is common to the greatest number," Aristotle maintained, "has the least care bestowed upon it."[11] If relations within the family and among intimates are
weak, wider civic virtue will suffer as well. This preference for the Aristotelian in contrast to the Platonic view of the origins of civic virtue was fundamental to most of Christian history, especially after Aquinas's synthesis
of Aristotelian philosophy with Christian theology. But the story is complicated, as we will soon see.

Wolfe's third point has to do with his proposed solution — the urgent

---

Citizenship," in *The Meaning of the Family in a Free Society*, ed. W. Lawson Taitte (Austin: University of Texas Press, 1991).

9. Wolfe, *Whose Keeper?* p. 20.

10. Plato, *The Republic*, ed. Alan Bloom (New York: Basic, 1968), bk. 5, pp. 461-65.

11. Aristotle, *Politics*, in *The Basic Works of Aristotle*, ed. Richard McKeon (New York: Random House, 1941), bk. 2, chap. 3.

need to revive civil society as a protection against the eroding effects of the state and market. Wolfe has a social interactional and social constructivist understanding of how civil society develops its culture and morality. Individuals in societies, in their interaction with one another and with groups on the margins, create their own rules. Learning and growth is important in this view of morality, which sees *"moral obligation as a socially constructed practice negotiated between learning agents capable of growth on the one hand and a culture capable of change on the other."*[12] In deriving his theory of society, Wolfe champions interactionalists such as George Herbert Mead, Erving Goffman, and Alfred Schutz more than he does sociological structuralists such Durkheim or Kantian structuralists such as Rawls and Kohlberg. His rejection of the latter is a matter to which I will soon return.

Some Foundations of Civic Virtue

Wolfe has a positive view of culture as a factor shaping human affairs. This is an attractive feature to a practically minded theologian, for where the concept of culture is developed, one generally finds tradition and religion trailing not far behind. But this is not so with Wolfe, and it is his thin view of culture that causes my first criticism of Wolfe's thought. His constructivist view of culture places heavy emphasis on how people create culture but little emphasis on the role of historical inheritance in the creation of culture. He gives some attention to how cultures are united by stories, but these stories seem to Wolfe more created by societies in the present than inherited from the past.[13] If he had paid more attention to how the past — what Hans-Georg Gadamer calls "effective history" — shapes the present, Wolfe would have called his view a reconstructive rather than a constructive theory of culture.[14] His view would have been closer to a hermeneutic theory which sees culture as reconstructing itself through a process of dialogue between the situation of the present and the classic religious and cultural sources of the past that have shaped that culture's history. In the additional criticisms that follow, we will see how classic expressions of our Western religious heritage have carried within them other crucial elements that Wolfe's important position neglects.

---

12. Wolfe, *Whose Keeper?* p. 22 (italics in original).
13. Wolfe, *Whose Keeper?* p. 94.
14. Hans-Georg Gadamer, *Truth and Method* (New York: Crossroad, 1982), p. 273.

My second criticism has to do with Wolfe's failure to fully account for why families are the most basic seedbed of civic virtue. Specifically, it has to do with his neglect of the biological grounds of altruism. Wolfe sees no need to give a biological grounding to the social self or to his constructivist view of civil society.

> The long debate in Western philosophy about the nature of human nature is, from the standpoint of the social construction position on morality, misplaced. It is not how we are in nature that matters. It is rather what we do with society that counts.[15]

But without saying more about the "nature of human nature," Wolfe cannot give an account of two of his most cherished assertions, that is, that families based on mother-father partnerships raise children on the whole better than nonfamilial settings and that generalized family affections make up the moral core of civic virtue. To show this, let us turn to a philosophically fine-tuned appropriation of insights from sociobiology. This will also, however, illustrate how biological insights have been used in that theological tradition that has had most to do with shaping family theory in the Christian tradition — the thought of Thomas Aquinas.

The theory of inclusive fitness associated with the name of W. D. Hamilton and popularized by E. O. Wilson, Michael Ruse, and Peter Singer is the biology that suits this purpose.[16] It has recently been integrated into economic theory by Judge Richard Posner[17] and into law by Richard Epstein, Posner, and others.[18] This perspective has argued, with the use of elaborate mathematical models, that the core of altruism is grounded in the unconscious tendency among all species to sacrifice for others in direct proportion to the number of genes shared between the altruist and the recipient of his beneficial acts. All animals, including humans, are more likely to sacrifice for their children, brothers, and sisters — because they share 50 percent of their genes with them — than they are for uncles, aunts, and cousins with whom they share only a fourth or eighth

---

15. Wolfe, *Whose Keeper?* p. 21.

16. W. D. Hamilton, "The Genetic Evolution of Social Behavior," *Journal of Theoretical Biology* 7 (1964): 1-52; E. O. Wilson, *On Human Nature* (Cambridge: Harvard University Press, 1978); Michael Ruse, *The Philosophy of Biology* (London: Hutchinson, 1973); Peter Singer, *The Expanding Circle: Ethics and Sociobiology* (New York: Farrar, Straus and Giroux, 1982).

17. Richard Posner, *Sex and Reason* (Cambridge, Mass.: Harvard University Press, 1992).

18. Richard Epstein, "The Utilitarian Foundations of Natural Law," *Harvard Journal of Law and Public Policy* 12, no. 3 (1989): 713-51; Richard Posner, *Economic Analysis of Law* (Boston: Little, Brown, 1986).

respectively. But they are also more inclined to sacrifice for any close kin sharing a reasonably high percentage of genes than they are for unrelated persons or strangers. This view of the fundamental ground of altruism is called "kin altruism."[19] Altruistic behavior, in this theory, is portrayed as a form of egoism. It is a complicated way of preserving oneself or, more accurately, one's genes.

Although biologists distinguish between reciprocal, group, and kin altruism, it is kin altruism which is said to account for parental investments in their children. Not only is kin altruism used to explain rudimentary parental investment, it is also employed to account for the relative absence of violence between parents and their children in comparison to acquaintances and strangers not related by blood. Martin Daly and Margo Wilson in their *Homocide* employ a sophisticated form of inclusive fitness and kin selection theory to explain ground squirrels' capacity to differentiate between full and half sisters and show less hostility to full sisters.[20] They also apply it to explain why out of the 512 homicides in Detroit in 1977 only 32, or 6.25 percent, were between consanguineous relatives. The theory throws light on why cohabitants who were not blood relatives were eleven times more likely to be murdered than cohabitants who are kin.[21] They believe it explains why in a study in Canada they found a 40 percent higher abuse rate for children raised by one natural parent and one stepparent than for children raised by both natural parents. It explains, they argue, why when homicide alone is considered, children under two years of age were seventy times more likely to be killed when living with one stepparent than when living with both blood parents.[22] All these strange facts, according to Daly and Wilson, can be explained by the theory of kin selection and what it predicts about the altruism of natural parents for offspring who share their genes.

Of course, it should go without being said that under a variety of circumstances, natural parents do kill and abuse their children as children do kill and abuse their parents. But they do it much less than in nonconsanguineous relationships. When Wolfe rejects the role of nature in human nature, he is depriving himself of this support for his case about the importance of families in creating a basic altruism that, when generalized, is the core of civic virtue.

19. Wilson, *On Human Nature*, pp. 53-56; Carl Degler, *In Search of Human Nature* (New York: Oxford University Press, 1991).

20. Martin Daly and Margo Wilson, *Homicide* (New York: Aldine de Gruyter, 1988), p. 11.

21. Daly and Wilson, *Homicide*, pp. 20-23.

22. Daly and Wilson, *Homicide*, pp. 87-89.

In addition, he need not be afraid that by including a biological dimension he is lapsing into determinism and undermining his constructivist view of society. Mary Midgley's philosophical reconstruction of sociobiological arguments in her *Beast and Man* has shown us the way out of this dead end. She contends that while humans have strong unconscious altruistic tendencies toward genetically related humans, they have other deep tendencies as well, such as drives toward autonomy, pleasure, rest, and defense. It is precisely because humans have conflicting tendencies that rationality and culture play such an important role in mediating between the different directions of our human nature.[23] This was an argument that William James made many years before.[24] With this model of soft determinism at hand, Wolfe's constructivist view of culture can be retained but revised. Social interaction does not create culture and civil society *ex nihilo*. Instead, social interaction creates culture and civil society to accommodate, balance, and find various ways to organize certain central tendencies in humans, one of which is to act altruistically toward genetically related persons.

Moral philosophy and moral theology often have made use of similar biological insights in both the philosophy of Aristotle and its influence on the thought of Thomas Aquinas. It is commonly known that Aristotelian biology was crude by today's standards and very bad in its misogynistic depiction of women as intellectually inferior, material, passive, and unspirited.[25] But, as recent studies have observed, when Aristotle's family theory is taken as a whole, both his biology and his regard for women look much better, especially in comparison to Plato.[26] Aristotle taught, as does sociobiology, that by nature humans want to leave behind images of themselves.[27] He objected to Plato's removal of children from parents because it would make love "watery"; the qualities that inspire regard and affection are that "a thing is your own and that it is your only one. . . ."[28]

---

23. Mary Midgley, *Beast and Man* (Ithaca, N.Y.: Cornell University Press, 1978), pp. 51-82.

24. For an interpretation of William James's view of humans as simultaneously the most instinctual and most rational of creatures, see Don Browning, *Pluralism and Personality* (Lewisburg, Pa.: Bucknell University Press, 1980), p. 164.

25. Maryanne Cline Horowitz, "Aristotle on Women," *Journal of the History of Biology* 9, no. 2 (1976): 183-213.

26. Arlene Saxonhonse, "Aristotle: Defective Males, Hierarchy and the Limits of Politics," in *Feminist Interpretation and Political Theory*, ed. Mary Shanley and Carole Pateman (University Park, Pa.: Pennsylvania State University Press, 1991), pp. 45-50.

27. Aristotle, *Politics*, bk. 1, chap. 2.

28. Aristotle, *Politics*, bk. 2, chap. 4.

Aquinas incorporated these insights into his explicitly Christian moral theology. Families, for him, were natural phenomena created to accommodate the unusually long period of infant dependency. This required that each child should have "certain and definite parents," specifically "a tie between the man and a definite woman."[29] Furthermore, in his reflections in the *Summa Theologica* on "The Order of Charity," Aquinas explicitly follows the Aristotelian line that we have both a natural inclination and a moral obligation to love our children first and give them special privilege among life's various loves. Aquinas could do this by distinguishing between different kinds of love. For instance, a man should *honor* his father as his "creative principle" or source and as being, for this reason, nearer to God. But Thomas held that we should love our children more than our fathers in the sense of *caring* for them. He echoed Aristotle and anticipated modern biology when he wrote, "a man loves more that which is more closely connected with him, in which way a man's children are more lovable to him than his father, as the Philosopher states."[30]

Neither Aristotle nor Aquinas derived his ethics from his biology. But they both allowed biology to inform their ethics by attempting to stay within, as Midgley has said, our "central human needs and tendencies."[31] And even though they both saw the family as a seedbed of virtue, they both taught the necessity of transcending the family. Aristotle saw political discourse and action in the democratic polis as a greater good, and Aquinas saw life in the kingdom of God as a greater good. Aquinas in particular saw family life as a good but not the final end of life. The enjoyment of the beatific vision of God was for him the final end, and love between family members was both grounded in and pointed toward this greater love.[32] Aquinas was aware that the author of the Gospel of Matthew had depicted Jesus as saying, "For I have come to set a man against his father, and a daughter against her mother. . . . He who loves father or mother more than me is not worthy of me; and he who loves son or daughter more than me is not worthy of me" (Matt. 10:35-37). But Aquinas, like most Christian writers since, did not believe that such words represented any fundamental contradiction between families and Christianity. He wrote that Jesus "commanded us to hate, in our kindred,

---

29. Thomas Aquinas, *Summa Theologica* (New York: Benziger Brothers, 1948), Supplement to the Third Part, q. 41, a. 1.

30. Aquinas, *Summa Theologica*, II.ii, q. 26, a. 1; Stephen Pope, "The Order of Love and Recent Catholic Ethics: A Constructive Proposal," *Theological Studies* 52 (1991): 257-62.

31. Midgley, *Beast and Man*, p. 193.

32. Aquinas, *Summa Theologica*, II.ii, q. 26, a. 9.

not their kinship, but only the fact of their being an obstacle between us and God."[33]

Wolfe's reluctance to incorporate a biological dimension weakens his case for the contribution of strong families to altruism. It also leads him to overlook ways that Western religious traditions used their primitive biological insights to good effect. My point is not so much to champion the specifics of the biology of Aristotle and Aquinas as to suggest that in their thought we may have a model of how psychobiological theories can inform moral thinking in ways profitable for contemporary issues.

Social Construction and the Ethics of Principle

Wolfe believes that the free interaction of civil society can generate a morality that will provide an alternative to as well as protection against the ethics of state coercion and market rational choice. I fully support him in attributing this potential to civil society. But I have reservations about his view of ethics and his rejection *in toto* of liberal ethics of the kind associated with Kant and Rawls (my third criticism). To suggest, as Wolfe's constructivist position does, that individuals in civil society "create their own moral rules through social interactions they experience with others" does not leave us with criteria for judging when these rules are genuinely moral and when they are not.[34] Wolfe describes the process but does not give us criteria. Therefore, his theory of civil society and what it implies for civic virtue leaves us without moral substance.

Wolfe rejects the liberalism of Rawls without attempting to reconstruct it for his purposes. He criticizes Rawls and his moral-psychological counterpart, Lawrence Kohlberg, for overemphasizing abstract models of justice and rights. Their kind of liberalism assumes the moral and affectional glue of civil society but does not have the concepts to account for it.[35] He echoes the criticism of Carol Gilligan that Rawls and Kohlberg are "formal and abstract" and not sufficiently "contextual and narrative."[36] He seconds the criticism of Rawls's deontological liberalism voiced in Michael Sandel's *Liberalism and the Limits of Justice;* deontological liberalism sees moral judgments as ends in themselves totally indepen-

33. Aquinas, *Summa Theologica*, II.ii, q. 26, a. 7.
34. Wolfe, *Whose Keeper?* p. 262.
35. Wolfe, *Whose Keeper?* pp. 103, 123.
36. Wolfe, *Whose Keeper?* p. 124; Carol Gilligan, *In a Different Voice* (Cambridge, Mass.: Harvard University Press, 1982).

dent of affects, desires, history, tradition, and the enhancement of particular nonmoral goods.[37] Against such a view, Wolfe writes, "In a world where people raise children, live in communities, and value friendships, a moral theory that demands rational cognition to the degree that Rawls's does is little help and may well be a burden."[38]

Wolfe does not realize that in rejecting Rawls and his understanding of justice as fairness, he has nothing to put in its place. His sociological description of how bonded members of a society create their own rules does not tell us how to distinguish moral from immoral rules; it overlooks the fact that members of a society sometimes happily make and accept, because of various manipulations, unjust rules. It also overlooks the truth that neo-Kantian concepts of justice, generalizability, and reversibility can be squared with positions that take genuine human affects, needs, and historical contingency into account. In these formulations — found in thinkers such as Frankena, Ricoeur, Etzioni, and Janssens — justice is not defined as totally independent of a concern to actualize the good. In these formulations, all attempts to satisfy desire, meet needs, or pursue finite goods have to be done in ways consistent with, and under the direction of, the dominant deontological principle of justice.[39] It is true that such an act of justice does entail some transcendence over appetite, need, and particular social locations, but it does not necessitate their suppression. On the contrary, it requires only that they be guided to conform to the specifications of justice as fairness.

It is true that we often fail to attain this kind of justice, but it is precisely approximations of it that tell us that communities are on track. Nor do obligations to kin necessarily conflict with the obligation to non-kin. But such formulations do require enlargement of the idea of justice, a sense of justice between kin groups rather than only between individuals. They mean that I must both allow and actively support the right of other families to discharge their duties to their children just as I claim the inclination and moral obligation to help my family.

It is also true that justice in this sense can be seen as quite inter-

---

37. Michael Sandel, *Liberalism and the Limits of Justice* (Cambridge, Mass.: Harvard University Press, 1982), pp. 15-65.

38. Wolfe, *Whose Keeper?* p. 125.

39. William Frankena, *Ethics* (Englewood Cliffs, N.J.: Prentice Hall, 1973); Paul Ricoeur, "Entre philosophic et théologie: La règle d'or en question," *Revue d'lmistoire et de philosophie religieuses* 69 (1989): 3-9; Amitai Etzioni, *The Moral Dimension* (New York: Free Press, 1988); Louis Janssens, "Norms and Priorities of a Love Ethics," *Louvain Studies* 6 (Spring 1977): 207-38.

actional and social rather than just a thought experiment of an isolated individual. Habermas in *Communication and the Evolution of Society* develops a communicative or dialogical model of justice in contrast to what he calls a "mononological" model. Justice is not simply what can be generalizable from the perspective of the individual thinker; it is what all who are part of the conversation freely agree can be justly generalized.[40] Habermas's theory of communicative justice and Wolfe's picture of civil society both have strong interactive features. But Habermas forcefully reworks Rawls's theory of justice into a communicative and interactive concept. I would add the need to see this communicative justice as guiding and measuring our affective quest for the good — including the central good of parental altruism toward children as the bedrock of later developmental and more public forms of altruism. Individuals who have the communicative capacity to participate in this kind of dialogical justice possess one of the central civic virtues. Possibly it is the most central civic virtue.

The neo-Kantian concept of generalizability and the sociobiological concept of kin altruism are not incompatible. The core of ethics may be the human capacity to generalize family affection and respect (the arena of our natural inclinations) to those outside the family. Stephen Pope in his important work on the relation of sociobiology to ethics has written that there are good biological and philosophical grounds for "affirming that relatively stable and secure bonds of love within the family create the emotional basis for a later extension of love to persons outside the family and that the utility of these early bonds continues powerfully to inform subsequent adult affectional bonds."[41] It would be entirely justifiable to substitute the more neo-Kantian word "generalize" for Pope's word "extension." One also can substitute the word "generalize" for the word "extension" in the following words written by Mary Midgley:

> [T]he development of sociability proceeds in any case largely by this extension to other adults of behavior first developed between parents and young. . . . [W]ider sociality in its original essence simply is the power of adults to treat one another, mutually, as honorary parents and children.[42]

40. Jürgen Habermas, *Communication and the Evolution of Society* (Boston: Beacon, 1979), pp. 80-93.

41. Pope, "Order of Love and Recent Catholic Ethics," pp. 257-62.

42. Midgley, *Beast and Man*, p. 136.

Peter Singer in his book *The Expanding Circle: Ethics and Sociobiology* makes the same point. Universal ethical systems are not based on suppressing family commitments; they evolve from the use of disinterested reason in expanding these particular affections outward. Singer argues:

> [E]thics evolved out of our social instincts and our capacity to reason. . . . [L]et us cling to the principle of equal consideration of interests . . . which relies on the fact . . . that we are rational enough to take a broader point of view from which our own interests are no more important than the interests of others. . . ."[43]

Although this line of thinking gives more ethical content to Wolfe's radically constructivist view of both civil society and civic virtue, this synthesis of sociobiology and neo-Kantianism needs the support of additional beliefs. For us to generalize family affections outward to others, we must have certain beliefs that make us take non-kin as seriously as our blood kin. Although we seldom do this in the full affective sense that we apply to our children or parents, when instinct and reason are supplemented by certain beliefs, we do sometimes, quite profoundly, treat non-kin with the same equal regard that we are more likely to apply to our brothers and sisters, mothers and fathers, sons and daughters. What are these additional beliefs that are needed to support reason and our affections?

Civic Virtue and Religion

Wolfe acknowledges that civil society must have its beliefs about the meaning of life. He believes these generally take the form of unifying stories that "define identity" and "emphasize the need for some kind of restraint on individual desires. . . ."[44] But Wolfe believes that in modern societies there is little role for religious stories. "Religion," he writes, "is no longer the source of moral authority it once was."[45] And religion is not the only thing that has lost its authority: "In looking to religion, philosophy, literature, or politics to find the rule of moral obligation," Wolfe writes, "we look in the wrong place."[46] The right place, he believes, is the free interaction of civil society as uncovered by sociology and conceived along Wolfe's constructivist lines.

43. Singer, *The Expanding Circle*, p. 111.
44. Wolfe, *Whose Keeper?* p. 94.
45. Wolfe, *Whose Keeper?* p. 3.
46. Wolfe, *Whose Keeper?* p. 6.

Religion is, for Wolfe, all but dead, and this is my fourth criticism of his thought. Wolfe does argue that civil society must have at least its secular stories. They must unify distant or nonconsanguineous people by emphasizing the need for mutual dependence and self-sacrifice. But there is another moral function of stories that Wolfe does not mention — they satisfy our need for beliefs about the moral status of individuals. Beliefs about the moral importance of other people, especially persons beyond our kin relations, are crucial, as I suggested above, to guide reason's extension of kin altruism to others.

According to the Kantian tradition, all persons are rational beings with the capacity for freedom and are deserving of universal respect. Such beings should be treated as ends and never as means only.[47] It can be argued that neo-Kantianism is a secular form of the Judeo-Christian narrative, which grounds respect for the other on the belief that God made humans in the image of God. Christians claim that the religious status of personhood is the ground of human worth. The sacred status of human personhood grounds morality, for Christians, even more profoundly than does human rationality.

Basil Mitchell has pointed out in his *Morality: Religious and Secular* that Judeo-Christian and Kantian ethics both base their ethics of justice on the status of persons as ends. The difference between them is that the Judeo-Christian tradition bases this status on the *imago Dei* in humans rather than on the thinner Kantian view of humans as rational beings.[48] Mitchell contends that the religious view adds moral weight and inclines those who base their moral action on this belief to take the other with even more seriousness.

My point is this: instinct and reason need the extension and reinforcement of unifying stories and their embedded beliefs. These stories, among other functions, must define the moral value of individuals. Beliefs about this, when deeply held, help reason generalize family affections and respect to distant relations. This is why civic virtue depends, in part, on narratives. Wolfe is perceptive in seeing the importance of stories for civil society and its civic virtue. But he is too optimistic in imagining that we can self-consciously invent new secular stories to take the place of the great religious stories that have shaped our culture.

Wolfe imagines society as creating itself something like Jean Paul

47. Immanuel Kant, *Foundations of the Metaphysics of Morals* (New York: Bobbs-Merrill, 1959), p. 7.

48. Basil Mitchell, *Morality: Religious and Secular* (Oxford: Clarendon, 1980), pp. 31-32.

Sartre envisioned the solitary individual defining herself. I recommend, instead, a hermeneutic model of historical reconstruction. Such a model sees societies standing in the present but, as Gadamer and Bellah have claimed, in a perpetual dialogue with the classics that have formed them out of the past.[49] Wolfe almost catches the spirit of the hermeneutical turn at the end of his book when he contends that modern persons will take social responsibilities seriously only when "society is understood as a gift."[50] One might think that Wolfe is speaking almost religiously about civil society or at least giving a strong pitch for the importance of inherited traditions. But what he gives, he also takes away. He soon adds a stunning qualifier: "Moreover, it is a gift that we give to ourselves, since no one put it in place for us."[51]

But is that true? Isn't it rather that all societies are built on layer after layer of contributions that still shape our lives as living histories? Isn't it more likely that any powerful attempt to reconstruct (not just construct) civil society will be done out of a vital interpretive conversation with the religio-ethical narratives that have unified civil society in the past?

Civil Society, Civic Virtue, and a Black Pentecostal Church

It may be true that no one religious tradition will dominate our public stories as certain traditions have in the past. Yet I am constantly amazed by those polls which say that between 80 and 90 percent of Americans are vaguely evangelical Christian in their beliefs and believe both in a personal God that listens to prayers and in the divinity of Jesus Christ.[52] But my claim is modest. I do not say that Christian stories can be the unifying center for the whole of civil society. I do want to illustrate, however, how one religious community appropriates its Christian story in ways that empower its members' participation in civil society. My motives are not apologetic in any narrow sense; I am not arguing for the truth or superiority of Christianity as such. Rather, as a long-time religious liberal, I am saying we can learn a great deal from this conservative church about how local

49. Gadamer, *Truth and Method,* p. 330; Robert Bellah, Richard Madsen, William M. Sullivan, Ann Swidler, and Steven Tipton, *Habits of the Heart* (Berkeley: University of California Press, 1985).

50. Wolfe, *Whose Keeper?* p. 25.

51. Wolfe, *Whose Keeper?* p. 25.

52. George Gallup and Sarah Jones, *100 Questions and Answers: Religion in America* (Princeton, N.J.: Princeton Research Center, 1989), p. 4.

religious expressions, feeding on commanding religious traditions, can support the revitalization of civil society.

For ten months during 1988 and 1989, I studied a black Pentecostal Church called the Apostolic Church of God. It was located eight blocks south on the very street I live on in Chicago's liberal Hyde Park. It is only two blocks beyond the southern edge of the University of Chicago where I teach. I give you the real name of the church as I do the real name of the pastor, the Reverend Arthur Brazier. I do this first of all because I have permission. I do it also because both the church and the pastor are famous as a result of their role in a widely studied community organization called the Woodlawn Organization (TWO). I do it, finally, because part of the meaningfulness of the story is the way the spheres of our lives, both theirs and mine, do and do not overlap even though we live in the same neighborhood.

This church's story illustrates elements that go into the creation of civil society and civic virtue, as I outlined these earlier. This church has been a key mover in attempting to protect the Woodlawn neighborhood from the moral logics of both the market and the state. Its theory and program illustrate the three elements of civic virtue that I discussed previously — generalized family affections and obligations, justice, and a unifying narrative. Specifically, restoring the black family is central to the mission of Apostolic Church. Furthermore, its official theology, devoid of the jargon of deontological liberalism, still promotes a version of justice that is analogous to it. Finally, its theological story helps its members handle the tensions between initiative and solidarity with distant others — a tension that besets its members as they seek to participate in the contradictions of a competitive democratic society with a liberal economic philosophy.

Apostolic Church of God is now approaching a membership of 8000.[53] It had fewer than 100 members when it was founded, and only 500 members in 1978. Arthur Brazier has been the church's pastor for over thirty years, and during its period of fantastic growth Brazier was, in addition to his ministry, the head of TWO — the Saul-Alinsky-style community organization that fought to keep Woodlawn, one of Chicago's worst urban slums and ghettos, from collapsing. He and his church were in the forefront of promoting the control of teenage gangs, improving public education, enticing government loans for housing developments, and en-

---

53. Don Browning, *A Fundamental Practical Theology* (Minneapolis: Fortress, 1991), pp. 243-77.

couraging businesses to return to the neighborhood. He was also in the forefront of a major battle with the University of Chicago in its efforts to develop North Woodlawn for its use, thereby displacing its poor residents. This activity brought fame and scholarly attention to Brazier and TWO.[54] Brazier was a Pentecostal minister with a political concern; this was unusual and attracted interest. But few of his scholarly admirers paid attention to where Brazier's heart really rested. It was not primarily in his political activity; rather, it was in his church and his message to those who attended Sunday and Wednesday services.

Brazier's ministry can be usefully interpreted in light of Wolfe's theory of the pressures on civil society from both the state and the market. As Woodlawn's population became almost totally black by the early 1950s, both government and the market had undermining effects. Markets, because of their cost-effectiveness mentality, began to withdraw. Pursuing business and industry in Woodlawn was not profitable, as William Julius Wilson has argued.[55] With jobs on the decline, men had less work and less to contribute to their families. Furthermore, the state-supported welfare systems had requirements that worked against male residency in families, in effect encouraging men to abandon their wives and children.

Apostolic Church is fully aware of the crisis of families in the black community. Its members are aware of teenage pregnancy, the fact that approximately 68 percent of all black children are born out of wedlock, and the growing feminization of poverty. The reconstruction of the black family is at the heart of its mission. Apostolic Church is a holiness church. Its official mission is to convert people, give them the gift of the Holy Spirit, turn them into sanctified saints, and help them live a life of moral purity. But a close second is its mission to reconstruct the black family and, within this, to reconstitute the role of black men in families.

In contrast to some political rhetoric of the 1992 presidential election, Apostolic Church spends little time speaking against single parents. Yet, it is clearly interested in reversing the trends toward single parenthood in the black community. Its strategy, however, is to concentrate on building up the self-image and responsibility of black men and enhancing their role in the black family. Its message seems successful; nearly 40 percent of the members of Apostolic Church are men, almost all of whom are under

54. John Fish, *Black Power/White Control* (Princeton, N.J.: Princeton University Press, 1973); Charles Silberman, *Crisis in Black and White* (New York: Random House, 1964).

55. William Julius Wilson, *The Truly Disadvantaged* (Chicago: University of Chicago Press, 1987).

age fifty. The women of the church are extremely supportive of the church's message to men and to families.

How are the three aspects of civic virtue discussed above stimulated at Apostolic Church? First, Apostolic Church's family theology and ministry seem on the surface to be patriarchal. But as I discovered during my time there, this patriarchy is subtle; the evidence for its presence is ambiguous and should remind us of the importance of context for the proper understanding of symbolic communication. Brazier's sermons and my various interviews with church members confirmed that men are depicted in this church as the moral and spiritual heads of their families. But, as in the classic verses of Ephesians 5, this headship is really one of servanthood, a concept quite different from standard patriarchal models in the Greco-Roman world that surrounded early Christianity.

Greek and Roman models of maleness emphasized the dominance and superiority of free men over women, slaves, and children. The message of Ephesians was different. It juxtaposed the message to spouses to "Be subject to one another out of reverence for Christ" (Eph. 5:21) with words such as "Husbands, love your wives, just as Christ loved the church and gave himself up for her" (Eph. 5:25). The members of Apostolic Church interpret the idea of mutual submission to mean that wives and husbands are "to be in tune with one another." For the husband to be the spiritual and moral head means that he is to take special leadership and responsibility for serving the family, parenting his children, and treating his wife and children with justice and respect.

In the end, the message is not so much one of male authority and power as it is one of male responsibility. An almost Rawlsian model of justice is supposed to reign, at this church, between husband and wife. Husband-wife relations, the church teaches, are not a matter of 50-50, they "are a matter of 100-100."

Brazier is fully aware of the social systemic deficiencies and patterns of discrimination that both state and market have inflicted on black males. He leads the church in trying to change these systems, both state and market. He is in favor of new jobs, humane welfare, better housing, job training, better transportation to take both men and women to where the jobs are — all the things that social-system reformers such as William Julius Wilson believe are important to cure the black ghetto of its ills.[56]

He also preaches a new family ethic, specifically aimed at men, and builds a community of support designed to implement it. In this way, his

---

56. Wilson, *The Truly Disadvantaged.*

church contributes to civil society and civic virtue. It is a religio-cultural contribution, and it seems to work. In addition to attracting large numbers of young men, Apostolic Church performs countless weddings each year, witnesses very few divorces among its congregation, sees few out-of-wedlock births among its teenagers, and supports large numbers of its children through high school and into higher education.

Apostolic Church is tolerant of alternatives to the blood-related mother-father partnership, but this family form is clearly the center of its emphasis. It does not, as some liberal feminists such as Judith Stacey do, champion so-called black matriarchy as a harbinger of the female-centered families of the future.[57] Nor does its rhetoric of male moral leadership in the family translate into a justification for the traditional (or, more properly, modern) breadwinning father and domestic and childrearing mother. The black wives in this church are nearly all employed outside the home and have been for decades. Parenting is something men are expected to be involved in; it is not just left to women. In spite of the church's lapse into patriarchal-sounding language, its families, I grew to believe, were on the whole egalitarian, equal-regard families, but with a very strong emphasis on male responsibility.

Second, Apostolic Church has a theory of justice that has formal similarities to the deontological liberalism found in Rawls. I refer specifically to the reversible and generalizing characteristics of neighbor love, "you shall love your neighbor as yourself" (Matt. 19:19). This ethic is applied both to the area of intimate relations and to that of public affairs. We saw this in the formula, quoted earlier, that husband and wife relations are not 50-50 (simple reciprocity) but 100-100 (full reversibility and equal regard). One sees this concern with justice in public affairs in the church's energetic support of liberal civil-rights organizations such as Operation Push.

In contrast to strict deontological liberal positions, in the theology of Apostolic Church the generalizability of neighbor love constitutes what I elsewhere have called the "inner core" of an ethic that is surrounded by a rich narrative "outer envelope."[58] The reversibility and generalizability of neighbor love guide affect and impulse. But this liberal-sounding ethic of neighbor love does not take over the church's entire ethical field. It is the highest and most abstract level of ethics for this church, but it is sup-

---

57. Judith Stacey, *Brave New Families: Stories of Domestic Upheaval in Late Twentieth Century America* (New York: Basic, 1990), p. 268.

58. Browning, *A Fundamental Practical Theology*, pp. 10-11, 171-207.

ported by many far more concrete ethical rules. Apostolic Church is a holiness church, and its members are "saints" who have been grasped by the Holy Spirit. Saints are people "who have been set aside." They are forbidden to drink, smoke, lie, cheat, have premarital sex, or commit adultery. Women, however, are now permitted to wear jewelry and cosmetics, and everyone, no matter what their income, tends to dress well. The members of Apostolic Church are, for the most part, political liberals in that they support most liberal political causes — equal rights, fair housing, welfare, affirmative action, freedom of speech, and so on. But they are cultural liberals in only certain limited ways. They preach an ethic of personal responsibility that leads them to temper their demands for government programs and guard against the temptations of a market-oriented popular culture. This is true even though, at the same time, the church works hard to prepare its members to work in business and industry — but to do so without conforming "to the ways of this world."

Third, the narrative outer envelope of Apostolic Church's religious ethic is complex and rich. It is the presence of this narrative that distinguishes this church's emphasis on justice from secular deontological liberalism in the strict sense. The theology of Apostolic Church is a synthesis of Calvinist themes of God's providence and the Wesleyan emphasis on sanctification. There is also a strong emphasis on both the goodness of creation and the doctrine of the atonement. The inner-core ethic of neighbor love (with all its analogies to deontological liberalism's emphasis on justice) is grounded, not on the rationality of humans, but in the faith that humans are created in the image of God and have added worth because Christ died for their sins. Furthermore, Brazier teaches that Christians are saved by the grace of God and not by their own actions. Nonetheless, moral behavior beneficial to others is a "sign" of salvation and a "mark" of the new freedom that Christians have in Christ.

Narrative and the Tensions of Modernity

I believe that the narrative outer envelope of Apostolic Church's ethic helps its people handle the tensions of life in a competitive democratic society. The members of Apostolic Church hear a message that empowers them to compete without turning either "winning" or "losing" in this society into an idolatry, a measure of their ultimate worth. Brazier's most paradigmatic sermon was preached on 2 Corinthians 8:9, "For you know the generous act of our Lord Jesus Christ, that though he was rich, yet for your sakes he became poor, so that by his poverty you might become rich." In interpreting this Scripture, Brazier began with an emphasis on the richness of God — the richness of Being, if you will. When God became human and poor, humans who accept him became rich. Brazier was not speaking of richness in terms of money, clothes, houses, or high-salaried jobs. He was speaking about a "richness at the core of your self-hood." This is the meaning of receiving the Holy Spirit; it is a kind of enrichment, empowerment, and liberation of the self. It is somewhat analogous to the kind of empowerment of the self that comes from a parent's love or a therapist's unconditional acceptance. As one convert said about his conversion, "My mind cleared, I felt at ease, I had new energy, I felt refreshed and clean, I had a new sense of power."

This religious vision seemed to help the members of Apostolic Church handle both their jobs and their human relations. For instance, Brazier said in this sermon that it was permissible for a Christian to pursue wealth. In fact, those with the gift of the Holy Spirit will have a richer and more powerful self to do that very thing. The Christian with the Spirit will have the strength to pursue a good job, education, and a decent salary. The "Christian can do this *freely* precisely because salvation does not depend on material riches," just as it does not depend on worldly success. Hence, one is free to pursue a comfortable life because, in the end, it is not all that important. Furthermore, all saints must tithe, which in itself is a check on measuring oneself by material success.

This same way of thinking was applied by Brazier to personal relationships. A person with a rich self will have better love relations. Indeed, one can pursue these relationships precisely because one's salvation does not depend on them. In fact, if love relations are threatened, "you will have the power to try again, either with the person you have loved or someone new." This is because one's ultimate justification does not depend on one's love relationships.

The theology of empowerment that Brazier preached worked to encourage energetic agency among his people in pursuit of both vocational and family goals. People are empowered to pursue these goods — yes, even to compete for them. But their competition is bounded by strong appeals to justice, a rich tradition of concrete moral rules, and a theology of grace that frees them from measuring themselves in any final way by their temporal successes or failures. I came to the conclusion that Apostolic Church was generally consistent with the great themes of the Christian tradition, but had reconstructed aspects of it to meet the unique needs of its situation. Its members were *reconstructing* both their religion and their civil society; they were not *constructing* them. This church had a rich sense of tradition — indeed, a "gift" from the past.

Apostolic Church was creating good citizens as well as sanctified "saints." Even today Apostolic Church is Woodlawn's most powerful force for social reconstruction and is indirectly a political force throughout the entire community of Chicago. This is true even though Reverend Brazier never issues a political endorsement.

In presenting this case study, I have illustrated ways in which religion contributes to the revitalization of both civil society and civic virtue in a nation increasingly beleaguered by the overreaching systems of the state and market.

Chapter 9

Narrative, Ethics, and Biology in Christian Family Theory (1996)

The article that forms the basis of this chapter was initially titled "Biology, Ethics, and Narrative in Christian Family Theory." I have changed the order of the terms because it now seems to me that putting "biology" first in the title suggested that the Christian theology of marriage and family works upward from biology to ethics and from ethics to religious story or narrative. In reality, it is just the reverse. The narratives of God's creation of Adam and Eve and of Christ's self-sacrificial love for the church as models for Christians' love of family were historically and logically prior to the psychobiology of kin altruism or the ethic of equal regard that can be found in Christian family theology. Yet these subordinate naturalistic and ethical arguments were part of Christian family theory, especially the theory of Thomas Aquinas, which I use, but in a distinctively Protestant way. I mean by this that I do not appropriate the theology of marriage as a sacrament.

With the title stated in the new order, the essay should be read as crucial to my entire constructive theology of marriage and family. In terms of the four steps of a fundamental practical theology, this chapter most explicitly illustrates steps two and three — the steps of historical theology and systematic theology. But notice: my analysis of the contemporary situation of families under the influence of the spread of market and bureaucratic rationality and of the consequences of this for father absence (the male problematic) is now brought to this historical and systematic inquiry in search of theological answers.

Notice as well that the five dimensions of practical-theological thinking also become visible in this chapter, especially the narrative, ethical, and premoral levels. But the contextual dimension is also seen not only in the analysis of the sources of the male problematic but also in my interpretation of Christian marriage narrative as uniquely powerful in addressing this problematic. Furthermore, the level of actual praxis (its rules and roles) is addressed in my discussion of the ethic of equal regard and the proposal that Christ's self-giving love for the church should be seen as a model for the sacrificial moment of *both* husband and wife (both father and mother) within a wider love ethic of equal regard.

Narrative and Biology in Christian Thomism

Christianity has had enormous influence on the marriage and family theory of Western societies. This influence, however, is not well understood. Furthermore, it is widely believed in most intellectual quarters that this influence is over. It is difficult to believe that this prediction is entirely accurate, especially in view of the continuing high percentage of individuals who consider themselves generally Christian, especially in the United States. Furthermore, Christian symbols and beliefs have had an extensive impact on wider aspects of our cultural understandings and institutions — especially the law. It is not widely understood that Christian understandings are complex and a product of several interacting lines of knowledge and judgment.

In this essay, I will illustrate how biological, ethical, and narrative dimensions of moral thinking have become interwoven in certain formative texts shaping Christian marriage and family theory in Western societies. I also will venture a hypothesis about an overlooked basic feature of Christian family theory, namely, that some of its classic formulations served to remedy what I will call the "male problematic." By the male problematic, I mean a central ambivalence in males about which of two evolutionarily successful ways of organizing their sexuality they will follow at any moment in history.

It will be useful to illustrate some contemporary manifestations of the male problematic and then go backward in history to Thomas Aquinas, then to the Gospels, to Aristotle, and finally to the Epistle to the Ephesians. I make these moves to demonstrate how these ancient sources may have addressed this male ambivalence. I must warn the reader now that, although we will spend much time investigating the role of sacrificial love in overcoming the male problematic, I will hold that equal regard is the deeper meaning of Christian love.

Allow me to gradually build the meaning of the male problematic by beginning with the contemporary experience of families in technologically advanced societies. The most dramatic change in families throughout the industrial world is the retreat of biological fathers from families and children.[1] This trend is integrally related to another, that is, the move of mothers — with the help of increased reliance on the wage economy, the government, and various informal networks — toward increasingly raising their children without significant presence of a father.[2] One-half of all children under eighteen today spend some time in a single-parent home, generally the mother's. One-third will spend as much as six years without an immediate father present.[3] The absence of fathers, plus their failure on average to pay adequate child support, has now been cited as a leading reason that one-fifth of all mothers and their children in our nation are poor.[4] Furthermore, children of absent fathers are now believed on average to do more poorly in school, become more involved in crime, and have poorer health.[5] The factor of the absent father seems to be an independent variable that functions, as well, across class and economic lines.

Various reasons have been advanced to explain the growing absence of fathers from children. The move of men in the eighteenth and nineteenth centuries out of the family farm and business into a wage economy separated the male spheres of public life from the private spheres of domesticity and child care.[6] This created the modern, industrial family — the family we mistakenly call the traditional family. When women in the twentieth century entered the wage economy, they became more economically independent from their husbands. With less economic dependency, both men and women resorted more frequently to divorce and non-

1. For popular but reliable accounts of this phenomenon, see Paul Taylor, "Life without Fathers," *Washington Post,* June 1992; Louis Sullivan, "Fatherless Families," *Television and Families* (Summer 1992): 34-36.

2. Sara McLanahan and Karen Booth, "Mother-Only Families: Problems, Prospects, and Politics," *Journal of Marriage and the Family* 51, no. 3 (1989): 557-80.

3. Frank F. Furstenberg Jr. and Andrew Cherlin, *Divided Families: What Happens to Children When Parents Part* (Cambridge, Mass.: Harvard University Press, 1991), p. 35.

4. Furstenberg and Cherlin, *Divided Families,* p. 45.

5. Victor Fuchs and Diane M. Reklis, "America's Children: Economic Perspectives and Policy Options," *Science* 255 (January 3, 1992): 42.

6. Jan E. Dizzard and Howard Gadlin, *The Minimal Family* (Amherst, Mass.: University of Massachusetts Press, 1991), pp. 25-67.

marriage.[7] Government programs are thought to have taken the place, for many poor women, of the husband's financial support, leading some commentators to speak of "state polygamy" — the marriage of millions of women to the state, which, indeed, some poor women sometimes call "the man."[8]

The post-Enlightenment cultural drive toward individualism is often cited as the great engine fueling these trends. Respected commentators as diverse as Robert Bellah, Christopher Lasch, Ron Lesthaeghe, and David Popenoe see modern individualism as an important underlying motive behind these economic trends — trends Western societies seem to have neither the desire nor the ability to reverse.[9]

Human Evolutionary Ecology and the Male Problematic

All these factors may be operating to produce this grand new issue facing postmodern families — the growing absence of fathers. Of course, there are powerful voices such as Judith Stacey, Judge Richard Posner, Stephanie Coontz, and more recently Iris Young, who believe that if the economic contributions of fathers can be replaced by higher incomes for mothers or better government supports, then father absence need not be a major threat to the welfare of children.[10] But others disagree.[11] Human evolutionary ecology (sometimes called sociobiology, evolutionary psychology, or behavior biology) throws light on both the male problematic (the tendency of men to drift away from families) and why the father's contribution to children is more than material benefits alone, as important as these may be. Furthermore, the general knowledge about the con-

---

7. Dizzard and Gadlin, *Minimal Family*, pp. 125-39; Richard Posner, *Sex and Reason* (Cambridge, Mass.: Harvard University Press, 1991), pp. 169-72.

8. Posner, *Sex and Reason*, p. 171.

9. Robert Bellah et al., *Habits of the Heart* (Berkeley: University of California Press, 1985); Christopher Lasch, *Haven in a Heartless World* (New York: Basic, 1977); Ron Lesthaeghe, "A Century of Demographic and Cultural Change in Western Europe: An Exploration of Underlying Dimensions," *Population and Development Review* 9, no. 3 (September 1983): 411-35.

10. Judith Stacey, *Brave New Families: Stories of Domestic Upheaval in Late Twentieth Century America* (New York: Basic, 1990), p. 268; Posner, *Sex and Reason*, p. 192; Stephanie Coontz, *The Way We Never Were* (New York: Basic, 1992), pp. 277-85.

11. David Popenoe, *Disturbing the Nest* (New York: Aldine De Gruyter, 1988); Irwin Garfinkel and Sara McLanahan, *Single Mothers and Their Children* (Washington, D.C.: Urban Institute, 1986); Barbara Dafoe Whitehead, "Dan Quayle Was Right," *Atlantic Monthly* (April 1993): 47-84.

ditions of male parental investment, I will argue, was known in the ancient world and provided the assumptive background beliefs to some of the key expressions of Christian family theory.

In recent years, human evolutionary ecology has developed powerful theories to explain the asymmetrical reproductive strategies of males and females and the conditions under which male parental investment emerges among Homo sapiens. Three concepts from evolutionary ecology are important — the theories of inclusive fitness, kin altruism, and parental investment.

The theory of inclusive fitness extends the official position in evolutionary theory that the individual is the basic unit of evolutionary survival. This is still held to be true, but since the work of W. D. Hamilton in 1964 it has been understood that the "individual" includes the genes a person shares with close kin (50 percent with one's siblings and children, 25 percent with nephews, nieces, and grandchildren, 12.5 percent with first cousins, and so on).[12] Individuals, according to this perspective, do not just fight for their own survival; they also work for the survival and flourishing of their biological relatives. They do this because these genetically related individuals are literally extensions of themselves.

This, then, is the meaning of kin altruism or kin selection: under some circumstances, individuals are willing to sacrifice their own inclusive fitness in direct proportion to the degree of genetic relatedness of the other and the degree of gain in the other's fitness in comparison to the loss of the one making the sacrifice.[13]

The concept of inclusive fitness also has relevance for a theory of parental investment, which is in fact our main interest here. Parental investment is a concept developed by biologists Ronald Fisher and Robert Trivers. Trivers defines it as "any investment by the parent in an individual offspring that increases the offspring's chance of surviving (and hence reproductive success) at the cost of the parent's ability to invest in other offspring."[14]

Evolutionary ecology is showing that both inclusive fitness and pa-

12. Pierre L. van den Berghe, *Human Family Systems* (New York: Elsevier, 1979), p. 14; W. D. Hamilton, "The Genetical Evolution of Social Behavior, II," *Journal of Theoretical Biology* 7 (1964): 17-52.

13. Hamilton, "Genetical Evolution," p. 17.

14. Robert Trivers, "Parental Investment and Sexual Selection," in *Sexual Selection and the Descent of Man,* ed. Bernard C. Campbell (Chicago: Aldine De Gruyter, 1972), p. 139. See also Martin Daly and Margo Wilson, *Sex, Evolution and Behavior* (Belmont, Calif.: Wadsworth, 1978), p. 56.

rental investment strategies are different for males and females of mammalian species. Females, because of their limited period of child-bearing capacity and the energy required to carry infants to birth, put their investment in relatively few offspring. The males of most mammalian species, on the other hand, follow a different strategy. They are inclined to mate with several different females, producing as many offspring as their life span permits, often a potentially limitless number.[15] Males of almost all mammalian species, including most higher primates, make little or no parental investment in their offspring. The human male for much of his evolutionary history has been an exception.

According to evolutionary theorist Don Symons, by the time hominids had left the forests and become hunter-gatherers in the open grasslands, males had left behind the promiscuous pattern of inclusive fitness typical of their chimpanzee ancestors and become attached for the most part to a single female, formed a relatively egalitarian nuclear family, and helped care for their children.[16] Their primary contributions to their children were protein (from food they provided) and protection, but studies of contemporary hunter-gathers such as the !Kung San suggest that these earliest fathers also may have cuddled their infants, fed them, played with them, and later taught them various skills.[17]

Since these earliest hunter-gatherers, human males have, on the whole, joined females and followed what evolutionary theorists call the "K" rather than the "R" strategy of inclusive fitness. Followers of the K-strategy invest a large set of resources into raising only a few children to adulthood. This contrasts with followers of the R-strategy, such as fish and frogs, which procreate a large number of offspring and leave it to luck as to whether a few survive.[18] The question is, how did this transition from what evolutionary theorists jokingly call the "cad" strategy to a "dad" strategy come about for the human male? How deeply grounded in

15. Van den Berghe, *Human Family Systems,* pp. 20-21; Helen Fisher, *Anatomy of Love* (New York: W. W. Norton, 1992), p. 63.

16. Donald Symons, *The Evolution of Human Sexuality* (Oxford: Oxford University Press, 1979), pp. 131-36.

17. Van den Berghe, *Human Family Systems,* pp. 131-40; David Popenoe, "The Fatherhood Problem" (New Brunswick, N.J.: Dean's Office, Rutgers University), pp. 17-19 (the materials in this paper appear in revised form as chapter 6 of Popenoe's *Life without Father: Compelling New Evidence That Fatherhood and Marriage Are Indispensable for the Good of Children and Society* [New York: Martin Kessler, 1996]).

18. Daly and Wilson, *Sex, Evolution and Behavior,* pp. 124-29; van den Berghe, *Human Family Systems,* pp. 25-26.

male human nature is the so-called dad strategy? Is the cad strategy lying just below the surface of the male ego, ready to manifest itself in actual social behavior?

Several factors worked together to bring the dad strategy into existence for males. First, there is the long period of dependency characteristic of the human infant and child, in contrast to other mammalian infants; this condition puts more pressure on the mother to both feed and care for dependent children for many years. Infant dependency stimulated females to turn to males for assistance, protection, and food — particularly sources of protein.

Second, conditions supporting paternal certainty began to emerge.[19] By parental certainty, I mean the recognition by a father that an infant is indeed his and not some other male's biological offspring. Although mammalian mothers are always certain that an infant is their biological offspring, males can hold only varying degrees of certainty about whether they are indeed the father. Trivers and others have argued that human males became parentally invested when they acquired the capacity to feel confident that a child was biologically theirs; they began to intuit that through their parental investment they were contributing to their own inclusive fitness by furthering the fitness of a child who carries their genes.[20] In those societies where parental certainty is difficult to achieve because of high degrees of female sexual freedom, the mother's brother, who of course is also genetically related to the child, often becomes the surrogate father.[21]

Third, male parental investment also seems to be a part of a wider pattern of male helpfulness to a female in order to gain sex. In addition, males help with infants and children in return for help from females in their daily tasks. All this means that paternal investment is a part of reciprocal helpfulness between males and females. According to evolutionary ecologists, paternal certainty is a necessary, but not sufficient, condition for the development of paternal investment. Sexual exchange and reciprocal helpfulness also seem to be necessary.

An example of the interrelation of these conditions can be seen in Aka

19. Barry S. Hewlett, ed., *Father-Child Relations: Cultural and Biosocial Contexts* (New York: Aldine De Gruyter, 1992); Robert Trivers, *Social Evolution* (Menlo Park, Calif.: Benjamin/Cummings, 1985), pp. 203-38.

20. Trivers, "Parental Investment and Sexual Selection," pp. 139-41.

21. Steven Gaulin and Alice Schlegel, "Paternal Confidence and Paternal Investment: A Cross Cultural Text of a Sociobiological Hypothesis," *Ethology and Sociobiology* 1, no. 4 (December 1980): 301-9.

pygmies of central Africa, who show the highest level of male infant care in the world. Aka husbands and wives fish together, and, according to Barry Hewlett, a male takes care of children as a trade-off for his wife's sexual favors and her help with the tasks of fishing.[22] From the standpoint of evolutionary theory, paternal investment is a result of paternal certainty, sexual exchange, and other forms of reciprocal altruism. Contrary to Stacey, Posner, Coontz, and other contemporary voices who downplay its importance, paternal investment in children among Homo sapiens appears to be important for the flourishing of children.[23] Others believe paternal investment was a key to the rise of civilization among Homo sapiens and that its decline is one of our society's greatest threats.[24]

Biology and Narrative in Aquinas's Family Theory

It would seem a long distance from contemporary evolutionary ecology to the family theory of the great father of the Catholic Church, St. Thomas Aquinas. The distance, however, is shorter than one might think. Aquinas's family theory depends, in part, on several crucial observations based on the comparative biology of his day — primarily the work of Aristotle — as well as on various refinements Aquinas found in the writings of his own teacher, Albertus Magnus.[25] In reading this great Catholic scholastic, we will begin to inhabit a world strangely close to and yet quite far from the powerful evolutionary ecological perspectives we have just encountered.

Aquinas had his version of what I have called the male problematic, and it was implicit in his theories of marriage and the family. The center of his theory of marriage was his belief that the symbol of Christ's union with the church described in Ephesians 5:20-33 was the foundation of marriage between baptized Christians. Paul Ricoeur's understanding of the relation of archeology and teleology in religious and artistic symbols gives a deeper understanding of the transformative meanings carried by that sym-

---

22. Hewlett, *Father-Child Relations,* p. 21; Barry Hewlett, *Intimate Fathers* (Ann Arbor: University of Michigan Press, 1991).

23. John B. Snarey, *How Fathers Care for the Next Generation* (Cambridge, Mass.: Harvard University Press, 1993), pp. 311-60, Hewlett, *Intimate Fathers,* pp. 151-66.

24. Popenoe, "The Fatherhood Problem," p. 38; James Q. Wilson, *The Moral Sense* (New York: Free Press, 1993); see also James Q. Wilson, "The Family-Values Debate," *Commentary* (April 1993): 24-31.

25. See James A. Weisheipl, ed., *Albertus Magnus and the Sciences: Commemorative Essays 1980* (Toronto: Pontifical Institute of Medieval Studies, 1980).

bol of Christ's union with the church. Ricoeur, in *Freud and Philosophy* and other writings, argued that in order to interpret a symbol, one must understand the unconscious archeology that is brought to the symbol and, to some extent, transformed by it. A symbol, he argued, has a "mixed language" containing a primitive archeology based in natural inclinations as well as a teleology pointing to a direction in which these inclinations are being called and, indeed, possibly transformed.[26] Ricoeur thought that the language of dreams, interpreted in part by the naturalism of Freud's theory of instinctual energies, might be a way of capturing this human archeology of desire.[27] In what follows, I will not use Freud, as did Ricoeur. I will use, instead, evolutionary ecology's theory of the asymmetrical patterns of inclusive fitness between males and females and determine what light it can throw on the archeology of human desire. The extent to which it is possible to find something like this same archeology of desire in Aquinas's theory of marriage and the family is surprising. It is important, however, to observe how this archeology of desire interacts with religious symbols and, at least to some extent, becomes altered by them.

Aquinas saw marriage as both a natural and a supernatural institution. As a natural institution, it is grounded in some deep inclinations — inclinations which must be refined by will, culture, and divine revelation if they are to become fully human. I will quote Aquinas rather heavily to convey the full flavor of his thought. In the Supplement to *Summa Theologica,* he writes that humans share with all animals an inclination to have offspring. Having asserted this, Aquinas introduces a very modern-sounding distinction.

> Yet nature does not incline thereto in the same way in all animals; since there are animals whose offspring are able to seek food immediately after birth, or are sufficiently fed by their mother; and in these there is no tie between male and female; whereas in those whose offspring needs the support of both parents, although for a short time, there is a certain tie, as may be seen in certain birds. In man, however, since the child needs the parents' care for a long time, there is a very great tie between male and female, to which tie even the generic nature inclines.[28]

26. Paul Ricoeur, *Freud and Philosophy* (New Haven, Conn.: Yale University Press, 1971), pp. 12-26.

27. Ricoeur, *Freud and Philosophy*, pp. 419-58.

28. St. Thomas Aquinas, *Summa Theologica*, vol. 3, "Supplement," trans. Fathers of the English Dominican Province (New York: Benziger Brothers, 1948) (hereafter referred to as

Aquinas, along with the modern evolutionary thinkers, believed that humans form families because of the long period of human infantile dependency. In the *Summa Contra Gentiles* he writes, "in those animals in which the female alone suffices for the rearing of the offspring, . . . the male and female do not remain together after coition."[29] The human female, he insists, is "far from sufficing alone for the rearing of children, since the needs of human life require many things that one person alone cannot provide."[30] For this reason, it is "in keeping with human nature that the man remain with the woman after coition, and not leave her at once, indulging in promiscuous intercourse. . . ."[31]

This last quote seems to suggest, as William James and Mary Midgley have argued so cogently in the twentieth century, that human beings (especially human males) are creatures of multiple impulses that sometimes conflict with one another.[32] Aquinas recognized that under certain conditions, males have inclinations to form families and assist females in raising children. But they also have other, possibly even more primal, inclinations toward promiscuity or something akin to what the evolutionary ecologists call the R-strategy of inclusive fitness. In the *Summa Contra Gentiles*, Aquinas writes that male animals desire "to indulge at will in the pleasure of copulation, even as in the pleasure of eating." For this reason, they fight with one another for access to females and they "resist another's intercourse with their consort."[33]

Aquinas recognized, as do today's evolutionary theorists, the role paternal certainty plays in forming monogamous relations between males and females. He held that human males have an instinct for paternal cer-

---

ST), q. 41, a. 1. I also want to express my thanks to Professor Stephen Pope of Boston College for his many excellent articles on the biological dimensions of Aquinas's thought and its analogues to modern biological theory. See particularly his article "The Order of Love and Recent Catholic Ethics," *Theological Studies* 52 (1991): 255-88. Although his unpublished essay titled "Sociobiology and Family: Toward a Thomistic Assessment and Appropriation" came into my hands after this chapter was complete, it was encouraging to see how closely our interpretation of Aquinas was converging, since he is the leading Aquinas scholar on these matters.

29. St. Thomas Aquinas, *Summa Contra Gentiles,* bk. 3, pt. 2, trans. the English Dominican Fathers (London: Burns, Oates and Washbourne, 1928) (hereafter referred to as *SCG*), p. 112.

30. Aquinas, *SCG*, p. 112.

31. Aquinas, *SCG*, p. 112.

32. William James, *The Principles of Psychology*, vol. 2 (New York: Dover, 1951), pp. 383-441; Mary Midgley, *Beast and Man* (Ithaca, N.Y.: Cornell University Press, 1978).

33. Aquinas, *SCG*, p. 117.

tainty. For modern evolutionists, however, paternal certainty is less a matter of instinct and more a necessary condition for paternal investment in one's children. Nonetheless, let us hear his words: "Man naturally desires to be assured of his offspring — and this assurance would be altogether nullified in the case of promiscuous copulation. Therefore the union of one man with one woman comes from a natural instinct."[34]

Of course, even in the framework of Aquinas's own argument, this union cannot be seen as a result of any one instinct; rather, it is the result of a compromise and reorganization of a wide range of inclinations which permit and enhance multiple satisfactions pertaining to pleasure, child-rearing, safety, and inclusive fitness. Although Aquinas had no concept of inclusive fitness in the technical sense we use it today, he did hold some features of that idea. For instance, he taught that fathers care for their children as a way of enhancing their own immortality. With a distinctively masculine bias typical of his day, he wrote, "since the natural life which cannot be preserved in the person of an undying father, is preserved, by a kind of succession, in the person of the son, it is naturally befitting that the son succeed in things belonging to the father."[35] Like both Aristotle before him and evolutionary ecologists today, Aquinas believed that, on the whole, parental investment (including paternal investment) follows parental certainty.

We already have heard the voice of the evolutionary ecologists. Let's consider Aristotle since he provides the intellectual background to Aquinas. In the *Politics* Aristotle wrote, "in common with other animals and with plants, mankind have a natural desire to leave behind them an image of themselves."[36] This sense that a child is a kind of copy of the parents, Aristotle believed to be, as a general rule, crucial for parental care and interest in one's children. This is why he opposed Plato's thought experiment in *The Republic* proposing that civil harmony would be enhanced if the state raised the children and parents were ignorant about which children were theirs. Aristotle believed this would lead to the general neglect of all children. He wrote, "that which is common to the greatest number has the least care bestowed upon it."[37] Hence, for Aristotle, parental investment comes with parental recognition. He thought that in Plato's state, "love will be watery. . . . Of the two qualities which chiefly inspire re-

34. Aquinas, *SCG,* p. 118.
35. Aquinas, *SCG,* p. 114.
36. Aristotle, *Politics,* in *The Basic Works of Aristotle,* ed. Richard McKeon (New York: Random House, 1941), bk. 1, chap. 2.
37. Aristotle, *Politics,* bk. 2, chap. 3.

gard and affection — that a thing is your own and that it is your only one — neither can exist in such a state as this."[38] Aquinas, it is clear, sided with Aristotle, not Plato, on this matter and incorporated the Aristotelian perspective into his Christian theory of the family.

Although Aquinas agreed with Aristotle that, as a general rule, parental recognition or certainty is a positive contribution to high levels of parental investment, he was close to contemporary evolutionary theorists in believing that this certainty is much easier to achieve for females than for males. Because females carry the infant and give birth to it, they know the child is theirs. Males never know with absolute certainty that a particular child is theirs, although there are some circumstances of procreation that provide higher degrees of certainty than others. Aquinas was in step, at least, with the general contours of evolutionary theorists when he wrote,

> In every animal species where the father has a certain care for his offspring, the one male has but one female, as may be seen in birds, where both unite in feeding their young. On the other hand where the male animal has not the care of the offspring, we find indifferently union of one male with several females, or of one female with several males: such is the case with dogs, hens, and so forth.[39]

In short, Thomas believed — as human ecologists Martin Daly, Margo Wilson, Donald Symons, and Robert Trivers do today — that paternal investment in children, paternal certainty, and monogamy tend to go together. Contemporary evolutionary ecologists are clearer than Aquinas about how paternal certainty is supplemented by two other conditions (sexual exchange and general reciprocal altruism between the couple) before paternal investment occurs. From the perspective of the modern discussion, however, Aquinas was playing in the right ballpark and, for his time, batting rather well.

Ethics and Narrative in Aquinas's Family Theory

Aquinas's theory of marriage and family does not remain at the biological level, as important as that is. There are really three major dimensions to his argument, paralleling the first three of five dimensions of practical

38. Aristotle, *Politics*, bk. 2, chap. 4.
39. Aquinas, *SCG*, p. 118.

moral thinking I have outlined in several of my books and essays.[40] The biological discussion orders what modern moral philosophers call the premoral level of his argument; it clarifies several questions pertaining to the ordering of a variety of premoral, natural goods in light of the needs created by the long period of infantile dependency. A more properly moral argument based on appeals to freedom, dignity, and the status of persons emerges when Aquinas argues for the superiority of monogamy over polyandry and polygyny. Polyandry is immediately rejected because it does not provide paternal certainty; that is the major reason it has not been widely used as a family form in the history of the world. Polygyny itself, according to Aquinas, does provide a degree of paternal certainty and hence at least some modicum of paternal investment in children on the part of males. But Aquinas's major criticism of polygyny is now advanced as a moral rather than a strictly biological argument. Polygyny is rejected by Aquinas because it is simply an unjust institution.

> Besides, equality is a condition of friendship. Hence if a woman may not have several husbands, because this removes the certainty of offspring; were it lawful for a man to have several wives, the friendship of a wife for her husband would not be freely bestowed, but servile as it were. And, this argument is confirmed by experience; since where men have several wives, the wives are treated as servants.[41]

The point is that women, for Aquinas, are made in the image of God just as men are. In this respect, they are equal to men. They are fit candidates for friendship with their husbands. He writes, "if the wife has but one husband, while the husband has several wives, the friendship will not be equal on either side; and consequently it will be not a freely bestowed but a servile friendship as it were."[42]

Aquinas concludes this part of his argument by quoting Genesis 2:24: "They shall be two in one flesh." This verse, of course, is repeated many times throughout the New Testament.[43] Aquinas interprets it to mean that husband and wife are to have a friendship of equality that binds them together in their task of raising and educating their children. This

---

40. Don Browning, *Religious Thought and the Modern Psychologies* (Minneapolis: Fortress, 187), p. 17.

41. Aquinas, *SCG*, p. 118.

42. Aquinas, *SCG*, p. 119.

43. See also Matt. 19:5; Mark 10:7; 1 Cor. 6:16; Eph. 5:31.

friendship and mutual assistance, as the "Supplement" says, is for Aquinas the second main task of matrimony in addition to the procreation and education of children.[44]

Of course, the equality that Aquinas has in mind is one of proportionality rather than the egalitarianism that moderns associate with liberal, contractual models of business and marriage. That is an issue, however, to be elaborated later in this chapter. The point for now is this: for Aquinas monogamy brought into existence a new level of care and investment by the father for his children, but it also created a new level of equality and friendship between the wife and her husband.

The third level of his argument about matrimony and the family is what I will call the narrative level. This is the level of supernatural grace and sacrament, but it is also the level where the narrative of Christ's sacrificial death on the cross is used as an analogy to the role of Christian fathers in their families. Even here, the biological dimension of the argument still shines through. It has to do with Aquinas's belief that the male-female tie that infantile dependency calls into existence must last longer than a few years — it must last for life. In fact, it must be indissoluble.[45]

Chapter 123 of the *Summa Contra Gentiles* is a key text on the indissolubility of marriage. It combines arguments based on several levels of debate — an analysis of human inclinations and natural law, a theory of justice between the sexes, and a rendering of the narrative implications of divine revelation. There are in humans, Aquinas believed, some natural, although unstable, inclinations toward indissoluble monogamy, which should inform and be consolidated by human law and then finally be perfected by divine revelation.[46]

The argument is stated from the male point of view and for this reason is grating to the liberal sensibility. On the other hand, it is clearly stated as a way of overcoming what we have called the male problematic — the tendency of males to mate without parental investment. Aquinas's arguments could be restated from the perspective of both parents, but there is value in first hearing his own logic. There are several points. Three arguments have to do with paternal investment. First, fathers care for their children, the argument goes, as a way of extending their own lives. Therefore, fathers should give appropriate degrees of care to their children indefinitely as a way of extending and enriching those who are literally parts

44. Aquinas, *ST,* q. 41, a. 1.
45. Aquinas, *SCG,* p. 114.
46. Aquinas, *SCG,* p. 115.

of themselves. Marriage should be indissoluble, he concludes, because it provides the context for this lifelong investment.[47] Second, because of the long years of human childhood dependency, children need parental (including paternal) authority indefinitely. Third, if couples exchange partners, paternal certainly is obscured.[48] And when this happens, fathers may care less or not at all for their progeny.

Three additional arguments are distinctively moral in character. To dissolve a marriage is an affront to equity and fairness. Aquinas assumes that men have a tendency to dispose of older women and take as mates younger, more fertile females. He writes, "if a man after taking a wife in her youth, while she is yet fair and fruitful, can put her away when she has aged, he does injury, contrary to natural equity."[49] Second, in addition to procreation, marriage is for friendship, and this friendship will be all the more stable if it is thought to be indissoluble.[50] Third (and most out of step with the liberal modern mind), Aquinas thought women were necessarily financially dependent on men and, furthermore, "naturally subject" to the man's superior wisdom. Therefore, neither women nor men should be allowed to initiate divorce since this would, in the end, deprive women of the resources and guidance they need.[51]

This last of Aquinas's reasons most strikingly points to the different situation of women in modern societies in contrast to their situation in all pre-modern societies. Women are far less economically dependent on men in modern societies. Furthermore, all that we know in the research of moral and cognitive development indicates that there are no significant differences between men and women in their deliberative capacities, at least not of a kind that necessitates male guidance. But the question remains: Do women need men to help raise children and do children need fathers to be strong? Aquinas could set aside this belief in female dependency and mental inferiority and still have grounds for arguing that women do need men's participation in child-rearing. The question being debated today is whether he is right and whether the reasons he advanced have backing.

Aquinas's final argument for the indissolubility of marriage makes a direct appeal to revelation and is the cornerstone of his understanding of marriage as a sacrament. It points to a paradigmatic narrative action

47. Aquinas, *SCG*, p. 114.
48. Aquinas, *SCG*, p. 115.
49. Aquinas, *SCG*, p. 115.
50. Aquinas, *SCG*, pp. 115-16.
51. Aquinas, *SCG*, p. 115.

which Christian men as husbands and fathers are charged to imitate in their relation to wives and children. Furthermore, it also shows how narrative about divine action was seen by Aquinas to supplement both natural human inclination and the positive law in regulating marriage. Both human law and divine revelation should be based on, yet remedy the defects of, natural inclination. Not only do divine laws "express the instinct of nature, but they also supply the defect of natural instinct."[52] Divine law adds to human law "a kind of supernatural reason taken from the representation of the indissoluble union of Christ and the Church, which is union of one with one."[53]

The analogy between the indissoluble union of husband and wife and Christ and the church refers, of course, to Ephesians 5:32. Here Aquinas follows the Vulgate in rendering the original Greek *mysterion* with the Latin word *sacramentum* rather than the more accurate *mysterium*, which we translate as "mystery." During the Patristic period, neither *sacramentum* nor *mysterium* communicated the idea that marriage was a source of supernatural grace in the way that Aquinas wants to assert.[54] In fact, this is what separates Augustine's three purposes of marriage set forth in "The Good of Marriage" from Aquinas's three purposes stated in Question 49 of the Supplement. Both say that marriage concerns (1) procreation and education of children, (2) mutual obligations in sexuality and other domestic affairs, and (3) *sacramentum*.[55] But *sacramentum* meant to Augustine only permanence or indissolubility and not supernatural grace. *Sacramentum* meant to Aquinas both indissolubility and supernatural grace.

Protestants, as is well known, returned to the idea that matrimony was primarily a natural, nonsacramental institution. That is, the act of marriage for them bestowed no special supernatural grace. Nor did the early Reformers see it as indissoluble, although there were strong constraints placed against divorce.[56] Of course, for Aquinas, matrimony was both natural (since it had been willed by God from the foundations of cre-

---

52. Aquinas, *SCG*, p. 116.

53. Aquinas, *SCG*, p. 116.

54. Rudolf Schnackenburg, *Ephesians: A Commentary* (Edinburgh: T. & T. Clark, 1991), pp. 255-56.

55. Augustine, "The Good of Marriage," in *Treatises on Marriage and Other Subjects*, trans. Charles T. Wilcox et al., ed. Roy J. Deferrari, vol. 15 of The Writings of Saint Augustine (New York: Fathers of the Church, 1955), p. 4.

56. Martin Luther, "The Estate of Marriage," in *Luther's Works*, vol. 45 (Philadelphia: Fortress, 1962), pp. 30-35; Steven Ozment, *Protestants: The Birth of a Revolution* (New York: Doubleday, 1992), pp. 151-69.

ation) and supernatural (when mutually consented to by baptized Christians, supernatural grace was infused into the marriage to overcome the weaknesses of the couple, especially the weakness of the male).[57]

There was another dimension of Aquinas's understanding of *sacramentum*. This aspect is far more dramatic and actional than the more mechanical idea of the infusion of grace to overcome our concupiscence and moral inadequacies, but it is still designed to help couples have a love adequate to the task of remaining in lasting marriages. This additional dimension invites imitation or participation in a model or archetypal pattern of divine action. It is closer to the true meaning of the Ephesians 5:20-33 passage which first stated the analogy between matrimony and Christ's relation to the church. This is the dimension of matrimony as sacrament that enacts the sacrificial love of Christ for the church. Aquinas is addressing this dimension when he writes, "Although Matrimony is not conformed to Christ's Passion as regards pain, it is as regards charity, whereby He suffered for the church who was to be united to Him as His spouse."[58]

This means, as the Ephesians passage instructs, that the husband is to imitate Christ both in his unbreakable commitment to the family and in his capacity for sacrificial love or charity (*caritas* in the Latin and *agape* in the Greek). Hence, when Aquinas invokes the narrative of Christ's passion for the redemption of the church, he doubtless has several of the Ephesians passages in mind. In this New Testament letter we read these words:

> Husbands, love your wives, just as Christ loved the church and gave himself up for her. . . . In the same way, husbands should love their wives as they do their own bodies. He who loves his wife loves himself. For no one ever hates his own body, but he nourishes and tenderly cares for it, just as Christ does for the church, because we are members of his body. For this reason a man will leave his father and mother and be joined to his wife, and the two will become one flesh. This is a great mystery, and I am applying it to Christ and the church. Each of you, however, should love his wife as himself, and a wife should respect her husband. (Eph. 5:25-33)

Aquinas's use of the Ephesians call to male sacrificial love and lifelong endurance in families must be understood in the context of his ar-

57. Aquinas, *ST*, q. 42, a. 2.
58. Aquinas, *ST*, q. 42, a. 1.

cheology of male sexual ambivalence (his pre-scientific version of the two strategies), the vulnerability of wives (males' possible decline of interest after their wives' childbearing years), and the needs of highly dependent human infants and children (who require, Aquinas thought, an indefinite commitment).

There is little doubt that Aquinas retains, in a qualified way, some of the patriarchy present in the Ephesians passage. Husbands are the heads of their families as Christ is the head of the church (Eph. 5:23). Both are carriers of an ethic of "love paternalism." This is a qualified and chastened patriarchy that emphasizes responsibility, commitment, and care; but the power, nonetheless, is still in the hands of the husband, in spite of the respect he is to have for his wife and children. Aquinas has mitigated the oppressiveness of ancient patriarchies, but he has not altogether done away with patriarchy. Nevertheless, to fail to place the symbolic relation between the servanthood of Christ and the husband against the background of Aquinas's analysis of the male problematic is to fail to recognize the potential richness of his contribution, both in the history of Western thought and even for today.

Is it possible that Aquinas formulated a powerful religio-cultural symbol that served to reinforce unsteady male inclinations toward paternal investment and the monogamy generally associated with paternal investment? Is it possible, as Margaret Mead once observed, that without powerful cultural incentives for men to invest in their children and remain with the women who give them birth, human males have deep inclinations to follow another sexual strategy?[59] Before Aquinas introduced the concept of the indissolubility of marriage and his version of marriage as a supernatural sacrament, he advanced mostly naturalistic and moral arguments about why men should be dedicated to their children and their wives. His concept of matrimony as a sacrament, both in its capacity to infuse grace and in its invitation to imitate the drama of Christ's sacrificial love, simply gives added cultural and religious reinforcement to what he has argued for on humanistic terms.

This reinforcement, however, is classically religious. It follows in considerable detail Mircea Eliade's widely respected phenomenology of the sacred. It makes matrimony a recapitulation of an act of divine beings in their creation of sacred space and time.[60] Aquinas may be wrong in believing that Ephesians 5:32 makes marriage a special conveyor of supernatural

---

59. Popenoe quotes from Margaret Mead on this subject in "The Fatherhood Problem."
60. Mircea Eliade, *The Sacred and the Profane* (New York: Harper and Row, 1961).

grace, but he certainly is not wrong in sensing that Ephesians makes marriage (especially the husband's role within it) a recapitulation of the cosmic drama of a divine being who creates from acts of *agape*, or self-sacrificial love, the marital bond between a man and a woman. Matrimony as a symbol of Christ's cosmic sacrificial union with the church is all the more striking when one understands it, following Ricoeur's dialectic between archeology and teleology, as the reinforcement of some, and the transformation of other, basic male inclinations. The symbol of Christ's steadfast and sacrificial love for the church becomes, as Ricoeur calls it, a "figure of the spirit" attracting inchoate male inclinations and shaping them into a new organization — an organization that is possibly even more satisfying for men than the older strategy, more productive for children, and more just to their wives.[61]

The modern papal encyclicals beginning with *Arcanum* in 1881 and ending with *Familiaris Consortio* in 1981 restated several times this understanding of marriage as a cosmic drama. *Casti Connubii* exemplifies this regularly repeated theme: "For matrimonial faith demands that husband and wife be joined in an especially holy and pure love, not as adulterers love each other, but as Christ loved the Church."[62] For men who actually believed that their marriages had this meaning and reality, this belief doubtless affected their behavior and self-understanding. Just how much and how deeply these powerful symbols affected men's actions and values, only good historical research, of the kind we do not presently have, can tell.

One can speculate, however, that these symbols may have set up two competing trends, one toward a reinforcement of a declining and defensive patriarchy but another toward a norm of male responsibility expressed in the care of their children and a respectful, lifelong commitment to their wives. The first possibility has been examined by a variety of hermeneutics of suspicion in recent decades; the second possibility has been largely ignored. More specifically, the particular archeology of human desire that Aquinas assumed and that was dialectically related to the symbol of Christ's love for the church has been mostly lost to history. It is certainly not retained in the papal encyclicals on marriage published in the twentieth century; there is no hint in these documents of Aquinas's view of the male problematic and its roots in natural male inclinations.

---

61. Ricoeur, *Freud and Philosophy*, pp. 462-68.

62. *Casti Connubii: Encyclical of Pope Pius XI*, in *The Papal Encyclicals*, ed. Claudia Carlen (Wilmington, N.C.: McGrath, 1981), par. 23.

The gradual disappearance of such powerful, religio-cultural rein-forcements for the symbol Christ's love for the church presents for the role of husbands and fathers raises an important question. Will our mod-ern, liberal, and contractual models of male-female relations (which in-creasingly do not include even the idea of formal marriage) address the male problematic with the same power as this older paradigm? Certainly no secular alternative to this older symbolic matrix comes immediately to mind. Furthermore, since both the forces of secularization and the ghost of patriarchy haunt the official teachings of the churches that still carry this symbolism, there seem to be few prospects for this symbol once again addressing the male problematic with the force that it may once have done.

The Male Problematic and Early Christianity

Is the dialectical relation between archeology and teleology in the symbol of Christ's love for the church something peculiar to Aquinas? Does it re-flect only a formulation that he stumbled upon but that has no visibility elsewhere in Christian teachings?

Martin Luther, of course, was greatly influenced by his Catholic prede-cessors yet revolted against the medieval church on a variety of matters, es-pecially issues pertaining to marriage and the family. It is widely known that he believed marriage was a worthier arena of Christian vocation than celibacy, that he rejected the sacramental view of marriage, that he emptied German monasteries and nunneries and encouraged marriage among Catholics, that he saw fatherhood (even the care of infants by men) as a di-vine vocation, and that he repudiated the medieval practice of secret mar-riage, seeing marriage instead as a public affair under the control of the state.[63] All of these steps were in tension with Catholic traditions.

But the formal outlines of his theory of marriage were very close to Aquinas's views. Luther did not correlate the disciplines of biology with Scripture in the fashion of Aquinas, but he believed Scripture alone *(sola scriptura)* supported his conclusions. He was more likely to quote the cre-

---

63. Steven Ozment, *The Protestants* (New York: Doubleday, 1992). Furthermore, it must be noted that much of Catholic canon law on marriage was taken over by the Protestant Reformation, but now administered by the state more or less as civil law rather than by the church itself and its courts, as it had been under Catholicism. See James A. Brundage, *Sex, Law, and Marriage in Christian Society in Medieval Europe* (Chicago: University of Chicago Press, 1989).

ation stories in Genesis and their restatement in the Gospels than he was to quote Ephesians or the Pastoral Epistles. He quoted Genesis 1:27, "So God created man . . . male and female he created them." Males and females were not to "be alone" (Gen. 2:18) but were to become "one flesh" (Gen. 2:24) and "be fruitful" (Gen. 1:28). These are not commands of God but "ordinances." They are stamped in creation and nature.

> It is a nature and disposition just as innate as the organs involved in it. Therefore just as God does not command anyone to be a man or a woman but creates them the way they have to be, so he does not command them to multiply but creates them so that they have to multiply. And wherever men try to resist this, it remains irresistible nonetheless and goes its way through fornication, adultery, and secret sins, for this is a matter of nature and not of choice.[64]

Luther wrote that the mundane and distasteful things that mothers and fathers do for their children — rocking the baby, changing diapers, staying up all night — are "adorned with divine approval." Like Aquinas, Luther aims his theology of parental responsibility even more toward fathers than toward mothers. In "The Estate of Marriage," he offers a prayer of thanks for his paternal vocation:

> O God, because I am certain that thou hast created me as a man and hast from my body begotten this child, I also know for a certainty that it meets with thy perfect pleasure. I confess to thee that I am not worthy to rock the little babe or wash its diapers, or to be entrusted with the care of the child and its mother. How is it that I, without any merit, have come to this distinction of being certain that I am serving thy creature and thy most precious will? O how gladly will I do so, though the duties should be even more significant and despised. Neither frost nor heat, neither drudgery nor labor, will distress or dissuade me, for I am certain that it is this pleasing in thy sight.[65]

Such divine approval is hardly on the same plane as participation in the cosmic drama of Christ's love for the church, but it does bestow divine weight to paternal investment. In addition, Luther did invoke the Ephesians drama and is aware that it is especially addressed to men. In Luther,

64. Luther, "The Estate of Marriage," p. 18.
65. Luther, "The Estate of Marriage," pp. 39-40.

this drama is more of a sign of the meaning of marriage than a sacrament that bestows supernatural grace, even though he occasionally used the word "sacrament." In his "Order of Marriage for Common Pastors," he gives prominence at the beginning of the text to the analogy between Christ and the church and the servant relation of husband to the family (Eph. 5:25-29). He then concludes with a prayer that thanks God for creating man and woman, ordaining them for marriage, blessing their fruits, and typifying "therein the sacramental union of the dear Son, the Lord Jesus Christ, and the church, his bride."[66]

Although Luther has no clear analysis of the male problematic in the fashion of Aquinas, the message seems very much the same. But it should be clear that in both Aquinas and Luther, this appeal to male responsibility was still formulated within the framework of a vigorous even though modified and mostly humane patriarchy. In his "Order of Marriage," Luther, using another side of Ephesians, can still instruct wives to submit "in everything" to their husbands (Eph. 5:22-24). The issue is this: Are there resources within the Christian tradition that make it possible to retain the symbolism of paternal and maternal investment but within a vision of marriage that sees it as more radically egalitarian? It is to this issue that I will turn in the remaining portions of this chapter.

The Greco-Roman Context of the Ephesians' View of Marriage

There is an unresolved tension in early Christianity between an ethic of equality and an ethic of male responsibility and servanthood. It is never satisfactorily resolved in the Scriptures of the early church. This tension looks less extreme if we carefully place early Christian literature in its historical context and compare it to surrounding Greco-Roman views on family, marriage, and sexuality. Early Christian teachings look more egalitarian than almost any religious or philosophical movement contemporary to early Christianity. On the other hand, Greco-Roman views were more complicated than we sometimes think and were themselves giving birth to new degrees of gender equality and male parental involvement.

Early Christianity spoke simultaneously of equality between the sexes (what I will later call an ethic of equal regard) and male "headship" or au-

---

66. Luther, "Order of Marriage for Common Pastors," in *Luther's Works*, vol. 53 (Philadelphia: Fortress, 1965), p. 115.

thority over the family. This is visible in the classic text from Ephesians 5:21-33; both elements can be found there. These two elements are reconcilable only if we remember two things: (1) that the husband as "head of the wife" is humbled and modeled after the sacrifice of Christ, and (2) that the equality of the wife even here contains some of the elements of "proportional" justice characteristic of the ancient world wherever Aristotle's philosophy influenced civic life. This happened almost everywhere in the Mediterranean world, including in most of the urban centers of Israel and Asia Minor. The Christian sacrificial husband could possibly see his wife as ontologically equal before God yet requiring male guidance because of her supposedly inferior deliberative capacities — or, at least, this was possible according to Aristotle.[67]

Hence, early Christianity in comparison to surrounding contexts made higher demands on male servant responsibility and enhanced the equality of wives but may still seem deficient from the perspective of our modern egalitarian views. But to leave it at that would be an error: there may be a realism about the male problematic in the early Christian view which is needed today. Furthermore, these remaining tensions in early Christianity may themselves be reconcilable when submitted to careful theological reflection. Achieving this coherence may be the task of theology, whether systematic or practical. I will take some tentative steps toward this reconciliation at the conclusion of this chapter.

A Discipleship of Equals

Early Christianity can best be thought of as a Jesus movement. It was, in its early years, a reform movement within Judaism consisting of a group of men and women who followed Jesus in his itinerant ministry of preaching and healing. Jesus' preaching announced that the kingdom of God, long awaited in Judaism, was in fact already beginning to unfold in the midst of the Jewish community.

This movement had a complicated relation to families. On the one hand, Jesus is depicted as an enthusiastic wedding guest and one who blessed the marriage wine; on the other, the Jesus movement is portrayed as in conflict with the patriarchal family structure of the Jewish and Greco-Roman worlds. Note the famous words, "For I have come to set a man against his father, and a daughter against her mother . . ." (Matt.

67. Aristotle, *Politics*, bk. 1, chaps. 12-13.

10:35; see also Matt. 10:21-23; Mark 13:12-13; Luke 21:12-17). But these passages are not attacks on families by the Jesus movement; they are instead reports of the divisions created in Christian families when Christians were arrested and jailed by civil authorities.[68] Family members, under such conditions, would literally disclaim each other. They are also criticisms of Jewish and Greco-Roman family clans who functioned as patriarchal religio-political units inhibiting their members from becoming a part of the kingdom Jesus was proclaiming. Early Christianity clearly relativized the patriarchal tribe as a family form, but it should not be thought that Jesus was against families as such. The tradition does represent him as wanting families, and individuals within them, to submit their lives to the rule of the kingdom of God rather than that of the tribal codes and cults which were the center of family clans throughout the Mediterranean world at that time.

Jesus is also portrayed as objecting to the patriarchal patterns of unilateral divorce of Jewish wives by their husbands, a practice that meant the ranks of the poor consisted primarily of women. Jesus is reported to have said that Moses allowed husbands to divorce their wives "because of your hardness of heart." But from the beginning of creation, "God made them male and female. 'For this reason a man shall leave his father and mother and be joined to his wife, and the two shall become one.' So they are no longer two but one. What therefore God has joined together, let not man put asunder" (Mark 10:5-9). Elisabeth Schüssler Fiorenza gives a particularly egalitarian reading of this passage when she argues that Jesus is claiming here that God did not create patriarchy, did not intend that women be given into the power of men to continue their house and family line, but intended instead "that it is the man who shall sever connections with his own patriarchal family and 'the two shall become one *sarx* (flesh).'"[69]

Fiorenza claims that the pre-Markan and pre-Q fragments of the Gospels depict the early Jesus movement as "a discipleship of equals" between men and women. As the Jesus movement became a missionary movement to the Greco-Roman world, evidence of this equality can be found in the prominence of women as leaders in the early house churches. Some of these women were wealthy and hosted meetings of these early Christian "clubs" in their homes. Some, like Prisca, were married but achieved dis-

---

68. Elisabeth Schüssler Fiorenza, *In Memory of Her: A Feminist Theological Reconstruction of Christian Origins* (New York: Crossroad, 1987), p. 74.

69. Schüssler Fiorenza, *In Memory of Her,* p. 143.

tinction independently of their husbands as founders of important churches throughout Asia Minor (Rom. 16:3) — a leadership role rare for women in the Greco-Roman world. These pre-Pauline house churches were scenes of important rites that enacted liminal dramas of radical equality, or, at least, radical for that day. Galatians 3:28 is thought to refer to a widely practiced baptismal formula that announces the new status of those who "have clothed yourselves with Christ." "There is no longer Jew or Greek, there is no longer slave or free, there is no longer male and female; for all of you are one in Christ." This formula is thought to reveal how relations between husband and wife, master and slave, Greek and Jew were restructured in these house churches. These redefined relationships may have radiated outward into broader public life. All of these pairs were equal in the house church because they were believed to be made in the image of God (thus having equal status before God) and to equally belong to Christ.

Several scholars believe that these little religious clubs enacted rituals that had egalitarian consequences for gender relations in the actual families of early Christians. Stephen Barton says it most forcefully when he writes,

> It is most likely that the potential created by church-in-house for the extension of the social range of female activity, represented at the same time a potential for redefining the women's social world generally (which, ipso facto, included that of their men as well). I mean by this that the ways in which women perceived themselves and expressed themselves within the sacred time and sacred space of the gathering-for-church-in-the-house will have *carried over* into secular time and space, especially because sacred time and space were linked so closely with secular time and space by virtue of the fact that church time constituted a segment of household time and church space was identical with household space.[70]

Entire families often joined these clubs. Although the house churches themselves functioned as a "new family of God" into which all members were adopted, these associations were not ascetic and natural family relations were rarely renounced.[71] Paul, in fact, specifically prohibited Christians from seeking divorce, even from their non-Christian partners (1 Cor.

---

70. Stephen C. Barton, "Paul's Sense of Place: An Anthropological Approach to Community Formation in Corinth," *New Testament Studies* 32 (1986): 74.

71. Schüssler Fiorenza, *In Memory of Her,* p. 214.

7:10-16). Family relations, however, may have received a new meaning through the acceptance of the baptismal formula as a model of more equal family relations. David Balch points out that although Paul's interest in equality between the sexes was less than that found in the pre-Pauline church, he still made egalitarian remarks that were unique in antiquity. In 1 Corinthians 7:4 he writes, "For the wife does not have authority over her own body, but the husband does; likewise the husband does not have authority over his own body, but the wife does." Balch says that the last half of this statement, giving the wife authority over the husband's body, was "astounding in Greco-Roman culture."[72] Furthermore, Paul agreed with most of antiquity that sexuality was somewhat dangerous and that for the sake of spiritual purity in the "eschatological endtime," it was better to be abstinent (1 Cor. 7:1-7). Nonetheless, marriage was natural and need not be sinful. In fact, Paul spent much time, as Balch points out, explaining the mutual obligations of Christian spouses (1 Cor. 7:1-16).

The pre-Pauline baptismal formula unleashed different consequences depending on the location of the Christian community. For instance, in the Corinthian church, the new gender equality inspired some women to experiment with wearing their hair loose, keeping their heads bare, and participating in provocative forms of ecstatic behavior. Such behavior was troubling to the outside pagan world. Christians were seen as undermining the normative model of the Greco-Roman family — powerfully stated by Aristotle in his *Politics* — which gave clear authority to the father over slaves, wives, and children.[73]

Paul, in an effort to minimize this criticism, made a distinction between inner and outer freedom. In public roles, he advised Christians to retain their pre-Christian positions: slaves should remain slaves, Jews should remain circumcised, and wives should remain obedient to their husbands. This external bondage was of little importance, Paul coun-

---

72. David Balch, "Theses about the Early Christian Family" (paper prepared for the annual seminar of the Religion, Culture, and Family project, located at the Divinity School of the University of Chicago and sponsored by the Division of Religion of the Lilly Endowment, 1993).

73. For the best discussion of the tensions of pre-Pauline and Pauline churches with the official household codes of the Aristotelian tradition, which dominated the urban life of Roman Hellenism, see David Balch, *Let Wives Be Submissive: The Domestic Code in 1 Peter* (Atlanta: Scholars, 1981); for the original statement of the household code outlining the respective obligations and rights of free Greek men over slaves, wives, and children, see Aristotle, *Politics*, bk. 1, chap. 12.

seled, in comparison to the deeper freedom and equality they enjoyed through their identification with Christ (1 Cor. 7:17-24). This advice, and Paul's attempt to deflect the criticism of the Greco-Roman world, suggests that Christians in the privacy of their house churches were experimenting with new freedoms and equalities that were affronts to the stability of the official order.

Although there was this impulse toward gender equality in the early Christian communities, and although this impulse had social consequences, it is best not to overstate these consequences or conceive of them in modern terms. In addition to the distinction between inner-ecclesial roles and outer-public roles, there was also the tendency to interpret the language of equality in terms of the widely influential Aristotelian concepts of proportional justice. In the *Nicomachean Ethics* Aristotle writes, "In all friendships between unequals, the love also should be proportional, i.e., the better should be more loved than he loves. . . ."[74] This is the form that equality was to take between people that were not of the same status, such as parents and children and, indeed, husbands and wives. Husbands and wives throughout the Hellenistic world were thought to have different degrees of excellence because men were believed to have higher powers of deliberation than women. We saw remnants of this belief in Aquinas, who taught that equity required that wives should not through divorce be deprived of the superior guidance of their husbands.

In early Christianity, equality between the sexes was thus a complicated matter. On the one hand, males and females were both made in the image of God, and, if the male and female were Christian, both of them were equal in their identification with Christ. On the other hand, after the early days of the Christian missionary movement, there was a gradual return of the language of male headship and the associated idea that wives required the guidance of husbands. Both Paul and the author of Ephesians said outright that the "husband is the head of the wife" (1 Cor. 11:3; Eph. 5:23). There was also, as we said above, the distinction between inner equality in one's relation to God and outer conformity to conventional public roles. This much can be said: early Christianity constituted an ambivalent challenge to the patriarchies — Jewish, Greek, and Roman — of the ancient world. It was a challenge that moved from the semi-private space of the house church to the public space of the polis.

Christianity was not the only challenge to this patriarchy. Certain Ep-

---

74. Aristotle, *Nicomachean Ethics*, in *Basic Works of Aristotle*, ed. Richard McKeon (New York: Random House, 1941), bk. 8, chap. 7.

icurean groups, for instance, accepted women as equals, but since the Epicureans were ascetics, they did not directly challenge the public relation between family and polis.[75] Early Christianity seems to have inadvertently challenged the Aristotelian model of the public father governing his private household made up of noncitizen slaves, wife, and children. Hence, in the early Christian era, transformative currents came from the domestic realm outward into the public. John Milbank says it well when he writes,

> Where neither women, slaves, nor children were citizens, then the relationship of *oikos* to *polis* was *external,* and mediated by the father. But where, on the other hand, women, slaves and children . . . are equally members *of an ecclesia,* then the relationship of every part of the *oikos* to the public realm is a much more direct one. . . . Inversely the domestic . . . becomes "political," a matter of real significance for law, education, religion, and government (although this has only been spasmodically realized in Christian history).[76]

Even though this significance has been only "spasmodically" realized, there still may be much to learn from the way these Christian domestically based associations indirectly influenced the wider public realm.

The Honor-Shame Codes and the Early Christian House Church

One issue remains. What was the meaning in the early church of the analogy between Christ's sacrifice for the church and the father's servanthood to the family? Did this cosmic analogy found in Ephesians and elsewhere only serve to bolster male authority, or was it a genuine reversal of ancient, heroic models of male authority in families? There is evidence that the second interpretation is the more accurate. To understand how this might be true, we must examine more closely the logic of male authority that functioned firmly throughout the Mediterranean world during the Hellenistic period and remained largely intact into Roman Hellenism. Some scholars now believe that this was an honor-shame code based on heroic military virtues of dominance and submission — virtues which had their roots in a culture reflected in the poetry of Homer.

In such a culture, individuals are thought of in relation to their families and their family's reputation or honor. Honor is maintained through

---

75. Schüssler Fiorenza, *In Memory of Her,* p. 75.
76. John Milbank, *Theology and Social Theory* (Oxford: B. Blackwell, 1990), p. 368.

the praise of respected equals.[77] It is established in political life and in war through achieving dominance in situations of challenge and riposte. Such interaction is a distinctively male activity: if the person who is challenged fails to respond, he is dishonored; if he responds but loses in either conflict or public debate, he is still dishonored. Honor is gained through winning, dishonor or shame through losing.

Anthropologists call cultures dominated by honor-shame ethics "agonistic cultures."[78] Public life is thought to be conflictual at its core and private life under constant threat of being dishonored by intrusive agents outside the family. Hence, a male's private sphere — his wife, children, mother, sisters, and slaves — are in constant threat of being insulted, molested, raped, seduced, and stolen. On the other hand, it adds to the honor of a man if he can penetrate the private space of another male outside his own family.

Men are shamed if their space is challenged and they lose. For women, on the other hand, shame is a positive thing; they are to "have shame" and to resist losing their shame or being "shameless."[79] For a man to avoid shame and for a woman to keep her shame, men must protect, control, guide, and circumscribe the lives of their women so that their private space will not be dishonored. Such an ethic celebrates the virtues of active dominance for males and passive conformity for females. The virtue of male activeness, as opposed to passivity, seems also to have been part of the widespread, but controversial, practices of pederasty whereby young adult males would take boys for their lovers until their own marriages, at which time such relations often subsided.[80] The honor-shame code also legitimated a double standard for male sexual activity after marriage; males could with ease have access to female slaves, possibly young boys, or even their neighbor's wife if they were clever enough to go unchallenged. It was a sign of their agency — their dominance.

Although this characterization of family relations under the honor-shame code is generally true, recent research qualifies it in several respects. While most women in Hellenistic societies led circumscribed lives,

77. Jerome H. Neyrey, *The Social World of Luke-Acts* (Peabody, Mass.: Hendrickson, 1991), p. 32; for an application of the honor-shame concepts to classical Greece, see David Cohen, *Law, Sexuality and Society* (Cambridge: Cambridge University Press, 1991).

78. Cohen, *Law, Sexuality and Society*, p. 29.

79. Neyrey, *The Social World of Luke-Acts*, pp. 41-44.

80. Eva Canterella, *Bisexuality in the Ancient World* (New Haven, Conn.: Yale University Press, 1992); for its controversial characterization of male bisexuality, see Cohen, *Law, Sexuality and Society*, pp. 171-201.

they had surprising freedom and power within these limits.[81] It is also wrong to believe that because men enjoyed extensive control of the domestic sphere and provided household security through public conflict, there was no genuine love, affection, or friendship between husbands and wives or fathers and children.[82] In spite of these qualifications, honor-shame patterns generally held true in the Greco-Roman world and provided the contextual background to an alternative family ethic (and an alternative understanding of the relation of *oikos* to the *polis*) that emerged in early Christianity, albeit fragmentarily.

The pagan world had a different form of the "male problematic" than that experienced in modern societies. The male problematic in modern societies is only superficially one of domination in the Greco-Roman sense. If our earlier analysis is correct, it is more a matter of neglect, absence, and failure of responsibility. Cultural individualism and technical rationality in both the market and state bureaucracies may be the more proximate social causes of this male neglect and absence. Domination and violence are part of the male problematic in modern societies, but now more capriciously — more as a way of asserting power in a social context that gives them increasing freedom but declining institutionalized control. In the shadows of both cases, however, we can detect the archaic inheritance of the ambivalent male reproductive strategy. The honor-shame code may be a particular cultural elaboration of ancient male reproductive strategies; it was a way of controlling wives, assuring paternal certainty, but also exploring the advantages of the R-strategy. The modern form of the problematic is different; as men increasingly renounce their control of women, they also renounce their concern with paternal certainty and paternal investment. Modern men seem increasingly unable to live by an ethic of equal regard that renounces control but maintains high degrees of mutual respect with spouses and paternal investment in children.

Was early Christianity exploring still another strategy? It may have been. In addition to its real but unsteady attempt to create an ethic of equal regard between husband and wife, there is evidence that it attempted to fracture the honor-shame code that dominated male behavior in families in the Mediterranean world. I use the word "fracture" to communicate that at best the Christian revolution was uneven, setting up certain ambiguous trends that even today we are still trying to resolve.

---

81. Cohen, *Law, Sexuality and Society,* pp. 133-69.

82. Richard Sallers, *Patriarchy, Property, and Death in the Roman Family* (Cambridge: Cambridge University Press, 1994).

The Epistle to the Ephesians, which influenced both Aquinas and Luther so decisively, can help us understand how early Christianity engaged the honor-shame culture. The author of Ephesians wrote this epistle to a group of second-century urban Christians living in cities in the Lysus Valley, attempting to save them from sinking back into the pagan existence of the surrounding culture. This pagan existence can be best understood as the continuing manifestation of the honor-shame code, with its belief in conflict and dominance as methods for achieving peace and respect. For rhetorical purposes, the author borrows from the metaphors of the male culture he opposes. In contrast to the armor and weapons of the heroic culture he criticizes, the author tells his readers to "take up the whole armor of God . . . the belt of truth around your waist . . the breastplate of righteousness. As shoes for your feet put on whatever will make you ready to proclaim the gospel of peace" (Eph. 6:13-15). The new male armor and the new male ethic is an ethic of peace. More specifically, it is an ethic "with all humility and gentleness, with patience, bearing with one another in love, making every effort to maintain the unity of the Spirit in the bond of peace" (Eph. 4:2-3). The opposing pagan ethic is an ethic of contest or "wrath" which follows the desires of the "flesh and senses" (Eph. 2:2-3). It is not just simple immorality that Ephesians opposes but a systematic male ethic that enshrined the virtues of courage, strength, dominance, and conflict as means for achieving domestic and civic order. Ephesians is in tension with the honor-shame code of the Greco-Roman world.

It is within this context that we must understand the way Ephesians addresses the male problematic by electing Christ's sacrificial relation to the church as a model for the husband's relation to his wife. It is, in effect, a reversal of the logic of the honor-shame ethic guiding male behavior in antiquity. Rather than being the agentive guarantor of domestic security through challenge and riposte in the public world and control over the private world, the husband is now admonished to imitate the peace of God and the self-giving love of Christ. It is against the heroic ethics of the Greco-Roman world that we should understand the words, "Husbands, love your wives, just as Christ loved the church and gave himself up for her" (Eph. 5:25). It is true that the model of male headship is retained in this passage, but the logic of the ancient heroic codes is at least fractured, if not overturned.

The struggle to state the grounds of gender equality between spouses typical of the pre-Pauline missionary movement is not totally absent in this passage. But its status is ambiguous. In 5:21 we read, "Be subject to one another out of reverence for Christ." Then we read admonitions for the wife to be subject to the husband. Shortly after this, the author tells husbands to love their wives as Christ loves the church. He adds, "Husbands should love their wives as they do their own bodies," a statement which seems to introduce the principle of neighbor love into the discussion of how husbands should love their wives. This principle, "You shall love your neighbor as yourself," is presented by Jesus in Matthew 22:39 (and also Mark 12:31 and Luke 10:27). It can be found in the Hebrew Scriptures, is repeated several times in the Pauline and Pastoral Epistles,[83] and is thought by many theologians to be the center from which all New Testament ethics should be understood. It first was thought to apply primarily to the neighbor (even the stranger) but not necessarily to family members themselves. In this passage, a variation is used to show just what it means for husbands to love their wives as Christ loves the church; it means that "husbands should love their wives as they do their own bodies." The author continues,

> He who loves his wife loves himself. For no one ever hates his own body, but he nourishes and tenderly cares for it, just as Christ does for the church, because we are members of his body. "For this reason a man will leave his father and mother and be joined to his wife, and the two will become one flesh." This is a great mystery. . . . (Eph. 5:29-32)

In short, husbands were to fulfill their servant roles by treating their wives equally to their own bodies.

One should conclude, I believe, that this text can be interpreted as fracturing the honor-shame codes of male conduct in the ancient world. It tried to do so within the patriarchal language game of antiquity. It also attempted to reconcile its view of male servanthood with the more egalitarian moments of the early Christian movement, but it accomplished this synthesis in an unstable way, leaving to posterity a passage difficult to interpret and susceptible to being read in a variety of ways. There is little doubt that it has been used quite frequently to bolster the crudest forms of Western patriarchal family ethics. It is unlikely, however, that such use was its original intent.

It is also clear that Aquinas's use of Ephesians was in keeping, for the most part, with its original spirit, if not its exact intent. Both Aquinas and

---

83. See, e.g., Gal. 5:14, James 2:8. The analogous Golden Rule is found twice: Matt. 7:12, Luke 6:31.

Ephesians address two different but overlapping versions of the male problematic. They may have supplied Western society with its most powerful statements as to why men should marry, stay married for a lifetime, treat their wives with respect, and serve the welfare of their children. As this powerful symbol of the marital relation declines in our culture, we must ask ourselves whether we will gradually sink back into a heroic ethic of dominance and submission or an even more archaic form of mammalian existence in which females raise children while males expansively sow their seeds with little or no paternal investment in their children.

If Aquinas and contemporary evolutionary ecology are correct, such a world is likely to be punctuated by intermittent fits of male jealousy, heightened domestic violence (which is not always the same as marital violence), male isolation from families, and lower states of child well-being. We must ask ourselves at this moment, when it seems that the last vestiges of this religious view of the family are losing their grip on the modern imagination and slipping into the safekeeping of books on library shelves, is this the condition of families we can expect for the indefinite future?

Some Tentative Proposals

So far my argument has been primarily historical. I have not asked whether the views I have described are right or wrong, good or bad. I simply have tried to tell the story of Christian family theory from a fresh perspective — from the perspective of how it coped with the male problematic. But has this led to a one-sided picture? Is not this entire story too oriented to the male point of view or, at least, the male problematic? Furthermore, is sacrificial love the complete understanding of *agape?* If so, is it true that self-sacrifice is the final goal of the Christian life? Finally, if there is a male problematic, is there not also a female problematic, and what would Christian family theory say about this?

From the perspective of human evolutionary ecology, there is a female problematic, but it is less well understood. If males have an inherited tendency to follow, under some conditions, the cad strategy of reproductive fitness, females, under some conditions, may have tendencies to raise children without paternal participation. This was, after all, the original mammalian condition — mothers raising children more or less on their own. Whereas fathers may have tendencies to drift away from their women and children, mothers may have tendencies, if other supports are in place, to drift away from fathers. For different reasons, mothers may need to value more the contributions of fathers and the importance of long-term (maybe lifelong) marital commitment, just as fathers may need to value more their wives and children.

Is the symbolism of Christ's marriage to the church a model of sacrificial love for wives and mothers as well as husbands and fathers? Could a sense of participating in the cosmic drama of Christ's relation to the church function as a counter to the primal female problematic just as it did the primal male problematic? Is Christianity, and probably other forms of religion as well, in tension with short-term evolutionarily adaptive strategies in the name of certain long-term, and ultimately more fruitful, strategies? Are there inner-theological grounds for asserting that as the husband can represent Christ's sacrifice to the family, so can the wife?

But this raises a troubling point: most of contemporary theological feminism has resisted, for good reasons, models of Christian love that overemphasize the features of self-sacrifice. They have resisted identifying Christian love too completely with the symbolism of the cross. Would claiming that wives as well as husbands can enact the Christian drama mean that women once again would be asked to play the role of sacrificial worker, denying their own selfhood, their needs and potentials, and assuming the role of endless servant to the other members of the family?

There is little said in the Pauline writings, Ephesians, or Aquinas about whether wives can be to the family as Christ was to the church. The problem in these texts was not principally the wife but rather the husband. Especially was this true of Aquinas and to a lesser extent Ephesians, which addressed an honor-shame culture where men by definition were assigned power, agency, and control. Although women from wealthy families did divorce in Greek and Roman societies during Roman Hellenism, on the whole, it was a male prerogative, as were the prerogatives of the double sexual standard.

Although he does not elaborate on it, Paul does imagine the possibility of wives being unto their husbands and children as Christ was to the church. They too could enact the drama of agapic love of which Christ was the supreme example. In his first letter to the Corinthians, Paul advises people facing marital issues to remain in their present state. The unmarried should remain unmarried. The married should remain married. These recommendations were due to his eschatological expectations that the end of this world and the beginning of a new creation were about to occur. These instructions were not commandments from the Lord but his personal opinion, which he believed was "trustworthy." This held even for Christians married to non-Christians; they should not divorce, and if they separate, they should not remarry. He writes,

> [I]f any believer has a wife who is an unbeliever, and she consents to live with him, he should not divorce her. And if any woman has a husband who is an unbeliever, and he consents to live with her, she should not divorce him. For the unbelieving husband is made holy through his wife, and the unbelieving wife is made holy through her husband. (1 Cor. 7:13-14)

What is remarkable about this passage is the idea that the wife can "make holy" (some translations say "sanctify") the unbelieving husband. Does this mean that the wife can be like Christ, who sanctifies and makes holy the church? If so, this suggests that Paul could imagine how women can mediate Christ's transforming and self-giving love to the family. Women too can participate in the christic drama.

In light of this possibility, I offer three suggestions for the reconstruction of Christian family theory. This reconstruction, I would claim, is consistent with the genius of Christian family theory and is little more than a systematic ordering, in light of contemporary conditions, of what is already there. Furthermore, I hope to order what is there as a general philosophy of marriage that might be attractive to people who do not consider themselves Christians. In short, I handle the Christian tradition as a classic of Western culture — a classic, like most classics, that may contain a deep wisdom of general significance beyond the confines of those confessional communities that call themselves Christian. Since Christian family theory has influenced many aspects of Western culture from law and imaginative literature to the visual arts, its deep truth should be of interest far beyond the confines of confessional Christian bodies.

My suggestions are as follows. First, both husbands and wives should take part in the drama of sacrificial or self-giving love needed to energize families for lifelong commitments. Second, sacrificial love is not the whole of love, even in the Christian tradition. Sacrificial love is an important moment within a wider context of love as equal regard. The appropriate relation of sacrificial love and love as equal regard can be stated in ways both consistent with the Christian tradition and philosophically adequate for a general theory of love within marriage. Third, to keep the proper balance between love as sacrificial and love as equal regard, it is useful to see love and marriage as life-cycle phenomena in which love takes slightly different forms depending on where a family is in its cycle. The brief words about these points which follow should be seen more as an agenda for further work than as a finished theology or philosophy of marriage.

With regard to the first point, we have already seen that there are grounds within the Christian tradition for saying that both husbands and wives can perform the christic drama. This means that both husbands and wives are called to moments of self-sacrifice, endurance, commitment, and forgiveness. For those who can step into the cosmic drama, as Christians are called to do, this may prove to be a great privilege and a source of strength. According to much of the Christian tradition, it endows the sacrificial moment with the power of the divine. Some theologians would argue that true and lasting self-sacrifice is not genuinely possible without participation in the divine power and vision, while other more liberal Christians can conceive of degrees of sacrificial love as standing independently of participation in this divine drama. I will not settle that issue here. Whether or not this is possible, however, it seems clear that no married relationship can survive over the long term without the husband and wife possessing some capacity for self-sacrifice. Needs of individual family members never totally synchronize, never completely fit. No matter what the degree of reciprocal altruism, something like this deeper capacity to love without the assurance of immediate return seems required. Both men and women, both husbands and wives, must have this capacity.

The male problematic may be particularly threatening to family commitment because it can, so easily, let slip the commitment to both wife and child. But the female problematic, with its easier commitment to the child but more ambiguous commitment to the husband, must also be acknowledged. Both parties must be inducted into a culture, religious or nonreligious, that celebrates the capacity for self-giving love — the capacity to extend commitment beyond the immediacies of reciprocal altruism as such. It is clear that in its classic expressions (Aquinas and Luther), Christian family theory, like much of the family theory of the ancient world, reinforced most of the conditions necessary for male marital and parental commitment — paternal certainty, monogamy, sexual exchange, and reciprocal helpfulness. What it added to all these elements, in addition to its blessing, was the understanding of love as *agape* and the drama of Christ's love for the church as a paradigm for the love of parents for one another and their children.

With regard to the second point, this much should be said now. Sacrificial love is an important element in Christian love as it is also for a love adequate for the demands of marriage. But it is not the whole of love in either context. It is more accurate to conceive of Christian love as a challenging requirement of equal regard of the kind expressed in the love command, "You shall love your neighbor as yourself" (Matt. 22:39). Christian ethicists have for generations studied the logic of this command. It is now widely agreed that the love command does not, first of all, require a life of perpetual self-sacrifice, self-abnegation, or self-denial. Neighbor love and its analogous Golden Rule ("so whatever you wish that men would do to you, do so to them"; Matt. 7:12) both mean something else. The Catholic moral theologian Louis Janssens gives us an insightful interpretation when he writes, "Love of neighbor is impartial. It is fundamentally an equal regard for every person, because it applies to each neighbor qua human existent."[84] "Valuing the self as well as others remains a manifest obligation" of the principle of neighbor love, according to Janssens.[85]

We saw a modified formulation of neighbor love in the midst of Ephesians 5:21-33. Remember verses 28-29: "In the same way, husbands should love their wives as they do their own bodies. He who loves his wife loves himself. For no one ever hates his own body, but he nourishes and tenderly cares for it, just as Christ does for the church, because we are members of his body." This remarkable passage demonstrates the close relation of the symbol of Christ's union with the church and neighbor love as models of Christian love in marriages. The husband loves his wife in the way he loves his own body. According to the extension that we are developing, the wife too should love her husband in the way she loves her own body.

Even in this passage, it is assumed that the husband has a natural inclination and right to cherish and nourish his own body. Even in this passage, considered to be the great passage in the Christian heritage that calls for sacrificial love in marriage, we have a full legitimation of the right of self-regard. Hence, self-regard is built into the principle of neighbor love; it is part of its logic to give equal regard to both the neighbor and the self *qua* existents — *qua* humans made in the image of God.

How then does the call for sacrificial love — for long-term endurance in marriage through hard times and even at some cost to the self — become a factor in marriage if we take this tradition seriously? Is there room for sacrifice within *agape* when it is first interpreted as equal regard?

---

84. Louis Janssens, "Norms and Priorities of a Love Ethics," *Louvain Studies* 6 (Spring 1977): 219.

85. Janssens, "Norms and Priorities of a Love Ethics," p. 220.

Janssens has a suggestive proposal. He holds that self-sacrifice is in fact not the ideal of the Christian life. Instead, love as mutuality and equal regard is the ideal, and sacrificial love, important as it is, is derived from equal regard. For Janssens, self-sacrifice is "justified derivatively" from the other-regard built into love as equal regard.[86] We sacrifice for the other, extend ourselves, and go the second mile not because self-sacrifice as such is the end of love, either within or outside of marriage. Rather, we do these things not as ends in themselves but to restore our relations with our spouses, and others, to the more ideal state of equal regard.

Christian realism holds that we live in a world of finitude and sin, and as long as this is true, perfect mutuality and equal regard will not prevail. There will always be degrees of imbalance, inequality, and injustice in relations, in and outside of marriage. Self-sacrifice is not in itself the goal of the Christian life. It is, rather, a transitional obligation designed to restore broken relations to mutuality once again. This self-sacrifice was first of all charged to the male in both Ephesians and Aquinas. But in both contexts, neighbor love as equal regard (with a genuine role for self-regard) is the larger context of meaning.

Because of the challenge, the strain, the near impossibility of this sacrificial moment, the Christian tradition has offered an additional resource — the belief that this sacrificial moment in marriage (with all of its attendant features of forgiveness, patience, and renewal) can participate in a deeper cosmic drama rooted in the divine life and manifest in Christ's love for the church. Husbands were first of all invited to participate in this drama, partially, I think, because of intuitions about the male problematic. It is a natural extension of beliefs implicit in the Christian story to offer this invitation to wives. For those who cannot accept this belief in this cosmic drama, either as reality or symbol, it is their task to find other grounds for justifying the sacrificial moment within a wider concept of love as equal regard.

Third, I am aware that love as equal regard seems to leave behind the biological and developmental features borrowed from evolutionary ecology and found, in pre-scientific form, in Aquinas and Aristotle. But we have not completely left behind this world. The sacrificial moment required from both husband and wife is there precisely, according to this model, to temper both the male and the female problematic, as different as they are. Love as equal regard, with its sacrificial moment, may help order the asymmetries of our reproductive strategies. Evolutionary ecology

---

86. Janssens, "Norms and Priorities of a Love Ethics," p. 228.

helps us understand the archeology of desire that fuels male and female behavior and that our religio-cultural symbols, when they have functioned well, have served to transform and redirect.

But evolutionary ecology has more to offer our constructive reflections. It also tells us that humans have a life cycle. It tells us that our evolutionarily grounded potentialities, in interaction with our environments and cultures, develop and subside in phases. These phases are marked with various tasks, opportunities, and responsibilities which must be met if our intertwined life cycles are to be strong and healthy.

Equal regard, as a model of marital love, can be fine-tuned when articulated within a theory of the marital life cycle. David Gutmann has shown us in *Reclaimed Powers* that throughout the world marriages entail an exchange of roles. He studied in depth Mayan, Navajo, and Druze societies and made observations about modern societies as well. In all societies he discovered that the active and protective roles of husbands generally last only through the period of the "parental emergency," during which mothers and infants are vulnerable and dependent.[87] As infants grow into maturity, women become more active, even agentive, and husbands relinquish their active and protective roles. Men become more contemplative, even religious. Women become, if social circumstances permit, more involved in work, community, and the wider family.

The human life cycle in families entails a reversal of roles, a kind of life-cycle process of taking turns. Potentialities that husbands or wives may sacrifice at one stage in life may be explored and reclaimed at another stage in life. Sacrifices, in the societies that Gutmann studied, were transitional. Equality was something achieved not so much moment by moment but over the life cycle as a whole.

What would this mean for a theory of marital love formed by Christian sensitivities? It would mean that husbands and wives should understand the rhythms of equal regard and self-sacrifice. Clearly, the principle of equal regard would be the pervasive guide to their attitudes and actions. But it may mean that for a moment, one or the other partner will carry a special role, delay the development of a talent or gift, take time out to give birth, or ask for leave from work to care for a child — with the trust that at later moments in the marital life cycle, a deeper actual equality will be restored. Sacrifice is not an end in itself but is what is done to contribute to an even deeper equal regard.

87. David Gutmann, *Reclaimed Powers: Toward a New Psychology of Men and Women in Later Life* (New York: Basic, 1987).

Furthermore, equal regard, when given a life-cycle interpretation, is an important guide for raising children. Raising children takes tremendous effort and some self-sacrifice. But it is important, even for the health of children, to realize that self-sacrifice alone cannot be the foundation of child care. Rather, self-sacrifice is what must be done to help children grow toward capacities for equal regard with others as well as their parents. Elements of equal regard must inform parental relations with children from the beginning, and acts of sacrifice should be constantly moderated as children's capacities for mutuality develop. Even here, sacrificial love is essential but serves the deeper goal of love as equal regard.

These brief constructive notes must remain incomplete. They are designed to illustrate how this tradition might be reconstructed both for Christians and for those who indirectly might learn from it. There are many issues that must be left untouched. These are the big issues that have plagued public debate — abortion, contraception, divorce, homosexuality, the limits of reproductive technology, the claims of biological parents in adoption, and so on. These important issues must be addressed if this theory can hold true.

As important as they are, however, these issues must not be allowed to wipe from consciousness this most basic discussion on the nature and meaning of marriage and the role that classic religious sources will play in informing this institution in the future. We may have tried for too long to address these sensational issues without fully developing our fundamental theories of marriage and family. I hope that these historical and constructive notes make a contribution to this deeper task.

Chapter 10

The Dialectic of Archaeology and Teleology in Christian Marriage Symbolism (2001)

This chapter not only illuminates why Christian marriage symbolism has such deep meaning to both men and women; it also throws light on the relation of science to religion. It was originally written for a festschrift for Professor Phillip Hefner, a leading contributor to the contemporary dialogue between science and religion.

It uses the work of the great French philosopher Paul Ricoeur to argue that all symbols have a double meaning — an explicit direction and an implicit (maybe even unconscious) background, that is, a teleology that reshapes an archaic archeology even as it is influenced by that archeology. To understand the meaning and work of a powerful religious symbol such as Christian marriage requires understanding its teleology (the world of meaning that is opened up to the believer) as well as its archeology (the fund of desires and tendencies that both contribute to the symbol and are reshaped by the symbol's direction).

This chapter further contends that science can throw light on the archeology of desire that is projected into a symbol but cannot itself uncover its teleology — its meaning. That requires an act of hermeneutics — an act of interpretation. It is precisely the virtue of critical hermeneutics or hermeneutic realism that it attends to both the realism of the archeology that science can illuminate and the possible truth and meaning of the teleology that hermeneutics can open. We can understand even better the work of the symbol by understanding the dialectical relation between its archeology and its teleology. The symbolism of Christian marriage illustrates this claim.

This chapter repeats material on Thomas Aquinas that appeared in the last chapter. Aquinas, as the reader will notice, appears frequently in these essays, but the different contexts of my use of him should prove illuminating. This chapter extends, and makes more central, brief remarks advanced earlier about the theory of symbolism in Paul Ricoeur. But this essay is much more explicit on the subject of the nature of Christian symbols and the relation of science and religion. Making these points more emphatically helps convey a message that I cannot repeat enough. To introduce the biological motivations brought to a religious symbol should not mean remaining at the biological level in interpreting the symbol's final meaning. Biology does not dominate the final transformative work of the symbol and its surrounding narrative. But biology does inform the meaning of the symbol even if it does not dominate the entire meaning. In the last analysis, the meaning of the symbol is revealed by attending to what the text and context uncover about both the desires brought to the symbol and the direction — the teleology — toward which the symbol transforms our basic motivations.

This essay is about three interrelated subjects. It is first about a theory of religious symbolism, that is, how religious symbols function to integrate mature and immature aspects of the human psyche. They do this, I will argue, by compensating or balancing certain tendencies of our immature selves. The meaning of the religious symbol cannot be fully understood unless the interpreter has insight into the archeology of immaturity for which the symbol is compensating.

Second, I want to illustrate this theory of symbolism by analyzing an important expression of the Christian theology of marriage, the views of Thomas Aquinas. I will demonstrate how Aquinas reveals the compensatory nature of religious symbolism. He does this by conceiving of the sacrificial love of Christ for the church as a model for male behavior and a balance for males' reluctance to bond with their children and wives.

Third, I will contend that this view of symbolism throws light on at least one way of understanding the relation of religion and science, a subject to which Philip Hefner has made significant contributions. There are several approaches to conceptualizing this relation; one of these centers on the idea that science, at least in the form of evolutionary psychology, helps us understand the archeology of religious symbols.

Ricoeur on Religious Symbolism

I will develop my argument by employing Paul Ricoeur's understanding of the relation of archeology and teleology in religious and artistic symbols. Ricoeur, in *Freud and Philosophy* and other writings, argued that in order to interpret a symbol one must understand the unconscious archeology of desire that is brought to the symbol and, to some extent, transformed by the symbol.[1] A symbol, he argued, has a "mixed language" containing a primitive archeology based on natural inclinations as well as a teleology that points toward the object of love that works to transform these inclinations or desires.[2] Ricoeur thought that the language of dreams, interpreted in part by the naturalism of Freud's theory of instinctual energies, was a way of capturing this human archeology of desire.[3]

Ricoeur developed his understanding of the dialectical relation of archeology and teleology in symbolism through a reworking of Freud's theories of identification and sublimation.[4] Desire construes the object of love through the mechanisms of projection. But Ricoeur uses Hegel's concept of "reduplication of consciousness" to suggest that the object of desire also shapes the desiring consciousness.[5] To say it simply, we love our parents, but in our effort to maintain our attachment to them, we internalize their images and in the process actually become like them. This process modifies our desires. It is in this way that the objects of our desires, including divine objects, transform our archeologies of love and carry us beyond our original wishes. The religious symbol, when adequately interpreted, reveals this tension between the archeology of the original wish and the teleology of the object toward which our desires are transformed. In mature symbols, teleology is dominant over the archeology of desire; in more regressive symbols, the archeology of the immature wish wins over the teleology of the object.

Ricoeur's theory of the symbol reveals what philosophers of science call a critical realist epistemology. On the one hand, the archeology of human desire — what Ricoeur sometimes calls the "embodied cogito" — is known only through its inherited language games.[6] From another perspective, Ricoeur retains the naturalism and realism of Freud's rather thin

---

1. Paul Ricoeur, *Freud and Philosophy* (New Haven, Conn.: Yale University Press, 1971).
2. Ricoeur, *Freud and Philosophy,* pp. xii, 65-67, 149-51.
3. Ricoeur, *Freud and Philosophy,* pp. 159-63.
4. Ricoeur, *Freud and Philosophy,* pp. 478-83.
5. Ricoeur, *Freud and Philosophy,* p. 461.
6. Ricoeur, *Freud and Philosophy,* pp. 42-47.

theory of libido. According to Ricoeur, we know our libidinous desires only through the mediations of language, but nonetheless it is precisely these natural strivings that language and symbol in fact reveal, although often in clouded and indirect ways.[7] In what follows, I will retain the outlines of Ricoeur's theory of religious symbol, but I will alter and expand his theory of desire through the use of the newly emerging discipline of evolutionary psychology. I will look at desire, not from the standpoint of Ricoeur's use of Freud, but from the thicker view of desire now emerging in the empirical and theoretical work of evolutionary psychology.

Marriage Symbolism in Thomas Aquinas

To analyze this dialectic of archeology and teleology in Christian symbolism, I start with the theology of marriage advanced by Thomas Aquinas. Along with Augustine's "The Good of Marriage,"[8] Aquinas's writings on marriage in the Supplement to the *Summa Theologica*[9] and the *Summa Contra Gentiles*[10] give expression to central themes in Western marriage theology.

Aquinas saw marriage as both a natural and a supernatural institution. We generally concentrate on the supernatural or, using the language of Ricoeur, the teleological features of marriage when we think of the contributions of Aquinas. Marriage, for Aquinas, was a supernatural sacrament modeled on the "indissoluble union of Christ and the Church."[11] This sacramental permanence — this teleology, so to speak — sticks in our mind when we first think of Aquinas on marriage.

But to leave our understanding of Aquinas on matrimony here is to grasp the teleological dimension of his view at the neglect of its archeology. Aquinas had a rich naturalistic theory of human motivation and family formation that constituted the background to the symbolism of his sacramental understanding of marriage. When rightly interpreted, Aquinas's marriage theology should be viewed as a symbolic narrative

---

7. Ricoeur, *Freud and Philosophy,* pp. 47-54.

8. Augustine, "The Good of Marriage," in *Treatises on Marriage and Other Subjects,* trans. Charles T. Wilcox et al., ed. Roy J. Deferrari, vol. 15 of The Writings of Saint Augustine (New York: Fathers of the Church, 1955), pp. 4-31.

9. Thomas Aquinas, Supplement to *The Summa Theologica,* trans. English Dominican Fathers, repr. ed. (New York: Benzinger Brothers, 1948), 3 (hereafter *Supplement*).

10. Thomas Aquinas, *Summa Contra Gentiles,* vol. 3, pt. 2 (London: Burns, Oates, and Washbourne, 1928).

11. Aquinas, *Summa Contra Gentiles,* vol. 3, pt. 2, p. 117.

about overcoming male reluctance to bond to infant and mother. It is as much about this as it is about marriage as a supernatural and unbreakable sacrament. Aquinas's marriage symbolism addresses and overcomes what I call the "male problematic."

Aquinas's marriage and family theory depends, in part, on several crucial observations based on the comparative biology of his day, primarily the work of Aristotle and commentary on Aristotle in the writings of Albertus Magnus. These observations constitute the archeology of his marriage symbolism and are surprisingly similar to contemporary evolutionary psychological views of the asymmetrical reproductive strategies of males and females. For example, in the Supplement to the *Summa Theologica,* Aquinas writes that humans share with all animals an inclination to have offspring. Then he introduces a very modern-sounding distinction. He writes,

> Yet nature does not incline thereto in the same way in all animals; since there are animals whose offspring are able to seek food immediately after birth, or are sufficiently fed by their mother; and in these there is no tie between male and female; whereas in those whose offspring needs the support of both parents, although for a short time, there is a certain tie, as may be seen in certain birds. In man, however, since the child needs the parents' care for a long time, there is a very great tie between male and female, to which tie even the generic nature inclines.[12]

Aquinas believed that humans form families because of the long period of dependency of their infants. The human female, he insisted, is "far from sufficing alone for the rearing of children, since the needs of human life require many things that one person alone cannot provide."[13] For this reason, it is "in keeping with human nature that the man remain with the woman after coition, and not leave her at once, indulging in promiscuous intercourse. . . ."[14]

This last quote suggests, as both William James and Mary Midgely have so cogently argued, that human beings (especially human males) are creatures of multiple impulses that conflict with one another.[15] Aquinas

---

12. Aquinas, Supplement, q. 41, a. 1.

13. Aquinas, Supplement, q. 41, a. 1.

14. Aquinas, Supplement, q. 41, a. 1.

15. William James, *The Principles of Psychology,* vol. 2 (New York: Dover, 1951), pp. 383-441; Mary Midgley, *Beast and Man* (Ithaca, N.Y.: Cornell University Press, 1978), pp. 261-66.

recognized that under certain conditions, males have inclinations to form families and assist females in raising children; but they also have inclinations toward promiscuity and the production of offspring with different mates. In the *Summa Contra Gentiles,* he writes that males have inclinations "to indulge at will in the pleasure of copulation, even as in the pleasure of eating," to "fight with one another for access to females," and to "resist another's intercourse with their consort."[16]

Aquinas also had a theory about what evolutionary psychologists today call "paternal certainty" and the role it plays in forming monogamous relations between males and females. He held that human males have an inclination or "instinct" to know that the child that they care for is their actual biological offspring. For evolutionary psychology, paternal certainty is less an instinct than it is a condition for a male's investment in raising children born to his consort. Nonetheless, let us hear the words of Aquinas: "Man naturally desires to be assured of his offspring: and this assurance would be altogether nullified in the case of promiscuous copulation. Therefore, the union of one man with one woman comes from a natural instinct."[17]

Of course, even within the terms of Thomas's own argument, this union cannot be seen as a result of any one instinct; rather, it is the result of a compromise and reorganization of a wide range of inclinations which enhance multiple satisfactions pertaining to sexual exchange, the rearing of dependent infants, safety, and the sense that the children cared for are also extending the substance of one's life. Although Aquinas had no concept of what evolutionary psychology calls "inclusive fitness," he did hold that fathers care for their children as a way of enhancing their own immortality. With a distinctively masculine bias typical of his day, he writes, "since the natural life which cannot be preserved in the person of an undying father, is preserved, by a kind of succession, in the person of the son, it is naturally befitting that the son succeed in things belonging to the father."[18]

Aristotle was the source of some of Aquinas's thinking on these matters. In one place Aristotle wrote, "in common with other animals and with plants, mankind have a natural desire to leave behind them an image of themselves."[19] He believed the sense that a child is an extension of the parent is crucial for the development of parental, especially paternal, care.

16. Aquinas, *Summa Contra Gentiles,* vol. 3, pt. 2, p. 17.

17. Aquinas, *Summa Contra Gentiles,* vol. 3, pt. 2, p. 118.

18. Aquinas, *Summa Contra Gentiles,* vol. 3, pt. 2, p. 114.

19. Aristotle, *Politics,* in *The Basic Works of Aristotle,* ed. Richard McKeon (New York: Random House, 1941), bk. 1, chap. 2.

Although Aquinas agreed with Aristotle on this matter, he also believed that this parental recognition was easier to achieve for females than for males. In holding this, he anticipated insights held by evolutionary psychology into conditions needed in the history of evolution for human males to connect with families. He wrote,

> In every animal species where the father has a certain care for his offspring, the one male has but one female, as may be seen in birds, where both unite in feeding their young. On the other hand where the male animal has not the care of the offspring, we find indifferently union of one male with several females, or of one female with several males: such is the case with dogs, hens, and so forth.[20]

In short, Thomas believed that paternal investment in offspring, paternal certainty, and monogamy — all three — tend to go together. But these for him were not the only natural conditions for family formation. Mutual helpfulness between a male and a female[21] and sexual exchange also contributed, he believed, to family formation and permanence.[22]

Ethics and Narrative in Thomas's Family Theory

Aquinas's theory of marriage does not remain at the biological level, as important as it is. There are, in fact, three levels to his argument: the premoral, moral, and narrative levels.[23] The biological discussion reveals what moral philosophers call the premoral goods of matrimony — the ones discussed above such as the goods sought by the dependent infant, the good of parents caring for a being that extends their lives, the good of mutual helpfulness, and the good of sexual exchange. A more properly moral argument for his theory of marriage emerges when Aquinas argues for the superiority of monogamy over polyandry (one woman marrying several men) and polygyny (one man marrying several women). Aquinas rejects polyandry because paternal care is diluted; fathers invest less in children when they do not know whether any given child is theirs.[24] On

---

20. Aquinas, *Summa Contra Gentiles,* vol. 3, pt. 2, p. 118.

21. Aquinas, Supplement, q. 41, a. 1.

22. Aquinas, Supplement, q. 64.

23. Don Browning, *A Fundamental Practical Theology* (Minneapolis: Fortress, 1991), pp. 105-9.

24. Aquinas, *Summa Contra Gentiles,* vol. 3, pt. 2, p. 118.

the other hand, he acknowledges that polygyny can provide a degree of paternal certainty and is likely to enlist a modicum of paternal investment in offspring.

But Aquinas's major criticism of polygyny is advanced as a moral rather than a quasi-biological argument based on the enhancement of premoral goods. Polygyny is rejected by Aquinas because it is simply an unjust institution. He writes,

> Besides. Equality is a condition of friendship . . . were it lawful for a man to have several wives, the friendship of a wife for her husband would not be freely bestowed, but servile as it were. And this argument is confirmed by experience; since where men have several wives, the wives are treated as servants.[25]

Aquinas believed that women are made in the image of God just as are men, although he did think women were less perfectly made in this image. Nonetheless, they were sufficiently close in dignity to men to be friends with their husbands. Thus, for Thomas, monogamy made possible a new level of care and investment by fathers for their children but also a new level of equality and friendship between wives and husbands.

The third level of his argument for monogamy is what I will call the narrative level and is the symbolic gathering together of the earlier lines of argument. This is the level that best illustrates the compensatory function of religious symbols — the subtle way they interweave archeology and teleology, the immature and the mature. In Aquinas's terms, this is the level of supernatural grace and sacrament, but it is also the level where the narrative and symbolism of Christ's sacrificial death is used as an analogy to the role required of Christian husbands and fathers in their families.

Even here, however, the biological dimensions of the argument shine through. These are evident in Thomas's belief that the male-female tie that infant dependency calls into existence must last longer than just a few years. It must last, he believed, for life. In fact, he argued that it must be indissoluble. But its indissolubility has a purpose, and this purpose is to overcome simultaneously human infant vulnerability, human male ambivalence about paternal investment, and a mother's vulnerability in the face of the demands of infant care.

Chapter 123 of the *Summa Contra Gentiles* is a key text on the indissolubility of monogamous marriage, and its arguments — including an analy-

---

25. Aquinas, *Summa Contra Gentiles,* vol. 3, pt. 2, p. 118.

sis of natural human inclinations, a theory of friendship between the sexes, and a rendering of the narrative implications of the divine revelation — make use of all three of these levels we have discussed. To begin with, Aquinas explains that there are in humans some natural, although unstable, inclinations toward indissoluble monogamy, which should be consolidated by human law and perfected by divine revelation. The naturalistic argument is stated from the male point of view but can be restated from the perspective of both sexes, as I have attempted to do elsewhere.[26] Aquinas also argues for the sacramental permanence of marriage. Some of his arguments have to do with paternal investment; for instance, fathers should care for their children indefinitely just as they do for their own bodies; children are highly dependent and need care for a very long time; impermanent conjugal arrangements lead to paternal neglect.

Some of Aquinas's arguments for marital permanence are more distinctively moral. They have to do with husbands' obligations to treat wives as friends, as we have seen. They also involve the duty of a husband not to exploit his wife's various vulnerabilities, some the result of the burdens of childbirth, and others — as was always the case in those days — the result of women's financial dependence.[27]

Aquinas's final argument for the indissolubility of marriage is the cornerstone of his symbolic and sacramental view. It is the command for Christian fathers and husbands to reenact the paradigm of Christ's sacrificial love in their relation to wives and children. This shows how narratives about divine action were seen by Aquinas both to supplement and to balance natural inclinations; both human law and divine revelation build on the regularities of natural inclinations yet remedy their ambivalence and excesses. Divine laws (and the symbols that express them) not only express "the instinct of nature, but they also supply the defect of natural instinct."[28] Or to say it differently, divine laws build on natural inclinations yet compensate and balance them toward a higher maturity.

It is important to focus on the dramatic features of Aquinas's sacramental symbolism; it invites imitation or participation in an archetypal pattern of divine action. This drama depends on the Ephesians 5:20-33 passage that first stated the analogy between matrimony and the sacrificial love of Christ for the church. Thomas is addressing this dimension

26. My colleagues and I extend the argument to wives and mothers in *From Culture Wars to Common Ground: Religion and the American Family Debate,* second ed. (Louisville: Westminster John Knox, 2000 [1997]), pp. 126-28.

27. Aquinas, *Summa Contra Gentiles,* vol. 3, pt. 2, pp. 114-16.

28. Aquinas, *Summa Contra Gentiles,* vol. 3, pt. 2, p. 116.

when he writes, "Although Matrimony is not conformed to Christ's Passion as regards pain, it is as regards charity, whereby He suffered for the church who was to be united to Him as His spouse."[29]

Aquinas's use of Ephesians to call for male sacrificial love and endurance in families should be understood in dialectical relation to his archeology of male sexual adventurism, male insecurity about paternal investment, the needs of dependent human infants and children, and the vulnerability of mothers when faced with the physical, emotional, and material demands of raising children. There is a range of relative goods at stake in the faithfulness of males. The logic of the recapitulation by the Christian man of the sacrificial love of God functioned in Thomas's mind to compensate for male ambivalence about commitment to these values. I use the word "ambivalence" because there are other natural tendencies in males which the sacrificial commitment was thought to build on and extend.

There is little doubt that Aquinas retains, in a qualified way, some of the patriarchy present in Ephesians 5:23. Both Ephesians and Aquinas are carriers of a "love paternalism" — a chastened patriarchy that also emphasizes male responsibility, commitment, and care. Yet to fail to place the symbolic dialectic of the servant husband against the background of Aquinas's analysis of the male problematic is to ignore the potential richness of his marital symbolism, both in the history of Western thought and even for today. Is it possible that Aquinas formulated in a systematic way a powerful religio-cultural symbolic that reinforced and guided unsteady male inclinations that are naturally but ambivalently oriented toward paternal investment and monogamy?

Aquinas's view of Christ's love as a symbol and model for the love of husband and father is classically religious. It illustrates Mircea Eliade's widely respected phenomenology of the sacred, making matrimony a recapitulation of divine acts in their creation of sacred space and time.[30] The symbol of Christ's steadfast love for the church becomes, as Ricoeur calls it, a "figure of the spirit" attracting inchoate male inclinations and shaping them into a new organization — an organization that is possibly even more satisfying for men, more productive for children, and more just to wives than the more archaic strategy.[31]

---

29. Aquinas, Supplement, q. 42, a. 1.

30. Mircea Eliade, *The Sacred and the Profane* (New York: Harper and Row, 1961).

31. Ricoeur, *Freud and Philosophy*, pp. 462-69.

Aquinas and the Modern Situation

Aquinas's analysis of the male problematic is consistent with contemporary insights from the social sciences and evolutionary psychology on male ambivalence about families but also their potential contribution to families. From a sociological perspective, the most dramatic change in families throughout the modern world is the growing absence of biological fathers from families and children. In many third-world countries, especially in sub-Saharan Africa and the Caribbean, father absence is even more dramatic than in Western industrial societies and is an active factor in producing poverty in these countries. In industrial countries, this trend is integrally related to another, namely, the move toward mothers — with the help of increased reliance on the wage economy, the government, and various informal networks — raising their children without significant presence of a father. Today, at least half of all children under eighteen will spend some time in a single-parent home, generally the mother's.[32] A third will spend as much as six years without residential presence of their fathers. The absence of fathers, plus their failure on average to pay adequate child support, has been cited as a leading factor associated with child poverty, mounting rates of violent crime, the declining health of children, and their decreased performance in school.[33]

Massive new evidence suggests that an absent father is not easy to replace. Research by Sarah McLanahan, Gary Sandefur, and others shows that children raised without both of their parents in the home — whether this is the result of divorce, single-parenthood, or living in a stepfamily — are two to three times more likely to have babies out of wedlock or have difficulties in school, job placement, and marriage formation. Equalizing financial resources only cuts these likely outcomes by one-half.[34]

Of course, there are many other factors producing father absence in addition to male inclinations not to bond. Fathers were pulled out of the home-based economy in the nineteenth century when they joined the wage economy. Women were made far less dependent on men, even the fathers of their children, when they too in the twentieth century joined the

32. Larry Bumpass and James Sweet, "Children's Experience in Single-Parent Families," *Family Planning Perspectives* 21 (November-December 1980): 256-60.

33. Nicholas Zill and Charlotte Schoenborn, "Developmental, Learning, and Emotional Problems: Health of Our Nation's Children," *Advance Data* (November 16, 1990), pp. 8-9.

34. Sara McLanahan and Gary Sandefur, *Growing Up with a Single Mother* (Cambridge, Mass.: Harvard University Press, 1994), pp. 1, 78-94.

wage economy and began earning their own incomes.[35] Western individualism, interacting with the forces of a market economy, has made men and women, husbands and wives, more concerned with their individual well-being and fulfillment.[36] But an accurate interpretation suggests that these cultural and social-systemic forces interact with, and indeed aggravate, male ambivalence about family formation — an ambivalence that historic Christian symbols tried to address and balance.

Modern evolutionary psychology throws light on the male problematic and the natural conditions that reinforce male paternal investment. On this point, evolutionary psychology and the ancient sources used by Aquinas are in surprising agreement, regardless of other differences. Evolutionary psychology basically affirms Thomas's archeology, although certainly not his teleology. From Bronislaw Malinowski to the team of Martin Daly and Margo Wilson, these disciplines depict an asymmetry between mammalian males and females in their reproductive strategies. Females are viewed as more easily knowing that the infant they birth is theirs and as expanding high energy in conception and birth. Males, on the other hand, do not expend energy in childbirth, are less certain that the infant of their partner is actually theirs, are more experimental sexually, and are more tentative about their commitments to offspring and partners.[37] Yet the long period of human infant dependency and the mother's need for assistance constitute for these contemporary theories crucial natural reasons, just as Aquinas observed, for male involvement in the mother-infant dyad. But these fragile natural tendencies need the reinforcement of symbols and narratives of the kind Aquinas developed.

Conclusion

The task of remedying the disruptions of the modern family entails uncovering the archeology of the male ego. It also entails investigating once again the great cultural symbols of the Western heritage that historically played a significant role in balancing that archeology.

35. Gary Becker, *A Treatise on the Family* (Cambridge, Mass.: Harvard University Press, 1991), pp. 356, 359.

36. Ron Lesthaeghe, "A Century of Demographic and Cultural Change in Western Europe," *Population and Development Review* 9, no. 3 (September 1983): 429.

37. Bronislaw Malinowski, *The Sexual Life of Savages in North-Western Melanesia* (London: Routledge, 1929); Martin Daly and Margo Wilson, *Sex, Evolution, and Behavior* (Belmont, Calif.: Wadsworth, 1978), pp. 77-110.

But another task must not be forgotten, even though its analysis lies beyond the scope of this essay. That has to do with rehabilitating male responsibility in marriage and family within an ethic of what I often have called the "equal-regard marriage." Is it possible to have male responsibility without patriarchy? I believe that it is. I have investigated this possibility at length with my co-authors in *From Culture Wars to Common Ground: Religion and the American Family Debate*.[38] Equality in sexual relationships without male responsibility (the direction our culture may be going) will be an ambiguous accomplishment — and, in the end, no real equality at all. The religio-cultural task of our time is to create a symbolic and social environment that will do both — produce responsible fathers and husbands as well as men and women capable of an equal-regard marriage.

Chapter 11

Can Marriage Be Defined? (2002)

The meaning and definition of marriage was once more or less commonly assumed. Not anymore. There is a great debate in our society, and throughout the world, about the definition of marriage. Social scientists sometimes reduce it to its health-producing consequences. The legal profession often reduces marriage to its contractual dimensions, even sometimes its private contractual dimensions. Even churches tend to see marriage only in terms of its religious meaning — its covenantal or sacramental dimensions.

This chapter argues that marriage is a multidimensional reality and that all of these dimensions should be held in tension. I both follow and slightly extend the creative work of legal historian John Witte in his important *From Sacrament to Contract.** I claim marriage is a *natural institution* that builds on, satisfies, organizes, and directs a wide range of natural premoral inclinations of an affectional, sexual, and procreative kind. It is a *contractual* institution between two consenting persons. It is a *social* institution that contributes to the public welfare. It has commonly been seen as a *religious* institution with covenantal or even sacramental significance.

I add to this list that marriage should also be viewed — especially in modern societies — as a *communicative* relationship. High levels of communicative skills are required if modern men and women are to achieve marriages of equal regard — an equal regard that also works

---

*John Witte Jr., *From Sacrament to Contract: Marriage, Religion, and Law in the Western Tradition* (Louisville: Westminster John Knox, 1997).

to actualize with justice the premoral goods of marriage for couples as well as social goods for the wider society.

Although I do not make this point explicitly in this chapter, one can discern in my discussion of this multidimensional view of marriage (that is, its natural, contractual, social, religious, and communicative dimensions) rough analogies to my five dimensions of practical reason discussed in Chapter I (namely, the premoral, the obligational, the contextual, and the narrative dimensions, all communicated in a concrete marital praxis, the various rules and roles of marriage).

What is marriage? The inability of our society to answer this question has led to a variety of unfruitful maneuvers. The churches are inclined to reply to the question on entirely religious grounds, thereby obscuring the legal, financial, health, and social functions of marriage. Some social scientists justify marriage by demonstrating its health, wealth, and sexual benefits.[1] Many therapists and educators justify it by showing its dependence on good communication; in developing this point, they fail to realize that communicative skills increase chances for a good marriage only for those who are already committed to that goal and have some sense of what a good marriage is.[2] American law has increasingly defined marriage as a private contract between affectionate and independent consenting adults, thereby reinforcing romantic and individualistic views widely held in the general population.[3] Many marriage experts equate marriage with a relational process that makes it indistinguishable from friendship. Even church documents have tended to equate marriage with a variety of intimate relationships.[4]

1. Linda Waite, "Does Marriage Matter?" *Demography* 32, no. 4 (November 1995): 483-504.

2. Leading books in the marriage communication field are John Gottman, *Why Marriages Succeed or Fail* (New York: Simon and Schuster, 1994); H. Markman, S. Stanley, and S. Blumberg, *Fighting for Your Marriage* (San Francisco: Jossey-Bass, 1994); S. Stanley, D. Trathen, S. McCain, and M. Bryan, *A Lasting Promise* (San Francisco: Jossey-Bass, 1998).

3. Nancy F. Cott, *Public Vows* (Cambridge, Mass.: Harvard University Press, 2000), pp. 198-99.

4. See Daphne and Terence Anderson's review of the situation in Canada in "United Church of Canada: Kingdom Symbol or Lifestyle Choice," in *Faith Traditions and the Family*, ed. Phyllis D. Airhart and Margaret Lamberts Bendroth (Louisville: Westminster John Knox, 1996), pp. 126-42; see also *Keeping Body and Soul Together: Report to the 203rd General Assembly* (Presbyterian Church, U.S.A., 1991).

The confusion about the meaning and nature of marriage is profound and is having negative consequences within and outside the church. There is growing evidence that both the marriage rate and the absolute number of people married in our society — and in most societies throughout the world — are declining. The growth of cohabitation now appears to be a more serious problem than most of us thought only a few years ago. Large numbers of cohabitors do not go on to marry, are more likely to divorce if they do get married, often have children while cohabiting, are more unstable in their parental commitments, and hence contribute to the increasing insecurity of children in nonmarital arrangements.[5] Debates in both church and society about whether gays should be permitted to marry are only one small part of the total crisis of marriage. For these and other reasons, it is time for a major social and ecclesial discussion about the nature of marriage.

I argue that marriage is a multidimensional reality consisting of affectional, legal, financial, procreative, cultural, and religious realities. It should not be reduced to any one of these strands in spite of contemporary pressures to do so. This view of marriage is a challenge to the churches. They must learn to think theologically about the affectional, legal, financial, cultural, and procreative aspects of marriage. Law and secular society also must broaden their tendencies to think about only the psychological aspects, or the financial aspects, or the legal and contractual aspects. Marriage must be seen in its multidimensional entirety.

The many definitions and justifications for marriage advanced through the ages can be organized along a continuum between its communal and personal dimensions. The march of history increasingly has subordinated the communal and elevated the personal, with the result that the idea of marriage as an institution has lost favor. Marriage is more and more viewed as an essentially private intersubjective agreement or "pure relationship" only incidentally sanctioned by state or church, if at all. In what follows, I argue that marriage historically has consisted of five dimensions, all of which are essential for an adequate understanding of marriage as both an institutional and an interpersonal reality. Marriage has been understood as consisting of natural, contractual, social, religious, and communicative dimensions.[6] Although its personal dimen-

---

5. Linda Waite, "The Negative Effects of Cohabitation," *The Responsive Community* (Winter 1999): 31-38.

6. For a similar list, see Council on Families in America, *Marriage in America: A Report to the Nation* (New York: Institute for American Values, 1995), pp. 10-11; also see Witte, *From Sacrament to Contract*, p. 2.

sions were always present, marriage in the past has been defined primarily as a social institution. Because of the important individual and social goods connected with marriage and marriage-like arrangements, society in the form of general community, extended family, or formal state always has guided, legitimated, and monitored marriage.

What is unique about marriage in Western societies since the Protestant Reformation is that church, state, and civil society have cooperated with one another in promoting, sanctioning, and celebrating marriage. This complex orchestration of various social sectors in support of marriage is now coming apart. States, communities, and religious institutions must now decide whether to preserve this cooperative relation in the future. The meaning of each of these five dimensions has varied over time. Which dimension was viewed as central and which as more peripheral also has shifted. To ignore any one of these five elements does violence to the full meaning of marriage.

Marriage as Organizing Natural Inclinations

To say that marriage is a natural institution means it has been viewed as giving form to persistent yet sometimes conflicting natural inclinations and needs. There is no instinct for marriage, but it does organize a wide range of our natural tendencies by elevating some and de-emphasizing others. A variety of natural inclinations are ordered by marriage — the desire for sexual union, the desire Aristotle believed humans share with the animals "to leave behind them a copy of themselves,"[7] and, following Aristotle again, the need to "supply" humans with their "everyday wants."[8]

These perspectives on the natural purposes of marriage from Greek philosophy were absorbed, especially in the writings of Thomas Aquinas, into Christian commentary on the creation accounts of Genesis 1 and 2. Genesis tells humans to "be fruitful and multiply" (Gen. 1:28). It also teaches that humans were made for companionship: "It is not good for man to be alone" (Gen. 2:18). For these reasons marriage was created: "Therefore a man leaves his father and his mother and clings to his wife, and they become one flesh" (Gen. 2:24).

Since Thomas Aquinas (1225-74) — the great synthesizer of Aristotle

---

7. Aristotle, *Politics,* in *The Basic Works of Aristotle,* ed. Richard McKeon (New York: Random House, 1941), bk. 1, chap. 2.

8. Aristotle, *Politics,* bk. 1, chap. 2.

with the Judeo-Christian tradition — marriage often has been defined and justified on two grounds, one drawn from Christian interpretations of the Genesis creation narratives and the other from the naturalism of Aristotle.[9] In the hands of Christian theologians, the theology of creation provided the deeper context surrounding Aristotelian naturalism. But Aquinas crystallized what had been gradually developing for centuries, that is, a double language — one religious and one philosophical and naturalistic — used to explain, define, and justify marriage.

Much of the Christian tradition has interpreted the early chapters of Genesis both as divine revelation to a particular community and as a "classic" that reveals general truths about human nature, both for believing Christians and for the wider community.[10] This made it possible to interpret this revelatory classic in ways that informed both the inner life of the church and the public philosophy shaping law and general culture. In much of the Western religious tradition, the philosophical language used to justify marriage was considered vital for the clarification of the religious language. One can see this in perspectives as disparate as Thomas Aquinas, John Locke, and the Roman Catholic marriage encyclicals of Pope Leo XIII.[11] Both Locke and Leo developed arguments for the institution of marriage similar to the one first put forth by Aquinas. Matrimony, Aquinas taught, is the joining of the father to the mother-infant relation. This was needed because of the long period of needful dependency of the human infant and child — a dependency so extended as to require the material and educational labors over a long period of both mother and father.[12] Locke wrote, with special reference to humans, that "the Father, Who is bound to take care for those he hath begot, is under an Obligation to continue in Conjugal Society with the same Woman longer than other Creatures."[13]

9. For a discussion of how Aristotelian naturalism is contextualized within Jewish-Christian doctrines of creation, see Don Browning, Bonnie Miller-McLemore, Pamela Couture, Bernie Lyon, and Robert Franklin, *From Culture Wars to Common Ground: Religion and the American Family Debate* (Louisville: Westminster John Knox, 1997), pp. 113-24.

10. For the idea of the classic, see Hans-Georg Gadamer, *Truth and Method* (New York: Crossroad, 1982), pp. 253-58; also see Paul Ricoeur, *Hermeneutics and the Human Sciences* (Cambridge: Cambridge University Press, 1981), pp. 59-61, 62-100.

11. For Leo XIII's version of the argument, see his "Rerum Novarum," in *Proclaiming Justice and Peace: Papal Documents* (Mystic, Conn.: Twenty-Third Publications, 1991).

12. Thomas Aquinas, *The Summa Contra Gentiles,* bk. III, ii, chap. 122 (London: Burns, Oates, and Washbourne, 1928).

13. John Locke, "Second Treatise," in *Two Treatises of Government,* ed. Peter Laslett (Cambridge: Cambridge University Press, 1991), chap. 7, para. 80.

The existence and importance of this double language about marriage is a point generally lost on fundamentalist Christians, much of the general public, and many leading secular intellectuals, all of whom seem to believe that marriage is a uniquely religious practice. This is not true. Although I have illustrated its philosophical and naturalistic dimensions by referring to Aristotle and Locke, I could have done much the same by turning to Roman law. Even Luther, who ostensibly repudiated the double language of medieval Roman Catholicism, derived his core ideas about marriage from the Genesis doctrine of creation. Since it was an institution of God willed at creation, and not in its essence an instrument of salvation, he saw marriage as a public and social institution that should be registered and witnessed by the state even though also blessed by the churches.[14] It was not, for him, a distinctively religious or Christian institution.

Marriage as Contract

Second, because of the great natural affective, sexual, procreative, and economic goods involved in marriage, marriage has been seen in most societies as requiring the regulation of contracts. The parties involved in the contracts, however, have varied over time. In ancient societies, the contracts were viewed as primarily between the families or clans of the husband and wife, with little if any reinforcement from king, prince, legislation, or courts.

The medieval canon law of the Roman Catholic Church made an extremely important contribution to the development of marriage in Western societies; it established that marital contracts were activated by the free consent of husband and wife. This made illegal, before the eyes of the Church, the patriarchal arrangement of marriage done primarily for political and economic advantage. Uncoerced consent was so central in defining marriage that the medieval Roman Church required no witness by family, church, or state as essential for the legitimation of marriage. The free consent alone of a baptized Christian man and woman put into effect both the binding codes of Catholic canon law and the efficacy of supernatural grace. Canon law was an amalgamation of Christian teachings

---

14. For the desacramentalization of marriage in Luther, see Martin Luther, "The Bablylonian Captivity of the Church," in *Luther's Works* 36 (Philadelphia: Muhlenberg, 1959), pp. 92-96. On the administration of marriage turned to the state and the "left hand of God," see Witte, *From Sacrament to Contract*, p. 51.

with Roman and German legal traditions.[15] These privately established contracts elevated the role of mutual consent between husband and wife, weakened the power of extended family, and strengthened the authority of church courts. Because of the disarray of civil law and secular powers during these centuries, the administration of the natural, social, and sacramental dimensions of marriage was exercised by the Church.

Making consent crucial to the definition of marriage was a major accomplishment of the Roman Catholic Church during this era. But it had an unforeseen consequence. It gave rise to the phenomenon of "clandestine" or "secret" marriages — unwitnessed marriages that were often fraudulent, the result of manipulation and deception, and frequently disputed.[16]

Marital contracts became fully public in the Protestant Reformation when marriage was defined as first of all a social institution requiring registration and legitimation by the state but also one deserving the blessing and confirmation of the church.[17] The mutual consent of the couple, confirmation by family and friends, registration before the state, and the blessing of the church were viewed as an orchestrated whole. All were deemed important for a valid marriage.

These various witnesses and legitimating voices turned the marriage contract into a multidimensional covenant with many different parties. This complex covenant understanding of marriage, as legal historian John Witte has pointed out, was developed even more decisively by John Calvin.[18] The establishment of marriage as both public contract and covenant in Protestant countries gradually ended the practice of clandestine marriage, which was a phenomenon that reminds one of the confusions of cohabitation today.[19]

This view of the complex public nature of marriage held sway until the Enlightenment view of contract narrowed the relevant covenant parties needed for a good marriage. As a result of this narrowed view, marriage more and more came to be seen as a private agreement. The Enlightenment inheritance finally gave birth to the idea of marriage-like "pure

---

15. Witte, *From Sacrament to Contract,* pp. 36-38; James Brundage, *Law, Sex, and Christian Society in Medieval Europe* (Chicago: University of Chicago Press, 1987), pp. 325-416.

16. Brundage, *Law, Sex, and Christian Society,* pp. 189-91; Steven Ozment, *When Fathers Ruled* (Cambridge: Harvard University Press, 1983), pp. 25-31.

17. Witte, *From Sacrament to Contract,* p. 51.

18. Witte, *From Sacrament to Contract,* p. 112; see also John Witte Jr., *Law and Protestantism* (Cambridge: Cambridge University Press, 2002), p. 232.

19. Lawrence Stone, *Road to Divorce: England 1530-1987* (Oxford: Oxford University Press, 1990), pp. 96-120.

relationships," as sociologist Anthony Giddens calls them, that are independent of the constraints of both public contract and the central tendencies of nature.[20]

Marriage as a Social Good

Third, marriage has been seen as a social good. The health of marriage and family, especially in their child-rearing functions, often has been seen as essential for the good of the larger society. Without marriage and strong families, Aristotle believed, children would grow up violent and the wider social fabric would be damaged. He taught that affection between children and invested natural parents inhibits the violent impulses of both adult and child. These restraining functions would decline, he predicted, if the stability and commitment of parents were weakened.[21] The Lutheran Reformation, however, gave us the most emphatic statement of the social view of marriage. Marriage, Luther taught, was not a sacrament for salvation but an institution given by God at the foundations of creation for the good of couples, children, society, state, schools, and common social life.[22]

One of the clearest manifestations of the social view of marriage was the Anglican commonwealth model that developed in England from the sixteenth to the late nineteenth centuries. This view absorbed the Reformation idea of the social good of marriage but extended it to include the ideal of an organic continuity and reinforcement between the married couple, wider family, church, and state.[23] The commonwealth model of marriage gradually became more egalitarian, utilitarian, and secular in the thought of John Locke and John Stuart Mill, but the idea that marriage was good for the social whole was constant throughout.[24] The belief that marriage is a social good is behind President Bush's plan to provide government support for pilot projects in marriage education for low-income and welfare groups. It is behind the moves into marriage preparation and education in Florida, Louisiana, Arizona, Oklahoma, and Maryland. The mass of marriage laws in the fifty states also demonstrates the belief that marriage is a public good requiring government support.

20. Anthony Giddens, *The Transformation of Intimacy: Sex, Love, and Eroticism in Modern Societies* (Stanford, Calif.: Stanford University Press, 1992).

21. Aristotle, *Politics*, bk. 2, chap. 4.

22. Witte, *From Sacrament to Contract*, pp. 2, 48-53.

23. Witte, *From Sacrament to Contract*, p. 131.

24. John Stuart Mill, *The Subjection of Women* (Indianapolis: Hackett, 1988).

Marriage as Religious: Sacrament and Covenant

Although marriage has been seen as organizing natural desires, requiring contracts, and serving the public good, it also has been seen as a profoundly religious reality. The dominance in the West of the religious view of marriage often blinds both the faithful and their detractors to marriage's natural, contractual, and social dimensions. Yet it is true that the early chapters of Genesis have been foundational for views of marriage in Judaism, Islam, and Christianity as well as for the cultures and laws of the societies that these religions have influenced. These texts establish marriage as an "order of creation" that expresses the will of God for all humankind. This order is preserved and enhanced through covenant promises between God and husband, wife, their families, and the wider community. As Leo Perdue points out, covenant in ancient Israel was simultaneously a religious, political, and familial concept.[25] The meaning of history, the rule of the king, and the order of marriage and household were all measured and given meaning by covenant faithfulness. The analogy between God's covenant faithfulness to Israel and Hosea's faithfulness to his wife Gomer has provided an archetypal pattern for marital commitment wherever Judaism, Islam, and Christianity have spread. It has elevated marriage to the status of recapitulating the dynamics of the divine life within the marital relation itself.

As an order of creation, marriage was not itself generally viewed, as I stated above, as a source of salvation. On the other hand, marriage conceived as a sacrament in medieval Roman Catholicism *was* viewed as a source of supernatural grace and a vehicle for salvation.[26] Both covenantal and sacramental views drape marriage with a royal robe of divine seriousness and approval. Furthermore, the ideas of covenant and sacrament do not necessarily exclude each other; nor do they require rejecting the natural, contractual, or social views of marriage. Catholic sacramental views assume and build on covenantal views. In addition, Aquinas organically linked his appropriation of Aristotelian naturalism to his sacramental theory. For instance, since his naturalism suggested that infant dependency required a long period of commitment from both mother and father, Aquinas assured this commitment by making marriage an unbreakable

---

25. Leo Perdue, Joseph Blenkinsopp, John Collins, and Carol Meyers, *Families in Ancient Israel* (Louisville: Westminster John Knox, 1997), pp. 239-44.

26. Thomas Aquinas, *Summa Theologica,* Supplement to the Third Part, q. 42 (New York: Benziger Brothers, 1948).

sacrament. His view of infant and childhood dependency and his under-standing of the natural fragility of male paternal investment led him to view marriage as needing to be permanent. His sacramentalism func-tioned to compensate for what his naturalism told him about the tenta-tiveness of male commitment to offspring.[27] Naturalistic understandings of the desires and needs organized by marriage also appear in the thought of Luther and Calvin. Both covenant and sacrament often went hand-in-hand with the idea of marriage as contract; these religious ideas strength-ened and deepened the contractual agreements, both public and private, that marriage entails.

A public philosophy of marriage cannot today be ruled directly by the ideas of orders of creation, covenant, and sacrament. But views of marriage guiding public policy and law must, nonetheless, understand our society's indebtedness to what these concepts did to form Western marriage. A pub-lic philosophy of marriage must take a generous and supportive attitude toward the way these great ideas worked in communities of faith and shaped both secular law and wider cultural sensibilities. Furthermore, this philosophy should allow these religious ideas to sensitize public debate on how the deep experiences of marriage tend to call forth the kind of tran-scendent aspirations generally associated with religion. Whether it is the deep metaphors of covenant as in Judaism, Islam, and Reformed Protes-tantism; sacrament as in Roman Catholicism or Eastern Orthodoxy; the ying and yang of Confucianism; the quasi-sacramentalism of Hinduism; or the mysticism often associated with allegedly modern romantic love, hu-mans tend to find transcendent values in marriage that call them beyond the mundane and everyday. Faith communities must cherish their reli-gious perspectives on marriage, constantly reinterpret them, yet under-stand how they can enrich the naturalistic, contractual, and social perspec-tives outlined above. Religious perspectives will function most powerfully in our society when they serve to frame, not necessarily compete with, these other perspectives on marriage. The language of covenant and sacra-ment should not try to rule the entire field of social discourse about mar-riage and family.

---

27. For an interpretation of this view of Aquinas, see Browning et al., *From Culture Wars to Common Ground*, pp. 120-24.

Marriage as Communicative Reality

There is a growing belief that marriage is a communicative reality between equals. But this idea has a history. The idea that marriage is for *mutual* comfort and assistance runs throughout the history of its various discourses.[28] The canon law view of contract assumed the personhood and autonomy of the consenting husband and wife. In early Christianity, the command to love your neighbor as yourself — what I have called elsewhere the love ethic of equal regard — is taken directly into the inner dynamics of the husband-wife relationship. An example of this can be found in the famous marriage passages of Ephesians telling us that "husbands should love their wives as they do their own bodies" (Eph. 5:28). Aristotle saw marriage as a kind of friendship, although one in which the male had the higher honor.[29] Stoics such as Musonius Rufus took additional steps toward viewing marriage as a union of equals.[30] Early Christianity went further still. Judaism, Christianity, and Islam all depended on the Genesis accounts of creation that portrayed *both* male and female as made in the image of God (Gen. 1:27). But, for the most part, it was not until the mid twentieth century that the social conditions necessary for the concrete realization of this long history of the ideal of marital mutuality fell into place.

As marriage evolves toward higher levels of economic, educational, and political equality between husband and wife, the demands for communicative competence between equal partners accelerate. It is one thing to proclaim an abstract ethic of equal regard between friends, neighbors, and strangers as was done in the Golden Rule and stated philosophically by Kant and others. It is another step to bring this abstract principle into the inner precincts of marriage, as happened in early Christianity and Stoic philosophy. It is another thing still to develop the actual communicative and intersubjective skills to implement this ethic in the countless small decisions of everyday life between husband and wife. This is the promise of marriage education. The skills of marriage education are real

---

28. Augustine, "The Good of Marriage," in *Treatises on Marriage and Other Subjects,* trans. Charles T. Wilcox et al., ed. Roy J. Deferrari, vol. 15 of The Writings of Saint Augustine (New York: Fathers of the Church, 1955), p. 12; Aquinas, *Summa Theologica,* Supplement to the Third Part, q. 41.

29. Aristotle, *Nichomachean Ethics,* in *The Basic Works of Aristotle,* ed. Richard McKeon (New York: Random House, 1941), bk. VIII, chap. 11.

30. Carolyn Osiek and David Balch, *Families in the New Testament World* (Louisville: Westminster John Knox, 1997), p. 115.

and profound. The founders of this movement — from Rogers and Buber to Hendrix, Markman, Stanley, Olson, and Gottman — have made real progress and major contributions.

The marriage education movement cannot, on its own, provide its guiding marital ethic, however. Nor can it alone provide us with a definition of marriage. It should develop its ethic and definition of marriage in dialogue with the classic sources that have shaped marriage as a public institution in the West. It should contribute to the enhancement of the personal and unitive aspects of marriage without reducing it to a simple communicative process.

The Use and Abuse of Marriage as a Public Institution

Marriage as a public institution, sanctioned by law, in service to the common good, and blessed by religion, must protect its private, personal, and intersubjective dimensions. Furthermore, we must never forget the procreative and educational functions of marriage. Not all persons will use marriage to balance the values of personal love, having and educating children, and increasing the social good. Some couples — as a result of intention, inability, accident, age, or other interruptions — will not have children. But the cultural, legal, and religious definitions of marriage must retain procreation as one of marriage's central values. In spite of the fact that some people who purchase automobiles seldom drive them, use them primarily for ostentation, or use them mainly on the back streets of small villages or for sightseeing in restricted venues, the cultural and statutory regulations of operating a car are built on the necessary competence and safety required for its heavy use in busy traffic. So it must be with marriage. It is beyond the capacity of law or society to monitor all the ways people might use this institution. But its explicit cultural, legal, and religious responsibilities and entitlements must continue to honor all of its historic dimensions, including the task of bonding parents to their children and to each other.

Among marriage's many functions and dimensions, the procreation and education of children give marriage as institution much of its special character. The fact that older people, disabled people, and people with special vocations want to marry even though they cannot or will not have children should not alter the strong association between marriage and procreation. The elderly should marry in order to *honor* the institution of marriage. The disabled who wish to become sexually involved, share economies of scale, enjoy a wide range of legal protections and privileges, and receive the social recognition of the status of marriage should also marry if at all possible. All of these acts honor marriage and its fuller functions. These gestures help keep the institution of marriage socially intact.

The issue of gay marriage raises the question of what does and does not honor the institution of marriage in all of its multiple dimensions. Does gay marriage reduce marriage to an interpersonal process? Does it suggest that natural parents are not important for child-rearing? Does it drastically broaden the meaning of marriage by giving all of its legal, religious, and social privileges to a certain type of friendship — friendships that involve the sharing of sexual intimacies, finances, and other interdependencies? Would gay marriage, by virtue of extending these privileges and recognitions to homosexual friendships, thereby discriminate against other classes of mutually dependent friends not involved sexually — older mother and daughter, two close friends, Catholic priest and housekeeper, the sick and their caretakers? Or, on the other hand, would gay marriage be like matrimony between the elderly or the impotent who want to honor marriage by becoming married?

This is the slender edge upon which the current debate about gay marriage hangs. But whatever the outcome of that great conversation, it should not be allowed to obscure the multidimensional and public character of marriage and its close relation to the responsibilities and privileges of giving birth, being parents, and raising children.

PART IV

Spheres, Strategies, and Praxis

Chapter 12

The Task of Religious Institutions in Strengthening Families (1999)

I begin Part IV of this volume, on the various spheres of society, with the church. After all, I am primarily a practical theologian. The angle of vision on the various sectors of society such as the economy, medicine, law, international human rights, and government should first of all be shaped by the life of the church.

Hence, even in this chapter (which was adapted, with extensive suggestions from the Communitarian Family Task Force, from chapter II of *From Culture Wars to Common Ground*),* I distinguish between the inner-ecclesial and public aspects of the task of the church in strengthening families, even though that distinction should not be made too absolutely. The new model of practical theology that I practice has tried to go beyond the captivity of the discipline to what Edward Farley once called the "clerical" or "ecclesial" paradigms of practical theology.** By these terms, he meant the view of practical theology that sees it as primarily about the theology of the ordained ministry or the theology of the church. Such theology is, in my view, well and good and indeed a fundamental aspect of the practical theological task. For several years, however, there has been a growing ecu-

*Don Browning, Bonnie Miller-McLemore, Pamela Couture, Bernie Lyon, and Robert Franklin, *From Culture Wars to Common Ground: Religion and the American Family Debate* (Louisville: Westminster John Knox, 1997). This is the summary book of the eleven-book Religion, Culture, and Family Series produced by a research project located at the University of Chicago and financed by a generous grant from the Division of Religion of the Lilly Endowment, Inc.

**Edward Farley, *Theologia: The Fragmentation and Unity of Theological Education* (Philadelphia: Fortress, 1988).

menical effort to introduce a public aspect to practical theology. This makes practical theology also a matter of the church's witness, action, and praxis in the world. Extending practical theology into public action inevitably requires being much more reflective about the ethical implications of the Christian faith — hence the extension of practical theology into practical-theological ethics.

Notice, however, that in this chapter I begin with what the inner life of churches and congregations, in their confessing and witnessing existence, should and can do to shape and strengthen families.

A communitarian family policy aspires to balance the good of society with the good of families and their individual members. It holds that the well-being of families, individual family members, and society is best guaranteed when the health of each is promoted equally. This principle is easy to state but difficult to actualize in concrete circumstances. The proposals we offer in this paper are designed to promote this goal.

In this paper, we ask what churches and synagogues as institutions of civil society should do to promote family well-being. What should they do for the families they immediately influence, and how should they work to shape public policy? We pursue these questions in this order because of our conviction that the strength of a society flows outward from its voluntary institutions — religious and civil — to public institutions and their policies. We hold, however, that government programs, religious institutions, and other institutions of civil society should be complementary in what they do for families. The state, market, churches and synagogues, and other voluntary organizations play different roles in relation to families, but these roles should be appropriately coordinated.

Our proposals are guided by three normative ideas.[1] First, although the various spheres of modern societies — government, business, religion, education, law, and the therapies — have unique responsibilities and privileges, they do not and cannot function independently from deeper ethical guidelines and constraints.

Second, family and local community should be allowed to exercise initiatives and natural capabilities in their spheres of immediate influence without undue interference from either government or market, even

---

1. For those interested in an explicitly theological elaboration of the three following ideas, see footnotes 1 and 2 for references.

though both of these have their rightful role in supporting families and local communities. This concept is close to what the Roman Catholic tradition calls the principle of subsidiarity — an idea that can be given religious meaning even though it also has ancient philosophical roots.[2]

Third, an ethic of "equal regard" should guide both the inner lives of families and family public policy. We realize that the idea of a family ethic of equal regard needs a definition.[3] We offer the following: *this ethic means that a husband or wife should (1) treat the other with unconditioned respect (as an end and never as a means only) and (2) within this mutual respect work to enhance the well-being of the other.* Concretely, the ethic of equal regard means that husband and wife should each in principle have equal access to the privileges *and* responsibilities of both public and private worlds, although this may be realized differently in specific households depending on individual interests and talents.

A familism guided by an ethic of equal regard is a "critical" familism — another term that requires definition. Critical familism is different from naive familism, which generally is interpreted as placing family togetherness above other values such as equality between husband and wife, the well-being of children, and the flourishing of individual family members. Critical familism balances family cohesion with the ethics of equal regard. It does this by uncovering and critiquing distortions in power in families which block the realization of equal regard among members.

The equal regard family does not relinquish parental authority; instead, it uses this authority to promote equal regard, dialogue, and the raising of children to gradually *grow toward* adult relations of mutual respect with their parents and others. In the case of relations between families, the ethic of equal regard holds that each family has the moral obligation to respect and work for the good of all other families. In turn, each family has the right to be respected and have its good promoted by others.

---

2. For a discussion of the Aristotelian roots of the concept of subsidiarity, see *From Culture Wars to Common Ground*, pp. 238-44, 363. For a more proximate source of subsidiarity in Roman Catholic thinking, see Pope Leo XIII, "Rerum Novarum," in *Proclaiming Justice and Peace: Papal Documents from Rerum Novarum through Centesimus Annus* (Mystic, Conn.: Twenty-Third Publications, 1991 [1894]).

3. The philosophical and theological grounds for the ethic of equal regard are extensively developed in the introduction and chapters 4, 5, and 10 of *From Culture Wars to Common Ground*. Chapter 8 also gives a discussion of the concept of subsidiarity and demonstrates how American Roman Catholicism, the thought of evangelical Ralph Reed, and the social philosophy of Senator Daniel Patrick Moynihan all have been influenced by this idea.

Civil Society, Religion, and State:
Toward a Critical Marriage Culture

With these principles in place, we affirm the emerging view that religious institutions are central to the health of civil society. They are major wellsprings of philanthropic action and seedbeds of civic, religious, and familial virtues. In light of their importance, we make the following recommendations.

The Retrieval of Marriage and Family Traditions

First, churches and synagogues should play a leadership role in stimulating the dialogue that creates a new familism. It is our judgment that, with few exceptions, religious institutions have not exercised this leadership in recent decades. To reclaim this role, they must retrieve their marriage and family traditions, even though they must do so critically. Religious institutions should examine their heritages, enter into dialogue with other denominations, work with secular institutions, survey the human sciences, and articulate a fresh vision of marriage and family — something close to what we have called critical familism.

This recommendation can be illustrated not only by the marriage theologies of various denominations but also by what Catholics and Protestants variously have called the "first" or "little" church. The continuity between the official church and the church at home has been a constant theme throughout Christian history. Because the early church met in homes, sacred actions around common meals in the gathered *ecclesia* were imitated in private home life. The importance of domestic rituals is even stronger in Judaism. When home rituals and the liturgies of church or synagogue reinforce each other, family life is made more cohesive and integrated more completely into the wider community. When these rituals or devotions are followed by free discussion between parents and children, they give rise to the reflective or critical assimilation of family traditions.

There is evidence that home-based rituals are extremely important for the creation of family cohesion. Family rituals at the dinner table, before bed, and on trips correlate with the effective communication of family traditions.[4] Rituals are important as well for families with a primarily secular identity. In these families, rituals may consist of carefully planned be-

4. William Doherty, *The Intentional Family* (New York: Addison-Wesley, 1997).

ginnings and endings to meals, family meetings, and other shared and regularly scheduled family activities.

Cooperation with Other Institutions in Helping Families

Second, religious congregations should join with other parts of civil society to foster a critical marriage and family culture. In some instances this cooperation might entail partnerships with the state. In establishing these cooperative ventures, religious institutions must seek to maintain their unique identity while at the same time striving to respect the separation of church and state. They can do this by searching for the points of analogy between their specific goals and the state's concern with the common good. The state, for instance, should be guided by an ethic of justice for individuals and families analogous to the ethic of equal regard promoted by religious institutions. Government also should abide by the principle of subsidiarity that respects the initiative and responsibility of families yet supports them when they need help.

Some cooperation between religious and public institutions already exists: witness the cooperation between churches and public health institutions. Catholic Charities and Lutheran Social Services both receive some state support. Note also the cooperation between churches and other institutions of civil society such as the Red Cross, a model that could be expanded and applied more directly to family issues. For example, a complex cooperative project between church, state, and other voluntary organizations can be found in recent efforts to expand the idea of a Community Marriage Policy. This program was first used to organize common marriage policies among local Protestant churches but has now been expanded in some communities to include judges, justices of the peace, and secular marriage counselors.[5] We say more about this policy below.

Public institutions should not become isolated from the energies and positive cultures of specific religio-cultural traditions. Sociologist James Coleman has argued that Catholic high schools provide better education than public schools because they receive more support from parents and church.[6]

5. As reported by Judge James Sheridan and Michael McManus at the "Smart Marriages: Happy Families" conference on July 10, 1997, Crystal Gateway Marriott Hotel, Washington, D.C.

6. James Coleman, "Schools, Families, and Children" (Ryerson Lecture, University of Chicago, 1985), pp. 9-18.

As societies organized around extended family have disappeared, Coleman believes, market, corporation, and government have expanded their influence on society, including schools. Catholic schools are succeeding, he argues, because they are an exception to this trend; they represent the values of families and their churches. Coleman urges us to abandon the idea that schools are solely agents of the state. Rather, they should more nearly reflect the values of the family and local community, including religious institutions.[7]

Our view is sympathetic to Coleman's but is somewhat different. We do not believe that family and church should dominate public schools. We hold that the family, religious institutions, market, and government each has its rightful expertise and authority for influencing the values and purposes of schools. Hence each of these spheres should conduct an intense dialogue about the direction of public schools and what they teach about marriage and family. *This dialogue should result in the development of new educational approaches to marriage and family life — approaches that have continuity with, but may not be identical to, the basic values of particular local families, traditions, and churches.*

Some proposals by William Bennett and Senator Dan Coats in their Project for American Renewal illustrate how state and civil society, including religious institutions, can cooperate. Coats and Bennett are mildly critical of programs that give welfare funds for families to the states. They also reject the idea of centering social programs for families mainly in the federal government. They call, instead, for funneling government support directly to the institutions of civil society, including the churches. They argue that these institutions are the conveyors of civic virtue, do most of society's moral education, and need to be revived in order to provide some of the cultural and institutional supports needed by families. They propose allowing individuals to give $500 of their tax liability to worthwhile nongovernmental charities that help poor families.[8]

They recommend demonstration grants for programs that match welfare families with religious communities that offer moral guidance and help. To encourage savings by poor families, demonstration grants would be provided for family deposits to be matched by churches, foundations, and corporations. Funds would be made available for pre-divorce counseling.

---

7. Coleman, "Schools, Families, and Children," p. 18.

8. Dan Coats, "Can Congress Revive Civil Society?" *Policy Review* (January-February 1996), p. 27.

It is not our intention to advocate these particular programs but rather to show that such proposals exist and deserve careful evaluation as possible ways for civil society, religious institutions, and the state to cooperate. Furthermore, we use them to illustrate the meaning of subsidiarity — the way large units of society such as government can support family and local communities without taking over the functions these smaller institutions perform best. Such cooperation also illustrates a dialogical view of authority, that is, how family, local community, state, and market can work together in creating a critical family culture.

Ecumenicity and Critical Familism

Third, churches must join with other churches and synagogues to create a new critical marriage culture. Seventy-five percent of all marriages, even today, are performed in synagogues and churches. This suggests that churches still have a significant role in marriage and should therefore work together in proclaiming and implementing a marriage and family culture.

But how can this happen? Michael McManus recommends that churches cooperate in adopting something like the Roman Catholic Church's coordinated program of premarital and marital support called the "Common Marriage Policy."[9] This program has been adopted by the vast majority of Roman Catholic dioceses in the United States. Because of this common policy, Catholic churches have a unified front on marriage issues. Young Catholic couples confront a common set of expectations and a common culture about what it takes to prepare for and thrive in family relations.

This common policy has five components: (1) a six-month minimum preparation period, (2) the administration of the new premarital questionnaires that have been tested for their capacity to predict marriages likely to end in divorce (PREPARE, the Pre-Marital Inventory, or FOCCUS), (3) the use of lay leadership and "mentoring couples" with the engaged and newly married, (4) the use of marriage instruction classes (weekend workshops, evenings for the engaged in the homes of mentor couples), and (5) engagement ceremonies held before the entire congregation.

McManus proposes bringing together Catholic, evangelical, and

9. Michael McManus, *Marriage Savers: Helping Your Friends and Family Stay Married* (Grand Rapids.: Zondervan, 1993), p. 131.

mainline Protestant churches (we would add synagogues) to create a "Community Marriage Policy"[10] — an ecumenical and interfaith common marriage policy that would help congregations across denominations to develop a united stance on marriage and family. Such a united front could help churches and synagogues counter the individualism and impatience of couples and parents who expect ministers to perform marriages on demand without careful preparation. The common elements McManus proposes look much like the Catholic model, but he suggests shorter waiting periods to adapt to more liberal customs among some denominations. Although the model needs further refinement, early reports suggest it is an idea moving in the right direction.

Youth and a Critical Marriage Culture

Fourth, churches and synagogues should take the lead in preparing youth for a critical familism. Large portions of society have retreated from guiding and inspiring youth in the areas of marriage and family. Many churches do not do adequate marriage preparation with engaged couples; they do even less with youth and teenagers. Churches have yielded leadership in these areas to public education, at both the college level and below.

As churches have retreated from sex, marriage, and family education, secular courses, often at the college level, have taken their place. A recent authoritative review of college textbooks by Professor Norval Glenn of the University of Texas has revealed that most of these texts are devoid of historical knowledge of the family, overly optimistic about the successes of alternative family forms, neglectful of children, and uninformed about new research on the benefits of marriage.[11] They tend to ignore evidence showing that married people are mentally and physically healthier, have more wealth, have much more sex, and are generally far more content with life than those who are not married.[12] Churches and synagogues should not only be concerned about this state of affairs but develop better alternative educational resources.

Religious institutions should be aware that there are very few adequate

10. McManus, *Marriage Savers,* p. 267.

11. Norval Glenn, "The Textbook Story of American Marriages and Families," Publication No. W.P. 46 (New York: Institute for American Values, May 1996).

12. Linda Waite, "Does Marriage Matter?" *Demography* 32, no. 4 (November 1995): 483-504.

educational resources addressing issues of marriage and family in secondary schools.[13] Sex education courses aim primarily to prevent disease and out-of-wedlock births.[14] Setting aside the question of their effectiveness in realizing these goals, it is important to note that they say little about marriage or family except to promote an attitude of tolerance for different family forms. One of the most competent sex education programs (designed by Marian Howard of Emory University) is not about education for marriage but about the delay of sexual activity until "maturity."

Existing educational programs emphasizing preparation for family life either are deficient in their use of religious resources or fail to present an adequately critical view of marriage, as do most fundamentalist religious programs. We believe that religious institutions should use the powerful new video technologies to teach their religious traditions, the best insights of the new marriage education programs (PREP, PREPARE/ENRICH, and so on), and realistic understandings of the economic, legal, and medical aspects of marriage.[15]

Addressing Family Pluralism from a Center

Fifth, churches and synagogues should develop theologies and programs that give priority to promoting the health of intact families while also helping other family forms. The cultural and social forces that are disrupting families are relentless, and high rates of family disruption are likely to continue in the foreseeable future. While we do recognize that family dissolution is often advisable in cases of violence, abuse, and addiction, religious institutions should recognize that many families could function well together if they had better supports.

There is much that can be done to mitigate strains on disrupted fami-

13. One of the best videos for high school education for marriage and family is prepared and distributed by the American Bar Association. It brings legal perspectives on marriage together with insights from the new psycho-education movement. See *Partners: An Interactive Televised Course* (Chicago: ABA Family Law Section).

14. There are few careful studies of the values clarification approach to sex education that show it to be successful. This is an approach in which teachers take no stand on moral issues. Decisions are left to students about how to use information. See Barbara Dafoe Whitehead, "The Failure of Sex Education," *Atlantic Monthly* (October 1994), pp. 55-80.

15. For information on PREPARE, write PREPARE/ENRICH, P.O. Box 190, Minneapolis, MN 55440-0190, and on PREP, write Professor Howard Markman, PREP, Inc., 1780 South Bellaire Street, Suite 621, Denver, CO 80222.

lies, be they never-married single parents, the divorced, or stepfamilies. Finally, we must recognize the advent of families with gay and lesbian parents and families consisting of heterosexual parents with gay or lesbian children. Although there is a range of positions in the churches about the nature and moral status of homosexual practice, almost all churches, conservative or liberal, wish to minister to these families.

Religious institutions should imitate those churches and synagogues that simultaneously and aggressively prepare people for stable and fulfilling marriages yet support and assist alternative family forms. For example, there is a burgeoning white Pentecostal church in the western suburbs of Chicago that has, in addition to its strong emphasis on marriage and opposition to divorce, a highly popular twelve-week post-divorce support program.[16]

Many African-American churches have such complex ministries. The Shiloh Baptist Church located in the poorer section of Washington, D.C., has a complex approach. It has delicately balanced programs designed to increase the number of intact families while, through its Family Life Center, it also reaches out to disrupted families in the community.

Churches, Synagogues, and the Balance of Work and Family

Sixth, religious institutions should address one of the major sources of strain on families — the tension between family needs and the demands of paid work. Mothers have joined fathers in the workforce, the average workweek has been extended, parents spend less time with children (the "parenting deficit"), and spouses spend less time with each other. Clearly, it *takes time and energy* to create an equal-regard family with parents guiding children into an ever-deepening dialogue with them, their faith traditions, and the wider society. We propose a model not exceeding a total sixty-hour workweek for a mother and father with young children. The compensated working hours could be divided between husband and wife as thirty-thirty, forty-twenty, or twenty-forty. There is evidence that the happiest families are those in which both husband and wife have some paid employment, share household chores and child care,[17] and work less

16. Paul Numrich, "A Pentecostal Megachurch on the Edge," in *Congregations and Family Ministry*, ed. Bernie Lyon and Archie Smith (Louisville: Westminster John Knox, 1997).

17. Rosemary Barciauskas and Debra Hull, *Loving and Working: Reweaving Women's Public Lives* (Bloomington: University of Indiana Press, 1989).

than two full-time positions.[18] Churches, in their theologies of work and leisure, should support such arrangements.

If the equal-regard family is to become a reality within the context of modern work demands, however, it will need to gain the skills of intersubjective communication (the ability to see and feel issues from the partner's point of view) required to define what is just and equitable. Church-sponsored day-care centers, support groups for working parents, church-sponsored baby-sitting networks, church-sponsored nursing support for parents of sick children — dozens of programs are possible. But more fundamental than any of these is a theory that sanctions the balance of work and parenting and the development of the communicative skills required to iron out the practical arrangements of everyday life.

Religious Institutions and Divorce

Seventh, religious institutions should do more to address the reality of divorce. While religious groups differ on the question of divorce, they all have tended to be either cautious, or genuinely restrictive, about this issue. Despite trends in secular society toward the easy acceptance of divorce, churches and synagogues should continue to be conservative in their attitudes on the dissolution of marriage. This does not necessarily mean an absolute prohibition of divorce, however.

We recommend four strategies that local churches can use to address the reality of divorce. First, prevention is the best cure. The best divorce prevention is extensive marital preparation of the kind envisioned by our proposal for a Community Marriage Policy and our suggestions for early church-based and school-based education for marriage and family.

Second, both church-based and secular marriage counseling should begin with a humane bias toward preserving marriages. William Doherty has written the following in reference to both the counseling pastor and the secular psychotherapist: "As therapists, we are moral consultants, not just psycho-social consultants. We should not try to impose our beliefs on undecided clients, but we can advocate in an open manner when appropriate."[19]

18. Rosalind C. Barnett and Caryl Rivers, *She Works/He Works: How Two-Income Families Are Happier, Healthier, and Better Off* (San Francisco: HarperSanFrancisco, 1996).

19. William Doherty, *Soul Searching* (New York: Basic, 1995), p. 33. See also Don Browning, *The Moral Context of Pastoral Counseling* (Philadelphia: Westminster, 1976), and

Counseling that presents theological and moral reasons for the importance of preserving marriage is entirely justifiable *as long* as it is not coercive, does not override the decision-making integrity of the individuals involved, does not suppress important dynamic and communicative issues that the couple should face, and does not ignore abuse, violence, and addiction. The idea that divorce is generally not good for children and that couples not involved in physical and mental violence may be able to learn to communicate and love one another again must be taken seriously in the counseling of churches.[20]

Recent social science research by Paul Amato and Alan Booth in their acclaimed *A Generation at Risk* indicates that only one-third of all divorces are preceded by high conflict of the kind destructive to children. This raises the question as to whether the less destructive remaining two-thirds might have avoided divorce had they found the proper help.[21]

Third, synagogues and churches should love, minister to, and sustain the divorced and their children. In spite of what worshiping communities do to discourage them, *divorces will occur,* although we hope less frequently. Churches and synagogues must also make a special effort to support children of divorced parents, whose experience of the divorce may be quite different from that of their parents and whose journey through childhood may be different from that of many other children. The religious communities that simultaneously promote a marriage culture, discourage a divorce culture, and promote a culture of care for the divorced, remarried, and their children,[22] are the ones that make full use of their theological traditions to hold authentic ideals together with a charitable sense of human weakness. Furthermore, these congregations help disrupted families create the networks — what sociologists call "social capital" — necessary for the support and enrichment of all families, especially those disrupted by transitions.

Finally, churches and synagogues, even at the local level, should join the national discussion about whether our divorce laws should be revised.

Bonnie Miller-McLemore, "Will the Real Pro-Family Contestant Please Stand Up? Another Look at Families and Pastoral Care," *Journal of Pastoral Care* 49, no. 4 (Spring 1995): 61-68.

20. Michelle Weiner-Davis, *Divorce Busting* (New York: Simon and Schuster, 1995).

21. Paul Amato and Alan Booth, *A Generation at Risk: Growing Up in an Era of Family Upheaval* (Cambridge: Harvard University Press, 1997), p. 220.

22. The Willow Creek Community Church, a megachurch in the northern suburbs of Chicago, is an example of a church with a strong marriage culture that promotes intact families but also has a wide range of services for the divorced, single parents, stepfamilies, and singles.

Churches, Synagogues, and Fathers

Eighth, churches and synagogues should do more to address the growing absence of fathers from their children. If the movement toward father absence is to be abated, nearly every aspect of civil society must address it, and religious institutions should take the lead. There is much to learn from black churches about restoring responsible fatherhood. The ten thousand–member Apostolic Church of God on Chicago's south side routinely and vigorously addresses father absence and discusses the positive contributions to children that fathers make. Another nearby church does all these things but with more consciousness of African themes. This church has rites-of-passage ceremonies for both teenage boys and girls that combine African themes and Christian meanings in defining adult male-female relations. It has an "adopt-a-school" program in which adult males relate to a neighborhood school, give courses on "responsible living," and help guide male students away from gangs and sexual involvement and toward their studies.

Critical Familism, Religion, and Public Policy: Beyond Value Neutrality

Churches and synagogues should become involved in public policy beyond the natural confines of their memberships and immediate communities. We hold that public policy should not and cannot maintain "value neutrality" on family matters. Furthermore, family issues cannot be solved strictly through technical and economic interventions by state and market. A critical familism is first a result of cultural visions — indeed religio-cultural visions — that come from the institutions of civil society, especially churches and synagogues. Nonetheless, economic measures from both state and market are also important for families.

The Economic Support of Families

First, religious institutions should explicitly support several economic strategies that can help families:

The tax structure should be far more family-friendly than it is. If the child exemption on federal income tax returns had kept pace with its value when first enacted in 1948, it now would be equivalent to $8,200 rather than its current $2,500.[23]

We applaud the recent adoption by Congress of a $500 per child tax credit. But it may need to be more. The 1991 report to the president of the National Commission on Children recommended a refundable tax credit of $1,000,[24] and William Mattox of the Family Research Council has called for a $1,500 credit.[25]

We support the earned income tax credit for poor families, which is generally believed to have contributed to the stability of low-income working parents.

The so-called marriage tax penalty — the fact that married couples often pay considerably more in taxes than they would if single — is both a real and symbolic assault on the social value of marriage and should be removed.[26]

Then there is the issue of welfare. We agree with those who argue that government's first obligation, at this moment in history, is to strengthen the institutions of civil society — churches, clubs, community organizations, voluntary service organizations — to carry more of our welfare system for families. But, at the same time, government must be involved in welfare to assure consistency, sufficient funding, and universality of some very fundamental programs.[27]

In this statement, we will not debate whether such goals should have been realized in a revised national welfare plan or through one administered by each of the fifty states, as established by the 1996 welfare reform. Instead, we are concerned about an issue in workfare, whether administered by states or by the national government. In keeping with our proposals that married couples with young children should not work in wage employment more than a total of sixty hours a week between them, we propose that single welfare parents with young children not be required

23. *Free to Be Family* (Washington, D.C.: Family Research Council, 1992), p. 35.

24. *Beyond Rhetoric: Report of the National Commission on Families* (Washington, D.C.: U.S. Government Printing Office, 1991), p. xxi.

25. William Mattox, "Government Tax Policy and the Family," a paper given at "The Family, Civil Society, and the State," a conference sponsored by the American Public Philosophy Institute, June 21-22, 1996, Washington, D.C.

26. *Free to Be Family*, pp. 34-43; Nick Rave, "Married Couples Feel Jilted by Uncle Sam," *Chicago Tribune* (March 17, 1995), p. C6.

27. John DiIulio, "Government Welfare to Support Families — the Right Way," a paper given at "The Family, Civil Society, and the State," a conference sponsored by the American Public Philosophy Institute, June 21-22, 1996, Washington, D.C.

to work more than twenty-five to thirty hours per week, roughly five to six hours a day.[28]

Even this time should be undergirded with state-supported child and medical care. The idea of thirty-hour working weeks for single parents and sixty-hour working weeks for married parents has been tried with success. For two decades, from 1930 to 1950, W. K. Kellogg ran his Corn Flakes plant in Battle Creek, Michigan, on a six-hour day. Recent research based on interviews with older employees reveals a high level of employee satisfaction with the arrangement.[29]

New welfare reform efforts should raise this model to public consciousness. A critical familism rewards family formation, gives social supports to those seeking gender equality, encourages paternal responsibility, discourages family welfare dependency, equips people for work, supports them with child care and medical care, and makes these policies as consistent as possible throughout the various states.

A Family-Friendly Workplace

Second, churches and synagogues should urge policy-makers to promote a family-friendly workplace. Some people advocate minimizing work strains with tax reductions that lower the need for families to have two incomes, thereby giving parents more time with their families; but many commentators argue that these proposals simply support the nineteenth-century model of an industrial family with its wage-earning father and domestic mother. President Clinton has tried to solve family-work strains with proposals such as better job conditions for parents, more flex time, an extension of the Family and Medical Leave Act, twenty-four hours a year for parents to keep school appointments and take children to doctors, portable family insurance, health insurance for poor families, compensatory time off in lieu of overtime pay, and new federal child-care programs.[30]

These proposals acknowledge women's desire to work and the reali-

28. Proposals for part-time work for single parents on welfare have been advanced by David Ellwood, *Poor Support: Poverty in the American Family* (New York: Basic, 1988), pp. 135-37, and Pamela Couture, *Blessed Are the Poor* (Nashville: Abingdon, 1991), pp. 178-84.

29. Benjamin Kline Hunnicutt, *Kellogg's Six-Hour Day* (Philadelphia: Temple University Press, 1996).

30. Alison Mitchell, "Clinton Prods Executives to 'Do the Right Thing,'" *New York Times* (May 17, 1996), p. C4; Alison Mitchell, "Banking on Family Issues, Clinton Seeks Parents' Votes," *New York Times* (June 25, 1996), p. C19.

ties of the postmodern family. We support both strategies — tax breaks *and* supports for family-friendly work conditions.

But these strategies do not go far enough. To implement the sixty-hour workweek, state and market must cooperate in creating the new twenty- and thirty-hour-a-week positions necessary for families to arrange the right combinations. These jobs should provide retirement and medical benefits. This raises the need for a basic universal health plan. We do not presume to settle here the best way to provide universal, cheap, and equitable health coverage for all workers, whether employed twenty, thirty, or forty hours a week. But to create flexible work arrangements that give parents sufficient time with their children, some such system of health care is required.

Child Care

Third, although there is a need for more and better care for the children of employed parents, some of the proposals we advocate should mitigate that need. If parents limit their employment outside of the home to sixty hours each week, fathers and mothers will have more time for child care. If the tax breaks listed above went into effect, couples would work fewer hours and have more time for child care, yet be able to afford better quality care because their overall income would improve.

Nonetheless, government initiatives to stimulate the development of more affordable quality child care are necessary. Government should invest in training and upgrading child-care workers, stimulate the development of minimum standards of care, encourage child-care provisions in parents' places of employment, and offer more flex time and home-based employment. Government-operated child-care facilities eventually may be necessary but should not be the country's first approach to meeting the needs of families.

State-Supported Marriage Education

Fourth, public policy should provide for marriage and family education. As we saw above, the state is already participating in marriage education, mainly through university-level courses on the family and elementary and high school sex-education classes. Much of this instruction is deficient on marriage and family and some is directly misleading. Although marriage and family life should not be reduced completely to simple public health issues, at this level alone the state has every right to promote marriage and family education. Other countries, such as Australia, sponsor marriage and family education courses. Sometimes these programs function through existing institutions of civil society. They emphasize communications skills, conflict resolution, and parenting skills.[31]

At the level of junior high and high school education, such programs would not be addressed to couples but would emphasize education in intersubjective communication skills that, later in life, would prove important for sustaining marriage and family.

Mothers, Fathers, and Public Policy

Fifth, religious institutions should support public policies that help both mothers and fathers with the new challenges they face. We advocate measures that go beyond finding ways to force deadbeat fathers to support their children. We agree that measures should be used to garnish wages, to collect delinquent payments through the use of federal and state income taxes, and to compel responsibility by canceling auto or professional licenses. But such policies, although necessary, are basically punitive.

The state should become a moral and financial partner of the initiatives in civil society to promote better fatherhood. Take, for instance, Charles Ballard's widely recognized National Institute for Responsible Fatherhood and Family Development, which receives some state support. Ballard's program is designed to reunite fathers with their children, help fathers support their children financially, and foster in these men an attitude of respect for former girlfriends or wives. Counselor-educators (called Sages) visit alienated fathers in their homes, help establish paternity, and model responsible fatherhood themselves.[32]

Other programs receive moral support from government even though they get no direct financial help. The National Fatherhood Initiative was founded during the autumn of 1994 with bipartisan support from Demo-

---

31. Margaret Andrews, "Developing a National Strategy of Marriage and Family Education," address given to the International Conference on the Family, University of Melbourne, July 1994; see also "Moving Counseling to Community Agencies," *Threshold: A Magazine about Marriage Education* 49 (December 1995): 3.

32. Brochure provided by the National Institute for Responsible Fatherhood and Family Development, p. 2. To contact, write the National Institute for Responsible Fatherhood and Family Development, 8555 Hough Avenue, Cleveland, OH 44106-1545.

crats Al Gore and William Galston as well as Republican William Bennett. It addresses the growing absence of fathers from their children by distributing information on the importance of fathers and the social costs of father absence.[33] Ken Canfield's National Center for Fathering is an older hands-on program with considerable grassroots impact.[34] Both organizations have more general audiences than Promise Keepers, and their messages are less laden with the language of a particular religious tradition. Both programs work intensively with religious organizations.

The situation of mothers in contemporary society has been very different from that of fathers. Fewer mothers have fled families, but they may instead feel trapped by them. Even today many women feel that they must choose between paid employment or time with their infants, a choice that often leads mothers to leave the workforce and fall behind in job and career advancement. This predicament has led economists Richard and Grandon Gill to propose what they call a Parental Bill of Rights.[35]

Just as American men who served in the armed forces during World War II were given the GI Bill to help them make up for lost career time, so should parents who take time to care for their children receive child-care payments, modest annual child allowances, job training, education, and other protections so that the years spent caring for their infants will not cause long-term financial, job, and career losses. The authors estimate that this Parental Bill of Rights would cost citizens no more than $200 per capita in 1990 dollars.

Divorce and Public Policy

Sixth, religious institutions should back the revision of divorce laws. Since the advent of no-fault divorce in the late 1960s and early 1970s, the marriage contract has become weaker than most business contracts. In many states, it can be broken unilaterally, and the dissenting partner has little recourse. From both a philosophical and a theological perspective, we hold that marriage agreements should be more like covenants, that is, binding agreements between a husband and wife, between them and the

33. Taken from a brochure titled "Creating a Father-Friendly Neighborhood: 10 Things You Can Do" (Lancaster, Pa.: National Fatherhood Initiative).

34. For information, write the National Center for Fathering, P.O. Box 413888, Kansas City, MO 64141.

35. Richard Gill and Grandon Gill, "A Parental Bill of Rights," *Family Affairs* 6, nos. 1-2 (Winter 1994): 1.

wider society, and, for the religious, between these two individuals and a transcendent power as they conceive it. Such multidimensional agreements should not be broken with ease. In reality, marriages should be conceived as both contracts *and* covenants. The system recently enacted in Louisiana which gives couples the option of choosing no-fault marriage contracts or more binding covenant marriages is a sound and noncoercive way to reestablish the legal seriousness of marriage.

The members of this task force do not agree as to whether the present system of no-fault divorce should be rejected completely by the several states. We do agree, however, that in cases where couples with children want divorce by mutual consent, they should undergo required counseling on parenting after divorce and on the potential impact of the divorce on the children. Furthermore, couples should be required to develop a long-term financial plan to cover the needs of children until they are eighteen and in some cases older. This plan would have to be accepted by the court before the divorcing couple could begin dividing property between them.[36]

Some members of the Task Force believe that the assignment of fault may not be necessary if waiting periods, required counseling, and long-term financial plans for child support are part of the proposal. However that issue is decided, we believe that marriage, even before the law, increasingly should be seen as a public covenant vital for individuals, children, and the common good.

The Media, Public Policy, and Civil Society

Seventh, the institutions of civil society and churches should join with government and the market to launch a critique of media images of marriage and family. The emphasis should be on providing criticism and well-grounded evaluations, not censorship. Nor should criticism be voiced in ways that obscure the good that educational television can do and the positive images that some programs and movies convey. But critiques of the unhealthy aspects of the media should be relentless, should come from many different voices, and must be heard.

36. To my knowledge, these suggestions were first put forth by Mary Ann Glendon, *Abortion and Divorce in Western Law* (Cambridge, Mass.: Harvard University Press, 1987), pp. 93-95. Later they were affirmed by Elaine Ciulla Kamarck and William Galston, "Putting Children First: A Progressive Family Policy for the 1990s" (Washington, D.C.: Progressive Policy Institute, 1991), p. 30.

From one perspective, the media are an expression of the overflow of cost-benefit, individualistic, and consumption-oriented patterns of the market that increasingly pervade our society. We are not against the market, but we do believe that the rational-choice and ethical-egoist motives of the market can and should be restrained by an ethics of equal regard for persons within and outside of families. This applies as well to a responsible critique of the family images found in movies, television, popular music, and popular journalism.

Rather than portraying the media as single-mindedly seditious,[37] however, we follow Kay Hymowitz's analysis of the dialectical relation of the media and social attitudes.[38] She points out that the values governing marriage and family have changed as a result of a variety of economic and cultural trends. The media, she explains, do not by themselves create these changes, but they do exploit and exacerbate them. Furthermore, in order to sell movies, TV series, and consumer products, the media use shock and excitement to create interest and viewing addiction to the more titillating aspects of these changes. The media give a stamp of normality to behavior and conditions once thought to be immoral and still deserving of analysis and moral criticism.

Censorship is not the answer. A new critical familism is the answer. But this familism and marriage culture should be supported by multiple voices critiquing and sometimes boycotting the media — voices no longer afraid of the charge of moralism. So far, the groups willing to do this are few in number. Such criticism is generally limited to the important reality of violence; addressing family and marriage issues seems to be more difficult.[39]

More needs to be done on both questions. The kind of criticism we have in mind is found in a long document by Roger Cardinal Mahony, archbishop of Los Angeles, in which he publicly urges the entertainment industry to "adopt general guidelines for the depiction of violence, sex,

37. See Michael Medved, *Hollywood vs. America: Popular Culture and the War on Traditional Values* (New York: HarperCollins, 1992).

38. Kay S. Hymowitz, "'I Don't Know Where This Is Going': What Teenagers Learn about Marriage from Television and Magazines" (New York: A Council on Families in America Working Paper, Institute of American Values, 1995).

39. An excellent program sponsored by the Family and Community Critical Viewing Project is unfortunately limited to violence. See *Taking Charge of Your TV: A Guide to Critical Viewing for Parents and Children*. For information on an extensive list of resources, write Family and Community Critical Viewing Project, 1724 Massachusetts Avenue, N.W., Washington, DC 20036-1969.

family, and the treatment of women."[40] Recent steps taken to adopt an industry-administered rating system that will later be reinforced by the parent-controlled V-chip may help.[41] Watchdog organizations such as the National Institute on Media and the Family should be encouraged.

But until a new artistic sensibility informed by a critical familism emerges, these suggestions will inevitably constitute partial measures. Just as Secretary of Health and Human Services Donna Shalala challenged Hollywood to live up to its creative potential by inventing stories not featuring people smoking cigarettes, so too should multiple voices challenge the media to tell more truthful and positive stories about human love, sexuality, marriage, and families.

Conclusion

There is no single cure for the family crisis in our society. There is no magic bullet. We have listed over a dozen strategies that religious institutions, voluntary associations, government, and market should take in cooperation with one another. The power of these strategies will become apparent not when they are viewed in isolation from one another, but when they become orchestrated into a new gestalt — a new critical familistic culture with accompanying social supports.

---

40. *New York Times* (October 1, 1992), p. B1.
41. Mark Caro and Steve Johnson, "Foes of New TV Ratings Worry about 'Forbidden Fruit' Factor," *Chicago Tribune* (December 23, 1996), A1, p. 4; Richard Morin, "Confronting Sex and Violence on TV," *Washington Post National Weekly Edition* (December 23, 1996), p. 38.

Chapter 13

Modernization: Critical Familism and the Reconstruction of Marriage (2003)

This chapter was originally written at the invitation of the Belgian journal known as *INTAMS (The International Journal of Marital Spirituality)*. I was asked to enter into a debate with my friend Professor Adrian Thatcher of the University of St. John and St. Mark of Plymouth, England. In 1999, Professor Thatcher had written a book titled *Marriage After Modernity*. In 2003, my book *Marriage and Modernization* was published. The editors of INTAMS were perceptive in noticing that Thatcher and I used the concepts of modernity and modernization in different ways. We were asked to clarify our respective views of how early Christianity could or could not be a resource for the equal-regard marriage. In addition, we exchanged views on the issue of cohabitation.

The reader will notice that I tend to have a more restricted definition of modernization than Thatcher. In addition, I do not believe we have gone beyond modernization into a sociological state called "postmodernity"; instead, I believe postmodernity is a philosophical concept and does not adequately describe a social process. I define modernization as the spread of technical rationality in the marketplace and in government bureaucracy. I claim, along with most social scientists, that both expressions of modernization create disruptions in marriage and family life. Although I do not treat the phenomenon of modernization as totally destructive, I believe it must be contained and guided by a complex "work of culture." Religion must be a part of this work of culture.

There are many massive social forces that disrupt families. Wars, famine, oppression, and racial discrimination all have their devastating effects on children, mothers, and fathers. I wish to address, however, the unsettling effects on families of world trends toward modernization and globalization.

Most social scientists now acknowledge that modernization, independent of factors such as war and famine, can by itself be disruptive to families. But many sociologists believe there is little to be done to allay these consequences; the social forces producing them are simply too deep and powerful. I do not share this view. Much can be done, but only if we understand the task as a complex cultural work — one that is like weaving a richly designed tapestry containing many threads. The threads needed for this cultural task are religious, political, legal, economic, and psychological. In addition, this cultural work must be worldwide in scope. Central to this effort is the worldwide revival and reconstruction of marriage. Admittedly, this is a big idea. And, of course, I do not envision this renewal and reconstruction happening tomorrow. My point, rather, is this: the worldwide disruption of families partially created by the processes of modernization cannot be addressed solely with policies emphasizing jobs, education, and the economic liberation of women — the favorite strategies of the United Nations, the World Council of Churches, and other international agencies. Such strategies are essential, but more is needed. Without the restoration of marriage, economic and development strategies can go awry. Notice that I do not speak of the revival of marriage; I call for the reconstruction of marriage. This would entail a culturally sensitive redefinition of the roles males and females play in this institution and in the rest of society. *I am pleading for a new international practical-religious dialogue between the major world religions designed to place the matter of marriage before the world community.* This proposal is an extension of the concept of critical familism that I first developed with my colleagues in *From Culture Wars to Common Ground* and more recently in my *Marriage and Modernization*.[1]

---

1. Don Browning, Bonnie Miller-McLemore, Pamela Couture, Bernie Lyon, and Robert Franklin, *From Culture Wars to Common Ground: Religion and the American Family Debate* (Louisville: Westminster John Knox, 1997, 2000); Don Browning, *Marriage and Modernization: How Globalization Threatens Marriage and What to Do about It* (Grand Rapids: Eerdmans, 2003); and for an extension of critical familism specifically into the arena of public policy, see Don Browning and Gloria Rodriguez, *Reweaving the Social Tapestry: Towards a Public Philosophy and Policy for Families* (New York: W. W. Norton, 2001).

Defining Modernization and Globalization

This raises the question, what do I mean by the terms modernization and globalization? For purposes of my argument, I offer a rather narrow definition of modernization. I define modernization as a kind of social process motivated by a cultural vision about the possibilities of progress in the improvement of life. Some people have expansive definitions of modernity, as does, I think, my good friend Adrian Thatcher in his important *Marriage After Modernity*.[2] Since I have been asked by the editors of *INTAMS* to address his point of view, I will say this. I understand Thatcher to be saying that modernity was born out of the Enlightenment romance with science, technology, and the cultural drive to improve the quality of life in this world,[3] and that it includes many cultural elements such as democracy, belief in human rights, the spirit of capitalism, and the values of bourgeois society.[4] Furthermore, Thatcher makes a strong separation between modernity and postmodernity. Postmodernity is for him primarily a variety of cultural and philosophical perspectives that have overturned the epistemological dominance of elements that make up modernity, principally science, technology, capitalism, bourgeois culture, patriarchy, and private rights.[5] He summarizes his review of various definitions of modernity and postmodernity with the following three points about why the category of postmodernity is of interest to theologians.

> First, they think there is, or has been, something called "modernity." Secondly, modernity is coming, or has come, to an end. And thirdly, the ending of modernity represents an opportunity for something else, perhaps a new beginning for Christian thought and practice.[6]

There is much in Thatcher's discussion of modernity and postmodernity that I affirm. Certainly modernity is associated with the rise of science and technology as both human activities and views of human knowledge. In recent years, strong philosophical perspectives have emerged that have questioned this dominance, such as American prag-

---

2. Adrian Thatcher, *Marriage After Modernity: Christian Marriage in Postmodern Times* (Washington Square, N.Y.: New York University Press, 1999).

3. Thatcher, *Marriage After Modernity*, pp. 25-26.

4. Thatcher, *Marriage After Modernity*, pp. 27-28.

5. Thatcher, *Marriage After Modernity*, p. 27.

6. Thatcher, *Marriage After Modernity*, p. 26.

matism and the practical philosophies of Heidegger, Wittgenstein, Gadamer, and Ricoeur.

But my position differs from Thatcher's in at least two respects. First, I think about modernity more narrowly than Thatcher. It is for me primarily the processes of technical rationality expressed in both market capitalism and government bureaucracy. It also includes the cultural vision that has motivated the rise of technical rationality, namely, the hope and belief that its widespread use will improve mundane existence for humankind. Thatcher's more expansive definition also strongly associates modernity with the cultural values of democracy and the spirit of capitalism. My position, however, holds that modernity defined primarily as the spread of technical rationality can easily be associated not only with democracy and rational capitalism but also with communism, rigid forms of socialism, or even various forms of theocracy. Modernization, as I use the term, is supple; it can swing from side to side — to capitalism and democracies on the one hand to planned economies, dictatorships, or even theocracies on the other. Technical reason can be used by a variety of political philosophies and polities.

Second, Thatcher sees a stronger discontinuity between modernity and postmodernity than I do. "[M]odernity is coming, or has come, to an end," Thatcher tells us. In contrast, I see the forces of technical rationality all the stronger even today, in spite of new and powerful postmodern philosophical objections to it. Furthermore, the forces of technical rationality expressed through neo-classical economic practices are themselves so strong that they have given rise to a special kind of globalization in the form of rational-market processes that now envelop the entire world. These market processes have developed a life of their own and unleashed new and unexpected cultural dynamics. These differences between Thatcher's and my views on the nature of modernization do indeed create some modest disagreements in our respective substantive views of marriage and families, some of which I will discuss below.

Modernization and the World Situation of Marriage

I will now amplify these initial remarks about the nature of modernization, the nature of globalization, and their consequences for marriage and family. I have not found it useful to make overly refined distinctions between modernization and globalization. Max Weber first defined modernization in the more narrow sense that I use it; he saw it as the spread of technical rationality into various domains of life.[7] Some theorists, including Weber himself, have seen this as a deterministic process that augurs well for the triumph of science, the narrow rationalization of all of life, and the final defeat of religion. The German social theorist Jürgen Habermas, however, has complicated Weber's theory of modernization by arguing that technical rationality can take the form of either market economics *or* bureaucratic control.[8] Within the context of market economics, technical rationality can be used to find the most efficient means possible for the production and sale of products that satisfy short-term wants and desires. When technical rationality is used within the context of powerful state bureaucracies, it functions to find efficient and powerful means toward the end of social control and the implementation of government policies. In either case, modernity has generally been thought to flow from the Western and the Northern hemispheres to countries in the Southern and Eastern parts of the globe.

There is much recent preoccupation with this first type of modernization — the global spread of capitalism in the form of free trade, money, and labor. It is better, however, to conceive of global capitalism as just one expression of technical rationality. Bureaucratic rationality — in the form of welfare policies and expanded legal control of formal and informal affectional unions — is also a form of modernization. These two kinds of modernization have technical rationality in common, that is, the belief that the efficient use of powerful technical means can increase our individual and collective satisfactions.

But the inevitability of modernization as the global triumph of technical rationality can be overstated. Cultural forces may emerge that will limit, guide, or even some day totally reject the hegemony of technical rationality. Furthermore, its worldwide spread in the form of market economies is not the only form of globalization. There is, as anthropologist Arjun Appadurai has argued, another form of globalization that is aided by but distinguishable from the worldwide spread of market rationality.[9]

7. Max Weber, *The Protestant Ethic and the Spirit of Capitalism* (New York: Charles Scribner's Sons, 1958), pp. 181-83.

8. Jürgen Habermas, *The Theory of Communicative Action,* trans. Thomas McCarthy, 2 vols. (Boston: Beacon, 1984, 1987).

9. Arjun Appadurai, *Modernity at Large* (Minneapolis: University of Minnesota Press, 1996). Roland Robertson also has warned against equating globalization with capitalism. See his "Globalization and the Future of 'Traditional Religion,'" in *God and Globalization,* vol. 1: *Religion and the Powers of the Common Life,* ed. Max L. Stackhouse with Peter Paris (Harrisburg, Pa.: Trinity Press International, 2000), pp. 53-68.

This is the move of cultural influences across the world in all directions that are communicated by the technologies of electronic communication — television, radio, email, travel, and computer processes of various kinds. This form of globalization is a product of human imagination and practical reason *(phronēsis)* rather than of the blind forces of technical rationality, even though it makes ample use of rationality's tools, gadgets, and computers. It is this form of globalization, perhaps conveyed by the electronic and digital revolutions, that would facilitate the worldwide reconstructive dialogue about marriage that I have in mind. I am calling for the imaginative creation of new micro-narratives to counter modernity's dominant message about the inevitable decline, and possible total collapse, of marriage.

William Goode: How Modernization Betrayed Families

I turn now to showing why many scholars of modernization have come to see it as a threat to marriage. On this issue, Thatcher and I agree. But since I hold that the world is not necessarily beyond modernization, as Thatcher seems to hold, I wish to both describe and counter its forces and consequences more directly than he does.

William Goode, a leading figure in American sociology who recently died, helps us understand the impact of modernity on marriage and family. In two massive books written thirty years apart, Goode fearlessly collected huge quantities of data and tried to account for family changes all over the world. In both of these books, he tried to explain what was happening by invoking the explanatory power of modernization as the spread of technical reason. In 1963, he wrote *World Revolution and Family Patterns*, which demonstrated the global movement away from extended-family patterns toward the convenient fit between industrialization and what he called the "conjugal" or "companionate" family.[10] Goode also shared a thesis developed even more powerfully by the historical sociologist Peter Laslett of Cambridge University, which holds that in the nineteenth century, England and Northern Europe exported to the world a modernizing trend that joined a wealth-producing industrialization process together with the four-centuries-old neo-local and relatively more companionate family of Northern Europe. In nearly every country he studied, he found

10. William Goode, *World Revolution and Family Patterns* (London: Free Press of Glencoe, 1963).

the extended family on the defensive. He also found trends toward smaller families, more women working in the wage economy, more equality between husband and wife, more education for both sexes (especially for women), and less control over the conjugal couple by extended family. This conjugal family pattern, he believed, had preceded, helped to create, and then served the emerging industrial and modernizing order. They fit like hand and glove.

In 1963, William Goode celebrated this new more individualized family pattern, not because it would bring more happiness, but because it would bring more freedom and the "potentialities of greater fulfillment."[11] Three decades later, however, when Goode published his massive *World Changes in Divorce Patterns* in 1994, his optimism about the triumph of the stable conjugal couple had become tempered. The comfortable fit between the neo-local conjugal family and industrialization that he described in 1963 was perceived as breaking down in the 1990s. Modernity's speed of change and its capacity to subdue intimate relations to the dictates of rational production had now made this old friend of the conjugal couple into a new enemy.

All Western and many non-Western societies are becoming what Goode calls "high-divorce societies."[12] Furthermore, Goode was aware that cohabitation and out-of-wedlock births have increased dramatically in Western societies and throughout the world. Hand-in-hand with these movements have been the growing poverty and declining well-being of significant percentages of women and children. This "feminization of poverty" has had negative social effects in wealthy countries, but it has had devastating consequences for poor ones.

There are, however, examples of stable high-divorce societies. Arabic countries, he claims, have historically had high levels of divorce and family disruption because of the unilateral divorce privileges of males. But in these countries, rejected wives were generally absorbed back into their extended families, often to marry again. Goode nominates Sweden as another kind of stable high-divorce and family-disruption society. Sweden's extensive system of social supports sustains divorced or never-married mothers, at least financially. Goode envisions shipping something like the Swedish system to all countries of the world, be they rich or poor, East or West, North or South.

---

11. Goode, *World Revolution and Family Patterns,* p. 380.

12. William Goode, *World Changes in Divorce Patterns* (New Haven, Conn.: Yale University Press, 1994), p. 336.

David Popenoe and Alan Wolfe

American sociologists David Popenoe and Alan Wolfe have reviewed these same trends. They analyze the forces causing the disruptions of modernization in ways similar to Goode, but they propose vastly different solutions.[13]

Here is an update of the kinds of statistics that concerned Popenoe and Wolfe when they wrote their books. Since the 1960s, the divorce rate has more than doubled in the United Kingdom, the United States, France, and Australia. During this same period, nonmarital births increased from 5 percent to 33 percent in the United States, from 4 percent to 31 percent in Canada, from 5 percent to 38 percent in the United Kingdom, and from 6 percent to 36 percent in France.[14] Since 1960, the rate of out-of-wedlock births in the United States has increased tenfold in the white community to 25 percent and threefold in the black community from 22 percent to a rate of 70 percent.[15] The marriage rate in all advanced countries has declined significantly. In the United States, there has been a 30 percent decline in the marriage rate since 1960, and overall there has been an 11 percent decline in the number of people over age fifteen who are married.[16] Much of this can be explained by later marriages and increased longevity. But some of this decline is due to increased lifelong singleness and cohabitation.

The number of couples cohabiting has increased eightfold in the United States since 1970.[17] Cohabitation is almost a universal experience in most Northern European countries. Studies in both the United States and Europe show, however, that cohabitation is much more unstable than

13. Alan Wolfe, *Whose Keeper? Social Science and Moral Obligation* (Berkeley: University of California Press, 1989).

14. Clarence Page, "When Marriage Goes Out of Style," *Chicago Tribune,* February 7, 2001, p. A17. Page is quoting statistics provided by Senator Daniel Moynihan in a September 2001 speech before the American Political Science Association.

15. Tom Smith, "The Emerging 21st Century American Family" (Chicago: National Opinion Research Center, University of Chicago, 1999), p. 3.

16. Barbara Dafoe Whitehead and David Popenoe, "Who Wants to Marry a Soul Mate: The State of Our Unions 2001" (Rutgers University, N.J.: The National Marriage Project, 2001), p. 18. The marriage rate is measured by number of marriages per one thousand of unmarried women age fifteen and older.

17. Linda Waite, "The Negative Effects of Cohabitation," *The Responsive Community,* vol. 10 (Winter 2000): 31. For a comprehensive summary of cohabitation trends in the United States, see R. Kelly Raley, "Recent Trends and Differentials in Marriage and Cohabitation: The United States," in *The Ties that Bind: Perspectives on Marriage and Cohabitation,* ed. Linda Waite et al. (New York: Aldine de Gruyter, 2000), pp. 19-39.

marriage and correlates with higher divorce rates for couples who do go on to marry.[18] Recent research has shown that in the United States, a significant portion of births out of wedlock actually occur in cohabiting relationships. There is evidence that the instability of cohabitation also contributes to the insecurity of care for children born to these unions.[19]

It appears that "responsible parenting" increasingly is becoming both the cultural norm and the government policy in European societies, with less interest in whether it takes place within or outside of marriage. According to one news account, some British social scientists are predicting that "marriage is doomed" and will soon be replaced by a "'constellation' of relationships where couples have a series of long-term relationships with children from each."[20] In the face of such statistics and trends, sociologist Linda Waite and journalist Maggie Gallagher strike a very different tone. They conclude in *The Case for Marriage* that a couple's public and legal commitment to the formal institution of marriage appears in itself to contribute to the stability of the union.[21] Along the same line, recent research by sociologist Steven Nock shows that couples choosing Louisiana's covenant marriage gain a stabilizing marital benefit simply from the multiple public commitments implicit in their marital vows.[22] The apparent importance to marriage of publicly witnessed promises has been overlooked by those advocating the delegalization and privatization of marriage.

Although these are the kinds of facts that concern Popenoe and Wolfe, they advocate a different strategy than Goode. Popenoe accepts William Goode's theory that modernization weakened first the extended family and eventually the conjugal couple — the core of the family itself. But he also believes that cultural values such as expressive and utilitarian individualism, independent of the social processes of industrialization, are the main factors fueling family disruption.[23] As the reader may have

18. David Popenoe and Barbara Dafoe Whitehead, "Should We Live Together? What Young Adults Need to Know about Cohabitation before Marriage: The State of Our Unions 1999" (Rutgers University, N.J.: The National Marriage Project, 1999); David Popenoe, *Disturbing the Nest* (New York: Aldine De Gruyter, 1988), p. 173.

19. Pamela Smock, "Cohabitation in the United States: An Appraisal of Research Themes, Findings, and Implications," *Annual Review of Sociology* 21 (Summer 2000).

20. Sarah Harris, "Marriage Will Be Extinct in 30 Years,'" *Daily Mail* (April 20, 2002).

21. Linda Waite and Maggie Gallagher, *The Case for Marriage* (New York: Doubleday, 2000), p. 18.

22. Steven Nock, "Report on Covenant Marriage," lecture given at the "Marriage, Democracy, and Families" conference, Hofstra Law School, March 14-15, 2003.

23. Popenoe, *Disturbing the Nest*, pp. 46-48; Robert Bellah et al., *Habits of the Heart* (New York: Harper and Row, 1986), pp. 32-35.

noticed from my remarks above, I have sympathies for Popenoe's formulation. The social processes of technical rationality are motivated by a cultural vision; individualism is doubtless an important factor in this vision, especially in Western market-oriented countries and the societies that recently have been influenced by them.

This observation leads Popenoe to see the world cure for family disruption in a massive cultural conversion — the birth of a new familism and a worldwide renunciation of over-determined individualistic aspirations. Handling world family disruptions by imitating Sweden, as William Goode would urge, is an option that Popenoe has considered but respectfully rejects as economically unfeasible and culturally destructive. Evidence supporting his rejection of the Swedish approach recently has been published in the British medical journal *The Lancet*.[24] In a study involving one million Swedish families, children from single-parent families were two to three times more likely to have psychiatric problems, be suicidal, and have problems with alcohol and drugs. The excellent financial supports of the Swedish welfare system probably undermine husband-wife interdependence and promote divorce and nonmarriage, but at the same time seem unable fully to deter the harmful consequences to children of high rates of family disruption in that country.

Alan Wolfe rejects the Swedish alternative as well; he contends that the system undermines marriage and family even as it attempts to save them. Wolfe uses the colonization theory of Jürgen Habermas to show how different expressions of modernization — whether in its market or bureaucratic forms — are almost identical in their negative effects on families. Colonization theory teaches that technical rationality enters into daily life from two perspectives — the efficiency goals of the marketplace and the control goals of government bureaucracy and law. Each of these forces disrupts the interactions of the "lifeworld" and the intimate spheres of marriage and family. From the market comes the increasing absorption of both men and women into the wage economy and the subsequent erosion of time for parenthood and stable marital relationships. From state bureaucracy comes increased control of the education of our children, the rise of the welfare state, its preemption of family functions, the subtle transfer of dependencies from family to state, and the increased juridification of both formal and informal affectional relationships.

---

24. Gunilla Ringback Weitoft, Anders Hjern, Bengt Haglund, and Mans Rosen, "Mortality, Severe Morbidity, and Injury in Children Living with Single Parents in Sweden: A Population-Based Study," *The Lancet* 361 (January 25, 2003): 289-95.

Wolfe argues that Sweden is the leading example of colonization of the lifeworld from the perspective of government bureaucracy, while the United States is the leading example of colonization from the perspective of market rationality.[25] In the end, the results for families of these two forms of colonization are approximately the same: more divorce, more out-of-wedlock births, and the declining well-being of children affected by these trends. It is this understanding of how modernization can colonize and disrupt family and marriage in both market-oriented and more socialist countries that led me to renounce an overly rigid coupling of modernization with capitalism and democracy. Modernization can be associated with either capitalist or socialist economies (democratic or totalitarian) yet have similar effects on families in both polities. This is the basis for the difference I have with the view of modernization in Thatcher's writings. It tends, as far as I can tell, to overly associate modernization with capitalism and liberal democracies.

Wolfe joins Popenoe in distrusting the Swedish model as a solution for the entire world.[26] They both have more faith in cultural change and reconstruction than socialist planning as ways to address the family issue. Indeed, Popenoe and Wolfe advocate a new moral conversation that would lead to a cultural rebirth of marital commitment, one tough enough and realistic enough to deal with the tensions of modernity.

Elements in a Critical Familism

Popenoe and Wolfe are close to my vision of the need for a new cultural work, initiated by the communities of civil society, that would revive and reconstruct the institution of marriage. Their vision, however, gives little attention to the role of religious institutions in this cultural work. If the family issue is first of all a cultural issue, as Popenoe and Wolfe believe, then religion, as it did in the past, must play a decisive role even today in the reconstruction of marriage and family ideals.

Christianity should be an important voice, though certainly not the only voice, in this cultural work because when rightly interpreted, Christianity is an important resource for the reconstruction of marriage and family theories in Western societies. My colleagues and I first set forth our ideas on marriage and family reconstruction — what we term a new

25. Wolfe, *Whose Keeper?* pp. 52-60, 133-42.
26. Popenoe, *Disturbing the Nest,* pp. 243-49.

kind of familism — in *From Culture Wars to Common Ground.*[27] Ours is not a familism that blesses and supports cohesive families at any cost. Family cohesion should not excuse physical and mental mistreatment, alcohol and drug abuse, or other forms of oppressive behavior within families. Critical familism promotes the ideal of the equal-regard, mother-father partnership where both husband and wife have, in principle, equal access to the responsibilities and privileges of both the public world of citizenship and employment and the domestic sphere of household maintenance and child care.[28] This is the critical principle that takes this new familism beyond the divided spheres and soft patriarchy of the so-called traditional family of the industrial era during the nineteenth and early twentieth centuries. Equal regard as a critical principle not only applies to the internal structure of families but also demands the reformation of society so that government, market, and education are more supportive of the formation and stability of justice in marriage and family. Critical familism closely associates the civil institutions of family and marriage with having and raising children, even though it fully acknowledges that within Christianity there is a dignified place for vocations of singleness and special marital vocations that do not include children. In addition, critical familism acknowledges that other religious traditions can contribute to this great cultural work. Parallel efforts to revive and reconstruct marriage along the lines of the equal-regard family can be found in other religious traditions and are underway in various scholarly quarters.[29]

Christianity provides excellent resources for the development of this new critical familism. Early Christianity, especially pre-Pauline and Pauline Christianity, was a family revolution. It significantly qualified, although it did not completely dismantle, the honor-shame codes that dominated family and marriage in the Greco-Roman world that consti-

---

27. Browning et al., *From Culture Wars to Common Ground*, pp. 2, 25, 30.

28. Browning et al., *From Culture Wars to Common Ground*, p. 2.

29. The project of the Religious Consultation on Population, Reproductive Health, and Ethics under the direction of Daniel Maguire works to retrieve something of an equal-regard understanding of male-female relations in the world religions. This project, however, does somewhat neglect marriage. See my critique of the project in *Marriage and Modernization*, pp. 223-44. For samples of the work of the Religious Consultation, see the following: Daniel C. Maguire, *Sacred Choices: The Right to Contraception and Abortion in Ten World Religions* (Minneapolis: Fortress, 2001); Patricia Beatie Jung, Mary Hunt, and Radhika Balakrishnan, eds., *Good Sex: Feminist Perspectives from the World Religions* (New Brunswick, N.J.: Rutgers University Press, 2001).

tuted the social and cultural context of early Christianity.[30] By honor-shame codes, I mean a family system in which free men gained honor through exhibiting qualities of dominance and agency and were shamed if they lost these virtues, generally in conflict with other men. Women, in these societies, gained honor by restricting their lives primarily to the domestic sphere and submitting to male protection. They were shamed if they went beyond these boundaries or were violated by the intrusion into their private space of other males outside their family and clan.

Early Christianity never completely disconnected from the honor-shame codes that surrounded it. It qualified them, however, by celebrating male servanthood rather than male dominance, by applying the Golden Rule and neighbor love to the relationship between husband and wife, by requiring males to renounce their sexual privileges with female slaves and young boys, and by elevating the status of women.[31] As the American sociologist Rodney Stark has argued in *The Rise of Christianity,* pagan women flocked to early Christianity because of its stand against infanticide, its restrictions on divorce (which in antiquity worked to the disadvantage of women), and its demand that men be responsible fathers and faithful husbands.[32] The famous Cambridge anthropologist Jack Goody argues that it was not only the Protestant Reformation that helped to give birth to the modern conjugal and companionate family, as has been suggested by Harvard historian Steven Ozment.[33] He believes that the seeds of the equal-regard marriage go back to the value of the individual found in early Christianity and its emphasis on "inter-personal, rather than inter-group, bonds."[34]

This emphasis on the value of the individual, along with insights from Roman family law, led eleventh- and twelfth-century Roman Catho-

---

30. For a review of the application of the insights of cultural anthropology on honor-shame societies to an understanding of the influence of early Christianity on families, see the following: Bruce Malina, *The New Testament World: Insights from Cultural Anthropology* (Louisville: Westminster John Knox, 1993); Carolyn Osiek and David Balch, *Families in the New Testament World* (Louisville: Westminster John Knox, 1997); Browning et al., *From Culture Wars to Common Ground,* pp. 129-54.

31. For amplification of these points, see Browning et al., *From Culture Wars to Common Ground,* pp. 129-56.

32. Rodney Stark, *The Rise of Christianity* (San Francisco: HarperCollins, 1997), pp. 98-118.

33. Steven Ozment, *Protestants: The Birth of a Revolution* (New York: Doubleday, 1992), pp. 151-69.

34. Jack Goody, *The Development of the Family and Marriage in Europe* (Cambridge: Cambridge University Press, 1994), p. 23.

lic canon law to make mutual consent between bride and groom the decisive factor defining marriage.[35] This move functioned to elevate the status of the conjugal couple over the power and control of the extended family. It limited the power of fathers to give their daughters in marriage for political and economic gain. According to the historian David Herlihy, this emphasis on the integrity and sanctity of the conjugal couple contributed to the downfall of polygyny, ended the monopoly of women by wealthy men, and introduced a new democratization of marriage whereby both poor men and rich men could find women to marry.[36] Although Luther and Calvin rejected the Roman Catholic idea of marriage as a sacrament, they accepted most of the other accomplishments of Roman Catholic canon law, especially the emphasis on marriage as requiring mutual consent by bride and groom.

My Major Substantive Difference with Thatcher

Luther and Calvin added one important element that societies influenced by the Protestant Reformation may be losing as a result of the deinstitutionalization of marriage reflected in increased cohabitation, nonmarital births, and movements in law designed to accommodate these trends. This points to a subject about which Thatcher and I appear to disagree — a difference that goes beyond our respective views about the nature of modernization. This has to do with the role of civil law in relation to Christian marriage.

Marriage, according to the Reformers, was understood as both a public *and* an ecclesial affair. It was for them first of all a natural and civic good that contributes to social flourishing. Marriage was of vital interest to a good society and therefore of interest to the state. The health and welfare of both children and adults depended in large part on sound marriages. The leaders of the Reformation thereby insisted that marriage be registered by the state and secondarily blessed by the church. The state registration of marriage gradually brought to an end the confusions of clandestine or secret marriages — marriages that were unwitnessed by friends, family, state, or church but still valid in the eyes of the church be-

---

35. John Witte Jr., *From Sacrament to Contract: Marriage, Religion, and Law in the Western Tradition* (Louisville: Westminster John Knox, 1997).

36. David Herlihy, *Medieval Households* (Cambridge, Mass.: Harvard University Press, 1985), pp. 61-62.

cause they were allegedly based on mutual consent. Since the Reformation, religion and state in most Western societies have cooperated in a great cultural work that made marriage simultaneously a public institution as well as a personal, consensual, and religious one. This step brought more public accountability into marital arrangements and limited the various manipulations of the marital process that ecclesial recognition of private and unwitnessed vows had often invited.

It is my belief that this grand cooperation between state and religious institutions on marriage was a major social accomplishment and should not be easily relinquished. It brought together theological and secular justifications for marriage in a complicated and sophisticated synthesis. The Reformers believed that the state, when properly conceived, should be sensitive to the will of God expressed in Scriptures. They also thought, as Luther scholar Brian Gerrish has so forcefully demonstrated, that government as an expression of the earthly kingdom is an appropriate arena for the exercise of practical reason, or what Aristotle called *phronēsis*.[37] Marriage as a civic good was revealed by God in the Genesis accounts of creation (Gen. 1:27; 2:24) but was also an institution that could be seen as a civic good by the natural processes of practical reason. The idea of marriage as a civic good of interest to both state and church seems undeveloped in the writings of Thatcher. Yet marriage as a civic and secular good is threatened just as certainly by the forces of modernization and globalization as is marriage as a covenant or sacrament within the precincts of the church.

Although the modern state today is less inclined to see its task as implementing the will of God, there is a place even within theology for trusting practical reason's capacity to see the wisdom of state registry and accountability for those entering and exiting marriage. Sound marriages contribute to the common good; they also contribute to the good of the individuals and couples involved. Recent studies show that marriage on average contributes to the mental health, physical health, sexual satisfaction, and wealth of the couples involved.[38] At the same time, there are great psychological, physical, and financial vulnerabilities that accompany both marriage and marriage-like arrangements. This includes the strong possibility of pregnancies (for example, the explosion of out-of-wedlock births even in this era of birth control), disease, or the precipitous loss of income (for example, divorced or never-married single moth-

---

37. Brian Gerrish, *Grace and Reason: A Study in Luther* (Oxford: Clarendon, 1962).
38. Waite and Gallagher, *The Case for Marriage*, p. 18.

ers who become poor). Cohabiting relationships may entail romance, mutual fascination, and perhaps real love and commitment. But they also entail extremely high material and psychological risks to adults, the children born of these unions, and society as a whole. These risks exist even when cohabiting relations are guided by what Thatcher calls the "norm of marriage" (the intent to someday make the public, legal, and religious commitments that marriage entails).[39] Marriage has these commitments, but it also enjoys the legal and communal protections that its public vows invoke. Cohabitation does not enjoy these protections. This makes its vulnerabilities all the more profound.

The vulnerabilities of cohabitation and other forms of sexual involvement are analogous to the dangers of driving an automobile. People can get hurt, maimed, and unsettled for life by car accidents and reckless driving, in spite of the best of intentions and the worthiness of the final destination. Societies seek to establish basic qualifications for receiving a license to drive. In the area of marriage and its equivalents, Western societies have not considered implementing analogous qualifications even though the gains and losses of the marital venture are nearly as serious as those of operating a vehicle on the open road. In driving an automobile, a license constitutes a framework for accountability for individual drivers that helps determine qualifications for insurance and, if necessary, the mediations and determinations of legal justice when infringements and accidents occur. Marriage and marital-like relationships are more like driving a vehicle than contemporary romantic and religious views of marriage fully acknowledge. But this romanticization and privatization of marriage in popular culture and popular Christianity is something new; both late medieval Roman Catholicism and the Protestant Reformers Luther and Calvin understood the civil, material, and health values at stake in marriage and saw a robust place for civil law as well as theology in defining its meaning.[40]

Thatcher has been insightful in seeing the worldwide trends toward cohabitation and nonmarital births as opportunities for evangelization. I believe, however, that he goes too far in normalizing cohabitation. In Chicago, a Roman Catholic Church composed primarily of poor Hispanics offers each year a free group marriage ceremony and celebratory party to its cohabiting couples who cannot afford society's image of a proper wedding. This parish also explains to these couples the full meaning of the Roman

---

39. Adrian Thatcher, *Living Together and Christian Ethics* (Cambridge: Cambridge University Press, 2002), p. 275.

40. Witte, *From Sacrament to Contract*, pp. 2-8.

Catholic understanding of marriage as sacrament, as indissoluble, and as a source of grace. In the process, the couples also become legally married and enjoy the clarity, public status, and protections of marriage as a civil contract. I agree with the policies of this church, but I am less clear that Thatcher is concerned about the role of legal marriage in our society.

I probably am more interested than Thatcher in maintaining the co-operative relation between church and state that was accomplished by the Protestant Reformation. He seems, at times, to be willing to decouple marriage from its legal and contractual dimensions. Bringing cohabita-tion under the norm of marriage by making it a part of the betrothal pro-cess does not give cohabitation these protections. The church can bless cohabitations, but that does not make the two individuals legally married unless they consent to be married before authorized persons. I am not op-timistic that the churches will be any more successful in bringing public and ecclesial accountability to betrothal than they presently are able to achieve with marriage itself.

This is Thatcher's principal constructive proposal; he wants to bring the marital norm to cohabitation and see it as the first step in a process to-ward an ecclesially blessed marriage. His proposal is novel and attractive. But will this broadening of the marital norm be any more likely to bring order and meaning to cohabitation than presently occurs with marriage? It is my argument that the spread of technical rationality into the realm of intimate relations makes it more difficult to baptize cohabitation with the marital norm than it would be to strengthen marriage more directly.

Thatcher is entirely correct that the cooperative arrangement between church and state did not always exist. In medieval Europe, the legal and the religious aspects of marriage were brought together under a single canopy — the sacramental theology and the canon law of the Roman Catholic Church. The secular state could not supervise marriage because, in fact, it did not exist. Although shreds of civil marriage law existed in Roman, Germanic, and Frankish territories, the Catholic Church was the major player controlling marriage as both a religious and a contractual re-ality. Thatcher is also correct that there was a differentiation between be-trothal and marriage in those days and that betrothal had, in many places, the greater binding power.[41]

But Thatcher does not understand the difficulties that would come

---

41. Thatcher brilliantly traces the differentiation of betrothal and marriage in the Bi-ble and in the early and late medieval church in chapters 4 and 5 of *Living Together and Chris-tian Ethics.*

in modern differentiated societies if betrothal, rather than marriage, were considered the beginning of a sexual and cohabiting process that eventually results in marriage. The strains of modernization make it more difficult to give public accountability to the marital process no matter where it begins. In view of the great absence of young people from the churches of England, I find it particularly puzzling to concretely and practically imagine how this proposal would be implemented. What are the grounds for believing that young couples would be attracted to the guidance of the church in turning their cohabitation into official betrothal understood as the first step toward marriage? And since there is little discussion of the role of civil law in Thatcher's understanding of betrothal, I find no instrumentalities with teeth that can enable cohabitors to mediate the conflicts over property, children, finances, and disease that their experimental unions might produce.

Early modernity changed the situation of the medieval church and its power over the contractual and sacramental aspects of marriage. The birth of the modern state made things different. Luther and Calvin identified the latent contractual and natural features of marriage that could be found in canon law and in the thought of Peter Lombard and Thomas Aquinas. They delegated these aspects of marriage to the supervision of the modern secular state. In the intervening centuries, the processes of modernization have rapidly expanded, as I described above. Today both state and church are having major difficulties implementing accountability in marriage and marriage-like relationships. The ravages of modernization, I predict, will make it more and more difficult for the church to enter the increasingly private, individualistic, and sequestered realms of modern sexuality for purposes of evangelism and the encouragement of ecclesial marriages. This is why the church must not attempt to order the field of human sexuality and marriage alone. *It must cooperate with other sectors of society.*

It is my view that churches should join with state, market, law, and various other institutions of civil society to restore the public understanding of and competence for marriage as both a religious and a legal-contractual reality. This cannot be accomplished by religious institutions alone. The forces of modernization function to undercut long-term marital dependencies, define intimate relations in terms of the cost-benefit logics of the market, and sequester sexual relations in the nooks and crannies of highly differentiated societies away from public visibility. These forces are simply too strong to be countered without an enormous cooperative cultural work involving several different sectors of society.

I have tried to elaborate what this complex cultural work might look like in a variety of my writings.[42] Describing them in detail would take this article beyond its appropriate scope. There is little doubt that there should be interest in the kinds of initiatives that Thatcher envisions for couples who cohabit outside the frameworks of legal marriage and ecclesial blessing. But more and more, marriage education in schools, universities, and welfare programs; tax policies that reward rather than penalize marriage; new work and family arrangements; better child-care arrangements; divorce reform that renders it more of a process and more child-centered; new cultural visions that honor marriage; critiques of popular culture that disparage marriage and glamorize nonmarriage; and more powerfully articulated theologies of marriage and family — all of these must interact in reconstructing social and cultural arrangements so that equal-regard marriages can enjoy both the protections of law and the rich meanings of the great covenantal and sacramental traditions of the Christian faith. Whether the church places a new emphasis on betrothal, attempts to renew marriage itself, or tries to go in both directions at once, it must see its work as part of a larger multidimensional work of culture that it can inform but not in itself either control or fully implement.

42. See particularly chapter 11 of Browning et al., *From Culture Wars to Common Ground;* chapter 8 of my *Marriage and Modernization;* and the entirety of Browning and Rodriguez, *Reweaving the Social Tapestry.*

Chapter 14

Egos without Selves: A Critique of the Family Theory of the Chicago School of Economics (1994)

Economic processes are highly influential on family dynamics and trends. One of the most powerful theories of how the economic structures of society shape families comes from my colleagues in the Chicago school of economics — Milton Friedman, Gary Becker, and law-and-economics scholar Richard Posner. Not only have they tried to give explanatory accounts of the field of economics, their theories have influenced several branches of the social sciences and shaped the general culture, including our views of family processes and functions.

This is why in the early phases of the Religion, Culture, and Family Project, I felt compelled to give this school a critical review from the perspective of practical theology and theological ethics — what I call in this chapter *practically oriented theological ethics* and in other contexts simply *practical theological ethics*. The Chicago school of economics reduces the family to a little engine of production — a "little factory," as Becker calls it — that produces a variety of commensurable satisfactions — meals, sex, warmth, wealth, and children.

Yet, behind this rather cold and calculative mode of speaking about marriage and family, one can find a vague but discernible narrative about the meaning of life. One scholar says the Chicago school contains an implicit Protestant ethic that views work, economic investment, and savings as morally good and self-indulgence and extravagance as morally bad. If it is true that this allegedly neutral and scientific economic theory actually contains an implicit religious narrative and ethic (and I believe it is true), then this school of economics is a fit candidate for review and critique by a practical-theological ethic of the kind that I advance in this chapter.

This paper is an exercise in theological ethics within a larger practical theological context. For some years, I have been investigating the relation of theological ethics and practical theology. When theological ethics attends to both the description of the contexts of action and the modes of transformation necessary for the realization of appropriate norms, it then becomes an instance of practical theology. For the purposes of this paper, I will call such an enterprise a "radically oriented theological ethics." Although this paper attends to the contexts of the contemporary family, issues pertaining to the transformation of the contemporary family must be addressed in a later paper.

I hold that a practically oriented theological ethics should be conceived as a revised correlational task. It should be seen as a critical conversation between an authentically conceived theory and practice of the Christian faith and the theory and practice of major competing secular voices. In this paper, I want to have such a critical conversation with the family theory of the Chicago school of economics. The Chicago school of economics is an extremely powerful social science perspective, which has, at least on occasions, defined itself explicitly over against what Richard Posner has called the "moral tradition" on these matters. By moral tradition, Posner means the legal and cultural traditions shaped primarily by Judaism and Christianity. It is because of this frontal challenge to the Western religious tradition that we are justified in bringing a theological-ethical analysis to the claims made by the family theory of the Chicago school.

I will concentrate on the contributions of economist and sociologist Gary Becker and legal theorist Judge Richard Posner. The prominence of these men can be seen in the Nobel Prize in economics recently won by Becker and the persistent rumors that Posner may someday become a judge of the United States Supreme Court.

The Chicago School and the Market Family

Gary Becker is the older man and the leading Chicago economist writing on the family. His 1981 *A Treatise on the Family* was recently reissued by Harvard University Press.[1] Becker is famous for expanding economic theories into a wide range of human activities generally thought to be non-economic in nature. Family affairs is just one of these. In his earlier *Hu-*

---

1. Gary Becker, *A Treatise on the Family* (Cambridge, Mass.: Harvard University Press, 1991).

man Capital and *The Economic Approach to Human Behavior,* Becker expanded the concept of wealth beyond money and property to include such things as human learning and skill, the use of time, children, and domestic or household work. He writes of a different form of capital: human capital in contrast to material capital or wealth.[2]

Posner follows Becker in this expansive concept of economics and wealth and brings these insights to the theory of law and jurisprudence. Judge Posner is a leading figure in the so-called law and economics movement, a movement that defines law in relation to its economic functions. He has been unbelievably prolific and continues to be so since leaving full-time teaching at the University of Chicago Law School and becoming a judge for the U.S. Court of Appeals for the Seventh Circuit. His most relevant books for this essay are *The Economics of Justice, Economic Analysis of Law, The Problems of Jurisprudence,* and his recent massive contribution to the legal theory of sex and family titled *Sex and Reason.*[3]

Both the power and the possible evils of the Chicago school, particularly on family matters, were first brought to my attention by Alan Wolfe in his *Whose Keeper? Social Science and Moral Obligation.*[4] Wolfe develops an argument, similar to Jürgen Habermas's, that various expressions of the systems world, notably markets and bureaucracies, are intruding upon and undermining the integrity of civil society — the world of free interaction between moral agents that creates the culture and social networks of local communities.[5] Uncontrolled government bureaucracies and uncurbed capitalist market systems, Wolfe insists, have almost equal capacity to undermine civil society. To persuade us of the truth of these charges, he attempts to document the decline of what he calls the "public family" under the impact of Sweden's welfare bureaucracy and the analogous decline of the "private family" under the impact of American market forces.[6]

The private family, he explains, increasingly understands intimate life in analogy to the cost-benefit logic of markets. Long-term commitments,

2. Gary Becker, *Human Capital* (New York: Columbia University Press, 1975), and *The Economic Approach to Human Behavior* (Chicago: University of Chicago Press, 1976).

3. Richard Posner, *The Economics of Justice* (Cambridge, Mass.: Harvard University Press, 1981), *Economic Analysis of Law* (Boston: Little, Brown, 1986), *The Problems of Jurisprudence* (Cambridge, Mass.: Harvard University Press, 1990), and *Sex and Reason* (Cambridge, Mass.: Harvard University Press, 1992).

4. Alan Wolfe, *Whose Keeper? Social Science and Moral Obligation* (Berkeley: University of California Press, 1989).

5. Wolfe, *Whose Keeper?* pp. 13-19.

6. Wolfe, *Whose Keeper?* pp. 52-60, 133-58.

mutuality, and parental self-sacrifice are increasingly giving way to short-term satisfactions, utilitarian individualism, and technical rationality, even in the intimate affairs of husband and wives, parents and children. This is where the Chicago school of economics comes in. Wolfe charges that this school gives intellectual justification to a culture-wide tendency to think more and more of the love life of families in analogy to the cost-benefit calculations of exchange markets.[7] Michael Walzer in his *Spheres of Justice* makes similar observations about the spread of market logics into non-economic areas of life such as the family.[8] Walzer regrets this emerging state of affairs as much as Wolfe. It is with their concerns in mind that I decided to study the amity theory of the Chicago school of economics. Wolfe and Walzer seemed at least half right; in recent years I had observed a chaplain at a professional conference present an ethical analysis of an abortion counseling case in cost-benefit terms. I also had observed marriage vows at weddings articulated in these terms. Finally, I had presented in my own writings a marriage counseling case of a couple who appeared to think of their relationship in a cost-benefit perspective.[9]

Becker and the Efficient Family

Becker is what is often called a neoclassical economic theorist. Neoclassical theory believes that humans always act rationally to maximize individual satisfactions or utility.[10] They do this, however, within the context of the satisfaction opportunities of various markets. A market is a context of exchange where an individual uses owned commodities or money to purchase commodities that satisfy enduring desires. Rational action is means-end action. It is also cost-benefit action; the rational individual always balances the satisfactions expected from a commodity with the costs expended to get the commodity.

Classical economic theory assumes that humans are driven by a relatively small but highly stable set of desires. In one place, Becker describes these desires as underlying preferences that inform a variety of more spe-

---

7. Wolfe, *Whose Keeper?* pp. 36-42.

8. Michael Walzer, *Spheres of Justice* (New York: Basic, 1982).

9. Don Browning, "Pastoral Theology in a Pluralistic Age," in *Practical Theology*, ed. Don Browning (San Francisco: Harper and Row, 1983), pp. 187-203; see also Don Browning, *Religious Ethics and Pastoral Care* (Philadelphia: Fortress, 1983).

10. Becker, *Economic Approach to Human Behavior*, pp. 3-14; see also Amitai Etzioni, *The Moral Dimension: Toward a New Economics* (New York: Free Press, 1988), pp. 1-19.

cific interests. They include the desire for "health, prestige, sensual pleasure, benevolence, or envy."[11]

Benevolence refers primarily to parents' concern for their own children. Both Becker and Posner agree with sociobiologists that this is an inborn human tendency. We love our natural children — as well as our blood-related brothers, sisters, nieces, and nephews — because they carry our genes and are, for that reason, partially us.[12] This is the sociobiological theory of "inclusive fitness," which recently has been incorporated into rational-choice theory.[13] Aristotle and St. Thomas, without benefit of modern genetic theory, long ago observed that we love the copy of ourselves that we find in our children.[14] Love of our children is one of the stable desires, according to both Becker and the classical philosophical tradition, that we want our various markets to satisfy.

Becker has distinguished himself by extending rational-choice theory into nonmaterial aspects of life. He does this, in part, by the metaphorical extension of the language of neoclassical economics into these nonmaterial areas. For instance, a home is a little "factory" that both "produces" and "consumes" wealth. Children are both "consumer" and "producer durables."[15] Children give "satisfaction" to their parents just like food, clothing, and a night at the movies. In this respect, children are like "commodities" and parents can be said to "consume" their children as they do other commodities. People bring "cost-benefit" calculations to the selection of their mates just as they do to their cars and even their decisions to have children. That is why we have fewer children today; their costs in relation to their satisfactions have gone up.

This expansion of the concept of wealth has the advantage of helping us perceive the importance of other forms of wealth besides property and money. Domestic labor-meal reparation, house cleaning, child care, and house and automobile maintenance all produce wealth, and to show how this is true, monetary values can be assigned to these activities. Because wealth refers to total produced and consumed satisfactions, two-person households with differentiated functions (especially men and women in marriages) produce more wealth than single-person households.[16] In ex-

---

11. Becker, *Economic Approach to Human Behavior*, p. 5.

12. Becker, *A Treatise on the Family*, p. 364; Posner, *Sex and Reason*, p. 189.

13. W. D. Hamilton, "The Genetic Evolution of Social Behavior, II," *Journal of Theoretical Biology* 7 (1964): 1-52.

14. Aristotle, *Politics*, bk. 1, chap. 2; Thomas Aquinas, *Summa Theologica* q. 1, a. 1.

15. Becker, *Economic Approach to Human Behavior*, pp. 169-75.

16. Becker, *Treatise on the Family*, pp. 20-79.

panding the concept of wealth in this way, Becker makes it nearly equivalent to the *ordo bonorum* (the order of the premoral or nonmoral good) as this concept functioned in the classical Aristotelian and Thomistic ethical traditions. What is different, however, is the prominent place Becker gives to individualistically conceived cost-benefit analyses within the constraints of available markets.

The Situation of Families

Practically oriented theological ethicists, I have argued, are interested as much in the way problems are defined as in the way they are answered. This is because, invariably, the way issues are defined goes far in determining what answers seem convincing. This raises the question, how does the Chicago school describe the situation of families today? Becker and Posner agree in their diagnosis, with Posner apparently accepting the earlier analyses of Becker on this question. The single most important fact about contemporary families in all modern societies is the move of women from domestic labor to wage labor in market systems outside the home. This trend was complemented by the move of governmental bureaucracy into the economic support of poor single mothers in the form of Aid to Dependent Children, Medicaid, food stamps, and so forth.[17]

These two trends have greatly decreased the economic dependence of women on men and have been a major factor behind the increase of divorce, the decline of the marriage rate, the decline of the birthrate, the growing number of births outside of wedlock, and the rise of single-parent families. Rational choice has often led women to realize that they are better off relying on their own earning power or on the paternalistic goodness of the state than on the capricious and arbitrary will of a husband. Furthermore, rational choice has led many men to feel that they can get most of life's sexual satisfactions and other comforts outside of the burdens of marriage.

Neither Becker nor Posner invokes cultural interpretations such as "expressive individualism" or feminism to account for these shifts, as is so frequently done in the analyses of Robert Bellah and Christopher Lasch.[18]

---

17. Becker, *Treatise on the Family,* pp. 356-57; Posner, *Sex and Reason,* pp. 171-72.

18. Robert Bellah, Richard Madsen, William Sullivan, Ann Swidler, and Steven Tipton, *Habits of the Heart* (Berkeley: University of California Press, 1985); Christopher Lasch, *Haven in a Heartless World* (New York: Basic, 1977).

Both individualism and feminism are best seen, according to Becker and Posner, as epiphenomenal to the interaction of rational-choice and the market opportunities of the last several decades.

Although neither Becker nor Posner strongly promotes his own practical solutions to these problems, normative orientations of interest to the practical ethicist are discernible in their writings. Becker tells an economic story that would return us to a higher appreciation for the discipline and differentiated labor of the classic modern family with its breadwinning father and domestic mother. Posner, as we will see, comes close to the line of certain feminists who want to create the cultural sanction, economic support, and political viability of what Andrew Cherlin calls the "feminization of kinship," that is, the growing prevalence of single mothers heading families and raising children with the aid of the state and their largely female networks.

Posner and the Bioeconomic View of Families

Posner advocates a view of law based on philosophical pragmatism. Law is not autonomous, as legal formalists would advocate. It is a function of society's efforts to maximize its utility. Economic analysis helps society adjudicate legal precedents and fresh legal conflicts from the perspective of the wealth-maximizing consequences of various legal decisions.[19] Once again, we must be reminded that wealth for Posner, just as for Becker, refers to the full range of human goods rather than just to property and money. With regard to legal matters pertaining to sexuality and the family, Posner refers to his position as "consequentialist" and "morally neutral."[20] In reality, it is "utilitarian" in ethical orientation and "libertarian" in social philosophy.[21] Posner is sophisticated enough to know that utilitarianism is not a morally neutral position — that it is indeed a very definite moral position rather than morally disinterested. But he believes that the utilitarian can more or less dispassionately analyze the consequences of various legal arrangements without prior religious or philosophical baggage. It is in this sense, he claims, that his view of the law is morally neutral, in contrast to all traditional moral points of view, the most prominent of which have been Judaism and Christianity. Posner treats these

19. Posner, *The Problems of Jurisprudence*, p. 26.
20. Posner, *Sex and Reason*, p. 85.
21. Posner, *Sex and Reason*, p. 3.

moral traditions with considerable respect and insight, but in the end he is quite clear that his pragmatist and utilitarian view should, and most likely will, replace their impact on both the law and society.[22]

Posner brings a well-developed theory of human sexuality to his utilitarian theory of family law. He calls it a bioeconomic theory. It is a synthesis of sociobiology and rational-choice theory. We saw this functioning to some extent in Becker, but in Posner the sociobiological aspects are worked out in more detail and presented more provocatively. Basically, he holds that human beings, both males and females, behave, whether they know it or not, in such a way as to promote their inclusive fitness within the context of the maximizing possibilities of various environments or markets.[23] This beginning point has many implications, only a few of which will I have space to illustrate.

For instance, males and females of most higher species have quite different ways of satisfying their inclusive fitness. The male's natural proclivity is to impregnate widely, almost without limitation, with little deep attachment to his various women or the progeny his multiple unions may produce. Females, on the other hand, are limited to approximately twenty births at most, which throughout most of evolutionary history have been hazardous for both women and infants. Hence, females, especially among Homo sapiens, have been far more cautious in their sexual liaisons and mate selection than have males, confining their sexual gifts, for the most part, to men strong enough and willing to provide some modicum of protection and support for them and their infants. In most of the societies in human history, rational choice has led men and women to organize marriage polygynously. According to Posner, this was a result not so much of the inequality between men and women as of the great disparity of wealth and power among men themselves. This disparity gave some men more resources to attract women and, indeed, meet their needs for protection during their vulnerable childbearing years.[24] This was true especially in the kinds of markets created in the shift from hunter-gatherer societies to the greater wealth-producing power of agricultural societies.

But modern societies are built around capital and wages. This makes it possible for both men and women to earn separate incomes. Such societies are also wealthy enough for governments to support poor women and their children — a form, as Posner calls it, of state polygyny where

22. Posner, *Sex and Reason*, p. 229.
23. Posner, *Sex and Reason*, pp. 88-98.
24. Posner, *Sex and Reason*, pp. 90-95.

many women, in effect, marry the state.[25] In such markets, men and women increasingly choose to work out their satisfactions and inclusive fitness independently of each other — witness in United States the 50 percent divorce rate and the 29 percent out-of-wedlock birthrate, 22 percent in the white community and over 65 percent in the black.

Posner believes that there is little that the law can or should do to change these trends. The companionate family, with its more or less equal mother-father partnership raising children, may be passing into a minority position in modern societies. Protecting and enhancing the companionate family can no longer be the central commitment of the law, as it has been under the impact of Christianity and the incorporation of Catholic canon law into secular law.[26] Since Posner believes that law should promote the wealth-maximizing goals of the larger society, he would have no objections to the law playing an advocacy role on behalf of this family form if it could be proved that it was essential for the maximization of wealth. But Posner is not sure that the companionate family is essential in today's societies for the production of wealth.

The experience of Sweden, he seems to argue, has shown that it is not essential. Family instability is extremely high in Sweden with extensive and generally transient cohabitation, fewer marriages, high levels of divorce, low birthrates, late marriages, and large numbers of people living alone. Because the salaries of working women are so high (90 percent of men's) and government subsidies for all families with children are so high, Swedish family instability has not translated into family poverty, with all of its associated damage to children.

The only issue remaining for Posner, then, is whether absent or unstable fathers are costly for children. If it could be proved that the presence of fathers in families is essential for the physical and psychological health (read "wealth") of children, independent of the economic supports that they provide, he would indeed think it fitting to lend the force of the law to the defense of the companionate mother-father family. But after a rather cursory review of the literature on this issue, he sees no solid evidence supporting such a vaunted role for the male of the species once its role in procreation has been exercised.[27]

25. Posner, *Sex and Reason*, p. 171.
26. Posner, *Sex and Reason*, p. 227. For a discussion of the formation of Catholic canon law on marriage and the family and how it, in turn, influenced the formation of secular family law, see James Brundage, *Law, Sex, and Christian Society in Medieval Europe* (Chicago: University of Chicago Press, 1987).
27. Posner, *Sex and Reason*, p. 192.

Of course, in recent months, evidence has been mounting at a furious rate that Posner is wrong on this issue. Fathers are important for their children, both sons and daughters, in other than material ways.[28] David Blankenhorn's research on this issue[29] and John Snarey's remarkable four-generational study of what working-class fathers did for their children are two important recent contributions to this debate.[30] Even more important is Posner's neglect of recent extensions of inclusive fitness theory. Robert Trivers, Margo Wilson and Martin Daly, Donald Symons, and Barry Hewlett use it to explain the conditions for the development of biological fathers' investment in their children's welfare.[31] Posner overlooks those discussions of how the human male is almost unique among mammals for paternal investment in children and what this may have meant for the evolutionary development of Homo sapiens. In short, the theory shows that paternal investment among male mammals tends to develop where the conditions for paternal certainty exist. When this paternal investment occurred, males began to exert great energy in providing the material and emotional supports necessary for the flourishing of infants who were literally extensions of their own selves — their own genetic mate-

28. The growing evidence for the importance of fathers, beyond the provision of material wealth, is now quite extensive. I have space to mention only a few facts and sources. The National Center of Health Statistics has reported the growing physical, educational, and emotional impairment of American youth (one out of five of all youth and one out of three teenage boys). It concludes that the growing number of single-parent families is a primary cause. (See N. Zill and C. A. Schoenborn, "Developmental, Learning, and Emotional Problems: Health of Our Nation's Children, United States, 1988," in *Advance Data* [U.S. Department of Health and Human Services, no. 190, 1990]). It is now widely quoted that 70 percent of men in our prisons grew up in homes where the father was absent. (See Louis Sullivan, "Fatherless Families," *Television* [Summer 1992]: 34-36.) It is also reported that 80 percent of children in psychiatric facilities come from broken homes, that three out of four suicides among teenagers come from households with one parent, and that youth of single-parent families are *20 to 40 percent* more vulnerable to illness. (For a summary of these and other statistics, see Joe Klein, "Whose Values?" *Newsweek* [June 8, 1992], pp. 18-20, and Myron Magnet, "The Family," *Fortune* [August 10, 1992], pp. 42-47.)

29. David Blankenhorn reviews Popenoe's research in *Fatherless America: Confronting Our Most Urgent Social Problem* (New York: Basic, 1994).

30. John Snarey, *How Fathers Care for the Next Generation* (Cambridge: Harvard University Press, 1993).

31. Robert Trivers, "Parental Investment and Sexual Selection," in *Sexual Selection and the Descent of Man, 1871-1971*, ed. Bernard Campbell (Chicago: Aldine, 1972); Martin Daly and Margo Wilson, *Sex, Evolution, and Behavior* (Belmont, Calif.: Wadsworth, 1978); Donald Symons, *The Evolution of Sexuality* (Oxford: Oxford University Press, 1979); Barry Hewlett, ed., *Father-Child Relations: Cultural and Biosocial Contexts* (New York: Aldine de Gruyter, 1992).

rial. This investment, in contrast to Posner's assumptions, seems important and not easily replaced.

Furthermore, Posner fails to recognize the many ways that men need families to channel their sexuality and aggression, to overcome their tendency to drift into isolation and self-indulgence, and to maintain their health.[32] Since Posner does not embrace this evidence for the negative effects of fatherless families, he, in dynamic contrast to what we can imagine being advocated by Milton Friedman, George Stigler, and other members of the Chicago school of economics, ends in advocating Sweden's form of welfare state with its extensive provisions for day care, medical insurance, paid pregnancy leaves, unemployment compensation, and other such supports necessary to assure that the feminization of kinship does not become, as it has in the United States, the feminization of poverty. Supporting, enhancing, or protecting the companionate family should no longer be, according to him, a central agenda of the law.

Posner's Critique of Christianity on the Family

Posner's presentation of Christian thinking about the family is quite sensitive and, indeed, instructive. This is all the more noteworthy in view of the admission that his economic theory of family law would, in the end, replace the last remnants of Christianity's influence on the law in family matters. Christianity was not the only historical force helping to create the companionate family. Movements in both Greek and Roman society parallel to the rise of Christianity were enhancing, he observes, the legal status of women and mitigating somewhat the harsher aspects of Greek and Roman patriarchy.

It is clear, however, that Posner believes that Christianity was the main force creating the companionate family. Christianity, building on Judaism, taught that both men and women were made in the image of God. This belief translated over the centuries into a variety of specific practices gradually more favorable to women. Christianity objected to arbitrary patriarchal divorce, which put women on the verge of humiliation and economic ruin. It rejected the double standard of Greek and Roman society which permitted sexual freedom for the man but confined women both politically and sexually. But rather than liberating women to func-

---

32. For a discussion of how families socialize male aggression, see James Q. Wilson, *The Moral Sense* (New York: Free Press, 1993), pp. 165-70.

tion like men, Christianity demanded the same fidelity from men that men had previously expected from women. This meant that it objected to all forms of extramarital sex, including the practices among free Greek men of taking boy lovers. It made procreation and the spiritual education of children a central, although not the only, justification for sex and marriage, thus making husbands central to the socialization process of their children.[33] These impulses were visible in primitive Christianity but became increasingly systematized in the synthesis between Christianity and Roman family law that went into the creation of Catholic canon law, and from there into the secular law of most modern societies.[34]

Although Christianity was implicated in the patriarchal structures of ancient Hebrew, Greek, and Roman societies, in comparison to these cultures it was, Posner admits, a positive force contributing to the creation of the modern egalitarian and companionate family. This admission is rather stunning for an economist to make, since, if true, it firmly establishes that religio-cultural factors may shape human behavior independently of the material motivations of rational choice and market opportunities. Posner even gives some credit to the rationality of the Catholic tradition of natural law.[35] And indeed he should, for after all, a biologically grounded rational-choice theory of the kind he is proposing must be seen as some kind of natural law theory, as colleague Richard Epstein correctly argues in his "The Utilitarian Foundations of Natural Law."[36]

Posner clearly values the companionate family. He probably lives in one himself. But there finally is deontological structure to the theory of the companionate family that no utilitarian rational-choice theorist can logically hold as absolute. The companionate family is based on a theory of respect for the selfhood and personhood of both marriage partners. This respect is an ultimate or determinative value; all other values, such as the maximization of wealth, are subordinate to the value of equal respect or equal regard. In the Christian tradition, this equal regard is grounded, as Posner rightly observes, in beliefs about the image of God in both husband and wife and, indeed, children as well. In more strictly liberal and secular theories of the companionate family, equal regard for the selfhood or personhood of marital partners is grounded in some theory about the rationality and self-reflexiveness of all human agents and what this im-

33. Posner, *Sex and Reason*, pp. 151-60, 220-36.

34. Brundage, *Law, Sex, and Christian Society in Medieval Europe*, pp. 576-94.

35. Posner, *Sex and Reason*, p. 227.

36. Richard Epstein, "The Utilitarian Foundations of Natural Law," *Harvard Journal of Law and Public Policy* 12, no. 3 (1989): 77.

plies for the moral necessity of treating all others, including spouses, as ends rather than means.

But Posner is consistent in his rational-choice utilitarianism. When faced with the worldwide drift toward the feminization of kinship and the declining role of fathers in families, he simply tries to calculate the consequences of this. This is where he believes Christianity, and its earlier foundations in Catholic natural law, has failed. It has overestimated the natural need for fathers to provide for and protect their children in companionate families. He writes, "under the social and economic conditions prevailing in modern societies such as that of Sweden, an insistence on compliance with the traditional marriage centered Christian morality may no longer be necessary for the protection of women and children."[37] Law can fulfill its role of enhancing the wealth-maximizing goals of society by providing the economic foundations required to neutralize the negative consequences of these trends toward the dissolution of the companionate family and the feminization of kinship.

Posner can hold such a position because, in the end, rational agents are for him egos and not selves. Humans are reality-oriented rational maximizers, not selves with identities, self-images, anxieties, fragmentations, self-deceptions, and profound needs for self-regard and self-cohesion. Humans are for him pervasively satisfaction seekers who readily sacrifice dignity, self-esteem, self-justification, and a sense of equal regard for increased utility. This seems true even in his picture of children, who seem not so much to need love, affirmation, and positive self-regard as to need financial, educational, intellectual, and medical resources and physical health. It seems simplistic and sentimental to say that children need both self-regard and wealth, but it is neither. Such a simple statement points to the basic difference separating the world of Christian anthropology from the view of humans found in market-oriented rational-choice theory. It is also precisely such an assertion that prepares us for the theological-ethical critique that follows.

A Theological-Ethical Response

Because Becker and Posner live in a world of egos without selves, they also live in a world of selves without narratives and stories. For this reason, they are blind to the narratives that are implicit in their own economic

---

37. Posner, *Sex and Reason*, p. 227.

theories. But there are such narratives, and that is why their theories are fit candidates for theological-ethical analysis.

In *Religious Thought and the Modern Psychologies*,[38] I have argued that contemporary psychotherapeutic psychologies contain a host of unthematized deep metaphors and implicit narratives. I was pleased recently to find an economist who makes a similar analysis of modern economic theory, especially the neoclassical school of the kind we have found in Becker and Posner. Donald McCloskey, in his engaging *If You're So Smart: The Narrative of Economic Expertise*, argues that, like other arts and sciences, economics uses what he calls "the whole rhetorical tetrad: fact, logic, metaphor, and story."[39] Neoclassical economists such as Becker, you will recall, are aware that they use metaphors, since they are constantly and self-consciously extending the terminology of markets, commodities, satisfactions, production, and consumption into nonmarket spheres of life. They also obviously use facts and logics. But they are unaware of their own stories — stories about the rise and decline of fortunes and wealth, and indeed about the rise and fall of what makes life good and meaningful.

McCloskey says that modern economists are ethicists and social philosophers, a point analogous to what I said in *Religious Thought and the Modern Psychologies* about psychotherapeutic psychology. As ethicists, however, economists make their moral points surreptitiously through implicit stories. They are, on the whole, stories in the realist mode of a Thomas Hardy or Henrik Ibsen about both the inevitability and moral permissibility of self-interest and greed.[40] The motivations and behaviors of Homo economicus that they describe also form an ethic that they implicitly advocate. McCloskey believes, however, that they advocate, to their credit, a restrained and prudent greed aimed primarily toward the production of wealth and not just its consumption. We certainly saw this in Becker's tendency to think of the family in analogy to a little factory. What McCloskey writes about neoclassical theory as a whole can easily apply to Becker's economic theory of the family.

> The ethical effect of paying close attention to economic behavior
> . . . is not entirely bad. Economics provides the rudiments of ethical
> thinking for a bourgeois age: accumulate, think ahead; be methodi-

---

38. Don Browning, *Religious Thought and the Modern Psychologies* (Minneapolis: Fortress, 1987).

39. Donald McCloskey, *If You're So Smart: The Narrative of Economic Expertise* (Chicago: University of Chicago Press, 1990), p. 1.

40. McCloskey, *If You're So Smart*, pp. 135-36.

cal if it suits the task; be as honest as is the local custom; above all, do not feel socially inferior to an impulsive aristocracy — their day is done.[41]

In this sense, the ethics of neoclassical economics is a variation of the Protestant ethic that Max Weber described so brilliantly.[42]

Applied to the family, Becker's economic theory is simply a Protestant ethic of families, at least as sociologists have described it. But Becker's ethics of self-interest is clearly different from Posner's. Becker's ethic of production tells us how families produce wealth. Two parents produce more wealth of all kinds than one parent. Investing in your children produces wealth, both human and material. Family division of labor produces wealth. Choose your spouse carefully so that he or she will be on a wealth-producing par with you. Be careful with your time; time is money. Do not have children out of wedlock; you will be poorer. We hear the echoes of Benjamin Franklin's *Poor Richard's Almanac* ring through these ideas, but now they have been applied directly and unambiguously to families.

Posner tells another moral story, even more realistic. Becker would restore not just the companionate family but maybe even the traditional (or modern) family — the breadwinning father, the mother producing material and human capital at home. Posner's moral story is, possibly, one that spells out more an ethics of consumption than an ethics of production. He tells a story of how both market and state will take the place of the father and between them produce the wealth necessary to keep the feminization of kinship from becoming the feminization of poverty.

In the end, I think that McCloskey would like Becker's story better than Posner's. But evaluating these stories is not his main point. His main point, and a very good one, is that societies need more than one story to make them work.[43] McCloskey obviously thinks that the neoclassical economic ethic of honest, hardworking, and prudent self-interest is not bad, as far as economics goes. He probably would agree that such an ethic would be relevant to the economic dimensions of families. With this point set aside for the moment, McCloskey's thesis about the need for multiple and complementary stories is something the practically oriented theological ethicist could not agree with more. It is with this point in mind that I conclude by briefly and tentatively outlining ways theological

41. McCloskey, *If You're So Smart*, p. 140.

42. Max Weber, *The Protestant Ethic and the Spirit of Capitalism*, trans. Talcott Parsons (New York: Charles Scribner's Sons, 1958).

43. McCloskey, *If You're So Smart*, p. 146.

ethics can discover the countervailing stories required to balance the implicit narratives of the Chicago school and the market forces it so forcefully rationalizes.

First, in their penchant for extending economic theory into nonmarket forms of wealth, Decker and Posner are taking a step toward the classical teleological ethical tradition identified with Aristotle, Aquinas, and Mill, as well as its pragmatist variation in thinkers such as William James. This tradition sees ethics as having to do with the realization of human needs and purposes. In their broadened paradigm, the Chicago school is simply acknowledging that humans pursue many purposes and many goods, not just the goods of property and the instruments of monetary exchange. In addition, one must acknowledge that it is sometimes useful to analyze the market value of all sorts of nonmarket goods or forms of wealth, such as education, marriage, and health. But it is the witness of almost all religions, and particularly Judeo-Christian traditions, that it is a tragic mistake to literally measure all the goods of life by their market or exchange value. This fundamental category error is often considered the essence of human sinfulness. No more powerful statement of this can be found than the parable of the rich man who built new barns to store his wealth and then measured his "soul," the essence of his self or personhood, by the ampleness of his possessions. God said to him, "Fool, this night your soul is required of you; and the things you have prepared, whose will they be?" The parable concludes with the words, "So is he who lays up treasure for himself, and is not rich toward God" (Luke 12:19-21). It would be wrong to interpret this and other parables as saying that there is no place in human life for the rational choice narratives of Becker and Posner. Indeed, the parables abound in references to landlords who hire and fire, who expect an honest day's work from their employees, and who hope for returns on their investments. These religious stories do not totally displace the economic stories of their day; they instead constitute a countervailing narrative that balances and relativizes them. If this is true, the Gospel parables would not displace or obscure the material aspects of marriage and families; they instead would relativize and balance them with another story that has primarily to do with the anxiety-driven excesses of the will, the inevitability of loss, and the possibilities of recovery, both material and spiritual.

Second, in spite of the relative truth of the economic story, it is not to be taken too seriously. As McCloskey says, the economic story of self-interest has the virtue of adding a note of realism into our view of life, including our view of intimate affairs. To this extent, the theological rele-

vance of the economic narrative is its particular interpretation of finitude. The Jewish and Christian traditions understand well the creaturely
and finite character of humans and their institutions. Marriages and families are finite and must organize themselves to cope with the material aspects of life. The economic story helps us understand some of the constraints created by the kind of economic order in which we live. But the
classic Jewish and Christian religious stories may also help us understand
the needs of the self, its anxieties, and the conflicting impulses it brings
to both the interpersonal and material aspects of intimate affairs.

Third, exchanges in markets or families appear to conform, on the
surface, to the utilitarian and cost-benefit logics so meticulously analyzed
in the neoclassical school of economics. But this school is neglectful of
the broader deontological logics that surround these utilitarian logics in
both the market and the family. Amitai Etzioni has argued this forcefully
in his *The Moral Dimension: Toward a New Economics.* Etzioni subsumes the
rational choice model to a larger deontological framework. He believes
that humans have multiple selves, both moral selves and rational-
calculating selves. Ideally, and in fact generally, our calculating selves are
bounded and guided by our moral selves. The moral self, according to
Etzioni, works on deontological principles of duty or reversible obligation. It treats others as ends and not as means only, and it regards others
and itself with equal seriousness. In the good society, and in the good
family, rational calculations are placed within, and limited by, a larger
ethic of fairness and mutual respect.[44] This is why in business we are interested in equal playing fields and why in families we are concerned with
equal power.

In some of his writings, Etzioni applies a more mixed deontological
economic ethic to families — an ethic that finds a place for certain teleological judgments within the context of a wider moral field defined by
deontological logics. Within this deontological framework, he inquires
into certain teleological considerations relevant to the importance of fathers for the well-being of children. Here he reads the empirical evidence
in ways diametrically opposed to Posner's reading. For Etzioni, fathers are
important for both the material and the psychological wealth of children,
and families in turn are important for the material and psychological
wealth of men. This was the point of the sections on the family in "The
Responsive Communitarian Manifesto" published in his journal *The Responsive Community,* a manifesto signed by many of the leading political

44. Etzioni, *The Moral Dimension,* pp. 11-13.

and social scientists of our day, including such luminaries as Robert Bellah, William Galston, Uric Bronfenbrenner, and Mary Ann Glendon.[45]

In recent writings, I have developed a theological ethic of Christian love similar to Etzioni's mixed deontological moral theory. Following the work of Louis Janssens, I have called it a love ethic of equal regard.[46] Janssens understands Christian neighbor love — "You shall love your neighbor as yourself" (Matt. 19.19) — as obligating us to take the needs of the other as seriously as we do our own. Janssens also argues that this same principle requires us to take our own needs as seriously as we do the needs of others. In other words, neighbor love is a reversible ethic requiring that both self and other be treated with equal regard. Self-sacrifice, in Janssen's view, is derived from love as equal regard, is not an end in itself, and is a transitional ethic designed to restore broken and unequal relations to a situation of equal regard. Self-sacrifice, in this view, cannot be used to justify a permanent sacrificial role for anyone. This also applies to the relation of husband and wife.

Janssens's interpretation of love as equal regard further agrees with Etzioni by including a teleological moment within a wider deontological or reversible moral logic. Love as equal regard (the *ordo caritatis*) permits the realistic pursuit of, and hierarchical ranking of, a wide range of premoral goods so long as this pursuit does not imperil the integrity of the wider deontological ethic. These premoral goods, according to Janssens, are consistent with the *ordo bonorum* (the order of the good) of the classic teleological tradition. They are also analogous, I would argue, to the expanded concept of wealth found in the Chicago school. Because of the parallels between Etzioni's philosophical ethic and Janssens's interpretation of Christian love, it is arguable that love as equal regard can advance much the same critique of the rational-choice theory of the family that Etzioni presents.

Posner, as we saw, flirted with the deontological constraints of an equal-regard ideal of the companionate marriage. With admirable consistency, however, he was willing to sacrifice it to the vision of utility that he believes the law should serve. Becker, on the other hand, speaks unwittingly in several places of "equality" in family relationships without fully

45. "The Responsive Communitarian Manifesto," *The Responsive Community* 2 (Winter 1992): 4-6.

46. Louis Janssens, "Norms and Priorities of a Love Ethics," *Louvain Studies* 6 (Spring 1977): 207-38; Browning, *Religious Thought and the Modern Psychologies*, pp. 117-60. See also Browning, *A Fundamental Practical Theology: Descriptive and Strategic Proposals* (Minneapolis: Fortress, 1992), pp. 139-70.

realizing that this is generally thought to be a deontological concept. To use it, without careful explanation, may compromise the purity of his rational-choice model.[47]

I will conclude with a word about the social importance of multiple stories playing countervailing roles. The law may indeed in the future take the direction that Posner envisions. This is because the forces that are destabilizing families in our society are so pervasive that much of what legislative law does is to provide material resources to minimize the poverty and other negative consequences associated with these family trends. But if the law does this, and only this, it will be a sad day for families in Western societies. Although Christianity can no longer in the present pluralistic context expect to use the law to protect its unique vision of life, the virtues of the equal-regard family integrating both fathers and mothers into the raising of children is a view that can be advanced not only theologically (with the use of Janssens) but also philosophically (as in the case of Etzioni). In contrast to Posner's view, the law should continue to encourage fathers to take their full responsibility in families, for the good of both their children and themselves, and they should do this within an ethic of equal regard. Christians can argue for this at the level of the law without insisting that the law give special privilege to the specific features of the Christian narrative. The narrative features of Christian family theory — dealing mainly with self-sacrificial giving, sin, grace, and forgiveness — play important counterbalancing roles, but a full amplification of these roles will have to wait for a later paper.

As a subordinate dimension of an equal-regard family ethic, the law should support a host of concrete legal and legislative incentives, which, for the most part, Posner ignores. These proposals include special tax credits for couples with children, incentives that would create better child care, pregnancy leaves both paid and unpaid, and more well-paying jobs

---

47. Becker, *The Economic Approach to Human Behavior*, p. 134. Here Becker defines "care" to mean, "M's utility would depend on the commodity consumption of F as well as on his own." Later he writes, "This concept of caring between married persons, therefore, does imply sharing — equal sharing when the caring is full and mutual — and is thus consistent with the popular belief that persons in love 'share'" (p. 235). Becker is on the borderline, here, of deontological thinking. What keeps him from falling over the edge is probably his belief that equal sharing pays higher dividends. A pure equal-regard thinker would say we are morally obligated to share equally even if it does not add to the joint utility. But it would be wrong to say that an equal-regard thinker is uninterested in joint utility. It is simply that maximizing joint utility or wealth would have to proceed within an ethic of equal regard.

for everyone, especially men in inner cities. Such proposals also would entail remedial supports such as federally mandated child-care payments from absent fathers and more carefully crafted divorces that make better long-term provisions for children. Legal supports for this companionate mother-father partnership, however, should not ignore the need for assistance to other family forms in raising children, especially in view of the present state of the family crisis.

Asking the law to provide these incentives and supports for the companionate family raising children should not obscure the special role of churches and synagogues as counterbalances to the ambiguous effects on families of both government and market. Religious institutions should not forget that their special task is not to control secular law but to present an alternative religio-ethical narrative that, among other objectives, will help prepare young men and women (but in our time especially young men) to appreciate the special vocation of parenting within the context of a love ethic of equal regard surrounded by forgiveness and grace. To this extent, a worthy model might be the great sexual revolutionary, Martin Luther, who developed a vocation of male parenting as an antidote to the medieval ideology that celibacy was a higher calling, especially for men.[48] In our time, the ideologies of masculinity are different, but the need for a new Luther may be as great.[49]

48. Martin Luther, "The Estate of Marriage," in *Luther's Works*, vol. 45, ed. Helmut Lehman (Philadelphia: Muhlenberg, 1962), p. 39; see also Thomas Aquinas, *Summa Theologica* III.41.1.

49. One of the strongest imaginable statements about the dignity of parenting, primarily addressed to men, can be found in Luther's "The Estate of Marriage," pp. 39-41. For excellent reviews of the contributions of Luther and the Protestant Reformation to a restructuring and elevation of men's roles in marriage and parenting, see two of Steven Ozment's books: *When Fathers Ruled* (Cambridge: Harvard University Press, 1983), and *Protestants: The Birth of a Revolution* (New York: Doubleday, 1992), pp. 151-68.

Chapter 15

Families and the Sixty-Hour Workweek: What It Means for Church, Society, and Persons (2002)

The preceding chapter demonstrates both the strength and weakness of the economic analysis of families and marriage. There is little doubt that market forces place enormous strains on families. Hence, addressing family disruption requires going beyond, although certainly including, attention to interpersonal dynamics and communication. I am a strong advocate of marriage education and believe it should flourish in both churches and the wider society, but the idea of the equal-regard marriage and family demands a prophetic critique of the economic patterns of modern societies. Societies must be organized to make the equal-regard family possible. One way to do this is to organize society to make the sixty-hour workweek for couples with children a genuine possibility.

This chapter was first prepared for a lecture at Garrett-Evangelical Theological School in October of 2002. But the idea of the sixty-hour workweek, first developed in *From Culture Wars to Common Ground,* has gained considerable attention. It was featured in the consensus statement by the American Assembly meeting on the family titled *Strengthening American Families* (2000) and in an article in *Business Week Online* (2001). Social scientist Jeffrey Hill and his colleagues have published a research article in *American Behavioral Scientist* (2006) that directly and self-consciously tests our sixty-hour workweek hypothesis with a survey covering 59,000 IBM employees in forty-eight countries. This study demonstrates that couples with children working in the wage economy no more than sixty hours each week between them have more satisfactions on a whole range of measurements of well-being than either couples in which one member stays home or couples in which both members work full-time.

The idea of the sixty-hour workweek has been one of the most popular proposals coming from the Religion, Culture, and Family Project.

I want to propose a simple idea that probably will not strike you as a theological idea at all. It is the importance to our society of developing a sixty-hour workweek for a husband and wife if they have children. I mean by this a sixty-hour workweek in the wage economy that husband and wife would in some way divide between them. Rightly understood, this little proposal is not only important, it also, as I will try to show, flows from Christian theological convictions. It is an idea with radical social implications.

This idea is one little suggestion in a relatively big book called *From Culture Wars to Common Ground: Religion and the American Family Debate*,[1] the summary book of the first phase of the Religion, Culture, and Family Project. The sixty-hour workweek was one small proposal in a list of seventeen or so recommendations on how to help families. But this was the idea that most attracted the attention of the public. The news media was particularly interested in the concept. I have been interested in why this recommendation gained so much attention. It often would be treated as a sound bite. "Tell us about the sixty-hour workweek," people would say to me, or, "I really like the sixty-hour workweek concept for couples with children."

I became a little disturbed that our various audiences never saw the theological-ethical significance of the idea. They always reduced it to a simple utilitarian proposal. "Would it really work?" they would ask. We live in a very efficiency-oriented society that doesn't like to pay attention to the assumptions that surround an idea; we are interested primarily in the payoff. This simple proposal about the sixty-hour workweek seemed, for many people, to be the whole payoff of our entire book.

At a time when almost all the churches, including the mainline churches, were preoccupied by the hot-button issues of abortion and ho-

---

1. Don Browning, Bonnie Miller-McLemore, Pamela Couture, Bernie Lyon, and Robert Franklin, *From Culture Wars to Common Ground: Religion and the American Family Debate* (Louisville: Westminster John Knox, 1997, 2000).

mosexuality, the Religion, Culture, and Family Project said something different. We said, "Oh, by the way, there are some other issues that deserve attention as well." Our project encouraged people in churches and society to talk about these other issues. We argued that the mainline should not let the religious right provide the only language for talking about the family. Nor should we turn the topics of family and marriage over to the field of economics, which is, in fact, dominating so much of the discussion in the academy. The mainline church should learn to speak more directly about the problems it has forgotten — the increase in out-of-wedlock births, the growing impoverishment of women and children, the increase of father absence in our society, the spreading influence of the market on families, and the decline of time available for parents to spend with their children. There ought to be other languages besides the dominant languages of economics or of the religious right to talk about these issues. There ought to be a new critical theological language.

But what does the sixty-hour workweek for couples with children really mean? It means that, in principle, such couples should not be in the wage economy between them more than sixty hours a week. It does not mean that one spouse should work sixty hours and the other not at all. But the idea does permit some variation. The arrangement might be thirty-thirty or it might entail a forty-twenty combination. But society ought to offer opportunities for couples to work out arrangements so that they both can enjoy the privileges and the responsibilities of the public worlds of paid employment and citizenship and the domestic sphere of home management and child care.

So that was the idea we proposed. But where did it come from? Quite early in the research of the Religion, Culture, and Family Project, we began to realize that there were some big-time social-systemic issues pertaining to families that both church and society were having difficulty grasping. When we read about ideas or programs that addressed these social-systemic issues, we clipped and filed them. While reading, clipping, and filing, we ran across a report about a study from the Harvard University medical system.[2] It was a pilot study that examined the marital and work satisfactions of a few hundred couples. The researchers studied marriages where, between husband and wife, they worked a total of eighty to one hundred hours each week. Then they examined marriages where, be-

---

2. Jacqueline Olds, Richard Schwartz, Susan Eisen, William Betcher, and Anthone Van Niel, "Part-Time Employment and Marital Well-Being: A Hypothesis and Pilot Study" (Belmont, Mass.: Department of Psychiatry, Harvard University McLean Hospital, 1993).

tween husband and wife, they worked in the wage economy only sixty hours a week. They also looked at couples where only one spouse worked — generally the husband — and the other stayed home managing the house and the children.

They found that the couples most satisfied with their marriages were those who between them worked no more than sixty hours each week. Within these couples, both married partners were stimulated by outside activity. They also had more time to spend with each other. They did not neglect each other, which is a major temptation for overworked parents, and they had more time for their intimate lives. They also, however, had more time for their children. Some of the extremes that afflict other patterns of work and family were eliminated. If one member of the couple stays home all the time or if both parents are out of the house for a total of eighty to one hundred hours each week, there are negative consequences for a variety of family issues: For couples where one spouse stays home and specializes in domestic activities, there is less actual marital satisfaction, possibly because of the boredom and inequality experienced by one of the partners. And for the couples who both work full-time or more, the deficit of time for fun, love, and parenting becomes a major problem. The sixty-hour workweek, it appears, produces a favorable combination of external stimulation and additional time; it also provides better access to the privileges and responsibilities of public and private life for both husband and wife.

We decided that this was a very suggestive study with profound implications for social reform. It also begged, we thought, for theological contextualization. We made the idea part of our theory of "critical familism." We used it to make a new critique of society — a critique and reform we thought was essential for implementing a new understanding of marital equality. Not only did radio commentators and journalists want to talk about this proposal, but I was asked to co-author the background book for the American Assembly in their effort to find a consensus on issues facing contemporary families.[3] The American Assembly is a think tank at Columbia University. They take on contentious issues in American life. To prepare for their assembly, the Assembly asks someone to write a background book. At the same time, they bring together sixty or so highly diverse leaders from religion, education, business, the academy, and the military. These leaders read this book, discuss the issues at hand,

---

3. Don Browning and Gloria Rodriguez, *Reweaving the Social Tapestry: Toward a Public Philosophy and Policy for Families* (New York: W. W. Norton, 2001).

and then produce a consensus statement. The book and consensus statement are then published together. The idea of the sixty-hour workweek for married couples with children floated to the top of the proposals put forth during that long weekend discussion and was featured in the final consensus statement that was distributed to the nation.[4]

That led to a telephone call from *Business Week Online,* the electronic version of the magazine by that name. The reporter commented that "This is a very interesting idea. Please tell us more about it." So we told him about the Harvard study and the research of Professor Benjamin Hunnicutt of the University of Iowa who actually wrote a book showing that the idea is feasible. The Kellogg industries during the 1930s, 1940s, and 1950s had thirty-hour workweeks, and they were very successful. This company even followed the thirty-hour workweek during the emergency years of World War II. Workers experienced many of the benefits in their home life that I described above. After several decades, the company finally gave it up, primarily because of the boom economy of the 1950s. Employees wanted to make more money even though they were very happy with what the thirty-hour week meant for their lives as a whole.

The Sixty-Hour Proposal and Social Analysis

An article on the sixty-hour workweek was finally published in *Business Week Online.* It was well done, and our project got lots of credit. But, once again, the theological aspects of the idea were neglected. The article went for the practical payoff.

In my view, however, to fully understand the sixty-hour workweek requires theological development. I will later in this article build the case for its theological and ethical significance. I want to show why one can, and should, talk about this concept in terms of Christian theology. The idea of the sixty-hour workweek is a very thick concept. I believe a Christian theological perspective should be part of that thickness.

But before I turn to this, I will address a question that may now be on your mind. You may be saying, "But our society has many problems. Why are you putting so much emphasis on work-family issues?" There are a number of reasons why the work-family relation should be considered as central. For one thing, the issue of families brings together so many disci-

---

4. The consensus statement itself was published under the title *Strengthening American Families: Reweaving the Social Tapestry* (New York: American Assembly, 2000).

plines and so many different sectors of society. Families can be examined from economic, psychological, communicative, sociological, or religious perspectives. All of the sectors of society — government, market, education, medicine, and law — come to bear on families. They are all part of the picture. I am convinced, however, that the theological perspective is the main point of departure — the main point of leverage.

The university where I have taught for most of my career, the University of Chicago, gives much attention to the economic analysis of families. As you may know, this is the university where the Chicago School of Economics reigns supreme among academic disciplines. A few years ago, I began to realize that my colleagues in the department of economics were writing and publishing a great deal about families. I said to myself, "I should pay attention to them. I should read them." I always have said that theology, especially practical theology, should be an interdisciplinary enterprise. If economic trends influence families, economics should not be ignored. So I read the works of my economist friends and neighbors. I spent the entire summer of 1992 reading the works of Nobel Prize winner Gary Becker and law and economics theorist Richard Posner.[5] We have a chapter critiquing these scholars in *From Culture Wars to Common Ground*.[6] Here are some insights that I gained — insights that any practical-theological perspective should keep in mind.

Much of the work of this school is actually historical; it analyzes the impact on families of changes in economic patterns. The first big shift in family patterns that the Chicago school writes about came in the early nineteenth century. Young families began to leave the farm and move to the cities. They left farm and craft economies and joined the wage economy. What effect did this have on families? Many historians and economists believe that these shifts disconnected the conjugal couple from financial dependence on extended family and the family farm or craft. These trends took the bread-earner — in this case, the husband — into the rhythms of the competitive wage economy. They served to split domestic life from financial activity — two parts of life that were held together in farm and craft economies. This was the first significant economic trend that affected the patterns of American family life.

The second momentous economic trend came in the middle of the twentieth century. Women rapidly began to join men in the wage economy.

5. Gary Becker, *Treatise on the Family* (Cambridge, Mass.: Harvard University Press, 1991); Richard Posner, *Sex and Reason* (Cambridge, Mass.: Harvard University Press, 1992).
6. Browning et al., *From Culture Wars to Common Ground*, chap. 9.

Gradually almost everyone — men and women, mothers and fathers — were working for a salary outside the home. The wage economy became the dominant force in the lives of people and gradually began to impinge on family life. Jürgen Habermas and sociologist Alan Wolfe claim that more and more the market began to intrude into the realm of intimate family life and change the very logic of these relationships.[7] Increasingly modern people began to think about their home life like a business, that is, in the terms of costs, benefits, and efficiency. It might be argued that Marx and Engels years ago made a telling point when they claimed that capitalism would eventually destroy the family.[8] The economic point of view says that families in the past stayed together because they were economically dependent on one another. Just as in the nineteenth century the conjugal family reduced its dependence on the extended family, in the twentieth century women and wives lowered their dependence on men and husbands. Both of these phenomena are happening today all over the world, not just in the United States.

We Christians like to think that couples stay together because they love each other or because they believe in the covenant or sacrament of marriage. As Christians, we should continue to hold such beliefs. The economic analysis can supplement the religious point of view, however, and in the end even Christians may need to be realists. Marriages may endure for at least two reasons — the covenant commitment of husband and wife *and* their practical economic dependency on one another. And good theological thinking about families should keep in mind both of these levels of analysis.

Some people, however, say that the problem is neither a matter of religious commitment nor a matter of economic dependency; it is, instead, a matter of communication. Couples get no systematic education, the argument goes, in how to communicate, solve conflicts, or express emotion. There is little doubt that this is true. At least, this is part of the problem. But it should be pointed out that the problem of communication can be exacerbated by these great shifts in economic dependency. When couples are no longer held together by economic dependency, skills in communication become all the more important.

There is one more reason why marriage and families are being dis-

7. Jürgen Habermas, *The Theory of Communicative Action,* trans. Thomas McCarthy, vol. 2 (Boston: Beacon, 1987), p. 196; Alan Wolfe, *Whose Keeper? Social Science and Moral Obligation* (Berkeley: University of California Press, 1989), pp. 52, 133.

8. Frederick Engels, *The Origins of the Family, Private Property, and the State* (New York: International, 1972).

rupted today. Some people will say, "Oh well, there's the cultural individualism issue. That is the major cause of family disruption. We're all individualists — into doing our own thing — and that's why families are not hanging together as they used to." I agree. As Robert Bellah and his colleagues argue in *Habits of the Heart,* this is a powerful — probably the most powerful — motivating force behind marital and family difficulties today.[9]

But it is useful to think about cultural individualism in relation to the economic transformations discussed above. If we are taught by our culture to be individualists and if we are not as financially dependent on each other as we once were, it follows that these economic and cultural trends interact and make things even worse. Market capitalism fosters individualism, at least at the level of tastes, consumption, and style. Market capitalism makes us less financially dependent on one another; it makes it easier for us to walk away from marriages and relationships, start a new life, and be a new independent person. For these reasons, it is helpful to think about cultural individualism in relation to the shifts in economic patterns I have described. Such connections make clear the way in which the work and family issue is a very important crystallization of the full range of issues facing families today.

Although the sixty-hour workweek is a simple idea, it is the result of a radical critique of the kind of society that is developing in Western countries and gradually spreading throughout the world. It is the result of a thesis claiming that market logics are spreading into all aspects of life — even intimate life. To critique this trend and to give it some teeth, there must be ways actually to say "no" to these trends. We as people need to do something that concretely helps redesign aspects of our society. We may not be able to accomplish such reform today. We may not be able to do it tomorrow. But we should gradually redesign our society so that the patterns and logics driving economic activity do not end in consuming everything that families and individuals do. One way to do that might be to develop something like the sixty-hour workweek for couples with children.

Theological Contributions to the Sixty-Hour Workweek

Behind this radical critique is the retrieval of two important theological concepts. The first has to do with what I call an ontology of equality,

---

9. Robert Bellah, Richard Madsen, William Sullivan, Ann Swidler, and Steven Tipton, *Habits of the Heart* (New York: Harper and Row, 1985).

which the Jewish and Christian traditions provide for the human imagi-nation. The second contribution is a compensatory understanding of gender equality. By a compensatory understanding of equality between the sexes, I mean a work or effort that addresses imbalances in equality — imbalances that require compensatory action to overcome.

First, the ontology of equality. Most interpretations of Genesis 1:27-28 today see these great passages about humans being made in the image of God as pertaining to both male and female. "So God created mankind in his image, in the image of God he created them, male and female he cre-ated them." The most trusted scholarly interpretations today tell us that this passage asserts the equal endowment of man and woman with the image of God. But it gets more interesting when you take into consider-ation Genesis 1:28. "Be fruitful and multiply, and fill the earth, and sub-due it and have dominion over the fishes of the sea and over the birds of the air and over every living thing that moves upon the face of the earth." Respected New Testament scholar Phyllis Trible interprets "Be fruitful and multiply and have dominion" as a religio-cultural mandate that gives equal opportunity and equal responsibility to male and female in both re-production and economic activity.[10] This grounds reproductive and eco-nomic activity in ontology — the structure of being — as this is established by God's will. This is something God wills in creation. The thin little idea that we should be equal in both production and reproduction has, ac-cording to the Genesis narrative, the weight of the Divine.

It is terribly important to keep this ontology of equality in mind be-cause our society tends to strip away these deeper ideals. Many Americans like to follow Kant, who believed that equality between humans depends on assumptions about their rationality, and that alone.[11] It may be that both Kant and the Genesis ontology can establish gender equality; philos-opher Basil Mitchell argued that both perspectives have weight. He con-tended, however, that more seriousness and profundity is found in grounding equality in an ontology that opens up the very nature of God and God's will for humans.[12]

Some Christians want to ground the economic and reproductive equality of male and female in principles such as the Golden Rule and neighbor love. It is more powerful theologically, I believe, to keep these

---

10. Phyllis Trible, *God and the Rhetoric of Sexuality* (Philadelphia: Fortress, 1978).

11. Immanuel Kant, *Foundations of the Metaphysics of Morals* (New York: Bobbs-Merrill, 1959), p. 49.

12. Basil Mitchell, *Morality: Religious and Secular* (Oxford: Clarendon, 1980).

principles in close association with this ontology of equality found in the creation story. Almost everyone resonates with the relatively thin idea that you should do unto others as you would have them do unto you — a concept found in Judaism, Christianity, and various religions around the world. According to moral-development psychologist Jean Piaget and Lawrence Kohlberg, humans have natural mental processes that lead them to gravitate toward this kind of reversible thinking about self and other in the field of ethics.[13] It is one thing to respect self and other on the basis of some thin humanistic belief about the dignity of all persons; it is another thing to base this belief on an ontology of equality of the kind found in Genesis 1:27-28.

I love the amendment that philosopher Paul Ricoeur gives to the Golden Rule. He amends this rule with some biblical authority, or at least with some authority from the tradition, referring to Rabbi Hillel. Ricoeur interprets Hillel as saying that doing to others as you would have them do to you actually means doing *good* to others as you would have them do *good* to you.[14] Those of you who are familiar with the history of philosophical and theological ethics know what Ricoeur has done in this formulation of the Golden Rule. He has brought together Kant's deontological reversible thinking with a subordinate Aristotelian statement about the importance of justice serving human goods and human flourishing. In this view, justice is more than simple Kantian respect for other and self. It is an active effort to respect and do good for both other and self.

When you do good to others as you would have them do good to you, it opens up the question, What are the goods of life? But this challenging question is one which most theology and philosophy have not addressed effectively. I remind you that in the Genesis passages, two types of goods are brought to our attention. These are the goods of human reproduction and the goods of material production. With Genesis in mind, to do good for others as you would have them do good for you means, at least minimally, granting equality to male and female with regard to the goods and responsibilities of both economic activity and having and caring for children. The Genesis ontology helps us see the religious and moral seriousness of these goods and our actions to have them.

But this leads to the second contribution of theology to the simple

13. Jean Piaget, *The Moral Judgment of the Child* (New York: Free Press, 1965); Lawrence Kohlberg, *The Philosophy of Moral Development* (New York: Harper and Row, 1981).

14. Paul Ricoeur, "The Teleological and Deontological Structures of Action: Aristotle and/or Kant," in *Contemporary French Philosophy*, ed. A. Phillips Griffiths (Cambridge: Cambridge University Press, 1987), pp. 99-120.

idea of the sixty-hour workweek. We need more than an ontology of the Golden Rule and neighbor love. We need insight into the compensatory symbols and actions needed to make gender equality a reality. I want to illustrate this rather obscure assertion with two brief commentaries. One will be on the context of early Christianity's remarks about families. The other will deal with a complex argument about marriage once made by Thomas Aquinas. Both will make more clear what I mean by compensatory symbols and actions in a Christian theology of families.

First, can we gain more insight into the context of early Christianity's statements about families? It is very difficult for contemporary Christians to properly interpret passages about families found in the Gospels, the Pauline letters, and the Pastoral Epistles. This is true because we have difficulty fully locating the context. With the help of biblical scholars, we are making progress on this task. I am impressed with insights into the context of early Christianity that have come from applying anthropological insights gained from studying honor-shame cultures.[15] We should remember that Roman Hellenism was pervasive throughout the Mediterranean world during the time of early Christianity. In the Greco-Roman world, there was a popular code of everyday behavior which anthropologists and classicists call an "honor-shame code." Applying primarily to male behavior, it helped define the responsible and respected man. According to the code, the strong and respected man should have honor and avoid shame. To have honor was to enjoy the capacity for dominance, freedom, and agency. Dominance also entailed the responsibility to protect those who depended on a man, especially his wife, mother, and daughters.

These dependent females were, in turn, to show shame. Shame meant that women should accept their roles in the domestic and private spheres of life. Women should understand their place in life, constrain their activities, and submit to the guidance of male protectors. If a woman under a man's protection was in any way assaulted or insulted, an honorable male would defend her honor with retaliation and, perhaps, an invitation to duel. Otherwise, he would be shamed. An honorable man was a dominant man and free man who avoided shame.

This pervasive ethic that guided male-female relations in the Mediterranean world also impinged on early Christianity. Many scholars believe that early Christianity subtly was bringing about a reorientation and reformation of this honor-shame culture, especially as it applied to male-

---

15. Halvor Moxnes, "Honor and Shame," *Biblical Theology Bulletin* 23, no. 4 (Winter 1993): 167-76.

female relations. Although early Christianity never completely escaped either antique patriarchy or the codes of the honor-shame culture, it clearly was in a struggle with them. Even the New Testament idea of the servant-husband and father was in tension with honor-shame codes in subtle ways. When Ephesians tells us, "Husbands, love your wives, just as Christ loved the church and gave himself up for her," we know that the patriarchy is not absent. But we should not miss the antithesis of that image of male responsibility to the honor-shame codes of its day. Nor should we miss hearing that "husbands should love their wives as their own bodies," a thought that applies the principle of neighbor love directly into the private sphere of marriage. This is a thought that was rare in surrounding religious and philosophical traditions of the day. The idea of the servant husband and father functioned to compensate for (in the sense of balance) the dominant male image of the honor-shame culture.

I now want to fast-forward to Thomas Aquinas. I am arguing that religious symbols and actions should be understood in dialectical relationship to the cultural distortions that they are trying to balance. Aquinas had insight into the compensatory work of Christian symbols but had a different way than Ephesians for making much the same point. Aquinas was close to contemporary evolutionary psychologists in his understanding of the relationship of males and females. Males, he argued, do not carry as much of the reproductive load as do females. They also have a more tentative relation with their own biological offspring. Aquinas and evolutionary psychology agree: males never know for sure that the child of their female partner is really theirs. One can find such statements by Aquinas in both his *Summa Contra Gentiles* and in the Supplement of the *Summa Theologica*.[16] The woman, on the other hand, always knows that the child she gives birth to is actually hers.

Males also expend far less energy in the reproductive process and, in that sense, have far less of an investment, at least in the beginning, than do mothers. Hence, males must gradually learn to think of the child as theirs and gradually learn how to take responsibility and be involved in the life of their offspring. Males throughout the world of mammals have, for the most part, allowed mothers to raise children, primarily because females are the source of nourishment. Human males are tempted to do this as well. And time and again, human females have accepted this bur-

16. Thomas Aquinas, *Summa Theologica* (London: R. & T. Washbourne, 1917), Supplement to the Third Part, qq. 41-42; Thomas Aquinas, *Summa Contra Gentiles* (London: Burns, Oates and Washbourne, 1928), vol. 3, pt. 2, chap. 123.

den and largely raised their children by themselves. *It was a great religious and cultural accomplishment when males accepted their responsibility and joined the mother-infant family.*

But the entire logic of both early Christianity and the Christian philosophy of Thomas Aquinas was to reverse that archaic asymmetry of the male-female relation. Everything that Aquinas said in interpreting Ephesians and developing his sacramental view of marriage was designed to balance this. The appeal by Aquinas for husbands to be like Christ was a call for them to build on this recognition that their partner's child is probably theirs and then to invest in the child, serving child and mother in analogy to Christ's love for the church. That was Aquinas's dialectical or compensatory understanding of the marital commitment. It compensated for a natural asymmetry that was not sinful as such but could be compounded by sin.

The task of our time is to make sure that in the process of stripping away the patriarchal power of the male we do not rob the male — the husband and father — of the servant responsibility that was developed in Ephesians against the background of the honor-shame codes of the ancient world. Nor should we fail to inform male responsibility with Thomas's even deeper insights into the asymmetrical reproductive strategies of males and females.

The Social Implications of Theological Ideas

These theological ideas should not be interpreted in overly narrow interpersonal categories. It is tempting to think only about how they apply to a particular husband and a particular wife in the privacy of their intimate domestic lives. And that is certainly theologically acceptable. Interpersonal relations are part of the object and field of theological affirmations. But these theological ideas should apply to social-systemic issues as well. Fathers and mothers are not simply in narrow dyadic relationships to one another. They occupy roles and statuses in particular kinds of social systems. If there is an ontology of equality and a compensatory function to the Christian symbols relating to marriage, these powerful theological ideas have consequences for both interpersonal and social-systemic realities. That is why my colleagues and I have recommended the sixty-hour workweek. That's what is required to bring this ontology of equality and this christological insight into our common everyday life. Christology can have ethical implications for the common good as long as its claims can be supported by additional publicly redeemable reasons of the kinds I have tried to advance in this essay.

Our society seems to be going in directions quite different from what is required in the sixty-hour workweek. Juliet Schor, a Harvard economist, wrote a book several years ago titled *The Overworked American*.[17] Recently she wrote an essay published in the *New York Times* in which she argued that Americans today are still overworked.[18] There are, of course, a few fathers who are working less and spending more time with their family, but the overall drift is still in the other direction. Americans have been working more and more for over three decades. Today, couples with children work in the wage economy 150 more hours a year than they did in 1990. Americans are in the wage economy far more than Europeans, and now exceed even the Japanese, whom we once thought were addicted to work. One reason why the United States is such an efficient country with such high levels of productivity is because industry is squeezing more and more out of its employees. In fact, Americans now work nine more weeks each year than their European counterparts.

Professor Schor also has an answer for those who think ideas such as the sixty-hour week are completely impractical after the events of 9/11 and the recent economic slowdown. She argues for seeing the silver lining in our economic hard times. She believes that we should create more jobs by reducing the workweek, an idea close to the sixty-hour concept. She recommends distributing jobs by making the forty-hour week into a thirty-five-hour or even thirty-hour week. She argues for using the present situation to work less and distribute the jobs more evenly throughout the population. This has implications for the poverty issue as well.

But even if there is no immediate way to implement the sixty-hour workweek, this does not mean it is a bad idea. Dreams that cannot immediately take effect are not necessarily bad ones. One can gradually work on constructing a society that is humane and beneficial. It may take five, ten, twenty, or thirty years to reorient our thinking about what is involved in a good society. But one must begin someplace.

17. Juliet B. Schor, *The Overworked American: The Unexpected Decline of Leisure* (New York: Basic, 1991).

18. Juliet B. Schor, "Why Americans Should Rest," *New York Times,* September 9, 2002, p. A17.

Chapter 16

The Language of Health versus the Language of Religion: Competing Models of Marriage in the Twenty-First Century (2002)

In this chapter, I continue developing the idea that reviving and reconstructing marriage in our day requires a great cultural work that integrates several different fields of knowledge and spheres of society. I do this by considering the important fields of health and medicine. More specifically, I address the significant work of social scientist Linda Waite that led to her publication with Maggie Gallagher of the book titled *The Case for Marriage*.* This admirable work collects social-science evidence that marriage is, on average, good for the health, wealth, and sexual satisfaction of both men and women, especially when married individuals are compared to singles of both sexes. This chapter of mine was written a few months before that work was published and addressed Waite's published research findings that were later incorporated into her widely read book.

In previous chapters I have argued that economic language cannot function properly without being surrounded and deepened by moral and religious language, and I make the same argument here with regard to health language. The concluding paragraphs of the chapter identify the health benefits of marriage as one of the several premoral goods of marriage; but these benefits are a good that needs the moral language of equal regard and the narrative language of Christian love for its proper realization in marriage and family.

---

*Linda Waite and Maggie Gallagher, *The Case for Marriage* (New York: Doubleday, 2000).

Strengthening marriages in our time must be conceived primarily as a cultural work. It is mainly a task of deepening and reformulating our understanding of the meaning of marriage. I call this task a cultural work because it must entail coordinating the efforts of a number of cultural disciplines — principally religion, law, economics, education, and psychotherapy. To be successful, this work cannot proceed from a single perspective; it requires the cooperative efforts of several major disciplines, each playing a distinct role.

This task faces many challenges. There is the challenge of putting marriage back on the agenda of these disciplines, the challenge of restraining each discipline from acting as if it were the only relevant perspective, and the challenge of placing the reconstruction of marriage within a sufficiently comprehensive historical, philosophical, and religious context.

With regard to this last point, this should be said: the cultural work of deepening marriage cannot be done on narrowly empirical grounds nor in terms of the slender ethical-egoist, utilitarian, or Kantian moral philosophies that rule much of modern life. Instead, the cultural reconstruction of marriage must entail the philosophical retrieval of the marriage classics — including the religious marriage classics — of the Western world and their refinement in light of modern social-science insights. These classics offer thick rather than thin moral perspectives. They provide general orientations to life (that is, ontologies), principles of moral obligation, and tested theories of basic human needs and goods. Most modern social sciences and moral philosophies either provide inadequate ontologies, theories of obligation, and indices of human needs or surreptitiously sneak more adequate ones into their frameworks from other sources, generally without taking responsibility for their acknowledgment or justification.

Retrieving these classics is not primarily a confessional theological task. The goal of academic discourse should not entail placing public deliberation about marriage under the control of Jewish or Christian theologies. Its goal, instead, should be to create a public philosophy about marriage — one that can give an account of the functions of religious language about marriage and how this language can be orchestrated with the descriptive and predictive concepts of the social sciences.

At the present, our cultural definition of marriage is in disarray. There are many reasons for this. First, there is the post-Enlightenment shift in cultural values, specifically the rise of Western individualism.[1] But

---

1. For perspectives that tie family disruption to the rise of individualism, see Robert

individualism, whether in its expressive or its utilitarian forms,[2] is not the only factor. Cultural individualism, as demographer Ron Lesthaeghe has argued, is disruptive of marriage and family because it is reinforced by market forces.[3] Economic individualism — a combination of market rationality and cultural individualism — is a major, although not the only, feature of modernization. Modernization, however, has ambiguous consequences for marriage and families. William Goode argued in *World Revolution in Family Patterns* that the modern conjugal family helped create modernization. Thirty years later when he wrote his *World Changes in Divorce Patterns* he admitted that modernization itself was now destroying the very family form that assisted in its birth.[4]

In an effort to address the disruptions surrounding marriage, several movements have emerged to repair it without necessarily developing commanding cultural visions of what marriage is. These movements should be supported, but they do not address the central issue about the nature of marriage. Three such movements come to mind — the marriage education movement, efforts by religious and social liberals to make marriage an equal partnership, and new efforts to document the health benefits of marriage. In this paper, I will discuss primarily the last of these — the emerging view of marriage as the royal road to health. What I say, however, should have implications for the other two movements as well.

Marriage as a Road to Health

To illustrate the health message, I will turn to the outstanding work of Professor Linda Waite, my colleague at the University of Chicago. The argument in her presidential address before the American Population Society — published as "Does Marriage Matter?" — is well-known. It has been

---

Bellah, Richard Madsen, William Sullivan, Ann Swidler, and Steven Tipton, *Habits of the Heart* (New York: Harper and Row, 1985), pp. 32-35, 46, 47, 142, 311; Jan Dizard and Howard Gadlin, *The Minimal Family* (Amherst, Mass.: University of Massachusetts Press, 1990), pp. 11-13; Edward Shorter, *The Making of the Modern Family* (New York: Basic, 1977), p. 21; David Popenoe, *Life without Father* (New York: Free Press, 1996), pp. 46-48.

2. Bellah et al., *Habits of the Heart,* pp. 32-35.

3. Ron Lesthaeghe, "A Century of Demographic and Cultural Change in Western Europe," *Population and Development Review* 9, no. 3 (September 1983): 429.

4. William Goode, *World Revolution in Family Patterns* (London: Free Press of Glencoe, 1963), and *World Changes in Divorce Patterns* (New Haven, Conn.: Yale University Press, 1993), p. 13.

extended in a book co-authored with Maggie Gallagher titled *The Case for Marriage*. She summarizes existing social-science data demonstrating that in contrast to never-married and divorced persons, married couples enjoy more of a wide range of goods. They have better psychological and physical health, live longer, have fewer heart attacks, have more satisfying sex, and accumulate more wealth. This is true for both men and women, although marriage is slightly better for men than for women.[5] This data has generated enormous attention and increasingly is used as a justification for the institution of marriage. In contrast to recent complaints charging that marriage is a bad deal, especially for women,[6] we now have reasons to think it is a vehicle, on average, for many of the basic goods of life.

This mode of thinking, typical of much of the reasoning in the contemporary social sciences, is similar to all social science efforts to track the individual and social consequences of particular social arrangements. It is similar to the implicit argument of Sara McLanahan and Gary Sandefur when they show the increased educational, marital, and employment risks to children who grow up with a single parent.[7] It is the logic of the recent Iowa State University study that contends it is not the family structure but the process of communication between divorced parents and their children that predicts outcomes for offspring.[8] A similar model of reasoning undergirds the rational-choice discussions of marriage found in the work of Nobel prize-winner Gary Becker and the entire law and economics approach to marriage represented by such writings as Judge Richard Posner's *Sex and Reason*.[9]

The health argument is important and has a place in the total cultural task of deepening and reformulating our understanding of marriage. But this language and moral logic should not be allowed to dominate completely our moral and cultural discourse about marriage. The health argument for marriage is a species of what moral philosophers call

5. Linda Waite, "Does Marriage Matter?" *Demography* 32, no. 4 (November 1995): 483-504.

6. Waite is specifically addressing the charges advanced by Jessie Bernard that modern marriage has not been good for women. See Bernard's *The Future of Marriage* (New York: World, 1972).

7. Sara McLanahan and Gary Sandefur, *Growing Up with a Single Parent* (Cambridge: Harvard University Press, 1994).

8. Ronald Simons, Kueli-Hsiu Lin, Leslie Gordon, Rand Conger, and Frederick Lorenz, "Explaining the Higher Incidence of Adjustment Problems among Children of Divorce Compared with Those in Two-Parent Families," *Journal of Marriage and the Family* 61 (November 1999): 1020-34.

9. Richard Posner, *Sex and Reason* (Cambridge: Harvard University Press, 1992).

a teleological view of moral reason. There are two dominant modern models of teleological moral reason — utilitarianism and ethical egoism.[10] Modern teleological views of moral reason, in contrast to the classical teleological views of Aristotle and Thomas Aquinas, see moral reason as calculative; moral thinking is a matter of computing whether an action will produce more nonmoral good over nonmoral evil for either self or the wider community. When an action is justified because it produces more nonmoral (or premoral) good for oneself, philosophers call this thinking a brand of philosophical ethical egoism. When an action is justified because it produces more nonmoral good for the majority of the wider community, this reasoning is called a brand of philosophical utilitarianism.[11]

The words "nonmoral" or "premoral" should not be confused with the word "immoral." Rather, the idea of nonmoral or premoral goods points to the myriad ways we use the word "good" to refer to the things and qualities of life that are pleasant, useful, or helpful for survival but that are not necessarily moral in the full sense of the word.[12] Food, wealth, health, transportation, shelter, and pleasure are goods in the nonmoral or premoral sense.[13] But such things and qualities are not moral goods as such; it would not be intelligible to speak of a moral steak, a moral automobile, or a moral house. These objects are goods that can be used either morally or immorally, depending on the intentions of the person using them and how they are organized with other goods sought by both self and neighbor.

Health is certainly one of these nonmoral or premoral goods. It is a good thing to enjoy sound health. Sex is certainly good in the premoral sense; it feels good, binds us with those who give us pleasure, and may make us healthy in other ways. Wealth is another premoral good. But we do not say that persons are moral simply because they have lots of health, good sex, and a good deal of money stashed in American or Swiss banks. We judge a person as morally good depending on how he or she resolves the inevitable conflicts between premoral goods — for example, the conflict between the good of sexual pleasure and the good of a costly and demanding baby, between the good of wealth and that of health, or between my wealth and the wealth of others.

The language of health, unqualified by further moral elaboration, can

10. William Frankena, *Ethics* (Englewood Cliffs, N.J.: Prentice Hall, 1973), pp. 14-16.
11. Frankena, *Ethics,* pp. 34-43.
12. Frankena, *Ethics,* pp. 9-11.
13. Frankena, *Ethics,* pp. 9-10.

end in justifying marriage on either ethical-egoist or narrowly utilitarian grounds. The first means that marriage is good because it is good for me; this view has generally been seen as an inadequate moral justification for anything, let alone marriage. The second utilitarian ground justifies marriage as a social utility, for reasons somewhat analogous to the reasons society values a gas or electric company.

Neither language constitutes sufficient grounds for the cultural renewal and reformulation of marriage. Ethical-egoist views of the health benefits of marriage make it a tool for individual fulfillment and provide little that helps us understand the commitment that makes marriage last. Utilitarian arguments for marriage justify it as good public policy, thereby ignoring the delight, rapture, struggles, moral obligations, and unique dramas that customarily have been associated with marriage. Furthermore, there is something oddly violent about ethical-egoist and utilitarian views of marriage, whether in their social science or moral philosophy wrapping. Ethical-egoist views make marriage analogous to a risky business investment where funds might be rapidly deposited or withdrawn, depending on one's judgment about the current prospects of maximizing one's gains — one's health. Utilitarian views end in losing the uniqueness of marriage and reducing it to one among many public goods deserving support or neglect depending on abstract calculations about its overall social utility. John Milbank has argued that the modern social sciences are, in fact, dominated by a vision (an ontology) of life that portrays it as fundamentally violent by rendering all of life as motivated by selfish genes (evolutionary psychology), tension-reducing libidinal energies (the early Freud), material motivations (Marx), or hardwired egoistic and individualistic interests (rational-choice economic models).[14]

Finally, both ethical-egoist and utilitarian justifications function to disconnect marriage from the classic religious and ethical languages once used, and to a degree still used, to express the reasons for marriage. However important health justifications — either individualistic or communal — are to the contemporary cultural reconstructions of marriage, when standing alone they are based on an inadequate style of moral reason. At the minimum, the contributions of the health justification for marriage must be placed within a more comprehensive cultural and moral framework.

For the cultural task of developing this more comprehensive framework, it is better to handle the religious language of Genesis, the Gospel

---

14. John Milbank, *Theology and Social Theory* (Oxford: Blackwell, 1991).

of Matthew, Ephesians, and other such texts as "classics" rather than as divine revelation. Of course, it is entirely justifiable for religious groups to treat these texts as revelation within their internal confessing and witnessing life. As the continental philosophers Hans-Georg Gadamer and Paul Ricoeur explain, however, such texts and the history of commentary on them are classics because they have in fact decisively shaped Western marriage theory and because they have been perceived as containers of truths that have repeatedly enlightened and enriched the cultural consciousness.[15]

What Is Marriage?

I turn now to a fuller exploration of the meaning of marriage as this can be seen through the eyes of the marriage classics of Western history. I do this to advance my argument that the modern teleological justifications for marriage must be kept in close relation to the classical Western languages about marriage. This task, as I have indicated, is primarily a philosophical enterprise designed to develop a public philosophy of marriage.

The classical Western marriage language, although not beyond criticism, provides ontologies and theories of moral obligation that modern views either lack or unconsciously appropriate from sources beyond themselves. The classics of the Western marriage tradition have portrayed marriage as a multi-dimensional phenomenon — a natural, religious, contractual, social, and communicative reality.[16] We must keep in mind this fuller picture as we proceed with deepening our understanding of marriage. In what follows, I will concentrate primarily on two of these five dimensions, marriage as a natural and a religious reality.[17]

Antiquity's view of marriage as a natural institution comes close to the modern justification of marriage as a means to health. Marriage in much of Greek philosophy was viewed as giving form to persistent yet

15. For the idea of the classic, see Hans-Georg Gadamer, *Truth and Method* (New York: Crossroad, 1982), pp. 253-58; also see Paul Ricoeur, *Hermeneutics and the Human Sciences* (Cambridge: Cambridge University Press, 1981), pp. 59-61, 62-100.

16. For similar lists, see John Witte Jr., *From Sacrament to Contract* (Louisville: Westminster John Knox, 1997), p. 2; *Marriage: A Report to the Nation* (New York: Institute for American Values, 1995).

17. Don Browning, "What Is Marriage? An Exploration," unpublished article prepared for a Consultation on the Marriage Movement, January 25, 2000 (New York: Institute for American Values).

sometimes conflicting natural inclinations and needs. A range of natural inclinations was viewed as ordered by marriage. These included the desire for sexual union and the desire Aristotle believed that humans share with the animals "to leave behind them a copy of themselves."[18] Following Aristotle again, marriage was also seen as meeting humans' natural need to be supplied with their "everyday wants."[19] The premoral values of sexual union, offspring, and the basic needs of life were seen by ancient Greek philosophy as the natural goods — indeed the health goods — that marriage satisfies. Aristotle's teleological form of moral thinking constituted the foundation of much of later thought on marriage in the West.

How did this happen? Aristotle's views were absorbed into Christian theology, especially the writings of Thomas Aquinas. This in turn had enormous impact on Roman Catholic thought, later on Protestant thought, and finally on marriage and family law in both Catholic and Protestant countries. In Aquinas, Aristotle's views were brought together with the creation stories of Genesis 1 and 2. Genesis tells humans to "be fruitful and multiply" (Gen. 1:28) and teaches that humans were made for companionship: "It is not good for man to be alone" (Gen. 2:18). For these reasons marriage was created: "Therefore a man leaves his father and his mother and clings to his wife, and they become one flesh" (Gen. 2:24). Procreation, mutual helpfulness, and companionship — these were the aims of marriage in the creation story of Genesis.

But in contrast to Aristotle and the modern teleological moral tradition — whether ethical-egoist or utilitarian — these premoral goods in the creation story are located within a larger narrative about God's acts in creating the world. These human needs and goods are seen as given by God and affirmed by God, and their responsible use as backed by divine command. Aristotle would say that humans *want* "copies" of themselves; Genesis depicts God as *commanding* humans to "multiply." Aristotle says humans are *naturally* social beings; Genesis states as a *pronouncement* of God that "it is not good for man to be alone." Aristotle sees the bonding of male and female as a consequence of these *natural tendencies;* Genesis combines *indicative* and *imperative* modes by saying, "And therefore a man leaves his father and mother . . . and becomes one flesh" with his wife. Genesis provides a vision (an ontology) of the fundamental goodness of the created world, including the inclination leading to the union of man

18. Aristotle, *Politics,* in *The Basic Works of Aristotle,* ed. Richard McKeon (New York: Random House, 1941), bk. 1, chap. 2.

19. Aristotle, *Politics,* bk. 1, chap. 2.

and woman, and backs this up as an expression of the will of God and therefore a moral obligation. In Genesis, the language of need and nature is placed within the larger context of the language of God's will for creation. Marriage is a product of God's command, but what God wills is also good for humans.

At least from the time of Thomas Aquinas (1225-74), the great synthesizer of Aristotelian philosophy with the Judeo-Christian tradition, marriage was often justified on two interrelated grounds. One was drawn from the Jewish doctrine of creation and grounded on the command of God. The other came from the naturalism and teleological thinking of Aristotle.[20] It is true that within the hands of Christian theologians such as Aquinas, Jewish and Christian theologies of creation provided the deeper context surrounding Aristotelian naturalism. But — and this is the point — Aquinas crystalized what had been gradually developing for centuries, that is, a double language — one religious and one philosophical or naturalistic — used to justify marriage.

It is my argument that the cultural work of restoring marriage must understand how these two languages worked together in the past and use this as a model for their fruitful interaction in the future.

In much of the Western tradition, the philosophical language accounting for the natural grounds of marriage was considered vital for the clarification of the religious language. One can see this in perspectives as different as those of Thomas Aquinas, John Locke, and the Roman Catholic marriage encyclicals of Pope Leo XIII. All three retain in some manner the Jewish and Christian creation stories. Yet all three make use of a naturalistic and philosophical language as well. All of them developed a subordinate naturalistic argument for the institution of marriage similar to the one first put forth by Aristotle. This naturalistic argument supplemented their view of the will of God in creation.

For instance, Aquinas taught that matrimony is the joining of the father to the mother-infant dyad. It was and is required by virtue of the long period of dependency of the human infant and child. This dependency is so burdensome to the mother that it necessitates the material and educational labors of both biologically invested procreators.[21] This partnership

---

20. For a discussion of how Aristotelian naturalism is contextualized within Jewish-Christian doctrines of creation, see Don Browning, Bonnie Miller-McLemore, Pamela Couture, Bernie Lyon, and Robert Franklin, *From Culture Wars to Common Ground: Religion and the American Family Debate* (Louisville: Westminster John Knox, 1997), pp. 113-24.

21. Thomas Aquinas, *The Summa Contra Gentiles* (London: Burns, Oates, and Washbourne, 1928), bk. 3, pt. 2, chap. 122.

secures the well-being of the child and secondarily that of the mother, who needs assistance. It also enhances the well-being of the father since the child also carries the "substance" of the father. Similarly, Locke, the author of liberal family theory, wrote with special reference to humans that

> the Father, Who is bound to take care for those he hath begot, is under an Obligation to continue in Conjugal Society with the same Woman longer than other Creatures.[22]

Arguments for marriage with similar health or well-being orientations can be found in the influential neo-Thomistic writings of Pope Leo XIII in the late nineteenth century.[23]

It was assumed by all three of these authors that God created humans as the kind of creatures whose infants have a long period of dependency. Nonetheless, this theological affirmation did not obscure their analysis of the concrete natural conditions that function to create matrimony at this basic level. In *From Culture Wars to Common Ground*, my colleagues and I show that these naturalistic observations are consistent with contemporary evolutionary psychology's view of how long-term human pair bonding occurs.[24] But we do not argue that this naturalistic explanation should supplant cultural appreciation for the wisdom of the founding marriage myths. Rather, the naturalistic explanation (I sometimes call it a "naturalistic moment") should be viewed as an index, sign, or signal of both the realism and profundity of the founding story.

The existence and importance of this double language about marriage is a point generally lost on the general public, who tend to believe that marriage is a uniquely religious and even distinctively Christian practice. This is not true. Although I have illustrated its philosophical and naturalistic dimensions by referring to Aristotle and Locke, I could have done much the same by turning to Roman law. Religious language adds breadth, seriousness, and transcendent grounds for commitment; but it need not exclude naturalistic explanations for marriage as long as they are not absolutized or allowed to dominate the entire field of meaning of this institution.

---

22. John Locke, "Second Treatise," in *Two Treatises of Government,* ed. Peter Laslett (Cambridge: Cambridge University Press, 1991), chap. 7, para. 80.

23. For Leo XIII's version of the argument, see his *Rerum Novarum,* in *Proclaiming Justice and Peace: Papal Documents* (Mystic, Conn.: Twenty-Third Publications, 1991).

24. Browning et al., *From Culture Wars to Common Ground,* pp. 106-14.

The Reformulation of Marriage: The Foundations of the Equal-Regard Marriage

So far I have been discussing how religious language and naturalistic language evolved into a double language about marriage — a double language important today for a public philosophy for marriage. Such a double language would make it possible for theologians, philosophers, and social scientists to cooperate in the cultural work of reviving marriage. Religion could become a partner in this work without reducing our public language to the confessionalism of specific religious traditions or the naturalism of the social sciences. The task of this public philosophy would be to position each discipline's specific contributions so that an orchestrated and holistic cultural vision could emerge.

I have called for an interdisciplinary cultural work and a double language for the deepening and reformulation of marriage. But what would this reformulation of marriage actually mean? *I have in mind the complex task of retaining male commitment to marriage and children but uncoupling this commitment from the lingering shadows of patriarchy.* Patriarchy, of course, has been on the decline in the West for centuries — since early Christianity repudiated the double sexual standard of the ancient world, since Roman Catholic canon law required the consent of both man and woman to establish a valid marriage (thereby breaking the power of fathers to select their daughters' mates), and since Lockean family and marriage theory influenced both England and the mothers of the American Revolutionary War.[25] Women's move into the wage market and their subsequent economic independence, as economists have demonstrated, were additional blows to patriarchy.[26]

All of these moves have created the need for what I have called a new critical familism and a new critical marriage culture.[27] By this I mean an equal-regard marriage where both husband and wife treat each other as equals, work for each other's well-being, and in principle give each other equal access to privileges and responsibilities of both domestic and public life.[28] This view does not mean, as some believe, that husband and wife must become identical and suppress the distinctiveness of being male and female. It means instead that husbands and wives must live by a strenuous

25. Linda Gerber, *Women of the Republic* (New York: W. W. Norton, 1980), pp. 15-23.

26. Gary Becker, *Treatise on the Family* (Cambridge, Mass.: Harvard University Press, 1991), pp. 356, 359.

27. Browning et al., *From Culture Wars to Common Ground*, p. 2.

28. Browning et al., *From Culture Wars to Common Ground*, pp. 273-79.

love ethic of regarding the other with equal seriousness to themselves just as they expect their partner to regard them. Within such an ethic, they should work together to determine their responsibilities and privileges in light of respective talents, inclinations, and realistic constraints.

Is such an ethic a pure fabrication of the liberal imagination or can it be buttressed by the marriage classics of the Western tradition? I believe that the seeds of the equal-regard marriage are deeply embedded within the founding marriage myths of the Western tradition. But the interpretive elaboration of these seeds needs to be sharpened, clarified, and completed. This is part of the cultural work of deepening and reformulating our understanding of marriage.

The creation stories of the Abrahamic religions suggest an ethic of equal regard. I call to your attention the suggestive work of Phyllis Trible, Mary Stewart Van Leeuwen, and Lisa Sowle Cahill.[29] These scholars remind us that in the Genesis account both male and female are made in the image of God: "in the image of God he created them: male and female he created them" (Gen. 1:27). These scholars further argue that male and female in this founding story are given joint and equal "dominion" over the reproductive and productive responsibilities of life: "God blessed them, and God said to them, 'Be fruitful and multiply, and . . . have dominion over the fish of the sea and over the birds of the air . . .'" (Gen. 1:28). Equal status before God, equal reproductive responsibilities, and equal productive responsibilities — this is the moral ontology behind the ethic of equal regard in the founding myths of the Abrahamic religions. These religions have not always been faithful to the full implications of this story, but the seeds of the equal-regard marriage are clearly there. Furthermore, it is against the background of a narrative that tells of God's primary purposes in creation that we must understand the subservience of Eve to Adam in the fall; the inequality, as this same group of scholars demonstrates, is a consequence of human brokenness and is not the primordial intention of God in creation.

Movement toward the deeper realization of the equal-regard marriage occurred when early Christianity brought the ethics of neighbor love ("You shall love your neighbor as yourself," Matt. 19:19) directly into mar-

29. Phyllis Trible, *God and the Rhetoric of Sexuality* (Minneapolis: Fortress, 1978), pp. 16-19; Mary Stewart Van Leeuwen, *Gender and Grace* (Downers Grove, Ill.: Intervarsity, 1990), pp. 42-47; Lisa Sowle Cahill, *Between the Sexes* (Philadelphia: Fortress, 1985), pp. 46-55. These views are basically confirmed by Leo Perdue's chapters in Leo Perdue, Joseph Blenkinsopp, John Collins, and Carol Meyers, *Families in Ancient Israel* (Louisville: Westminster John Knox, 1997), pp. 223-59.

riage itself: "husbands should love their wives as they do their own bodies" (Eph. 5:28). Furthermore, we now know that early Christianity must be interpreted against the background of the honor-shame ethic of much of the ancient world, especially the Roman Hellenism that surrounded it. This was an ethic of male honor associated with male agency, dominance, and sexual freedom; it also entailed an ethic of shame for women if they broke out of their confinement to the domestic realm and their restriction from public life. Early Christianity, while never completely escaping the honor-shame ethic of antique paganism, rejected the Greco-Roman double-sexual standard, confined male sexual activity to their wives, emphasized an ethic of male servanthood, and greatly increased the stature and visibility of women.[30]

But a double language justifying the equal-regard marriage begins to emerge most strikingly, once again, with Thomas Aquinas. It was Aquinas who synthesized the Genesis accounts of how both male and female were created in the image of God with Aristotle's philosophical view of friendship. Marriage, for Aquinas, was partially a naturalistic process of incorporating males into the task of raising children, as we saw above. But marriage was also about friendship, and friendship implies equality.[31] Aquinas could simultaneously use and blend the philosophical language of friendship with the theological language of the image of God in both male and female. Of course, Aquinas was too much an Aristotelian to make this a *fully* equal friendship of the kind he believed possible only between free and educated males. But he did set the stage for viewing marriage as a friendship — an idea that has been developed and extended by various contemporary philosophical and theological perspectives and is consistent with Genesis and the ethic of neighbor love applied to marriage. The idea of marriage as friendship is the precursor for understanding it as a "conversation," as John Milton proclaimed,[32] or as a "dialogue," as we put forth in *From Culture Wars to Common Ground*.[33] Such ideas are also behind the view of marriage as communication and conflict resolution which undergirds the present-day marriage education movement.

---

30. Browning et al., *From Culture Wars to Common Ground*, pp. 141-46.

31. Aquinas, *Summa Contra Gentiles*, vol. 3, pt. 2, p. 118.

32. John Milton, "The Doctrine and Discipline of Divorce," in John Milton, *Selected Prose*, ed. C. A. Patrides, new and revised ed. (Columbia, Mo.: University of Missouri Press, 1985), p. 124.

33. Browning et al., *From Culture Wars to Common Ground*, p. 298.

The Equal-Regard Marriage and Society

Marriage as a conversation and dialogue of equal regard should not exclude viewing marriage in terms of its health benefits for husband, wife, and children. It does mean, however, that in the equal-regard marriage, neither husband nor wife, parents nor children, should ever be reduced to the level of being viewed primarily as an instrument of health.

More concretely, if marriage is an institution of equal regard that also raises children, some dramatic changes must be made in our society. Here are a few of these changes. Education that prepares individuals for an equal-regard marriage must be widespread. Furthermore, government and market should cooperate in making it possible for couples to be simultaneously parents, wage-earners, and citizens. All three roles should be possible without couples' working eighty to ninety hours each week outside the home, as some do today. This entails institutionalizing something like the sixty-hour workweek as the maximum combined time couples with children should work in the wage economy. These sixty hours can be divided as the couple sees fit — an idea we developed at length in *From Culture Wars to Common Ground.*[34] It certainly should not mean, however, that one member of the couple work the entire sixty hours.

Supporting the equal-regard marriage means privileging marriage in a variety of cultural, political, and economic ways. It means removing all penalties — such as the so-called marriage penalty in the federal income tax. But the question of how one organizes a culture and society to support the equal-regard marriage is a huge topic and must be addressed more fully at another time.

My argument has been that the vision of life, the narratives that convey it, and the ontologies of personhood found in the key texts of the Western marriage tradition should play a role today in the cultural work of reviving this institution. This can be done best when these texts inform a public philosophy of marriage as classics — classics that have time and again proven themselves as carrying deep truths. These truths can place naturalistic discussions of the goods of marriage into wider contexts of meaning.

Justification for retaining in public discourse the mythic framework of Western family theory has several dimensions to it, more than I can cover here. But one justification has to do with acknowledging the difficulty that all thought has in escaping mythic horizons. I have spent much

---

34. Browning et al., *From Culture Wars to Common Ground*, p. 317.

of my scholarly life arguing that all theories of action, including social-science theories, contain within them deep metaphors, generally unthematized, about the origins, meanings, and purposes of life. The social sciences are riddled with implicit metaphors (and corresponding ontologies) of strife (rational-choice), harmony (humanistic psychology, Jung), life against death (Freud), care (Erikson, Kohut), husbandry (Skinner), and more.[35] These hidden metaphors function analogously to the faith stances of the classic Western religious traditions. If this is true, it seems only fair that visions of life surrounding the religious classics of the past should be allowed to continue to inform the public conversation about marriage and be tested in terms of how they illumine the full meaning of this fundamental institution that we seek to better understand.

---

35. Don Browning, *Religious Thought and the Modern Psychologies* (Minneapolis: Fortress, 1987).

Chapter 17

Critical Familism, Civil Society, and the Law (2004)

This chapter was originally presented at a conference on Family and Democracy held at Hofstra Law School during the spring of 2003. More specifically, it was presented as part of a concluding panel that also included the feminist sociologist Judith Stacey (whose work I treat in Chapter 6), critical-legal feminist Martha Fineman, conservative legal scholar Lynn Wardle, and family-law scholar Linda McClain. My task was to explain and defend critical familism to an audience of legal scholars.

I first explained that critical familism is a family and marriage theory that primarily applies to the sphere of civil society and only secondarily has implications for the law. Nonetheless, I argued that law should do nothing to undermine the ideals of critical familism, given their broad public validity. Furthermore, law should develop statutes, legal policies, and social programs that support the goals and values of critical familism.

I also discussed a variety of concrete social programs that should be enacted by law to withstand the disruptive effects of modernization on families. These should include the idea of a workweek of no more than sixty hours total for a married couple with children, to be divided thirty-thirty or forty-twenty as suits their circumstances, aptitudes, and tastes. These legislative programs should also include higher tax benefits and exemptions for couples with children and more child-centered divorce laws. For an informative summary of the panel (which also constitutes something of an introduction to contemporary family law), see Professor Linda McClain's "Intimate Affiliation and Democracy: Beyond Marriage?"*

*Linda McClain, "Intimate Affiliation and Democracy: Beyond Marriage?" *Hofstra Law Review* 32, no. 1 (Fall 2003): 379-422.

C ritical familism is a concept that my colleagues and I developed to
summarize our thinking during the first phase of the Religion, Culture, and Family Project — a research project located at the University of
Chicago that deals with the possible relevance of the Western religious
traditions to contemporary family issues. It is a summary of what we
thought were the most abiding themes of that tradition — both Judaism
and Christianity — as well as the best insights of contemporary human
sciences such as sociology, psychology, and economics. It is a normative
theory of family and marriage primarily intended to provide culture and
civil society their ideals and practical strategies for family formation and
marriage.

Critical familism only indirectly has implications for family law. On
the other hand, family law should do nothing to undermine this normative model and, in fact, should do some things to support it. Critical
familism acknowledges the central importance of religio-cultural aspirations and supports the equal-regard mother-father team with equal privileges and responsibilities in both the public worlds of politics and employment and the more private realms of home, child-rearing, and
intergenerational care.[1]

Critical familism is "critical" in that it attempts to expose, critique,
and reform distortions of social, economic, and political power that function to block or undermine the free formation and support of the equal-
regard mother-father partnership. It holds that the principles supporting
such critique can be found within both the Jewish and Christian traditions and gleaned as well from insights drawn from contemporary moral
philosophy. Even though critical familism fully acknowledges that mar-

---

1. The basic sources of critical familism are the summary book of the first phase of the
Religion, Culture, and Family Project by Don Browning, Bonnie Miller-McLemore, Pamela
Couture, Bernie Lyon, and Robert Franklin, *From Culture Wars to Common Ground: Religion
and the American Family Debate* (Louisville: Westminster John Knox, 1997, 2000). Also see
Don Browning and Gloria Rodriguez, *Reweaving the Social Tapestry: Toward a Public Philosophy
and Policy for Families* (New York: W. W. Norton, 2001); this book was the background book
for the American Assembly's consultation on families held in September of 2000. Critical
familism influenced the consensus statement developed by the fifty-three diverse individuals attending that conference and published under the title "Strengthening American Families: Reweaving the Social Tapestry: The 97th American Assembly, September 21-24, 2000."
The arguments in this chapter may take critical familism in directions that some of my co-
authors would not share, and must be regarded primarily as my own. The theory of critical
familism is also extended into a wider international discussion in my *Marriage and Modernization: How Globalization Threatens Marriage and What Should Be Done about It* (Grand Rapids:
Eerdmans, 2003).

riage is not always chosen by everyone for the purposes of procreation and child care, as an institution with certain cultural, social, and legal entitlements and responsibilities, marriage should be defined primarily with its child-rearing tasks envisioned as central.

Critical familism has a variety of other names in the current literature. Sociologist Brad Wilcox in a recent review of the family strategies of the mainline churches refers to it as "progressive familism" in contrast to the "traditional familism" of the 1950s or the "expressive liberationist" approaches of some religious groups today.[2] Sociologist William Doherty, partially influenced by critical familism, has developed a perspective on family issues that he calls a "critical promarriage" point of view with implications for cultural, social, and legal reform.[3]

Critical familism is not primarily a legal theory, although it has implications for the law. It is basically a cultural strategy — indeed a religio-cultural strategy — to be carried out principally by the institutions of civil society. It envisions the task of reconstructing family and marriage along its theoretical lines as a complex cultural work that requires a delicate set of collaborations between civil society, government, market, and the specialized field of family law.[4]

Religious Thinking and Public Discourse

Critical familism holds that family theory informed by religious traditions has a right to contribute to public policy. It holds this because of the often overlooked symmetry of religious and so-called secular thought. Critical familism holds that all moral, political, and legal thinking — as expressions of practical wisdom *(phronēsis)* — are complex interweavings of several dimensions of thought. These include (1) deep metaphors conveying fundamental views of reality, (2) general principles of moral obligation (for example, utilitarian, ethical-egoist, Kantian, the Golden Rule,

2. Brad Wilcox, "For the Sake of the Children? Family-Related Discourse and Practice in the Mainline," in *The Quiet Hand of God: Faith-Based Activism and the Public Role of Mainline Protestantism,* ed. Robert Wuthnow and John H. Evans (Berkeley: University of California Press, 2002).

3. William Doherty and Jason Carroll, "Health and the Ethics of Marital Therapy and Education," in *Marriage, Health, and the Professions,* ed. John Wall, Don Browning, William Doherty, and Stephen Post (Grand Rapids: Eerdmans, 2002), p. 216.

4. For the idea of marriage reconstruction as a cultural work, see Browning, *Marriage and Modernization,* pp. 24-29.

neighbor love), (3) assumed theories of premoral goods that satisfy central human needs, (4) theories of natural and social-systemic patterns and constraints, and, finally, (5) assumptions about preferred concrete practices, rules, and social roles.[5] These five dimensions of practical wisdom can be uncovered through a process of empirical reconstruction of concrete instances of actual practical thinking similar similar to Jürgen Habermas's method of uncovering his three validity claims.[6] This is to say that a careful analysis of concrete instances of practical reason invariably demonstrates assumptions and judgments at these different levels.

Critical familism holds that the deep metaphors of all practical thinking have the status of faith-like assumptions. Deep metaphors may illuminate experience but are not subject to definitive proof short of metaphysical arguments that are themselves generally thought to be inconclusive. Since such metaphors (for example, organic, mechanistic, monistic, harmonistic, dualistic, or theistic) can be uncovered in all instances of practical thinking, the distinction between explicitly religious practical thinking and so-called secular moral, political, or legal practical thought is not categorical. Both allegedly secular and religious forms of practical rationality float on a veritable ocean of assumed metaphors about the basic structures of life, their directions, and their trustworthiness or lack of it.[7] This rough commensurability of so-called religious and secular forms of practical reason means that positions on family theory informed by explicitly religious sources have the right to enter into deliberations aimed to shape public policy. Of course, in contrast to confessional criteria that have their authority within their respective traditions, for explicitly religiously informed family theories to gain a hearing in policy debates, they must advance their arguments in publicly accessible ways.

This can happen when religiously informed perspectives present themselves as mixed discourses in which faith affirmations expressed in metaphor and narrative are interwoven with moral arguments about the right and the good that can be expressed in publicly recognizable forms of philosophy and social theory. Most axial religions contain clear examples of such articulate blends of religious narrative and metaphor with philosophically identifiable forms of argument about the nature of the moral

---

5. For a fuller discussion of the five dimensions of practical reason, see Don Browning, *A Fundamental Practical Theology* (Minneapolis: Fortress, 1991).

6. Jürgen Habermas, *Moral Consciousness and Communicative Action* (Cambridge, Mass.: MIT Press, 1990), p. 79.

7. George Lakoff and Mark Johnson, *Metaphors We Live By* (New York: Oxford University Press, 1959).

and premoral goods relevant to public policy; for example, Roman Catholicism is informed by Aristotelianism, while liberal Protestantism has been variously informed by Kantianism, American pragmatism, and existentialism. Furthermore, historical research reveals that the family theories of early Christianity contained insights from Aristotelian and Stoic philosophy. Mature forms of axial religions are almost always mixed discourses blending explicitly religious metaphors and narrative with moral-philosophical arguments that sometimes merge into political and economic judgments as well. The problem of linking the deep metaphors of practical thought to its more articulate moral and premoral judgments is a challenge not only for religious thinking but for so-called secular practical thought as well.

Critical familism, with its vision of the equal-regard mother-father partnership, is grounded on a complex, mixed religio-philosophical discourse of this kind. At its most abstract formulation, the idea of equal regard is what William Frankena called a "mixed-deontological" concept.[8] It defines the marital contract as a complex social covenant. The covenant between husband and wife is to treat each other as ends and never as objects or means of satisfaction alone. Used as a mixed-deontological concept, it also contains a strong teleological subdimension that entails the obligation to actively work for the good of one's marital partner in all spheres of life, both private and public. The equal-regard covenant or status is a theory of mutuality and is thoroughly reversible; it applies with equal force to both husband and wife. But because of the asymmetrical nature of male and female investments on certain matters such as procreation and child care, the equal-regard covenant does not necessary imply moment-by-moment identical treatment, although it does require equality over the marital life cycle.

The equal-regard covenant is primarily a religio-cultural ideal to be promoted and implemented by the institutions of civil society. It should be a guide to socialization in family, schools, and religious institutions in their various forms of marriage education, preparation, and support. Government and market should do nothing to undermine the equal-regard covenant and should do what they reasonably can to support it. Law in its various forms does not have the primary responsibility for promoting it but should be seen as a source of friendly assistance.

8. William Frankena, *Ethics* (Englewood Cliffs, N.J.: Prentice-Hall, 1973), p. 43.

Sources of Critical Familism and the Equal-Regard Covenant

Even though at its core, the equal-regard covenant is a mixed deontological concept, it also has many sources and several levels of additional meaning adhering to it. It takes seriously what Hans-Georg Gadamer would call the written "classics" of Western religious and philosophical traditions on marriage and family. For instance, it honors the Ur-myth of Genesis 1 that gives the dignity of the *imago Dei* (Gen. 1:27) to both male and female and that also grants equal responsibility to both in procreation and "dominion" (generally interpreted as economic responsibility) (Gen. 1:28).[9] In addition to the classic texts of Judaism, Christianity, and Islam, the equal-regard doctrine of critical familism takes seriously the Aristotelian theory of friendship between husband and wife as the sharing of utility, pleasure, and virtue[10] — especially the Thomistic enrichment of these concepts with Aquinas's attribution of the *imago Dei* to the wife as well as the husband.[11] This was a significant yet still incomplete step toward balancing Aristotle's theory of proportional justice between husband and wife.[12] Critical familism also values medieval canon law and Thomistic accomplishments that made uncoerced consent on the part of both husband and wife central to the definition of marriage.[13]

Thomas Aquinas provides critical familism with some additional insights. Aquinas could agree with those contemporary feminists who hold that the primordial family is the mother-infant dyad.[14] For both Aquinas and contemporary evolutionary psychologists, however, the question is this: *What are the conditions which led to the momentously important cultural accomplishment of human males joining the mother-infant dyad and contributing provision and care for their offspring and consorts?* Aquinas's answer (parallel

---

9. Phyllis Trible, *God and the Rhetoric of Sexuality* (Philadelphia: Fortress, 1978), p. 19.

10. Aristotle, *Nicomachean Ethics,* in *The Basic Works of Aristotle,* ed. Richard McKeon (New York: Random House, 1941), bk. VIII, chap. 3.

11. Thomas Aquinas, *Summa Contra Gentiles* (London: Burns, Oates, and Washbourne, 1928) 3, ii, p. 118 (hereafter referred to as SCG.).

12. Aristotle, *Nicomachean Ethics,* bk. VIII, chap. 7.

13. John Witte Jr., *From Sacrament to Contract: Marriage, Religion, and Law in the Western Tradition* (Louisville: Westminster John Knox, 1997), pp. 26, 32-33; James Brundage, *Law, Sex, and Christian Society in Medieval Europe* (Chicago: University of Chicago Press, 1987), pp. 361-64.

14. Thomas Aquinas, *Summa Theologica* Supplement to the Third Part (Boston, Mass.: Benziger Brothers, 1948), q. 41, a. 1 (hereafter referred to as ST); Martha Fineman, *The Neutered Mother: The Sexual Family and Other Twentieth Century Tragedies* (New York: Routledge, 1995), p. 5.

to that given by contemporary evolutionary psychology, but of course without its theory of evolution) contained several elements. The long period of human infant dependency, the father's recognition and certainty that the child was his (what evolutionary theorists call "paternal recognition" and "paternal certainty"), sexual exchange, and mutual assistance between father and mother gradually brought the human male to assist the mother-infant dyad.[15] These are the naturalistic foundations of matrimony, which religion and culture sanction and stabilize but do not directly create.

Both Aquinas and much of contemporary evolutionary psychology assume that this was an enormous social and cultural achievement that distinguishes humans from almost all other mammals.[16] My research suggests that other medieval scholars from different faith traditions such as the Jewish Nachmanides and the Islamic al-Ghazali also recognized something like this naturalistic archeology of the marital institution.[17] Marriage as sacrament for Aquinas and marriage as a one-flesh covenant for Nachmanides and al-Ghazali gave this male connection with the mother-infant dyad the additional stability and reinforcement of sacredness. The sacred character of sacrament and covenant convert the logic of mutual advantage (the logic of costs and benefits) to the logic of mutual obligation and respect; costs and benefits are not ignored but they now become secondary. For most of the period since the Protestant Reformation, marriage law in most Western societies has in some way recognized the priority of the logic of sacred obligation in the marital contract and covenant.

15. For references to these various moves by Aquinas, see the following texts: ST, Supplement to the Third Part, q. 41, 1; SCG, vol. 3, pt. 2, pp. 112-18. For analogous points made in evolutionary psychology, see Pierre Van den Berghe, *Human Family Systems* (New York: Elsevier, 1979), pp. 20-21; Donald Symons, *The Evolution of Human Sexuality* (Oxford: Oxford University Press, 1979), pp. 131-36; Barry Hewlett, ed., *Father-Child Relations* (Hawthorne, N.Y.: Aldine de Gruyter, 1992); Robert Trivers, *Social Evolution* (Menlo Park, Calif.: Benjamin/ Cummings, 1985), pp. 203-38. For a more detailed summary of this comparison between the naturalism of Aquinas and evolutionary psychology, see Browning et al., *From Culture Wars to Common Ground*, pp. 111-27.

16. I say *almost* all other mammals because there are a few other primates, such as gibbons, where this happens, although in quite different ways than with humans. See Martin Daly and Margo Wilson, *Sex, Evolution, and Behavior* (Belmont, Calif.: Wadsworth, 1983), p. 142.

17. Nachmanides, *Commentary on the Torah Genesis*, vol. 1 (New York: Shilo, 1971-76), p. 8; al-Ghazali, *Book on the Etiquette of Marriage*, in *Marriage and Sexuality in Islam*, ed. Madelin Farah (Salt Lake City: University of Utah Press, 1984), p. 45. For extensive commentary on these texts, see Browning, *Marriage and Modernization*, pp. 117-25.

Sacred concepts endow with intrinsic value the human arrangements that they bless. These arrangements are seen to have such intrinsic value that they are regarded as protected and sanctioned as *termini* for entire ranges of important but less valuable instrumental goods. Until recent decades, Western thought developed certain legal and philosophical concepts that honor understandings of marriage as sacrament (Catholicism, Hinduism), covenant (Judaism, Islam, Protestantism), or "one flesh" union (Judaism, Catholicism, Hinduism, and Protestantism), without sanctioning any one model of the sacred. The legal concepts of marriage as a "status" or a secular legal "covenant" are designed to serve this legal and cultural function of supporting and stabilizing this human accomplishment of joining the father to the mother-infant dyad.

There are additional sources for the ideal of the equal-regard mother-father marital covenant, including, of course, Kant and his followers, such as John Rawls and Susan Okin.[18] But critical familism adds additional twists to the Kantian formulation. First, it holds that it is precisely the task of both husband and wife in the equal-regard covenant to promise publicly before the state, friends, extended family, and, if religious, before relevant communities of faith that they will treat one another as ends and never only as means.[19] Hence, the equal marital covenant is also a covenant with other spheres of society beyond the husband-wife dyad. This makes the equal-regard covenant simultaneously both thoroughly private and thoroughly public. It is public in that its promises start with the conjugal couple but also include a variety of spheres beyond it. It is thoroughly private in that neither state nor market should interfere except in emergencies and to support; both state and market must avoid disrupting or replacing the tasks of the conjugal couple as parents and lovers.

Second, in contrast to Kant, the mixed deontological logic of the equal-regard covenant implies that this public pledge also entails equally strong efforts to actualize the welfare of the other (the good of the other) as well as the good of any offspring of the marital union.[20] But, as Kant himself recognized, his categorical imperative had its predecessors in the Golden Rule, the Jewish and Christian principle of neighbor love, and

18. Immanuel Kant, *Foundations of the Metaphysics of Morals* (New York: Bobbs-Merrill, 1959); John Rawls, *A Theory of Justice* (Cambridge, Mass.: Harvard University Press, 1971); Susan Okin, *Justice, Gender, and the Family* (New York: Basic, 1989).

19. Kant, *Foundations of the Metaphysics of Morals*, p. 47.

20. For the neo-Aristotelian Janssens and a neo-Thomistic statement of the meaning of equal regard closer to what I subscribe to, see Louis Janssens, "Norms and Priorities of a Love Ethics," *Louvain Studies* 6 (Spring 1977): 207-88.

their various analogues in other religions. Finally, it should be emphasized that the equal-regard marital covenant is about the conjugal couple
and not necessarily the neo-local nuclear family isolated from the rest of
society. The equal-regard covenant and critical familism are ecological
concepts designed to define families as democracies of work and affection
interacting with, contributing to, and supported by wider social and natural networks.

Critical Familism as Antidote to Modernization

The ideal of the equal-regard covenant also is informed by various historical and sociological trends. The development of democratic polities and
modernization in Western societies gradually has been interpreted to require something like the equal-regard covenant. In the nineteenth century, the processes of early modernization drew into the wage economy
and out of dependence on the farm and craft-based economies centered
in the extended family.[21] In the twentieth century, modernization and industrialization drew women into the wage economy and away from exclu-
sive economic dependence on husbands. These social processes decreased
forced economic dependencies and have had a democratizing influence
on marriage and family.

It should be noted, however, that the concept of the equal-regard marital covenant is both compatible with modernization and an antidote to
its excesses. Both husband and wife have access to the fruits of the modernizing process, but Habermas argues that the blind processes of modernization also tend to "colonize" the lifeworld of face-to-face social interactions (neighborhoods, families, and marriage) and reduce them to the
cost-benefit logics and functional universalism of efficient market productivity.[22] The equal-regard marital covenant places strong limitations
on the disruptive excesses of market forms of modernization. Although
critical familism supports appropriate welfare measures, it also places
strong limitations on bureaucratic forms of modernization that attempt
to remedy the disruptions of families with dependency-inducing forms of

21. Gary S. Becker, *Treatise on the Family* (Cambridge, Mass.: Harvard University Press,
1991), pp. 348-56.

22. For descriptions of both market and bureaucratic forms of rationalization, see
Jürgen Habermas, *The Theory of Communicative Action,* trans. Thomas McCarthy, vol. 2
(Boston, Mass.: Beacon, 1987), pp. 182-96; Alan Wolfe, *Whose Keeper? Social Science and Moral
Obligation* (Berkeley: University of California Press, 1989), pp. 52-60, 133-41.

assistance that actually encourage further family fragmentation. Critical familism follows the thinking of Roman Catholic subsidiarity teaching; neither government nor market should interfere with or attempt to replace the investments of kin altruism located in the mother-father team.[23] Both spheres of society — but especially government — should be willing to assist families (and this includes all families with children, be they intact yet poor, or single-parent families) when the need is clear and beyond remedy by other means.

Practical Strategies

Since critical familism is primarily a theory and strategy for the culture-building and socializing tasks of the institutions of civil society, recommendations for concrete strategies should begin there. The first task is to both recover and reconstruct our inherited marriage and family traditions. Neither the general public nor the specialized professions of law, medicine, education, or therapy understand these traditions. Most people do not comprehend the complex interweaving of Jewish and Christian teachings, Greek philosophy, Roman and German law, and Enlightenment philosophy that has gone into the formation of Western marriage and family traditions. But the retrieval and reconstruction of these traditions also will require a nuanced dialogue between them and more newly visible traditions within Islam, Hinduism, Buddhism, and Confucianism in Western societies. Critical familism holds that neither our family culture nor our public policies should be developed in such a way as to marginalize either the classics of the Western religions that have shaped our culture or the traditions that were once thought to be exotic but are now part of our daily lives and may have insights to contribute.

The task of the future is to retrieve and reconstruct all these traditions and to find fruitful analogies (not necessarily identities) between them for the purposes of rough cultural consensus.[24] Research and scholarship by both the Emory Center for the Interdisciplinary Study of Religion and the Religious Consultation on Population, Reproductive Health, and Ethics

---

23. Pope Leo XIII, *Rerum Novarum*, in *Proclaiming Justice and Peace: Documents from Rerum Novarum through Centesimus Annus*, ed. Michael Walsh and Brian Davies (Mystic, Conn.: Twenty-Third Publications, 1991), para. 12.

24. For a discussion of the distinctions between analogy, identities, and non-identities in correlational thinking, see David Tracy, *Blessed Rage for Order* (Minneapolis: Seabury, 1975), and his *The Analogical Imagination* (New York: Crossroad, 1981).

suggest that all these classic religions have significant strands that are roughly analogous to the central ideas of critical familism.[25] The goal of this ecumenical retrieval and reconstruction should not be to dictate either public policy or the details of family law. The purpose instead should be to help develop a loose cultural consensus to which public policy and law would be sensitive and, indeed, respectful.

Critical familism holds that our society should retain the accomplishment of the Protestant Reformation that made marriage a public institution but also an institution that could be blessed by religious traditions. This achievement should be preserved now, however, with broad sensitivity to the variety of religious traditions that make up the American social reality.

The development of a powerful culture of critical familism requires more than historical retrieval and reconstruction. It also necessitates effective systems of socialization. Marriage is a complex intersubjective communicative process that needs advanced levels of "communicative competence."[26] Furthermore, there are skills, privileges, and responsibilities associated with marriage and child-rearing — skills, privileges, and responsibilities somewhat analogous to those that come with driving an automobile. To take the comparison further, there are similar material and economic costs and benefits to health, safety, pleasure, and utility in both marriage and driving a car. Hence, just as we train people to drive well and safely, society through its various educational and religious institutions should teach people to handle the communicative, cultural, and bioeconomic realities of marriage. This is primarily a task for the institutions of civil society rather than law or government, although both can, in limited ways, support this cultural task.

The market is not the primary locus for promoting critical familism.

---

25. For sample publications of the Religious Consultation on Population, Reproductive Health, and Ethics, see Howard Coward and Daniel Maguire, *Visions of a New Earth: Religious Perspectives on Population, Consumption, and Ecology* (Albany: State University of New York Press, 2000); John Raines and Daniel Maguire, *What Men Owe to Women* (Albany: State University of New York Press, 2001); Daniel Maguire, *Sacred Choices: The Right to Contraception and Abortion in Ten World Religions* (Minneapolis: Fortress, 2001). For a publication that reviews the religious consultation that comes from the Emory Center for the Interdisciplinary Study of Religion, see Browning, *Marriage and Modernization,* pp. 223-44.

26. Although Habermas develops the idea of communicative competence in relation to his discourse ethics and its implications for political procedures, in an era when economic dependence no longer unifies marriage, communicative competence and discourse ethics are relevant to family dialogue as well. See Habermas, *Moral Consciousness and Communicative Action,* pp. 120, 209.

But it can make essential contributions. In addition to a broad array of family-friendly provisions, business and industry should take rapid steps toward implementing what critical familism has called the sixty-hour workweek option for married couples with children, to be divided between husband and wife thirty-thirty or forty-twenty. It follows that single-parents should be offered thirty-hour workweek options and that work requirements for single parents on welfare should not exceed thirty hours per week.[27] These options should be offered with health benefits, and in the case of welfare, single parents also should receive child care, medical insurance, and transportation supports. Through the instrument of the sixty-hour workweek option, critical familism simultaneously supports the modernizing process but also limits its mindless spread into family life.

This proposal reveals the radical edge to critical familism. Limiting the time and energy that parents dedicate to the wage economy is essential for shaping a society in which the privileges and responsibilities of the public and private spheres of life are equally available to all parents. This recommendation makes critical familism truly progressive in contrast to other contemporary options. The conservative political and religious right wants to contain the spread of the market into private life by retaining the nineteenth-century solution of the divided spheres that placed men in the public realm and women in the domestic realm. Critical familism differs from liberal feminism that would give women full access to the market but has few proposals to radically contain it other than government and business support for child care. Critical familism differs from gynocentric legal feminists who emphasize the elevated status of mothering before law and government but have few proposals to limit the demands of market rationality.

Critical Familism and Family Law

Finally, critical familism has proposals relevant to the law even though law and government are not its primary points of leverage for marriage and family reform. Critical familism is fully aware that the modernizing

---

27. For further discussions of the sixty-hour workweek for couples with children and the thirty-hour workweek for single parents, see Browning et al., *From Culture Wars to Common Ground*, pp. 316-18, 327-28; Browning and Rodriguez, *Reweaving the Social Tapestry*, pp. 128-30; and the final consensus statement of the Ninety-Seventh American Assembly attached to *Reweaving the Social Tapestry*, p. 190.

process has done much to break down old cultural pressures and economic dependencies that functioned to support stable marriage formation. As a consequence, divorce, nonmarital births, and alternative family patterns have become more common in modernizing societies. Abundant social-science research accumulated since the early 1990s demonstrates that these marriage and family disruptions have not been good for the health and well-being of either children or adults.[28] These negative trends are now showing signs of slowing in the United States, although in many other parts of the world they seem to be gaining momentum.[29]

Whether coming or going, these trends are serious enough to require government policies and family law to develop fair and equitable ways for handling family disruption and the strains of divorce, custody, single parenthood, and out-of-wedlock births. But in addressing these issues, law and public policy should not attempt to develop alternative family and marriage cultures that would require heroic redefinitions of inherited cultural patterns. Efforts to delegalize the marital relation and grant legal status only to parenthood, or perhaps mainly to mothers, would be ineffective and culturally destructive from the perspective of critical familism. They also would arrogate far too much cultural and social power over family matters to law and public policy.[30]

There are, however, steps that law and policy should take to encourage and support the equal-regard marriage and family and, at the same time, provide a range of universal supports and remedies for all families with children. Policies that would remove the marriage penalty from the tax code can be recommended. The increase of child tax exemptions and child credits for all families regardless of their form is also clearly in order. Advances in marriage education have been made that are sufficiently re-

28. Recent texts that demonstrate the social costs of family disruption include Frank Fuerstenberg and Andrew Cherlin, *Divided Families* (Cambridge, Mass.: Harvard University Press, 1991); Linda Waite, "Does Marriage Matter?" *Demography* 32, no. 4 (November 1995): 483-507; Paul Amato and Alan Booth, *Generation at Risk* (Cambridge, Mass.: Harvard University Press, 1997).

29. For summaries of the new international trends, see Linda Waite and Maggie Gallagher, eds., *The Ties that Bind: Perspectives on Marriage and Cohabitation* (New York: Aldine de Gruyter, 2000).

30. For an emphasis on parenthood as the center of family law, see "Principles of the Law of Family Dissolution: Analysis and Recommendations" (American Law Institute, 2002), and June Carbone, *From Partners to Parents: The Second Revolution in Family Law* (New York: Columbia University Press, 2000). For an emphasis on motherhood as the center of family law, see Martha Fineman, *The Illusion of Equality* (Chicago: University of Chicago Press, 1991), and Fineman, *The Neutered Mother.*

searched to justify making such education widely available to teens and young people throughout society.[31] Government support of experiments in marriage education, generally offered by various agencies of civil society, is consistent with centuries-old state interests in marriage as a civil institution. From the perspective of critical familism, state-mandated marriage education at the level of secondary schools, as now exists in Florida, is an acceptable idea,[32] just as are experiments in covenant marriage now being conducted in Louisiana, Arizona, and Arkansas.[33] State encouragement of cooperation on marriage education between religious bodies, the field of medicine, welfare agencies, and schools, as is being pursued in Oklahoma, is also worth studying.[34] "Children first" legislation that would require the filing of long-term financial plans for children at the time of divorce, as proposed by Mary Ann Glendon, Katherine Spaht, and William Galston, has considerable merit as well.[35]

Finally, government should pass legislation that encourages business and industry to provide more twenty- and thirty-hour workweeks with benefits to make more widely attainable the sixty-hour workweek for couples with children and the thirty-hour week for single parents. Government should take the radical step of curtailing the spread of market demands into the intimate rhythms of families and child care.

As indicated above, the equal-regard covenant recognizes the existence of male-female asymmetries in their respective investments in procreation and child care. In fact, an ethic of equal regard demands additional protections for vulnerable mothers during childbirth and the early

31. John Gottman, *What Predicts Divorce* (Hillsdale, N.J.: Lawrence Erlbaum, 1994), and *Why Marriages Succeed or Fail* (New York: Simon and Schuster, 1994); Howard Markinan, Scott Stanley, and Susan L. Blumberg, *Fighting for Your Marriage* (San Francisco: Jossey-Bass, 1994).

32. Pam Belluck, "States Declare War on Divorce Rates, Before Any 'I Dos,'" *New York Times* (April 4, 2000), p. A1.

33. Amitai Etzioni and Peter Rubin, *Opportuning Virtue: Lessons of the Louisiana Covenant Marriage Law* (Washington, D.C.: Communitarian Network, 1997).

34. Christina Johnson et al., *Marriage in Oklahoma: 2001 Baseline Statewide Survey on Marriage and Divorce* (Oklahoma State University: Bureau for Social Research, 2002).

35. See Katherine Shaw Spaht's discussion of this proposal in "The Family As Community: Implementing the 'Children-First Principle,'" in *Marriage in America: A Communitarian Perspective,* ed. Martin Whyte (New York: Rowman and Littlefield, 2000), pp. 235-56: see also Mary Ann Glendon, *Abortion and Divorce in Western Law* (Cambridge, Mass.: Harvard University Press, 1987), pp. 93-95; William Galston, "A Liberal-Democratic Case for the Two-Parent Family," *Responsive Community* (Winter 1990-91): 2325; Elaine Kamarck and William Galston, "Putting Children First: A Progressive Family Policy for the 1990s" (Washington, D.C.: Progressive Policy Institute, 1991).

years of child care. Similarly, critical familism recognizes the need for additional cultural and social inducements for fathers and husbands to commit to child and spousal support. Because of these asymmetries, it is reasonable for culture and law to give preferential rights and support to mothers in custody matters. But this should not be done at the expense of exempting fathers from their legal responsibility to assist in guiding and financially supporting their offspring, except in clear instances of incapacity or unfitness. Of course, in some instances, these features of incapacity and unfitness may equally apply to the mother, thereby overriding legal and cultural presumptions in her favor.

But it is best for those of us who do not specialize in the law not to become buried in the legal details. It is safer for me to stay at the level of general frameworks, reasserting my belief that marriage and family matters are primarily works of culture to be addressed in civil society and only secondarily matters that can be promoted or remedied by government policy, the market, or the details of family law.

Chapter 18

The Meaning of the Family in the Universal Declaration of Human Rights (2004)

This chapter is an extension of my efforts to make sense of critical familism with reference to the law — in this instance, the human rights movement that shapes so much of modern international law. The chapter was originally written as a plenary address for the Asian Pacific Dialogue on the Family Conference held in October of 2004 in Kuala Lumpur, Malaysia. It was a conference held in preparation for the United Nations's Second International Year of the Family that was celebrated in Doha, Qattar, in late November of that same year.

This celebration was the occasion for a bit of self-reflection by both the United Nations and various nongovernmental organizations that participate in the discussions centering at the United Nations. Many of the human rights statements of the United Nations discuss not only the rights of individuals but also the rights of families, mothers, and children. But what is meant, or at least assumed, in these statements by the word "family"?

This question is especially important for the mother of all United Nations human rights documents, the Universal Declaration of Human Rights. This chapter tries to answer how the term "family" was used in the Declaration and also discusses what claim this use might have on contemporary trends in international and national family law.

What was the meaning of the concept of family in the Universal Declaration of Human Rights (UDHR) and what was the family's connection with marriage? I ask this question because of the importance of the Universal Declaration for the wider field of international law and its struggle to define the legal status of families in our changing world. Documents such as the UDHR and the wider field of international family law are having increasing influence on family theory and family culture throughout the world. If there is wisdom on family issues in the UDHR, this wisdom should be made more available. If there are confusions, they should be clarified and remedied.

This essay will argue that the UDHR was not so much confused about the meaning of family and its relation to marriage as it was pragmatic and open-ended, hence not entirely definitive. Nonetheless, I will argue that an outline of the UDHR's general direction can be discerned and developed for use in a variety of cultural, political, and legal contexts. In short, I believe that returning to the Universal Declaration and clarifying its implicit directions can provide orientation for the future.

Historians give us the following picture of the accomplishments and compromises on issues about the family in the Universal Declaration. We are told that a certain air of practicality came to dominate the Commission on Human Rights. It was significantly inspired by the Confucian P. C. Chang, who was one of the leaders of the Commission, and to some extent by philosophical advisors such as Jacques Maritain, who served on the Committee on the Theoretical Basis of Human Rights.[1] With the endorsement of Eleanor Roosevelt, the Commission's first chair, attempts to ground the basic concepts of the UDHR with reference to the transcendent (concepts such as Creator, God, or the divine) gradually were rejected. Also largely excluded were efforts to ground concepts on the idea of nature. Roosevelt said the Universal Declaration "left it to each of us to put in our own reason" for the justification of its central concepts.[2]

The Lebanese philosopher and statesman Charles Malik resisted these expediencies. At one point, he proposed inserting the sentences, "The family deriving from marriage is the natural and fundamental group unit of society. It is endowed by the Creator with inalienable rights antecedent to all positive law and as such shall be protected by the State and Society."[3] Malik wanted the words "natural" and "endowed by the Creator" in the text to assure that the concept of the marriage-based fam-

---

1. Mary Ann Glendon, *A World Made New* (New York: Random House, 2001), pp. 77, 134.

2. Glendon, *A World Made New*, p. 147.

3. Johannes Morsink, *The Universal Declaration of Human Rights: Origins, Drafting, and Intent* (Philadelphia: University of Pennsylvania Press, 1999), p. 254.

ily was seen as endowed with its own "inalienable rights" and not viewed as a human invention subject to the caprice of either State or current public opinion.[4]

For the most part, Malik was not successful in getting his stronger natural-law type arguments into the text of the UDHR. The Commission followed the strategy of discovering the points of concrete agreement and bracketed matters of deeper justification. Article 16 did retain part of his formulation, however, when it stated, "The family is the natural and fundamental group unit of society and is entitled to protection by society and the State" (Article 16.3).[5] This is less than Malik wanted, but more than first meets the eye.

The connection between marriage and family was deleted, principally out of the fear that it stigmatize children born out of wedlock.[6] The idea that the Creator guaranteed the family as "the natural and fundamental" unit of society was also removed. But the words "natural," "fundamental," and "group unit" were retained and are not meaningless. Furthermore, they point to some model of natural law. Since society and state are to protect the family, it is clear that Malik's formulation deprives society and state of the power to grant the family its basic rights. These rights are in some way independent of these social entities.

New Models of Natural Law

It is widely acknowledged that Malik was a kind of natural law philosopher and tried to ground the Universal Declaration in natural law theory. He was not completely successful, but he did not entirely fail. I do not plan to resurrect Malik's view of natural law. It is clear that his colleagues on the Commission felt it was too rigid and could not fully capture the foundations of the great variety of religious and cultural systems. In fact, I agree to some extent with the strategy of the Commission that led it to resist invoking a particular view of the transcendent as a way of protecting human rights. Some views of the transcendent are relevant to human rights, but it is better to provide flexibility for various religious systems to bring their visions to the field of human rights rather than asserting the dominance of a particular view.

---

4. Morsink, *The Universal Declaration of Human Rights,* p. 255.

5. Universal Declaration of Human Rights, in Glendon, *A World Made New,* p. 312.

6. Morsink, *The Universal Declaration of Human Rights,* p. 256.

But appeals to nature may have a more important intermediate role to play. I will argue that a flexible natural law theory is in fact implied by the Universal Declaration, even as it stands. Furthermore, I want to develop this flexible theory in contrast to a fixed teleological metaphysical view that ties natural law in an invariant step-by-step manner to some final end. I believe this flexible theory can be found in antiquity. I hold that the Universal Declaration is consistent with this flexible view and that its ideas can, in fact, be found in a variety of Western philosophical and religious systems. An aspect of this view has to do with the importance to the strength and health of families of kin attachments and kin altruism. Rightly understood, however, kin altruism is a finite good, in contrast to an ultimate good. It is not the measure of all goods but rather simply a highly central good that we should seek to maximize if at all possible by finite human arrangements. Religious systems may carry, and indeed, strengthen the value of kin altruism, but its importance to human life can also be arrived at as a consequence of natural observation and rational analysis. The importance of kin altruism to family well-being is something philosophy, law, and religion frequently have cooperated to articulate, defend, and implement. The Universal Declaration of Human Rights reflects this grand tradition, and the Declaration's role in shaping culture, law, and public policy would be even stronger were the importance of kin altruism to family stability made even clearer.

It is a matter of cultural variability as to whether families are patriarchal or egalitarian; extended, joint, or nuclear; multigenerational households or two-generational parent-child systems; polygamous or monogamous; built around divided spheres of public and private or flexible in allowing both males and females access to domestic as well as nondomestic pursuits; and specialized in their economic activity or built around a single-household economy. But within all this pluralism of family forms and functions, there is a rather persistent core value that is widely cherished and protected around the world. This is the importance of the people who procreate the infant also being, as nearly as possible, the ones who care for it. This value was based on the widely held assumption that people who conceive a child, when they recognize their relation to it, will on average be the most invested in its nurture and well-being.

There are various languages designed to communicate this truth. Religious and theological languages often do this around the language of divine creation and divine command. Some philosophical systems have made this point using a combination of biological and philosophical arguments. Then there are a surprising number of instances in which a dual language combining both religious revelation and the naturalistic philosophy come together to create powerful synthetic arguments supporting the importance of kin altruism and even buttressing its central role in family formation by channeling it into the institution of marriage.

I hope to demonstrate how the language of kin altruism functioned in antiquity to form the implicit family theory of societies influenced by Greek philosophy and the Abrahamic religions of Judaism, Christianity, and Islam — hence, the legal, cultural, and religious theories of much of the modern world. I will not touch on non-Islamic Asian and Eastern societies, although I think my argument also would hold there. I will claim that the Universal Declaration was right to resist the grounding language of religion, not because it is irrelevant, but because a variety of religious systems, rather than any single system, may lend support to its position. It also was right to retain its slender reference to family as a "natural and fundament group unit." It is now time to clarify what this could have meant, or better, what it should now be thought to mean in light of deeper historical and social-science research. This discussion will throw light on the enduring relation between marriage and family and the role of religion in supporting, but not necessarily fully creating, the grounds for family formation built around natural kinship and marriage.

The Double Language of Kin Investment

Aristotle is the place to begin: He provided much of the naturalistic and philosophical language for the centrality of kin attachment and altruism in the theory of family formation in philosophy, law, and religion. His insights were used to reinforce folk observations in Christianity, Judaism, and Islam. His arguments have influenced both religious and secular law and the powerful theory of subsidiarity that constitutes the philosophical core of Roman Catholic social teaching. This great tradition was a possible source for Charles Malik's view of the family as "the natural and fundamental group unit of society."

Aristotle had considerable insight into what evolutionary psychologists today call "kin altruism." This is our tendency to invest ourselves more in those to whom we are biologically related. His pre-scientific theory of kin altruism can be found throughout his writings. In his *Politics,* Aristotle begins to move toward a theory of kin altruism when he writes, "in common with other animals and with plants, mankind have a natural desire to leave behind them an image of themselves."[7] It was simple comparative observation that formed Aristotle's belief that humans share this impulse with other animals and that it thereby constitutes a basic framework within which behavior proceeds.

We see this idea developed more in his critique of Plato's *Republic*. Plato tells us that Socrates believed that nepotism (the preferential treatment of kin by blood relatives) was the fundamental cause of divisiveness within a city. This factionalism could be decisively lessened, Plato believed, if the more elite men of the city coupled and had offspring with women who were held in common. These offspring would then be raised by state nurses, with neither parents nor children knowing their biological ties with one another. In such a state, everyone woulf "apply the terms 'mine' and 'not mine' in the same way to the same thing" — especially to children, thereby undercutting the divisive consequences of nepotism.[8]

Aristotle, however, believed that Plato's experiment would fail. In developing his case, we see Aristotle's theory of kin altruism argued even more fully. He wrote,

> Whereas in a state having women and children in common, love will be watery; and the father will certainly not say "my son," or the son "my father." As a little sweet wine mingled with a great deal of water is imperceptible in the mixture, so, in this sort of community, the idea of relationship which is based upon these names will be lost; there is no reason why the so-called father should care about the son, or the son about the father, or brothers about one another. Of the two qualities which chiefly inspire regard and affection — that a thing is your own and that it is your only one — neither can exist in such a state as this.[9]

Aristotle believed that such a society would water down and undermine parental recognition and investment. Furthermore, he believed it would unleash violence because the inhibiting factor of consanguinity would be removed. He wrote,

> Evils such as assaults, unlawful loves, homicides, will happen more . . . for they will no longer call the members of the class they have left brothers, and children, and fathers, and mothers, and will not,

7. Aristotle, *Politics*, in *The Basic Works of Aristotle*, ed. Richard McKeon (New York: Random House, 1941), bk. 1, chap. 2.

8. Plato, *The Republic* (New York: Basic, 1968), bk. 5, par. 462.

9. Aristotle, *Politics*, bk. 2, chap. 4.

therefore, be afraid of committing any crimes by reason of consanguinity.[10]

Aristotle believed that, for the developing child, the family is more fundamental than the state. Yet with regard to the more inclusive good, the state for him was more fundamental.[11] Either way, Aristotle is certainly an early champion, long before Malik, of the idea that the family is a basic group unit of society and that without a good amount of investment between biologically related individuals, family love will run thin, violence will rise, and social well-being and cohesion will decline.

Kin Altruism in the Ancient World

Aristotle was not the only thinker who developed a theory of marriage and family that centered around the idea of kin altruism. The Stoic Musonius Rufus believed that this natural inclination led parents to feed their children, even in hard times amidst poverty and other adversities.[12] The medieval rabbinic scholar Nachmanides, without the benefit of Aristotle, used the biblical concept of "one flesh" (Gen. 2:24) to communicate the value of kin altruism for parental care. At the human level, however, not only are mother and father "one flesh" with the child but through marriage they are symbolically one flesh with each other. The natural kin altruism that exists between parent and child became for Nachmanides the symbol for the relation between wife and husband. "The female of man," Nachmanides writes, "was bone of his bones and flesh of his flesh." For him, this double one-flesh relation (one biological, between parents and child, and one symbolic, between husband and wife) is why human parents work together to take care of their children through their many years of dependency. Another example can be found in the Islamic scholar al-Ghazali. He actually rejected the Islamic Aristotelianism of his day. Nonetheless, he could sound like Aristotle in celebrating the importance of both "lineage and marriage" and linking them to the preservation of one's "descendants."[13]

---

10. Aristotle, *Politics*, bk. 2, chap. 4.

11. Aristotle, *Politics*, bk. 1, chap. 2.

12. Cora Lutz, *Musonius Rufus: The Roman Socrates* (New Haven: Yale University Press, 1947), p. 99.

13. Nachmanides, *Commentary on the Torah*, trans. Charles B. Chavel (New York: Shilo, 1971-76), vol. 1, p. 80. Al-Ghazali, "Book on the Etiquette of Marriage," in *Marriage and Sexuality in Islam*, ed. Madelain Farah (Salt Lake City: University of Utah Press, 1984), p. 45.

The great Roman Catholic theologian Thomas Aquinas stated the role of kin altruism in family formation and marriage with remarkable clarity. He developed his point of view with a double language that was simultaneously religious and biophilosophical. The biophilosophical view was informed by Aristotle, and the specifically religious language principally came from Genesis and New Testament commentary on Genesis. Although his biology and philosophy of family formation — his natural law thinking — was informed by his theology, in many crucial respects it functioned independently of religious grounding. His biophilosophical insights also constituted the core ideas supporting one of the most powerful theories of the relation of family to the state that is available, namely, subsidiarity theory as it functions in Roman Catholic social teachings and secular family law in such modern countries as Germany. It probably influenced the thinking of Charles Malik and his concept in the UDHR that the "family is the natural and fundamental group unit of society. . . ."

It is clear that Aquinas thought that his view of marriage and family was a product of reason. He called marriage in its primordial form an "office of nature." At this level it could be illuminated by the natural law, especially that aspect of natural law that identifies those natural inclinations that are further guided by interventions of "the free will" and "acts of virtue."[14] But marriage also was revealed in Scripture, specifically the Genesis account of creation. In the "Supplement" to the *Summa Theologica,* he quotes Matthew 19:4, "Have ye not read that He Who made man from the beginning 'made them male and female,'" a verse which itself refers back to Genesis 1:27. Nearby he refers to Genesis 2:21 and claims that before sin and from the foundations of creation, God "fashioned a helpmate for man out of his rib."[15] This implies what the full Genesis passage makes explicit: "It is not good that the man should be alone; I will make a helper as his partner" (Gen. 2:18).

But Aquinas's full argument about marriage and family does not stay at the level of scriptural interpretation. This is an extremely important observation. Religious perspectives are not always advanced on narrowly religious grounds, just as so-called secular arguments often contain in their horizons quasi-religious assumptions about the depth of human experience.

We generally think of Thomas Aquinas as one of the architects of the

14. Thomas Aquinas, *Summa Theologica,* Supplement to the Third Part (London: T. and T. Washbourne, 1917), q. 41, a. 1.

15. Aquinas, *Summa Theologica,* Supplement to the Third Part, q. 42, a. 3.

sacramental view of marriage that has been of such decisive influence on marriage theory in Christian nations in recent centuries. Although this is true, we should not blind ourselves to his naturalistic theory of the origins of family formation and its link with marriage, especially in view of how similar it is to modern scientific views of family formation found in the emerging new field of evolutionary psychology. Aquinas defined matrimony as the joining of the male to the primordial mother-infant family. He saw this happening for four natural reasons. First, the long period of human infant dependency makes it very difficult for mothers to raise infants by themselves. Hence, they turn for help to their male consorts. Second, the likely fathers are much more inclined to attach to their infants if they have a high degree of certainty that the infant is actually theirs and hence continuous with their own biological existence. Third, males attach to their infants and consorts because of the mutual assistance and affection that they receive from the infant's mother. Finally, Aquinas realized that sexual exchange between mother and father, even though he talked about it as paying "the marital debt," helped to integrate the male to the mother-infant dyad.[16] Of course, Aquinas could not support his biophilosophical theories with the scientific explanations that are available today. We should note, however, that these four conditions are almost perfectly parallel to those now held in the fields of evolutionary psychology and anthropology to have led humans, in contrast to most other mammals, to form families and long-term attachments between fathers and mothers for the care of their children.[17]

Kin altruism was at the core of this naturalistic model of family formation. When Aquinas said that the human male "naturally desires to be assured of his offspring and this assurance would be altogether nullified in the case of promiscuous copulation,"[18] he was echoing Aristotle's belief that parental investment is more intense and durable between natural parents and their offspring. We see it again when Aquinas offers naturalistic reasons for the permanence of marriage, referring to the long period of

16. For Aquinas's explanation of these reasons, see his *Summa Theologica,* Supplement to the Third Part, q. 41, a. 1.

17. For a summary of these four conditions as they can be found in the literature of evolutionary psychology, see Don Browning, Bonnie Miller-McLemore, Pamela Couture, Bernie Lyon, and Robert Franklin, *From Culture Wars to Common Ground: Religion and the American Family Debate* (Louisville: Westminster John Knox, 2000), pp. 111-13. See also Don Browning, *Marriage and Modernization: How Globalization Threatens Marriage and What to Do about It* (Grand Rapids: Eerdmans, 2003), pp. 109-11.

18. Aquinas, *Summa Theologica,* Supplement to the Third Part, q. 41.

care that is required for a parent to raise to maturity the child who is in, fact, "something" of the parent.[19]

Aquinas's ethical and sacramental arguments for marriage and family build on these naturalistic reasons, which themselves are significantly in debt to ancient observations about the role of kin altruism in family formation. His moral and religious ideas simply extend, guide, and reinforce his naturalism. His naturalistic theory of family formation gains consolidation from the reinforcements of his theology, but can stand independent of them. Indeed, this Aristotelian-Thomistic naturalism has been a powerful force in subsequent legal and religious developments for centuries, ever since Thomas gave them such a powerful articulation in the double language of theology and philosophy.

It is important to notice the flexibility of Aquinas's naturalistic argument. He was fully aware that humans have conflicting natural tendencies with no single fixed aim. The world of nature is full of proximate causes, an insight that Charles Malik held as well.[20] But when human sexuality is guided by the needs of child-rearing, then the inclinations toward kin altruism, reinforced by culture and religion, can and should have a commanding role in ordering our unstable natural tendencies. Hence, Aquinas gave us a flexible natural law argument, not a rigid one. It is consistent with the images of natural law developing in the thought of contemporary philosophers and theologians such as Mary Midgley, Jean Porter, Stephen Pope, Larry Arnhart, and Lisa Sowle Cahill.[21] It probably was the view of natural law that Charles Malik was also trying to articulate. Mary Midgley says it well when she writes that in spite of our plural and flexible human desires and needs, "The central factors in us must be accepted, and the right line of human conduct must lie somewhere within the range they allow."[22] It is

---

19. Aquinas, *Summa Theologica,* II-II, q. 10, a. 12.

20. Charles Malik, "The Metaphysics of Freedom," in *Freedom and Man,* ed. John Courtney Murray, S.J. (New York: P.J. Kenedy and Sons, 1965), pp. 184-85. Malik's form of natural law could find a place for "proximate causes," although he warned against a preoccupation with them at the expense of contextualizing them within the context of ultimate ends. He writes that "at its best throughout the ages the West was faithful to both realms" (p. 184).

21. Mary Midgley, *Beast and Man* (Ithaca, N.Y.: Cornell University Press, 1978); Jean Porter, *Natural and Divine Law* (Ottawa, Ont.: Saint Paul University Press, 1999); Stephen Pope, *The Evolution of Altruism and the Ordering of Love* (Washington, D.C.: Georgetown University Press, 1994); Larry Arnhart, *Darwinian Natural Right* (Albany: State University of New York Press, 1998); Lisa Sowle Cahill, *Sex, Gender and Christian Ethics* (New York: Cambridge University Press, 1996).

22. Midgley, *Beast and Man,* p. 81.

clear that for Aristotle, Aquinas, and most of contemporary evolutionary thought, kin altruism is a central tendency that both biology and moral sensibilities have honored as being one of these "central factors." There is evidence that when Malik and the Commission on Human Rights referred to the family as "the natural and fundamental group unit of society," they were influenced by this historic line of thought.

Kin Altruism in Roman Catholic Social Teaching

One can see scattered evidence of this Aristotelian-Thomistic emphasis on kin altruism as a central feature of family formation in modern Protestantism and various expressions of modern law. But its most visible manifestation is in the outlines of subsidiarity theory that began to take shape in the writings of Pope Leo XIII at the end of the nineteenth century. The 1880 papal encyclical *Arcanum* is considered to have been the great statement of Leo XIII on marriage, but his 1891 *Rerum Novarum* on Catholic social teachings is the more revealing. This was a tradition that both Charles Malik and Jacques Maritain understood. It was a philosophical system nestled within a theological context but also in many respects independent from it.

Leo XIII saw an analogy between parents' relation to their children and laborers' rights to the fruits of their bodily blood and sweat. He believed it to be a law of nature — one that he found in Aristotle — that humans should have certain *prima facie* rights and responsibilities to both the fruits of their bodily labor *and* the issue of their procreative activity. With regard to natural parents, this was partially true because they by nature were the most invested in their children. Natural parents would care for their children more because they would see themselves in their children; they therefore should have both the primary responsibility to discharge this care and the rights needed to do this without undue interference from the outside forces of society, state, and market. Leo paraphrased Thomas Aquinas, but unfortunately perpetuated Aquinas's theory of patriarchal paternal authority, when he wrote,

> A most sacred law of nature ordains that the head of a family should provide for the necessities and comforts of the children he has begotten. That same nature leads him to want to provide for his children — who recall and in some sense extend his personality.[23]

23. *Rerum Novarum,* in *Proclaiming Justice and Peace: Papal Documents from Rerum*

Leo recalled Aquinas's implicit theory of kin altruism when he wrote, "Children are naturally something of their father . . . they are held under the care of their parents until they acquire the use of free will."[24] Of course, as we have seen, nature is not as single-minded about programming parental care as Aquinas thought; it is more that nature provides parenting tendencies that can be developed and built upon, even though, at the same time, they can be easily disrupted. Furthermore, to rescue Leo's and Aquinas's point, we today would certainly acknowledge that mothers as well as fathers have these inclinations to care for their children. But since, in so many parts of the world, fathers more than mothers have become detached from the parental task, it is helpful to be reminded by Leo and Aquinas of the natural, although fragile, grounds of this male inclination and responsibility.

In these passages, however, Leo XIII established the framework for the Catholic theory of subsidiarity. Let us hear his early statement on this teaching.

> It follows that to want to see the state's power arbitrarily at work within the intimacy of household is to make a great and pernicious mistake. Of course, when a family happens to be in a state of great distress, helpless and utterly unable to escape from its predicament, it is right that its pressing need be met by public aid. After all, every family is a part of the state. Similarly when within a family there is grave dispute about mutual rights, it is for the public authority to insist upon each party giving to the other its due. In doing this, the state does not rob citizens of their rights, but rather strengthens them and supports them as it should.[25]

This is the meaning of subsidiarity. State and market should give support (*subsidum*) to both intact and disrupted families when they are in situations of special need or stress. But, at the same time, neither should do anything to disturb, undermine, or take over the natural and fundamental inclinations and capacities of families to care for one another. This is doubtless what Malik and the UDHR meant when they referred to the family as the natural and fundamental "group unit" that is "entitled to

---

Novarum through Centesimus Annus, ed. Michael Walsh and Brian Davies (Mystic, Conn.: Twenty-Third Publications, 1991), para. 11 and 12.

24. *Rerum Novarum*, para. 12. (The quote from Aquinas comes from *Summa Theologica*, II-II, q. 10, a. 12.)

25. *Rerum Novarum*, para. 12.

protection by both society and the State." The phrase "group unit" invokes this rich tradition that refers to the web of natural inclinations toward the sense of solidarity, continuity, and deep attachment that spring from bonded mother-father partnerships and their children.

But if the state and law go too far and replace the responsibilities and privileges of parents in the fashion of Plato's *Republic,* then Leo XIII does not approve. Sounding quite Aristotelian, he writes, "Thus, when socialists set aside parental care and put that of the state in its place, they offend against natural justice and dissolve the bonds of family life."[26] In these statements, Leo is criticizing the excesses of both state and market when they disrupt the initiatives and responsibilities of families and workers. In taking this stand, a position later amplified by Pius XI in *Casti Connubii* (1931) and *Quadragesimo Anno* (1931), he sets the stage for a critique of the two contemporary and competing grand solutions to the world domestic crises — the family dominated by the state and the family dominated by the market.[27]

Covenant and Nature in Protestant Thought

I have been arguing that there is a substructure of naturalistic and philosophical thinking, mainly built around the investments of kin altruism, that undergirds much of Western family thinking, even thinking that ostensibly appears to be religious or theological. The religious symbolism gives moral amplification and ontological grounding to this thinking, but it does not completely swamp these more naturalistic insights and their usefulness in public discourse. Modern Roman Catholic social teachings on the family exhibit these patterns, and some modern Protestant theologians, although by no means all of them, do so as well.

Protestant theologies of marriage and family are often believed to emphasize biblical covenant themes in contrast to the ideas of sacrament and natural law typical of Roman Catholic thinking. Although this is partially true, there are in Protestant theology important examples of a blend of covenant and flexible models of natural law. The best example of this is the theology of the mid-twentieth-century European Emil Brunner. Brun-

---

26. *Rerum Novarum,* para. 12.

27. Pius XI, *Casti Connubii* (New York: Barry Vail Corporation, 1931), and Pius XI, *Quadragesimo Anno,* in *The Papal Encyclicals,* comp. Claudia Carlen (Wilmington, N.C.: McGrath, 1981).

ner honored the classical Protestant tradition of grounding its theology of marriage and family on the so-called orders of creations, namely, the differentiation of male and female of Genesis 1:27, the idea that it is not "good for the man to be alone" (Gen. 2:18), and the declaration that a man leaves "his father and mother and clings to his wife, and they become one flesh" (Gen. 2:24). These theological affirmations, based on the Genesis doctrine of creation, are fundamental to all of the great religions of the Book — Judaism, Christianity, and Islam.

But Brunner did not anchor his view of family and marriage on these biblical affirmations alone. He believed that the fundamental social spheres of life — marriage, government, and market — evolved out of basic human interests that could be known and analyzed by reason.[28] Government comes from the natural interest to achieve security and social order, economics from the natural interest to earn a living, and marriage from the psychophysical interests of sex and procreation. From the perspective of human reason, these sphere-specific institutions function to meet human needs; from the perspective of faith, they are gifts of God in creation.[29]

Brunner, like Aquinas and today's evolutionary psychologists, emphasizes the importance for the emergence of monogamy of parental "recognition," that is, the human recognition that this child is mine, someone I brought into the world, and indeed someone who is literally part of my very being. But it is for Brunner a three-way recognition entailing father, mother, and child. Aquinas and the evolutionary biologists would agree, as we saw above, that the mother's recognition that the child is hers comes more easily and that a father's recognition of this fact is more a matter of probability and hence subject to a variety of additional contingencies. Brunner affirms the importance of these various recognitions but emphasizes not only the husband's and wife's recognition of their mutual responsibility for the child's physical life, but also their recognition of their responsibility for the child's social existence and development. Brunner adds the importance of the child's recognition that this woman and this man are responsible for his or her existence. The trinity of recognitions of this bio-existential reality throws mother, father, and child together in irrevocable ways. Brunner writes,

> Since I, the father, as well as the mother and the child, know irrevocably that this fact is irrevocable, then we three persons are bound

28. Emil Brunner, *The Divine Imperative* (Philadelphia: Westminster, 1957), p. 335.
29. Brunner, *The Divine Imperative*, p. 336.

together in a way in which no other three persons have ever been bound together, in an unparalleled and indissoluble relation. . . . This trinity of being we call the human structure of existence.[30]

In short, Brunner brings nature and biblical revelation together with the following formula. Nature itself anticipates the recognition of the one-flesh union of mother, father, and child. But its normative status is revealed in the biblical creation account fundamental to Judaism, Christianity, and Islam. Nature and revelation are not identical, but they correlate and complement one another. Although Brunner's views are not literally shared by the three great religions, they offer a suggestive model for how these religions can be interpreted. They also offer another example of a double language — simultaneously naturalistic and religious — that can give precision to the contributions of religious traditions in the emerging world discourse about marriage and family.

We saw analogues to Brunner's style of thinking in the Stoic Musonious Rufus, the rabbinic Nachmanides, the Islamic al-Ghazali, the Christian Thomas Aquinas, and the modern Roman Catholic social teachings of Leo XIII and Pius XI. All of these thinkers thought at multiple levels — naturalistic levels, moral levels, and religious levels. These different dimensions enrich each other but also can be seen to have a degree of autonomy from one another. The Universal Declaration of Human Rights in its celebration of the natural family as the fundamental group unit of society developed the naturalistic and moral dimensions of this tradition and omitted the religious background dimension. I will not debate whether this expediency was wise or not. The omission of the religious dimension should not, however, obscure one of the major sources of the Declaration's insights or the right for these religions to once again bring their broad, flexible, and multidimensional thinking to world deliberations about the rights of families.

Philosophical and Legal Reflections

The idea that the natural family was the fundamental group unit of society contained within it the idea of kin altruism. The ancients developed a folk psychology and biology which linked procreation and parental care, whether placed within the context of monogamy or polygamy. They devel-

---

30. Brunner, *The Divine Imperative*, p. 346.

oped law, philosophy, religious institutions, and symbolic systems that channeled human inclinations into a stable alignment of at least four goods — sexual desire, affection, procreation, and child-rearing. The stable integration of these four goods builds on natural inclinations but requires additional powerful social, legal, cultural, and religious reinforcements. *Marriage and family as public institutions are designed to integrate these goods.* The integration of these four goods enhances care of children by parents, care between father and mother, intergenerational care between the young and the elderly, and care throughout the extended family. Public recognition of who is partnered with whom, who is the procreator of this child, who is the spouse of this person, and who is the son or daughter of this elderly person are essential for the social and legal assignment of responsibilities of care and provision. In this fragile and vulnerable finite world, there will be a variety of failures and exceptions to the normative complex integration of these four goods, but in order even to make adequate provision for the exceptions, the institutions that promote this central integration must be energetically protected by law, culture, and traditions of human rights. Law must complete and refine the inclinations of nature.

Common sense observations into the investments stemming from kin altruism traditionally have linked procreation and child-rearing. This linkage not only reinforced parental affections but integrated parents and offspring with grandparents, uncles and aunts, and the wider extended families. The family as a group unit has been and remains today an intergenerational reality that spreads mutual care outward into society and forward into the future cycle of the generations. It is, of course, the greatest welfare system ever devised by the human race, the one upon which all other support systems, either private or governmental, finally depend and only modestly enhance.

The power and function of kin altruism have been clarified by recent advances in evolutionary psychology. From ants, to mammals, to those unique mammals and primates called humans, contemporary evolutionists have discovered the proclivity of biological parents to invest in, favor, and even sacrifice themselves for their biological offspring.[31] Modern ge-

---

31. For the basic study that literally founded the fields of sociobiology and the later evolutionary psychology, see W. D. Hamilton, "The Genetical Evolution of Social Behavior, II," *Journal of Theoretical Biology* 7 (1994): 17-52. For a study that brings these theories into the sociology of family, see Pierre van den Berghe, *Human Family* (New York: Elsevier, 1979). For

netics helps us explain this process more concretely, but, as we have seen, the ancients understood it on the basis of simple naturalistic observation.

The Universal Declaration of Human Rights gave considerable weight to this insight, but not to the point of being prejudicial to single-parent families and other possible family patterns. Mothers and their infants — which Aristotle, Aquinas, and evolutionary psychology all hold to be the primordial family — rightly receive special protections in the UDHR (Article 25.2). *My reflections in this essay lead, however, to the following question: What weight should the family built on the kin altruism of the mother-father-child triad have in international documents on human rights and the legal influence that they have?* Kin altruism is, after all, a relative value. It is an exaggeration to argue that biological attachment alone converts humans into good and nurturing parents. We all know of exceptions to this rule. Good parenting and nurturing family life depend on a variety of goods — for example, consistency of behavior on the part of parents, their economic circumstances, their health, and the social stability that surrounds the family. Poor parents that are overworked and perhaps sick often cannot find the time, energy, and emotional tranquility to give expression to their natural attachments and inclinations. Some natural parents are emotionally damaged themselves and project their wounds onto their children. Furthermore, the inclinations of kin altruism at the human level are fragile and need the reinforcements of culture, powerful symbols, compelling rituals, public promises, stable supporting communities, and adequate material resources.

In view of the fact that the inclinations of kin altruism must finally be seen as a relative good amidst a variety of goods, to what extent should international rights, national cultures, political institutions, and legal codes give special privilege and support to assuring kin altruism's social viability and institutional embodiment? To what extent must it have legal and political stability in the form of the privileges and protections of marriage and the supports of various political and legal entitlements?

The answer to this question depends on two considerations. First, how decisive is the factor of kin altruism in the mix of goods and supports that make for good family life and child-rearing? Second, what is the role of law, either human rights law or the family codes of particular societies?

---

authoritative studies from within the field of evolutionary psychology, see Martin Daly and Margo Wilson, *Sex, Evolution, and Behavior* (Belmont, Calif.: Wadsworth, 1983), and Donald Symons, *The Evolution of Human Sexuality* (Oxford: Oxford University Press, 1979).

The answer to the first question is this: There is convincing evidence that children raised by their married natural parents on average do significantly better in their schoolwork, are less likely to have children out of wedlock, are more likely to have stable marriages themselves, are less likely to become involved in criminal behavior, and are more likely to have stable employment as adults.[32] Data supporting these generalizations are not available from every corner of the world, but in those countries where social-science surveys do exist, they hold up. In addition, there is significant evidence, as Aristotle predicted, that in those families where children are raised by nonbiological parents, children are far more subject to violence, physical harm, and sexual molestation. Much of this data has been collected by evolutionary psychologists who explain what they find with the theory of kin altruism and what it implies for parental care, less parental violence, and less sexual exploitation.[33] There is, however, voluminous data summarized by the legal scholar Robin Wilson that does not rely on the explanatory perspectives of evolutionary psychology and that amply demonstrates on sociological and statistical grounds much higher levels of the sexual abuse of young girls living with stepfathers, their mothers' cohabiting boyfriends, and other such family arrangements.[34] Of course, all such statistics deal with averages and probabilities and should not be used to stereotype all such family arrangements. But the mounting evidence of the difficulties and vulnerabilities of children in such arrangements at least should alert us that, for the purposes of the

---

32. For a review of the pertinent findings, see Sara McLanahan and Gary Sandefur, *Growing Up with a Single Parent* (Cambridge, Mass.: Harvard University Press, 1994); Paul Amato and Alan Booth, *A Generation at Risk: Growing Up in an Era of Family Upheaval* (Cambridge, Mass.: Harvard University Press, 1997). For a significant study that combines evolutionary psychology and the sociological study of contemporary family decline, see David Popenoe, *Life without Father: Compelling New Evidence That Fatherhood and Marriage Are Indispensable for the Good of Children and Society* (New York: Free Press, 1996).

33. For a summary of the findings of evolutionary psychology on child abuse in families with one or more biologically unrelated parent, see Martin Daly and Margo Wilson, *Homicide* (New York: Aldine de Gruyter, 1988), and their book *The Truth about Cinderella: A Darwinian View of Parental Love* (London: Weidenfeld and Nicolson, 1998).

34. For a review of social science studies of the significantly higher incidence of sexual abuse of young girls in stepfamilies, cohabiting families, and situations after divorce, see the important summaries by legal scholar Robin Fretwell Wilson: "Children at Risk: The Sexual Exploitation of Female Children after Divorce," *Cornell Law Review* 86, no. 2 (January 2001): 251-327; "Fractured Families, Fragile Children — The Sexual Vulnerability of Girls in the Aftermath of Divorce," *Child and Family Law Quarterly* 14, no. 1 (2002): 1-23; and "The Cradle of Abuse: Evaluating the Danger Posed by a Sexually Predatory Parent to the Victim's Siblings," *Emory Law Journal* 51, no. 1 (Winter 2002): 242-308.

law and public policy, some family arrangements are generally more worthy of encouragement than others. Whatever equality of treatment means with regard to families, it should not blunt social awareness about the likely overall effectiveness of different arrangements.

Second, there is the question of the role of the law on family issues. Should the law be neutral with regard to family patterns and only provide remedial supports as equally as possible? Should it be concerned with which patterns correlate more positively with human flourishing and for that reason warrant encouragement? Space permits only the following observations in response to these questions. The very existence of the Universal Declaration of Human Rights points to a model of law that should be widely followed. The need that motivated the Universal Declaration and the purposes to which it has been put make it an exemplary instance of a proactive use of law. The UDHR is, of course, not a binding legal document as such. But it was written to inspire the law and shape a more coherent and unified universal system of legal rights among the nations of the world. With regard to family issues, it was both normative and inclusive. If my interpretation of the phrase saying the "natural family is the fundamental group unit of society" is reflective of the direction the UDHR was going, then the document has clear and decisive normative implications that should be reflected in more particular national legal codes and cultural sensibilities. But notice also the inclusiveness of the UDHR. When it says that "Everyone who works has the right to just and favourable remuneration ensuring for himself and his family an existence worthy of human dignity," there is little doubt that this includes all families with responsibilities for children and other dependents (Article 23.3). A basic provision of this kind, however, should not be confused with the channeling functions of culture and law designed to encourage optimal arrangements for human flourishing. This dual approach can be illustrated by the statement of the Declaration that "Motherhood and childhood are entitled to special care and assistance. All children, whether born in or out of wedlock, shall enjoy the same social protection" (Article 25.2). Thus, all children, regardless of the circumstances of their birth, should be protected from the contingencies of life; at the same time, the potential negative consequences for children of family patterns, the accidents of history, or the intentions of adults should be minimized by just societies as much as possible.

But even then, the Commission's rightful concern not to stigmatize children born out of wedlock may have been excessive and misplaced. It led it to reject Malik's desire to have his famous sentence read, "the family *deriving from marriage* is the fundamental group unit of society" (my italics). Although concern about stigmatizing children is both understandable and justified, it is even more important that children be protected from the damaging and debilitating realities of the breakdown of marriage. Since the ratification of the UDHR, there has been a worldwide explosion of children born outside the protective bonds of publicly certified marriages. This factor alone has contributed to their poverty, anxiety, and lack of protection and supervision. Children need universal protections, but this should not come at the price of inadequate theories of human rights and law which themselves contribute to the weakening of family as their primary institution of care.

The direction on family issues of the Universal Declaration of Human Rights was fundamentally sound. This direction should be further clarified, strengthened, and used to influence the broad field of international law and the family legal codes of particular societies throughout the world.

Chapter 19

Adoption and the Moral Significance
of Kin Altruism (2005)

Much of my writing on family has been designed to promote the reconstruction of modern marriage and family in order to enhance both family cohesion and an ethic of equal regard. I have hoped to do this in spite of the powerful forces of modernization that make these two values of equality and cohesion increasingly difficult to hold together.

This raises the question, How does one handle exceptions to the equal-regard intact marital couple with their biological children? One of these exceptions is the case of children needing adoption. I ask in this chapter, Why should we adopt? What are the moral grounds for adoption, especially in light of the centrality I place on the relative and finite value of kin altruism? My answer is this: The moral grounds for adoption rest on the needs of the child to be loved and given a home and only secondarily on the needs of adults to fulfill their parental inclinations, although these deserve some moral recognition as well. This chapter elaborates that point of view.

Adoption is a delicate issue. This is true for public policy and even more so for the fields of theological ethics and practical theology. I hold that these theological disciplines have a twofold task: They should first state a critically developed confessional view of the meaning of adoption and then articulate the implications and amendments that are appropriate and defensible for the wider public in a pluralistic society.

These are not easy tasks, especially in the present social context. The purpose, use, and justification for adoption in the face of roaring debates over the health of contemporary families and the appropriate use of reproductive technology make it analogous to the ball in a heated game of soccer. First it is captured by one team and used to make a goal; next it is stolen by the other side in its drive to score its own point. At one moment in the cultural debate, adoption can be invoked to justify all manner of family patterns alternative to the intact mother-father partnership. Arguments for adoption also can be employed to justify a much more expansive use of reproductive technologies. On other occasions, adoption can be used to exemplify one of the few justifiable alternatives to the intact conjugal couple with children and employed to discourage almost all other alternatives.

The political and theological elasticity of the practice of adoption is due to certain failures in our moral and theological thinking. For example, many who enter the adoption debate have shortcomings in their wider analysis of the social and cultural context of the family; they have difficulties in understanding the meaning of adoption within broad cultural and social trends. Second, many contributors to the conversation are reluctant to make use of certain important distinctions, for example, the difference between moral and premoral goods and the difference between what Christians should rightly demand of themselves and what they can justifiably expect from the wider pluralistic culture. Even theological ethicists differ significantly in how they handle the question of adoption, although they all would claim to rely on the authority of the Christian tradition.

In this chapter, I hope to bring some order to the tensions in the moral-theological dialogues on adoption, or at least illustrate how order might be injected. I will do this by reviewing a small but influential number of contemporary Christian theological voices on the adoption issue.

Before launching into this discussion, I want to share a formative experience that has shaped my thinking about family and adoption. In the spring of 1991, the National Council of Churches sponsored a major conference on the family. It was held in Chicago, and large numbers of people from all over the country attended. A consistent theme ran through many of the carefully selected plenary addresses. The message went like this: Sure, families are changing. There are more single-parent families, more divorces, more cohabiting couples, more children born out of wedlock, and more gay and lesbian families. Furthermore, there are many lonely single people who have no families at all. But do not worry. The church can and should become a big superfamily ready to receive and accept all disrupted families and all lonely individuals. One speaker drew analogies between a local neighborhood bar and the church. Just as a bar would accept, support, and kind of adopt all of its lonely customers, the church could do even better. It could become a great surrogate family offering symbolic and functional adoption to all isolated individuals and fractured families. The metaphor of adoption was used to promote a vague ideology of therapeutic acceptance as the cure for family disruption.

I was struck by the remarkable inadequacy of this solution. For years, I monitored the impact of the modern psychotherapies on culture, ecclesial practice, and modern theology itself. I believed in the power of psychotherapeutic acceptance and even the analogy that Tillich and others drew between it and Christian doctrines of grace and forgiveness.[1] I also believed that the church should invite, accept, and support all persons and all families willing to hear its message. But I also had become impatient with the overextension in Christian theology of Carl Rogers's theory of therapeutic acceptance or "unconditioned positive regard" and the way it worked to blunt ethical analysis and personal responsibility.[2] Therapeutic acceptance, as well as theological grace, was only effective, I believed, if it functioned against a clear ethical background that could articulate criteria for moral adequacy and therefore assign responsibility to individuals and communities. Under the cover of the idea of spiritual adoption, this conference was promoting a form of therapeutic acceptance as both the main and the only ecclesial and public policy for addressing the mounting problems facing families.

I noticed that the conference presented no real analysis of what was happening to families; we were told that society was changing, that societies always change, that change is generally good, and that change should not be resisted. No explanation of these changes was offered and no evaluation of these changes was presented. In the minds of the conference leaders, there seemed to be no qualitative differences between intact families and divorced families, children born within marriage and children born outside, children with fathers residentially present and those without their fathers, or single-parent families and two-parent families — that is, no differences that acceptance (i.e., adoption) by the church could not remedy. Isolation and stigmatization were the central problems of fami-

---

1. Paul Tillich, "The Impact of Pastoral Psychology on Theological Thought," *Pastoral Psychology* 2, no. 101 (February 1960): 17-23. For my early favorable response to this line of thought, see Don Browning, *Atonement and Psychotherapy* (Philadelphia: Westminster, 1966).

2. Carl Rogers, *Client-Centered Therapy* (Boston: Houghton Mifflin, 1951), and "A Theory of Therapy, Personality, and Interpersonal Relationships," in *Psychology: A Study of a Science*, vol. 3, ed. Sigmund Koch (New York: McGraw-Hill, 1959).

lies, and loving inclusion was the cure for these problems. There were no more specific recommendations offered about how to lower the divorce rate, how to address teen pregnancies, how to bring fathers back into the lives of their children, how to prepare young people for better marriages, and how to create higher levels of equal regard and mutuality in marriages. There was no effort to address the growing tensions between work and family — what Habermas, to ratchet up the level of analysis, calls the colonization of the lifeworld by the technical rationality of market and state.[3] The interaction between acceptance and the metaphor of adoption had become, it seemed, a recipe for ecclesial and societal inaction. I was troubled.

Critical Familism and Adoption

The main concern of my early writing on families was the issue of family disruption itself. What is it? Is it a problem? What are the causes? What is an adequate practical-theological and moral-theological analysis of and response to current claims about growing family fragmentation? This was the concern of *From Culture Wars to Common Ground: Religion and the American Family Debate,* the so-called summary volume of the first phase of the Religion, Culture, and Family Project.[4] The question of adoption was not at the center of our attention in that volume, although it was to some extent addressed. We certainly acknowledged that there is an important place for adoption in the Christian life.[5]

We hung a tag on the theological position on family issues that we developed; we called our position "critical familism." I have developed this concept in subsequent writings, principally in *Reweaving the Social Tapestry*[6] and *Marriage and Modernization.*[7] Social-cultural analysis and theological-ethical retrieval has led me to believe that both church and society should promote the "committed, intact, equal-regard, public-private

---

3. Jürgen Habermas, *The Theory of Communicative Action,* trans. Thomas McCarthy, vol. 2 (Boston: Beacon, 1987), p. 196.

4. Don Browning, Bonnie Miller-McLemore, Pamela Couture, Bernie Lyon, and Robert Franklin, *From Culture Wars to Common Ground: Religion and the American Family Debate* (Louisville: Westminster John Knox, 1997, 2000).

5. Browning et al., *From Culture Wars to Common Ground,* pp. 2, 178.

6. Don Browning and Gloria Rodriguez, *Reweaving the Social Tapestry: Toward a Public Philosophy and Policy of Families* (New York: W. W. Norton, 2001).

7. Don Browning, *Marriage and Modernization* (Grand Rapids: Eerdmans, 2003).

family."[8] I have envisioned this primarily as an *ecological* task requiring preparations by and resources from several interacting sectors of society.[9] The church should take leadership, but families also need the support of market, government, law, and the secular professions. By "intact," my colleagues and I meant that both church and society should attempt to encourage and support the husband-wife partnership and the offspring of such partnerships. "Intact" does not necessarily mean the modern nuclear family in its neolocality from extended family and its frequent isolation from other sources of social support. It means instead the integrity of the conjugal couple in either nuclear or joint-family arrangements. By using the phrase "critical familism," we wished to convey the task of vigilant critique of centers of power and distortion in culture, tradition, market, government, and civil society that function to block or distort the free exercise of the love ethic of "equal regard," both within and between families. In asserting that this new family should be "public and private," we meant that husband and wife should in principle have full access to the privileges and responsibilities of both the public world of citizenship and the wage economy *and* the domestic world of intimacy, child care, and family maintenance.

The equal-regard family points to a theory of Christian love, one that can also be stated as philosophically relevant to society at large. We followed Louis Janssens, Paul Ricoeur, and several neo-Thomistic feminist theological ethicists in our understanding of Christian love as an ethic of equal regard.[10] Love as equal regard was for us what moral philosophers call a *mixed-deontological* concept. Meditations on the Golden Rule, the principle of neighbor love, and their extension into early Christian family ethics (Eph. 5:28) led us to see love as equal regard as the core of Christian ethics within the church, in the family, and in public affairs. It first means regarding the other as an end and never as a means alone; this principle is

---

8. Browning et al., *From Culture Wars to Common Ground*, p. 2.

9. Browning et al., *From Culture Wars to Common Ground*, pp. 2, 306; Browning, *Marriage and Modernization*, pp. 24-29.

10. Louis Janssens, "Norms and Priorities of a Love Ethics," *Louvain Studies* 6 (Spring 1977): 209-37; Paul Ricoeur, "The Teleological and Deontological Structures of Action: Aristotle and/or Kant?" in *Contemporary French Philosophy*, ed. A. Phillips Griffiths (Cambridge: Cambridge University Press, 1987), pp. 99-112; Barbara Andolsen, "Agape in Feminist Ethics," *Journal of Religious Ethics* 9 (Spring 1981): 69-81; Christine Gudorf, "Parenting, Mutual Love, and Sacrifice," in *Women's Consciousness, Women's Conscience: A Reader in Feminist Ethics*, ed. Barbara Andolsen, Christine Gudorf, and Mary Pellauer (New York: Harper and Row, 1985), p. 185.

reversible and was interpreted by us to apply equally to other and self — "You shall love your neighbor *as* yourself" (Matt. 19:19). But we followed Janssens, Ricoeur, and some neo-Thomist feminists in going beyond a more strictly Kantian interpretation of equal regard after the fashion of Gene Outka[11] and attributed a strong teleological subdimension to the concept. *This was a move, as we will soon see, relevant to the adoption issue.*

We liked Ricoeur's way of stating the case for the mixed-deontological nature of love. With reference specifically to the Golden Rule, he follows Rabbi Hillel's formulation. Hillel argues that to do unto others as we would have others do unto us means doing *good* to others as we would have others do *good* to us.[12] Notice here the abstract reversibility of self and other; one finds this in both the biblical principles of the Golden Rule and neighbor love *and* Kant's categorical imperative that emphasizes respect for the humanity of both self and other.[13] But our view of love as equal regard went beyond abstract reversibility. Love as equal regard entails not only respect for other and self, it also requires theories of the *goods of life that actively should be promoted* within the context of this mutual respect.

This formulation opens the very important question of the *goods* of families and the *goods* of marriage, a question also relevant to the issue of adoption. The classic Christian tradition has listed three goods — fidelity between the conjugal couple, children and their education, and permanence (Aquinas meant by this sacramental permanence).[14] We tried to deepen this discussion of the goods of marriage and families. We were struck by the presence in the tradition of an implicit, and sometimes quite explicit, theory of kin altruism. This is the idea that in both creation as God intended it and in the rhythms of nature as revealed through naturalistic observation, it was commonly assumed that "natural" parents were more deeply invested in their children and, on average, more consistent sources of care and nurture than all substitutes. One can see this most distinctively where Aristotelian ethics influenced religious

---

11. Gene Outka, *Agape: An Ethical Analysis* (New Haven, Conn.: Yale University Press, 1972).

12. Ricoeur, "Teleological and Deontological Structures of Action," pp. 107-8.

13. Immanuel Kant, *Foundations of the Metaphysics of Morals* (Indianapolis: Bobbs-Merrill, 1959), p. 47.

14. Augustine, "The Good of Marriage," in *Treatises on Marriage and Other Subjects,* trans. Charles T. Wilcox et al., ed. Roy J. Deferrari, vol. 15 of The Writings of Saint Augustine (New York: Fathers of the Church, 1955), pp. 9-51; Thomas Aquinas, *Summa Theologica,* "Supplement to the Third Part," q. 42.

thought, whether in the ethics of the Christian Thomas Aquinas, the Jewish Maimonides, or the Islamic al-Ghazali.[15] There was no significant departure from this assumption in Protestant thought even though Aristotle's naturalism played a less significant role. This assumption emerges once again in the Catholic encyclicals from Leo XIII to Pius XI.[16] These Christian thinkers had no technical theory of kin altruism of the kind that today we find in evolutionary psychology. They had no theory of how shared genes between parents and offspring intensify the parental sense of investment in the children — parents' sense of identification with their offspring and the capacity to endure the hardship of parenting. But these thinkers did have everyday, naturalistic observations that children tend to look like their parents, and that this motivates parents to care for offspring out of a sense of preserving what is partially the parents themselves — what extends their "personality" and their "substance."

Kin Altruism as Finite Premoral Good

My colleagues and I handled kin altruism, whether derived from the theology and biopsychology of the tradition or from the insights of contemporary evolutionary psychology, as an important yet finite premoral good. We followed the definitions of "premoral good" that one can find in Janssens, Mary Midgely, and William Frankena.[17] Premoral goods are various finite objects, experiences, or tendencies that we experience as good in the sense of satisfying and enjoyable. They are the opposite of premoral evils or disvalues — objects, experiences, or tendencies that are unsatisfying or harmful. *Premoral goods are not fully moral goods.* A moral good, according to this line of thinking, is a disposition of the will to fol-

15. Thomas Aquinas, *Summa Contra Gentiles,* vol. 3, part 2, chap. 123; Maimonides, *The Code of Maimonides,* Book Four: *The Book of Women,* in *The Book of Marriage: The Wisest Answers to the Toughest Questions,* ed. Dana Mack and David Blankenhorn (Grand Rapids: Eerdmans, 2001), pp. 500-509; al-Ghazali, *Book on the Etiquette of Marriage,* in *Marriage and Sexuality in Islam,* ed. Madelin Farah (Salt Lake City: University of Utah Press, 1984), pp. 48-126.

16. Leo XIII, *Rerum Novarum,* in *Proclaiming Justice and Peace: Papal Documents from Rerum Novarum through Centesimus Annus,* ed. Michael Walsh and Brian Davies (Mystic, Conn.: Twenty-Third Publications, 1991), pp. 3-39; Pius XI, *Casti Connubii,* in *The Papal Encyclicals,* ed. Claudia Carlen (Wilmington, N.C.: McGrath, 1981).

17. Janssens, "Norms and Priorities of a Love Ethics," p. 210; Mary Midgley, *Beast and Man* (Ithaca, N.Y.: Cornell University Press, 1978), pp. 182-83; William Frankena, *Ethics* (Englewood Cliffs, N.J.: Prentice-Hall, 1973), pp. 9-10.

low some principle that, if acted upon, would justly and productively organize a range of potentially conflicting premoral goods. That is the
point: Premoral goods can conflict and in this sense harm, if not destroy,
one another. The moral good seen as a disposition and principle of free
moral action is moral precisely in its capacity to organize, hierarchize, and
harmonize competing premoral values, both within one's own life and in
our lives with others.

The authors of *From Culture Wars to Common Ground,* although we
were all liberal Protestants, followed the Catholic Thomas Aquinas and
certain modern Thomists in viewing kin altruism as a highly important
premoral good that should be protected and enhanced.[18] But it also was
regarded as a finite good that can easily conflict with other finite goods.
Hence, it is not an ultimate good that can always and everywhere trump
all other goods.

It is not clear that the readers of *From Culture Wars to Common Ground*
always understood our discussion of kin altruism as a finite, and even relative, good. For some readers, the fact that we even mentioned the importance of the kin altruism of natural parents was enough for them to conclude that we were deeming as grossly inferior if not morally defective all
other family patterns where parents and children are not biologically related, including adoptive families. When properly interpreted, however,
viewing kin altruism as a very important premoral good should allow one
to give it a degree of centrality as a religio-cultural value without squeezing out all other organizations of affection and child-rearing. Affirming it
as a highly important premoral good should not lead to the automatic
denigration of the relative goods found in other patterns.

On the other hand, acknowledging the relative goods in a variety of
family patterns beyond the intact mother-father partnership should not
make us disregard the importance of careful comparative analysis of the
relative goods of different family patterns. This is why both church and
society should take seriously recent research by Sarah McLanahan and
Gary Sandefur,[19] Paul Amato and Alan Booth, [20] David Popenoe,[21] Mavis

18. In addition to the position of Lisa Cahill, whom I will review in this article, see Stephen Pope, *The Evolution of Altruism and the Ordering of Love* (Washington, D.C.: Georgetown
University Press, 1994).

19. Sarah McLanahan and Gary Sandefur, *Growing Up with a Single Parent* (Cambridge,
Mass.: Harvard University Press, 1994).

20. Paul Amato and Alan Booth, *A Generation at Risk* (Cambridge, Mass.: Harvard University Press, 1997).

21. David Popenoe, *Life without Father* (New York: Free Press, 1996).

Hetherington,[22] and Mary Parks[23] showing that, on average, children growing up under the care of two biologically related parents do better in performing at school, relating to the job market, avoiding teen pregnancies, and forming marriages than those raised by single parents or stepparents. These too are goods that most people accept as important. Of course, it must be quickly added that many who grow up in disrupted families, even without regular contact with one of their biological parents (generally the father), often still do quite well in the external achievements of their lives.[24] Furthermore, recent research demonstrates that adopted children do well on objective indices when compared to children raised by their biological parents.[25] This is explained partially by the high motivation of adoptive parents as well as the careful screening and preparation given them by adoption agencies. Also, from an evolutionary-psychological perspective, it is believed that humans have been selected for kin altruism over such long periods that the innate mechanisms for responding and bonding with children are in humans and can be activated, even if the child is not one's biological offspring.[26] But even then, as Judith Wallerstein has shown, many children of divorce separated from their biological parents have long-term subjective worries and doubts.[27] In addition, it seems to be a matter of continuing debate as to whether adopted children suffer inward anguish, self-doubts, and longings as a result of not knowing their biological parents.[28]

The distinction between moral and premoral goods can be used to clarify the claims about the moral relevance of the discoveries of

22. E. Mavis Hetherington and John Kelly, *For Better or for Worse* (New York: W. W. Norton, 2002).

23. Mary Parks, "Are Married Parents Really Better for Children?" Center for Law and Social Policy, Policy Brief, May 2003, no 3.

24. It should be noted that although children from intact families are two to three times more likely to do well in school, marriage, and work, the majority of children from disrupted families still do well. McLanahan and Sandefur, *Growing up with a Single Parent,* p. 43.

25. Peter Benson, Anu Sharma, and Eugene Roehlkepartain, *Growing Up Adopted* (Minneapolis: Search Institute, 1994).

26. Martin Daly and Margo Wilson, *Sex, Evolution, and Behavior* (Belmont, Calif.: Wadsworth, 1983), p. 291.

27. Judith Wallerstein, Julia Lewis, and Sandra Blakeslee, *The Unexpected Legacy of Divorce* (New York: Hyperion, 2000).

28. Betty Jean Lifton, *Twice Born: Memories of an Adopted Daughter* (New York: Penguin, 1977). For a more balanced statement of this point of view, see D. M. Brodsinsky, M. D. Schecter, and Robin Henig, *Being Adopted: The Lifelong Search for Self* (New York: Anchor, 1992).

sociobiology and evolutionary psychology. Ever since the early writings of sociobiologists such as E. O. Wilson, Richard Dawkins, and Richard Alexander;[29] philosophers such as Mary Midgley, Elliot Sober, and David Sloan Wilson;[30] and evolutionary psychologists such as David Buss, Robert Wright, and Steven Pinker,[31] these fields have made strong claims about the moral relevance of biological inclinations. More specifically, evolutionary psychologists have insisted that the twin realities of kin altruism and inclusive fitness (the tendency to preserve not only one's own genes but also those of offspring, siblings, and cousins who carry our genes) are the foundations of morality.

Criminologist James Q. Wilson probably states this claim better than some of the evolutionary biologists. He believes that our preferential inclinations toward our own children and blood relatives sparked by kin altruism and inclusive fitness are the foundations of sympathy and thereby the main source of morality.[32] Kin altruism leads us to identify in special ways with the pain and elation of those who are partly us — our children, siblings, and so on. It leads us to regard them as we do ourselves. This is the core, he argues, of other important moral sentiments such as a sense of fairness, self-control, and duty.[33] These rudimentary sentiments can be analogically extended outside blood relations to others in wider social circles and therefore become the foundations of a more generalized social reciprocity. Frans de Waal in *Good Natured: The Origins of Right and Wrong in Humans and Other Animals* makes a similar argument.[34] Basically, Wilson and de Waal turn Richard Dawkins's "selfish gene" concept — the idea that our genes are interested only in their own individual well-being and immortality — on its head. The ideas of kin altruism and inclusive fitness show that creatures, even those who reproduce through sexual selection, have capacities for investment and sympathy in others, especially their

29. Edward O. Wilson, *On Human Nature* (Cambridge, Mass.: Harvard University Press, 1978); Richard Alexander, *The Biology of Moral Systems* (Hawthorne, N.Y.: Aldine de Gruyter, 1987); Richard Dawkins, *The Selfish Gene* (New York: Oxford University Press, 1989).

30. Midgley, *Beast and Man;* Elliott Sober and David Sloan Wilson, *Unto Others: The Evolution and Psychology of Unselfish Behavior* (Cambridge, Mass.: Harvard University Press, 1998).

31. David Buss, *The Evolution of Desire: Strategies of Human Mating* (New York: Basic, 1994); Robert Wright, *The Moral Animal* (New York: Pantheon, 1994); Steven Pinker, *How the Mind Works* (New York: W. W. Norton, 1997).

32. James Q. Wilson, *The Moral Sense* (New York: Free Press, 1993), p. 30.

33. Wilson, *The Moral Sense,* pp. 31-129.

34. Frans de Waal, *Good Natured: The Origins of Right and Wrong in Humans and Other Animals* (Cambridge, Mass.: Harvard University Press, 1996).

own kin. This, Wilson and de Waal argue, is the foundation of other-regarding sentiments in general.

One does not have to determine either the scientific or moral adequacy of these arguments to examine their logic. *Claims about the importance of kin altruism to both parental investment and the development of moral sentiments are basically arguments at the premoral level.* The realities of kin altruism may prompt natural parents to be, on average, more invested in their offspring, but this investment does not automatically convert to full parental adequacy. In fact, in some cases, it may feed narcissistic strategies of manipulation and control that can be overtly destructive. In other cases, it can feed nepotism and tribalism. It may be true that kin altruism and inclusive fitness feed a primitive sense of sympathy, but a fully mature sense of equal regard, fairness, and duty requires many social and cultural refinements beyond this elemental beginning.

Hence, in both cases — parenthood and more general morality — kin altruism may be a very important premoral good that is in some sense foundational. It is not exhaustive, however, of the full moral meaning of either parenthood or the mature ethical life. Nonetheless, kin altruism must be taken seriously as worthy of central cultural and religious appreciation and encouragement, as our religious traditions for the most part have tended to do.

Adoption and the Situation of Families

It is important to address the adoption issue with a careful analysis of the situation of families in rapidly modernizing countries such as the United States. In *From Culture Wars to Common Ground,* we dedicated a long chapter to this task. Personally, I am struck by how often scholars rush into family issues without careful analysis of what is happening. Many scholars see patriarchy as the major cause of, and its dismantling as the major solution to, all family difficulties. This is an important part of the analysis, but this phenomenon needs to be set within a larger context. As Weber saw years ago, and Habermas and others more recently, the spread of technical rationality in market and government bureaucracy is clearly the most unsettling force today on families throughout the world.[35] A new means-end logic for the efficient enhancement of short-term satisfactions

---

35. Max Weber, *The Protestant Ethic and the Spirit of Capitalism* (New York: Charles Scribner's Sons, 1958), p. 182; Habermas, *Theory of Communicative Action,* vol. 2, pp. 304, 307.

increasingly has colonized or dominated the lifeworld of day-to-day interactions — home, love, neighborhood, civil society — and led all of us to
think more about mundane decisions in analogy to the cost-benefit logics
of technical efficiency in market and bureaucracy. Rational-choice theorists explain family changes in terms of the declining economic dependence in the nineteenth century of the conjugal couple on extended family, and then, in the last half of the twentieth century, of the lessening
financial dependence of wives on husbands because of women's entry
into the wage economy.[36] These pressures, plus the customary problems
of poverty (the recent relative decline of the salaries of working-class
males), have undermined the role of economic interdependence in supporting marital and family stability.

Accompanying these economic and social-systemic transformations
has been the increasing power, at least since the Enlightenment, of cultural individualism. This is a view of life that sees individual satisfactions
and fulfillment as the primary goal.[37] Cultural individualism and the
logic of market rationality should not be equated, but they clearly reinforce each other. Both function to destabilize the kin altruism and parental investments of the conjugal couple, and the consequences help explain
the discouraging family trends summarized above. In addition, all of
these changes unleashed new psychological turmoil. A profession of psychotherapy arose to help individuals and families cope with the ceaseless
pressures of technical rationality and individualism. But psychotherapists
generally rendered their assistance in terms of the very rationality and individualism that gave rise to these unsettling forces to begin with. Psychotherapy itself is in part a *techne,* and its guiding values, for the most part,
have been distinctively individualistic.[38]

These changes mean that there are more broken families with children to adopt, more older childless couples who have waited too long and
have missed the parental fulfillment of having children, and more unmarried singles who think about adoption as a way to fulfill their parental inclinations. Some commentators, such as Stephen Presser, say that the

36. Gary Becker, *Treatise on the Family* (Cambridge, Mass.: Harvard University Press,
1991), pp. 347-61.

37. Robert Bellah, Richard Madsen, William Sullivan, Ann Swidler, and Steven Tipton,
Habits of the Heart (New York: Harper and Row, 1986), pp. 35-36.

38. See Don Browning, *Religious Thought and the Modern Psychologies* (Minneapolis: Fortress, 1987); Frank Richardson et al., *Re-envisioning Psychology* (San Francisco: Jossey-Bass,
1999); Philip Cushman, *Constructing the Self, Constructing America: A Cultural History of Psychotherapy* (Cambridge, Mass.: Perseus, 1995).

adoption process itself is being sucked into the social and cultural dynamics of market and bureaucratic technical rationality.[39] Furthermore, some have cogently argued that the entire process of procreation, birth, and child-rearing increasingly has come under the control of medical technology — that it has, in short, become "medicalized."[40]

The forces of technical rationality and individualism have inserted themselves into the realm of human procreation. Various birth control procedures have been available for decades. Now a whole slew of assisted reproductive technologies (ARTs) are obtainable, such as artificial insemination (AI), artificial insemination by husband (AIH), artificial insemination by donor (AID), in vitro fertilization (IVF), surrogacy, and still others. All of these technologies are available from many clinics for married or unmarried heterosexual couples, singles, and gay and lesbian couples in a new individualistic culture of "procreative liberty."[41] These technologies interacting with market rationality and cultural individualism have led, according to Brent Waters's excellent analysis, to a series of separations: the disconnection of sexual intercourse from marriage, procreation from sexual intercourse, parenthood from procreation, and child-rearing from parenthood.[42]

All this means that the question of adoption must be located within the fuller context of significant new family disruptions as well as a new culture of procreative freedom. From one perspective, I would argue that this situation all the more requires new emphases on and methods for enhancing the integrity of the married conjugal couple and the on-average higher levels of the premoral good of kin altruism associated with this form of the family. On the other hand, in view of the actual reality of family disruption and larger numbers of homeless, abandoned, and suffering children needing care and support, this situation may require an *equally strong* cultural emphasis on the importance and dignity of adoption.

It is not a contradiction, as we will see below, to emphasize both directions simultaneously. Some analysts promote adoption but then fail to make the wider analysis of the reality and causes of more general family disruption. Hence, they regard a cultural emphasis on the equal-regard in-

---

39. Stephen B. Presser, "Law, Christianity, and Adoption," in *The Morality of Adoption: Social-Psychological, Theological, and Legal Perspectives,* ed. Timothy P. Jackson (Grand Rapids: Eerdmans, 2005), pp. 219-45.

40. Brent Waters, *Reproductive Technology: Towards a Theology of Procreative Stewardship* (Cleveland: Pilgrim, 2001), p. 14.

41. Waters, *Reproductive Technology,* p. 19.

42. Waters, *Reproductive Technology,* pp. 15-17.

tact family as almost a threat to the cause of rendering adoption more culturally attractive. Others are so anxious to push for the revival and reconstruction of the intact family that they forget to address the importance of adoption. Both positions are finally wrongheaded. But if there is a need for adoption in face of the numerous reasons leading to family disruption, how does one build the case from a theological point of view — a case for the life of the church and a theological case for the role of adoption as a public practice in a pluralistic society?

In the remaining sections of this chapter, I wish to bring the concepts of critical familism into conversation with four recent theological-ethical views on the meaning of adoption. I do this, first, to make both appreciative and critical commentary on these important positions. I do it as well to enrich and extend critical familism on a topic about which it needs to say more.

Ted Peters and an Eschatological Ethic of Adoption

Lutheran theologian Ted Peters in his *For the Love of Children: Genetic Technology and the Future of the Family* is a wonderful example of a position that draws advocacy of adoption into a collateral defense of progressive perspectives on the use of reproductive technologies.[43] There are few if any assisted reproductive technologies (ARTs) that Peters would not allow. This is because Peters sees no solid theological reasons for maintaining the unity between what the Christian tradition has called the *unitive* (the one-flesh melding of wife and husband) and the *procreative* (the birthing and education of children) aspects of covenanted marital love. For this reason, Peters is quite ready to allow into church and society Brent Waters's list of separations between sex and marriage, sex and procreation, procreation and parenthood, and parenthood and child-rearing. Peters believes that traditional theological grounds for keeping these aspects of life in some kind of unity or interaction no longer have validity.

These reasons for keeping the unitive and procreative together have principally included natural law arguments widely used in Roman Catholic theology and "orders of creation" arguments used in Protestant theology. Roman Catholics actually use both kinds of arguments. For instance, Thomas Aquinas assumed that Genesis 1:28 ("Be fruitful and multiply")

43. Ted Peters, *For the Love of Children: Genetic Technology and the Future of the Family* (Louisville: Westminster John Knox, 1996).

was addressed to male and female in the marital arrangement. Hence for him, marriage and procreation were willed by God at the foundations of creation — something of an order of creation.[44] But Aquinas spent much more time developing his natural law arguments for marriage. These said that the long period of human infant dependency requires the father to recognize that the child is part of his substance and should be cared for as he would care for himself. Furthermore, to address the dependency of both infant and mother, the father should join the mother-infant dyad, bond with consort and child, and assist with material and spiritual nurture.[45] Aquinas insisted that we love our children for two reasons — because they are part of us (both mother and father), and because they are part of the goodness of God (God's children) and should be cherished as such.[46] Clearly, the latter reason — the status of all children as reflective of the goodness of God — was the weightier reason for both Aquinas and the Christian tradition as a whole. From Aquinas's perspective, however, both reasons were theological. God was seen to work through the tendencies of nature just as God reveals the divine purposes in the history of creation and salvation.

Both reasons, I might add, are central theological grounds for the love of our children from the standpoint of critical familism. Both reasons help us understand why marriage and procreation based on kin altruism should be central to church and public policy, but why, as well, we need to cherish, preserve, and adopt all needy children, whether or not they are our own. Luther, it should be added, based his argument for the love of children principally on appeals to God's intentions in creation, but many commentators still detect remnants in his thought of classic natural law arguments as well.[47] I believe that Protestants and Catholics have available to them both of these theological arguments for the love of children. Of course, the naturalistic argument can be more readily used in public argument even if secularists reject the idea that God works through our kin-altruistic inclinations. This does not mean that the Christian framing of natural law argument is not valuable; indeed, it may be crucial for keeping the natural law argument from taking destructive directions.

But Peters is willing to jettison both types of theological argument — orders of creation and natural law. He is especially concerned to reject

44. Aquinas, *Summa Theologica,* Supplement to the Third Part, q. 42, a. 2.

45. Aquinas, *Summa Contra Gentiles,* vol. 3, part 2, chap. 123.

46. Aquinas, *Summa Theologica,* vol. 2, part 2, q. 26, aa. 3, 8, 9.

47. John McNeill, "Natural Law in the Teaching of the Reformers," *Journal of Religion* 26, no. 3 (1962): 168-82.

anything approaching a natural law argument. He derides what he calls the "inheritance myth" — any argument that the preferential attachments of parents for their children are due to a biological or genetic link.[48] Parenthood, especially fatherhood, is for him a completely social concept; it applies to those who actually love children and this incidental to their biological ties. Peters grounds the theology of adoption — his theological grounding for the love of all children — on eschatology. He writes,

> It is my proposal that the field of Christian ethics should be founded on our vision of the promised Kingdom of God. Ethics should be founded on eschatology. The world that constitutes our present reality is slated for transformation, a transformation promised to us by God and proleptically anticipated in the Easter resurrection of Jesus Christ.[49]

But Peters does not view eschatology as fulfilling creation and nature, although much of the tradition actually does. For him, the transformations of God's kingdom that come from the future are totally disconnected from creation and nature. "We pass from being people of dust to people of heaven. We pass from being the children of Adam and Eve to becoming brothers and sisters of Christ."[50] Then we hear the culminating point: "Our definition or identity as human beings is determined not by the DNA we have inherited but rather by our vision of the network of relations that will constitute the Kingdom of God."[51]

What is this eschatological ethic that comes from the future and works without reference to nature or creation? It is first of all an ethic that assumes, and even celebrates, our increased freedom to make "choices" independent of the constraints of creation, nature, or tradition.[52] But choice, Peters acknowledges, requires criteria if it is to be responsible. He brings eschatology and Kant's categorical imperative together in a grand synthesis that emphasizes God's covenant with humans — but mainly a covenant that comes to us in God's eschatological action. Covenant is "a freely entered into promise to remain faithful . . . and should be applied to the relationship parents enter into with their children."[53] The content of this cove-

---

48. Peters, *For the Love of Children*, pp. 25-27.
49. Peters, *For the Love of Children*, p. 155.
50. Peters, *For the Love of Children*, p. 155.
51. Peters, *For the Love of Children*, p. 155.
52. Peters, *For the Love of Children*, p. 3.
53. Peters, *For the Love of Children*, p. 3.

nant goes like this: "God loves each of us regardless of our genetic makeup, and we should do likewise."[54] Or again, "[A] covenant to love children means that we will treat children as ends and not merely as means to fulfill someone else's desires."[55] It is striking that this position, in the final analysis, gives humans the freedom to choose, without constraints, whether to have children the "old-fashioned way" or use adoption, artificial insemination by donor (AID), surrogacy, gamete intrafallopian transfer (GIFT) (where neither the egg nor the sperm belongs to the parents who will raise the child), or even cloning. Notice that adoption is lumped together as just one additional alternative reproductive strategy. Peters believes that his eschatologically stated imperative to love all children blocks the possibility of using these technologies to manipulate children for the sake of adult interests or to commodify them as we do our automobiles and clothes, always looking for the best model.

But this grand democracy of reproductive methods, as generous and attractive as it at first glance seems to be, has enormous problems. Peters is motivated to lift the cultural onus on adoption, and this is laudable. Certainly there is a range of reproductive technologies that can be used to enhance committed marital parenthood and the investments of kin altruism without resulting in Brent Waters's list of separations in the reproductive process. But the difficulties in Peters's position are of such magnitude that one cannot avoid the judgment that he has gone too far — too far for the praxis of the church and too far for the policies of the wider society.

First, Peters avoids developing his case within the context of a careful analysis of what is happening to families in modern societies. His position is, in brief, short on careful social analysis at either the theoretical or empirical level. He is concerned about the potential commodification of children but seems to have little interest in what the general forces of technical rationality, either in their market or in their state-bureaucratic form, are doing to promote family disruption, especially at the level of the integrity of the conjugal couple. He seems to have little understanding of how his lumping together adoption with all other presently possible assisted reproductive technologies could function as the crowning victory for technical rationality's colonization of the lifeworld. At the empirical level of analysis, he pays very little attention to the emerging social science literature that shows how, on average, children raised by biologically related parents in an intact relationship seem to do better in life on a variety of criteria.

54. Peters, *For the Love of Children*, p. 4.
55. Peters, *For the Love of Children*, p. 3.

Closely related to this is how Peters discerns our moral obligation to children. It is God's command from the future that we love children as ends and never treat them as means only. But should we be concerned about what is the *good* for children? Peters's eschatological Kantianism has the weakness of all forms of pure Kantiansim — it begs the question of the good for children other than the goal of respecting them as ends. In short, Peters has no theory of the premoral good for children. He claims that tradition, through such concepts as the orders of creation, does not show us what is good for children. Nature in the form of natural law arguments does not tell us what is good for children. Finally, the social sciences in their measurement of the conditions and consequences of various family arrangements do not for him tell us what is good for children. In the end, this leaves the ideas of love and respect as vacuous and without content, hardly enough to protect children from the commodification and manipulation that he fears.

Such a position, I fear, is not faithful to the Christian tradition. It is, however, even more fragile as a basis for public policy. It would seem to suggest that all of society would need to be converted to the expectations and moral predicates of Christian eschatology. Furthermore, his position is without definitions of the premoral goods for children — what makes them flourish, grow, and become mentally and physically healthy. If this is true, Peters's views would result in a public policy (especially in the present situation of growing technological dominance) that would sow even more seeds of reproductive disruption and confusion.

In the end, it would be better if Peters retained both the argument from created orders and the argument from nature. It is true that the idea of orders of creation can be misused. But it also can be employed by Christians as a powerful hypothesis of faith — one that can direct the imagination as it looks for other collaborating insights about the goods of life to be appreciated and preserved. The idea that covenant marriage is one of these orders — one of these plausibilities of faith — can be defended confessionally. It also is a fundamental human good that can be argued philosophically with the use of hermeneutic philosophy and the subordinate arguments of natural law and the human sciences. Philosophically, the idea of covenanted marriage has functioned, to use the terminology of Hans-Georg Gadamer, as a religio-cultural "classic" that has time and again been confirmed by intuition, reflection, and experience.[56] Natural law arguments of the kind used by Aquinas (the importance to dependent

56. Hans-Georg Gadamer, *Truth and Method* (New York: Crossroad, 1982), p. 254.

human infants of the supporting factors of parental certainty, kin altruism, and the bonding of parents) are a heuristic index or diagnostic, to use a phrase from Paul Ricoeur, about the natural energies taken up and organized by the covenanted marital relation.[57] These two resources help guide our "love of children" and give it content.

Clearly Peters is to some extent right: The element of respect for children as ends is the central component of love. Love as equal regard — so crucial to critical familism — holds this insight in common with Peters's position. But the covenant of equal regard requires a teleological submoment — some view of the premoral goods of life and the premoral goods for children. I believe that the glorious title of Peters's book, "For the Love of Children," requires such teleological submoments before it can become an intelligible and trustworthy guide to family policy. Accepting my recommendations would lead him to cherish more the intact mother-father partnership, but at the same time to also honor adoption, appreciate ARTs that enhance covenanted marriage, and modify his enthusiasm for those ARTs that would undermine this relation.

Premoral and Moral Goods in Waters

There are a variety of contemporary positions that are closer to the sensibilities of critical familism. But these positions are not identical to each other and not consistent with critical familism in all respects. Commenting on these admirable positions will teach us much and provide me with the opportunity to render critical familism's underdeveloped comments on adoption a bit more mature.

All of these perspectives share one thing in common; this is an emphasis on the religious and cultural centrality of what I have called the intact, equal-regard, mother-father partnership, *along with* commendation for the importance of adoption as a Christian obligation when needy children are at hand. Hence, the dual commitment that Peters finds contra-

---

57. The concept of diagnostic is Ricoeur's way of positioning the illuminating insights of natural explanation without obscuring the beginning of reflection in history and linguistic heritage. It is an anti-foundationalist way of handling natural sciences and would apply to the use by theological ethics of natural law. See Paul Ricoeur, *Freud and Philosophy* (New Haven, Conn.: Yale University Press, 1970), p. 346. For an introductory discussion of the concepts of diagnostic and "distanciation" in Ricoeur, see Don Browning, "Ricoeur and Practical Theology," in *Paul Ricoeur and Contemporary Moral Thought*, ed. John Wall, William Schweiker, and David Hall (New York: Routledge, 2002), p. 260.

dictory is precisely what these thinkers believe the Christian faith makes possible. But this raises a variety of related questions. How do they each understand the appropriate theological grounds for adoption? How do they handle the crucial question of the relation of premoral and moral goods as these apply to the motivations for adoption? And, finally, how do they relate adoption to a variety of other strategies, methods, and technologies for reproduction?

In his recent *Reproductive Technology: Towards a Theology of Procreative Stewardship,* Brent Waters has burst on the theological scene with a commanding perspective on these questions. His thesis is in the subtitle of his book. The fields of sexuality, love, procreation, adoption, and ART should be guided for Christians by the concept of procreative stewardship. What does it mean? First, it is the opposite of positions such as that of John Robertson, who would order procreation with the principles of procreative liberty — individual autonomy, individual fulfillment, and a sense of the ownership of one's body and one's offspring.[58] Procreative stewardship is based instead on the biblical idea that life (the life of the child and one's own life) is not our possession to be disposed of as we please. It is, instead, a gift of God that is on loan from God and given to us to be cherished and nurtured.[59] The God-given context for the birth and nourishing of children is the covenanted marital relationship between husband and wife. Waters writes, "In being drawn toward each other as women and men, it is the one-flesh unity of marriage that expresses the fullest and deepest dimension of their fellowship. We may point to marriage as a sign, covenant and vocation bearing witness to a creation being drawn toward the expansive and enfolding love of its creator and redeemer."[60]

Furthermore, this one-flesh covenant between man and woman also includes the "unique one flesh of the child beyond them. In marriage a woman and man give birth to a child to whom both are related and drawn together in love and fidelity."[61] Humans — both parents and children — are not divisions of body and soul; rather they are "embodied souls and ensouled bodies."[62] We are more than our biology and more

---

58. John Robertson, *Children of Choice: Freedom and the New Reproductive Technologies* (Princeton, N.J.: Princeton University Press, 1994).

59. Waters, *Reproductive Technology,* p. 3; many of these same points are made in Waters's "Adoption, Parentage, and Procreative Stewardship," in *The Morality of Adoption,* ed. Jackson, pp. 32-51.

60. Waters, *Reproductive Technology,* p. 41.

61. Waters, *Reproductive Technology,* p. 42.

62. Waters, *Reproductive Technology,* p. 3.

than our social relationships; we are creatures of God intended in creation to find our reproductive fulfillment in covenanted relations that include yet transcend both biology and finite loves in our relation with God. Waters admits that parenthood based on biological relatedness is important and should be promoted, but he does not directly employ the idea of kin altruism in either Aquinas or evolutionary psychology to amplify its relative importance. Biology, moreover, does not exhaust the meaning of parenthood, according to Waters. Waters makes a vague and unsystematic use of the concept of premoral goods when he describes the moral meaning of covenant. He writes, "A covenant entails the ordering of goods that are both internal and external to a relationship, binding its parties together by its imposed terms."[63] Waters seems to imply that the investment of kin altruism is one of those goods given organization by the marriage covenant, but he nowhere directly develops this idea. This will have consequences for a small reservation that I have about his position.

Waters believes in the moral obligation of Christians to adopt needy and abandoned children. But the Christian does this as a matter of "charity"; it is not a matter of personal fulfillment. "Adoption . . is not a reproductive option, but an act of charity (*caritas*)." Waters continues even more emphatically:

> The overriding consideration is the welfare of the child, not the plight of natural or adoptive parents. The intent is not to relieve natural parents of a burden they are unable to bear or to satisfy the parental desires of an infertile couple, but to find a suitable place of timely belonging for a child who would otherwise have none. This is why adoption is not restricted to infertile couples, for its purpose is not to obtain children but to place them in families.[64]

Waters is mildly critical of Roman Catholic moral theologians such as Germain Grisez and Lisa Cahill for recommending adoption as an alternative to third-party reproductive assistance for couples to fulfill their "generative" tendencies.[65] But let me be clear. Waters agrees with these thinkers: Adoption is more Christian than the use of third parties. It is Grisez and Cahill's moral grounding that he questions. Charity should be the Christian motivation for adoption, not parental or generative self-

63. Waters, *Reproductive Technology*, p. 41.
64. Waters, *Reproductive Technology*, p. 73.
65. Waters, *Reproductive Technology*, p. 71.

fulfillment. All Christians should be willing to adopt when the need arises, not just the childless.

But this raises a series of important questions. Are we to conclude that when couples turn to adoption with the desire to fulfill their parental longings that they are always suspect from a Christian perspective? Does this mean that Christians should discourage this motivation in the general public? Should the charity that motivates adoption stand completely uninfluenced by our generative interests? Can charity build on, transform, and guide our generative interests? This raises the analogous questions: *What is Waters's understanding of love? Where does he stand in the great debate about the relation of* eros *and* agape, *of self-fulfillment and self-sacrifice, in Christian love?* It is with these questions in mind that I turn to a review of the commanding natural law perspective of Catholic moral theologian Lisa Cahill and the important covenantal position of Protestant Stephen Post.

Natural Law and Covenant in Cahill and Post

Cahill and Post share many things in common, but they develop their theological arguments in somewhat different ways. Both of them emphasize the religious and cultural priority of the covenanted conjugal couple.[66] Marriage is central for sexuality and child-rearing for both of them. And each of them in some fashion takes seriously the good of kin altruism. Cahill does this by affirming the Aristotelian and Thomistic strand of thought that views the affections of natural parents as a seedbed of more generalized other-regard.[67] As does critical familism, Cahill also invokes the insights of evolutionary psychology about the nature of kin altruism; it is for her a naturalistic substratum of parental love, although it does not capture the full character of this love.[68] Post also makes considerable use of the idea of kin altruism but often invokes the paradigms of history and the Bible more than either ancient or modern biology, although he gives modest attention to both. Post is struck by the innumerable uses of parental metaphors — God the father, God the mother, the solicitude of mother love, the forgiving father, and so on — that run

---

66. Lisa Sowle Cahill, *Family: A Christian Social Perspective* (Minneapolis: Fortress, 2000), p. xi; Post, *More Lasting Unions* (Grand Rapids: Eerdmans, 2000), p. 119.

67. Lisa Sowle Cahill, *Sex, Gender, and Christian Ethics* (Cambridge: Cambridge University Press, 1996), p. 71.

68. Cahill, *Sex, Gender, and Christian Ethics*, pp. 92-95.

throughout both ancient Hebrew and early Christian texts.[69] In fact, for Post, parental love and the male-female relation in covenant marriage reflect the very image of God as caring and loving parent — *in imagine Dei.*[70] Post makes much of the Greek concept of *storge,* a concept that points to the preferential and self-giving care and concern that parents have for their offspring.[71] We see this, he tells us, in the images of God delivered by tradition, and we experience it in our lives in families. This parental love is the foundation for the analogical spread of love to others outside the family. We first experience love in our own particular families and gradually learn to love others outside the family — especially if we believe that, in the end, like us they are all children of God and part of the grand family of God. And, as we will see, a similar view is held by Cahill.

Even though they both emphasize the priority of conjugal love and parenthood, they are both strong advocates of the Christian duty to adopt. In contrast to Peters, they do not see these two mandates as being in opposition. Both Cahill and Post, like Waters, are opposed to the rush toward using the marvels of assisted reproductive technology. It should be observed, however, that Cahill pushes the limits of official Catholic teachings; she would permit the use of selected technologies that they have discouraged or forbidden. For instance, she approves the judicious use of contraception if it works to enhance the marital relationship and helps to space births for the good of the family as a whole. She also goes beyond church teachings in approving artificial insemination by husband (AIH), since it does not disturb marital commitment and can actually enhance the parental relationship. She agrees with Post, and indeed Waters, however, that any use of these technologies that introduces third parties or detracts from the integral relation between covenanted marital love, procreation, and child-rearing should be resisted, both by the church and by the wider society.[72]

On the other hand, both Post and Cahill, in contrast to Waters, are proponents of the use of adoption for the realization of frustrated parental inclinations.[73] Post goes even further. He works hard to show why adoption is in no way inferior to parenting in intact families, and even ar-

---

69. Stephen G. Post, *Spheres of Love* (Dallas: Southern Methodist University Press, 1994), pp. 60-63. See also Stephen Post, "Adoption: A Protestant-Based Perspective," in *The Morality of Adoption,* ed. Jackson, pp. 172-87.

70. Post, *Spheres of Love,* p. 20.

71. Post, *Spheres of Love,* p. 63.

72. Cahill, *Sex, Gender, and Christian Ethics,* pp. 252-53.

73. Cahill, *Sex, Gender, and Christian Ethics,* p. 246; Post, *More Lasting Unions,* p. 123.

gues for the moral acceptability of some parents voluntarily relinquishing their children for adoption when they do not have the means to sustain them.[74]

Cahill and Post use slightly different sources and theological methods in arriving at their respective positions. Cahill uses the resources of sacramental theology and natural law.[75] Post uses natural law thinking as well, but positions it as a subdimension of his covenant theology.[76] These dual foci permit both Cahill and Post to give priority to "natural parents" but also to organize their kin investments into the more universalistic moral framework of the justice of the kingdom of God. This dual language also permits them to speak directly to the confessional life of the church as well as to the broader public. As a natural law theologian, Cahill takes the empirical needs and experiences of both children and adults with great seriousness. She believes that there are universal needs that cut across differing cultures, and, in contrast to Martha Nussbaum (with whom she otherwise has much in common), Cahill believes that kin-relatedness in parenting is one of those universals.[77] But Cahill is not a foundationalist. She does not move from the empirical analysis of experience directly to the assertion of norms.[78] Cahill assumes the historically mediated Genesis story of creation as a beginning point, that is, its affirmation of the male-female relation as reflective of *imago Dei* and its command to both men and women to multiply and have dominion. Natural law and empirical analysis are subordinate indices for her that provide further "good reasons" that help us see the plausibility of revelation and tradition.[79] These good reasons can and should be defended before wider, non-Christian publics and may often prove relevant to public policies in pluralistic societies.

Post, on the other hand, uses natural law and the empirical analysis of the social sciences in much the same way but within his covenant theology that puts the primary emphasis upon the command of God and our

---

74. Post, *More Lasting Unions*, pp. 137-38. Post agrees with those spirited defenses of adoption such as Elizabeth Bartholet, *Family Bonds: Adoption and the Politics of Parenting* (New York: Houghton Mifflin, 1993). He is also for adoption for the good of the child rather than the legacy interests of the parents. For a history of these two motivations in culture and law, see Stephen Presser, "The Historical Background of the American Law of Adoption," *Journal of Family Law* 11, no. 2 (1972): 443-516.

75. Cahill, *Sex, Gender, and Christian Ethics*, pp. 46-50.

76. Post, *Spheres of Love*, pp. 85-88.

77. Cahill, *Sex, Gender, and Christian Ethics*, p. 59.

78. Cahill, *Sex, Gender, and Christian Ethics*, p. 235.

79. Cahill, *Sex, Gender, and Christian Ethics*, p. 235.

human response to this command. These moves by Cahill and Post make it easier for them to address their position on family and adoption to both ecclesia and public policy. They can do this with more ease than is the case with the more strictly confessional positions of Peters and Waters. The presence of a double language in Post and Cahill gives them extra flexibility in public debate.

This brings me to the last commonality of Cahill and Post: their understanding of the dialectical relation of kin altruism to more universal love and, as well, the dialectical relation of *eros* to the self-transcending character of Christian *agape.* Post has for several years investigated the relation between *agape* and *eros* — the relation of sacrificial love to self-love and the quest for self-fulfillment.[80] Post generally has opposed the view, often associated with Anders Nygren's magisterial interpretation of the history of Christian love,[81] that Christian love is mainly self-sacrificial love that completely transcends self-regard and self-love. To the contrary, Post identifies Christian love with the mutuality of the love commandment to "love your neighbor as yourself" (Matt. 19:19). This is close to the view in critical familism of love as equal regard. Post's view of love also retains, as does critical familism's theory of equal regard, a strong teleological subdimension. Post's view of love as mutuality builds on and analogically extends the motivations of kin altruism — the affections, investments, and solicitude of parental love extended outward from one's own offspring to all children everywhere. In contrast to Nygren, and in contrast to Peters and even Waters, the Protestant Post follows the core of the Catholic tradition that views universal love — even the love that leads to adoption — as the analogical generalization of kin altruism. *Eros* and *agape,* as well as kin altruism and self-transcending love, are dialectically related for Post. Post is also close to critical familism in holding a theory of mutuality and equal regard that requires the cross. He believes, as critical familists do, that the cross is required in order to endure in the midst of sin and brokenness so that love as mutuality can be renewed and reinstated when threatened. For Post, the love that motivates adoption should build on our innate, and sometimes frustrated, tendencies toward kin altruism, even though it must extend and stabilize these energies with the endurance of love inspired by the symbol of the cross. The two motivations can be brought together.

Cahill's view is similar. Cahill and Post allow the energies of kin altru-

---

80. Stephen Post, *A Theory of Agape* (Lewisburg: Bucknell University Press, 1990).
81. Anders Nygren, *Agape and Eros* (Philadelphia: Westminster, 1953).

ism to come into play in adoption. Cahill writes about this in ways that, as we have seen, have elicited the critical response of Waters. In an effort to discourage forms of reproductive technology that undermine the one-flesh unity of the marital relation, Cahill believes that parents should see adoption as a creative way of "satisfying their generative impulses."[82] Waters believes that this dilutes the motivation of charity. It should be noticed, however, that Cahill holds that adoption should not be motivated for Christians by parental needs alone; it must be motivated by our sense of solidarity with others as children of God and persons for whom Christ died — truths symbolized in the Christian common meal.[83]

In short, Cahill and Post implicitly maintain the distinction between premoral and moral goods that I developed earlier in the chapter. This helps them both appreciate kin altruism as a very important premoral good — a good that more fully Christian moral acts build on, analogically extend, and in partial ways transcend. For these two theologians, the satisfaction of generative inclinations can be a partial ground for adoption for Christians *and* for wider public policy. But kin altruism always needs to be extended, both for the task of parenting our own biological children and as a ground for adoption. As Waters says, the adoption element must enter for Christians into the parenting of their own offspring. Our children are both products of our own genes and gifts of God. Fully to recognize them as gifts is also to acknowledge the element of adoption in every act of parenting.

Christians should support public policies that promote adoption. In the present context of world family disruption, the need is great. But this raises the question, what can be the grounds for adoption, other than fulfilling generative needs alone, in public policy? Cahill believes rational deliberation is a resource. She believes that the expansion of altruism beyond our own children is possible on other than Christian grounds. She writes, "A judgment in favor of inclusive altruism can, of course, be supplied by a religious tradition like Christianity. I maintain that it can also be arrived at inductively, consensually, and experientially by public and dialectical reflections on nature and conditions of a humane society."[84]

82. Cahill, *Sex, Gender, and Christian Ethics*, p. 247.

83. Cahill, *Family: A Christian Social Perspective*, pp. 42-44. It is my reading of Timothy Jackson's position that he too would place the primary emphasis on the needs of the child and the agapic love of the adopting parent but would not necessarily eliminate as a secondary ground for adoption the needs for generative fulfillment of the adopting parent. See his "Suffering the Suffering Children: Christianity and the Rights and Wrongs of Adoption," in *The Morality of Adoption*, ed. Jackson, pp. 188-216.

84. Cahill, *Family: A Christian Social Perspective*, pp. 10-11.

This may be true. Christians can, and should, acknowledge that there may be other than Christian ways to justify and inspire the adoption of the needy. Admitting this should not undercut the Christian belief that acknowledging children as gifts of God, God's children, and objects of Christ's love — hence as persons we too should love and cherish — provides even profounder reasons for adoption.

Chapter 20

Domestic Violence and the Ethic
of Equal Regard (2005)

This chapter was prepared for a conference on domestic violence held at the University of Leuven, Belgium, in February of 2005. I accepted the invitation to prepare this paper for two reasons. First, I had not addressed the issue of domestic or family violence from the perspective of critical familism. It was time to do that. Second, Leuven was the academic home of Louis Janssens, whose love ethic I have used so extensively in my writings on marriage and family. Janssens, who lived well into his nineties, was dead when I made my visit to Leuven. But my hosts had been trained by him and shared my respect for his contributions to theological ethics. This chapter also gives me the opportunity to attempt to untangle the knotty distinctions between domestic violence, family violence, and marital violence — distinctions not well made in popular discourse and the popular press. These phenomena are sociologically and ethically not exactly the same things. When the distinctions between them are properly made, marriage — at least the equal-regard marriage — becomes something of a cure for, rather than a cause of, domestic violence.

In this chapter, I hope to demonstrate how an adequate Christian view of love can inform and help remedy the reality of family violence. I also hope to show how even good theology must be accompanied by accurate understandings of both human nature and contemporary social realities. Without clearly comprehending the kind of social, economic, and legal world that modernity is injecting into our midst and how these modernizing dynamics interact with the kind of creatures we humans happen to be, both obvious family violence and more subtle forms of family disruption will grow and become more destructive.

One of the most powerful contemporary theological statements on the nature of Christian love can be found in the writings of the Louvain moral theologian Louis Janssens. It may seem strange that an American liberal Protestant practical theologian could turn toward the resources of a Catholic moral theologian, but that is most certainly the case with me. I have used extensively in my writings his understanding of Christian love as equal regard, and this has been especially true in my writings on marriage and family. The term "equal regard" was a phrase Janssens openly acknowledged appropriating from the American theological ethicist Gene Outka's seminal book *Agape: An Ethical Analysis.*[1] But Janssens added to Outka's view of Christian love some extremely important — in fact, crucial — insights gleaned from his interpretation of the Thomistic tradition. Outka was a bit too much of a Kantian for Janssens, and I think that Janssens was right.

When Outka and Janssens reflect on the commandment "you shall love your neighbor as yourself," which is stated no less than eight times in the New Testament, they interpret it in very similar ways. Janssens states their understanding well when he writes, "Love of neighbor is impartial. It is fundamentally an equal-regard for every person, because it applies to each neighbor *qua* human existent."[2] Janssens employs the basic Christian metaphors that tell us that every person is a child of God and redeemed by Christ to ground his affirmation that all humans are of "irreducible worth and dignity."[3]

Janssens was as emphatic as Outka in insisting that Christian love as equal regard applied equally to self and other; in fact, both asserted that Christians had a moral obligation to regard themselves as ends and never as means alone. Furthermore, Christians also had the obligation to expect other people to treat them as ends, or children of God.[4] This idea of Christian love as commanding self-regard on an equal par with love of other has, as we will soon see, an enormous implication for the entire field of family violence.

1. Gene Outka, *Agape: An Ethical Analysis* (New Haven, Conn.: Yale University Press, 1972).

2. Louis Janssens, "Norms and Priorities of a Love Ethics," *Louvain Studies* 6 (Spring 1977): 219.

3. Janssens, "Norms and Priorities," p. 219.

4. Outka, *Agape,* pp. 209-91; Janssens, "Norms and Priorities," pp. 219-20.

But Christians should become uncomfortable if Outka's and Janssens's view of Christian love as equal regard were to end here. We need to know how they handle the self-sacrificial aspects of Christian love. What place does the cross have in their understanding of Christian love? Janssens says it best when he claims that self-sacrifice is not the goal or norm of Christian love, as it was for Anders Nygren and even for the American theologian Reinhold Niebuhr. According to Janssens, the self-sacrifice of the cross is what is needed in this sinful and finite world when mutuality and equal regard deteriorate and become unbalanced. The idea of bearing the cross of Christ points to the extra effort — indeed, the sacrificial effort — that is required to bring broken relations back to mutuality, equal regard, and full community. "In short," Janssens writes, "self-sacrifice is not the quintessence of love. . . . Self-sacrifice is justified derivatively from other regard."[5] By "other regard," he means the regard for the other that is part of the equal regard of genuine mutuality.

These observations about the true nature of Christian love are extremely relevant to the field of family violence. Family violence is often justified and maintained because of faulty and easily exploited norms that people carry in their minds about the appropriate ratios of other-love, self-love, and self-sacrifice that should be followed in family life. Clarifying what Christians should say to themselves and to the rest of society about the obligations of love is at least part of the answer to the reality of family violence.

Domestic Violence: Some Generalizations

We need a description of the field of domestic violence before we can become more concrete about the theology and appropriate practical response to the phenomenon. You will be happy to learn that I will not burden you with a large number of statistics to support some generalizations that I want to make.

First, I find the phrase "domestic violence" preferable to "family violence" as a way of defining our subject matter. The concept of domestic violence covers a very wide range of physical and sexual assaults that go on between people living in close proximity to one another; it includes the situation of single mothers and their children; cohabiting, sexually involved adults; extended families living under a single roof; and groups of

5. Janssens, "Norms and Priorities," p. 228.

adults and children sharing a single house or apartment. Statistics about domestic violence, at least in the United States, do not apply only to married couples and their children, even though the press and the wider public often interpret them that way. Official statistics about domestic violence cover this entire field of intimate living arrangements, but reports on domestic violence in popular news media often neglect to make careful distinctions between these various settings.

When domestic violence is understood to cover this wide field of living arrangements, some interesting surprises appear. In the United States, studies show that men and women in intimate relations attack each other with about equal frequency; it is simply that women get hurt more severely than men.[6] Live-in boyfriends and men in cohabiting relationships are more violent, on the whole, than married husbands.[7] One of the highest rates of domestic violence occurs between single mothers and their children, probably for understandable reasons of parental frustration and stress.[8] Economic stress appears to be a factor in domestic violence since the poor and unemployed have higher rates than the middle and upper classes.[9] Religion is often thought to be a primary carrier of violence by husbands toward wives and children, and although that may be true in some very special circumstances, it does not appear to be true on the whole, at least not in the United States. When religious groups are distinguished between active and nominal participants, actively involved religious men are less violent toward their spouses than secular men.[10] And although evangelical and conservative fathers may physically discipline their children more than religiously liberal or secular men, recent research by sociologist Brad Wilcox shows that they also are more deeply involved in their children's lives and more emotionally expressive with their children.[11]

Sexual abuse must also be seen as a form of domestic violence. The sexual abuse of children is far greater in cohabiting families and step-

---

6. M. A. Strauss and R. J. Gelles, "Societal Changes and Change in Family Violence from 1975 to 1985 As Revealed by Two National Surveys," *Journal of Marriage and Family* 48 (August 1986): 470.

7. Linda Waite and Maggie Gallagher, *The Case for Marriage: Why Married People Are Happier, Healthier, and Better off Financially* (New York: Doubleday, 2000).

8. Richard J. Gelles and Claire P. Cornell, *Intimate Violence in Families* (Beverly Hills, Calif.: Sage, 1985), p. 57.

9. Gelles and Cornell, *Intimate Violence*, p. 57.

10. W. Bradford Wilcox, *Soft Patriarchs, New Men: How Christianity Shapes Fathers and Husbands* (Chicago: University of Chicago Press, 2004), pp. 113-17.

11. Wilcox, *Soft Patriarchs*, pp. 113-17.

families, possibly because of the absence of the inhibiting factor of consanguinity. As we will see at some depth later in this paper, when murder statistics are collected and carefully analyzed in local communities, murder rates are several times higher among nonbiologically cohabiting individuals than among those who are related by biological kinship. And, as we will also see later in more detail, the sexual abuse of a daughter is much more likely to be perpetrated by a stepfather or stepbrother than by a male in an intact married family.

But what do these patterns of domestic violence suggest for a practical marital and family ethic? I hold that the love ethic of equal regard has crucial relevance for domestic violence. Not only should this ethic restrain all violent acts in the name of mutual respect, but it should function to empower the weak to demand that they be treated as ends — as children of God — and never as means or objects of exploitation. The love ethic of equal regard is not an ethic for the submissive, weak, and downtrodden. Janssens believes it is an ethic of empowerment that can undergird the demands for equal respect expressed by women, minorities, and exploited children.[12] As New Testament scholar Luise Schottroff has argued, the ethic of equal regard undergirds the nonviolent movements of resistance promoted by Gandhi and Martin Luther King.[13] It is an ethic that not only resists exploitation but also demands the transformation of the exploiter. But we cannot fully see how the love ethic of equal regard might be implemented within the various contexts of domestic violence without speculating about the various causes of the complex patterns of violence that I outlined above.

The Sources of Family Violence

I come to you as a person who wanders between the hazardous terrain of practical theology and the rocky path of theological ethics or, as Catholics call it, the field of moral theology. I believe that practical theology (often called pastoral theology in Catholic circles) needs the norms of theological ethics and that theological ethics needs the descriptions of contexts and situations that practical theology can provide. There are at least four

12. Janssens, "Norms and Priorities," p. 220.
13. Luise Schottroff, "Non-Violence and the Love of One's Enemies," in *Essays on the Love Commandment*, by Luise Schottroff et al., trans. Reginald H. Fuller and Ilse Fuller (Philadelphia: Fortress, 1978), p. 20.

prominent nominations for the cause of domestic violence that deserve review if we are to understand better the various contexts of this phenomena.

First, there is the cultural hypothesis built around the history of patriarchy and the legacy of male dominance that it has bequeathed to most societies. This view says that domestic violence is largely perpetrated by men as a result of the cultural bias that says males are superior to females. There is little doubt that there is some truth in this point of view, although it might fail to explain why battering perpetrated by women is equal to that by men but just less effective. (It is possible that battering on the part of females may be done principally for defensive reasons.) Since Christianity has much to do with forming the cultures of Western societies, Christianity is often cited as a principal carrier of male dominance and therefore male violence.

But the native impulses of early Christianity, when properly understood, do not support this charge. Several of the world religions, including Christianity, have gone through periods of distortion when they were co-opted and corrupted by monarchical or feudal cultural forces, thus making them appear to be carriers of patriarchy, authoritarianism, and male violence toward wives and children. But early Christianity certainly did not support male violence toward wives and children and probably, in its very earliest period, did not even support male headship or dominance. I have been influenced by the new school of cultural anthropology and New Testament scholarship that interprets early Christianity in light of the honor-shame codes that governed male behavior in the surrounding Greco-Roman Mediterranean area.[14] According to these schools of thought, honor for men in these areas was associated with agency and dominance while shame was associated with passivity and submission.

The earliest phases of the Jesus movement inverted this male ethic of dominance and planted the seeds of a new male ethic. The command to "love your neighbor as yourself" (Matt. 19:19) not only was applied to neighbor, stranger, and enemy but also was eventually applied to home and spouse. We see this in Galatians where it says that in Christ "there is no longer male or female" (Gal. 3:28) and in Ephesians: "husbands should love their wives as they do their own body" (Eph. 5:28). These passages

---

14. For a summary of the use of honor-shame categories in New Testament studies, see H. Moxes, "Honor and Shame," *Biblical Theology Bulletin* 23, no. 4 (1993): 167-76. For a summary of the research in cultural anthropology, see David D. Gilmore, *Manhood in the Making: Cultural Concepts of Masculinity* (New Haven, Conn.: Yale University Press, 1990).

point to an emerging love ethic of equal regard. Furthermore, the earliest strands of the Jesus movement associated Christian manhood with the servanthood and self-sacrifice that Jesus showed for the church, further reversing the ancient male honor-shame code of the Greco-Roman world (Eph. 5:25).

Of course, the Jesus movement's reversal of the honor-shame ethic was unsteady. Male headship reemerges in the pastoral epistles,[15] and it becomes once again a stable teaching in many of the medieval and early modern Christian theological classics, reflecting the feudalism of the societies of those periods. But even then, my search of Catholic canon law, Aquinas, Luther, and Calvin indicates that the concept of male headship that can be found in these sources was always circumscribed by powerfully articulated rules that seldom legitimated male violence.

Thus, when Christian teachings are invoked to legitimate male violence in the family, this must be seen as a significant distortion of the basic directions of primitive Christianity, reflecting external social and cultural trends rather than the heart of the Christian faith. Furthermore, it is worth reiterating that recent social-science research in the United States indicates that when distinctions are made between active male Christians and nominal ones, religiously active Christian men even today are less violent than secular men.[16]

Second, the forces of modernity themselves may help cause domestic violence. Max Weber and Jürgen Habermas defined modernization as the spread of technical rationality into both the free market of capitalist societies and the bureaucratic state of more socialist countries.[17] Both forms of technical rationality tend to reduce more and more of life to efficient means toward short-term satisfactions and function to undermine the cohesion-producing interdependencies of families, civil society, and communities of faith. Under the impact of modernization, the regulation of sexual, marital, and family life decreases as communities of tradition deteriorate. Sexual exploitation and violence tend to increase throughout society. For instance, in residential colleges and university settings in the United States, it is often difficult to distinguish between informal sexual relations referred to as "hooking up" and the more serious matter of date

---

15. Elisabeth Schüssler Fiorenza, *In Memory of Her: A Feminist Theological Reconstruction of Christian Origins* (New York: Crossroad, 1983), p. 289.

16. Wilcox, *Soft Patriarchs*, pp. 113-17.

17. Max Weber, *The Protestant Ethic and the Spirit of Capitalism* (New York: Charles Scribner's Sons, 1958), p. 182; Jürgen Habermas, *The Theory of Communicative Action*, trans. Thomas McCarthy, vol. 2 (Boston: Beacon Press, 1987), p. 333.

rape, as a variety of recent reports, books, and novels are now bringing home to the American public.[18]

But modernity also creates dramatic divisions in society between the rich and poor, between those who are educated to handle the tools of technical reason in an increasingly digital society and those who are not. Poverty clearly is associated with domestic violence, especially among those poor who are also alienated from supportive and culture-building communities of tradition.[19]

Third, the forces of modernization undermine marriage itself, a development which may in turn contribute to domestic violence. I have investigated this process at depth in my recent book *Marriage and Modernization*.[20] The comparative sociological evidence shows us that when marriage declines, divorce increases, cohabitation increases, more formal and informal stepfamilies emerge, and more physical and sexual domestic violence occurs as well. I realize this sounds harsh to the ears of many people living in progressive modern societies, but the best social-science research supports this generalization, at least in the United States.

For instance, Martin Daly and Margo Wilson in their significant book *Homicide* studied the murder statistics of Detroit; their research demonstrates a truth that Aristotle knew well, namely, that consanguinity protects against violence.[21] They examined the 508 closed murder cases in Detroit, Michigan, in 1972. They found that only 127 or 25 percent were between "relatives." Of the relatives, 80 were spouses (36 women killed by their husbands and 44 men killed by their wives). Only 32 victims were blood relatives of the perpetrator — there were 8 children killed by their parents, 11 parents killed by children, 9 brothers and 1 sister killed by a sibling, 1 girl killed by her male cousin, a fifty-two-year-old man killed by his sixty-five-year-old uncle, and an infant boy killed by his twelve-year-old uncle.[22] Only 6.3 percent of the total of 508 homicides actually involved bi-

18. See, for example, Norval Glenn and Elizabeth Marquardt, *Hooking Up, Hanging Out, and Hoping for Mr. Right: College Women on Dating and Mating Today* (New York: Institute for American Values, 2001); Tom Wolfe, *Hooking Up* (New York: Farrar, Strauss, and Giroux, 2000).

19. Murray A. Straus and Richard J. Gelles, *Physical Violence in American Families: Risk Factors and Adaptations to Violence in 8,145 Families* (New Brunswick, N.J.: Transaction, 1990), p. 359.

20. Don Browning, *Marriage and Modernization: How Globalization Threatens Marriage and What to Do about It* (Grand Rapids: Eerdmans, 2003).

21. Aristotle, *Politics*, in *The Basic Works of Aristotle*, ed. Richard McKeon (New York: Random House, 1941), bk. 1.2.

22. Martin Daly and Margo Wilson, *Homicide* (New York: Aldine de Gruyter, 1988), p. 19.

ologically related individuals.[23] This data was found to be consistent with similar studies in Philadelphia and Miami.[24]

These statistics seem to suggest that, in general, anything that a society can do to consolidate the prevalence of biological relatedness in family groups will decrease violence, and anything that increases biological unrelatedness in family groups will also increase domestic violence. The facts seem to support this generalization. In their book titled *The Truth about Cinderella: A Darwinian View of Parental Love,* Daly and Wilson review data on stepfamilies. This leads them to report that, "according to our calculations, a child under three years of age who lived with one genetic parent and one stepparent in the United States in 1976 was about seven times more likely . . . to become a validated child-abuse case in the American Humanitarian Association records than one who dwelt with two genetic parents."[25] When the criterion of abuse was made more stringent and limited to cases of actual murder, Daly and Wilson write that "rates in stepparent-genetic-parent households had grown to approximately *one hundred times* greater than in two-genetic-parent households."[26] Their explanation for this reality is nothing more than an update, from the perspective of contemporary evolutionary psychology,[27] of an insight that goes back to Aristotle and that became a central feature of Roman Catholic family theory in the thought of Thomas Aquinas: Biological parents on average are more invested in their children and less likely to harm them, just as they are less likely to harm their own flesh.[28]

Much the same story is found when one concentrates primarily on the phenomenon of sexual abuse. Legal scholar Robin Wilson summarizes the data well when she writes,

> Although children of all economic and racial backgrounds are at risk, sexual abuse is not distributed randomly through the child population. Instead, childhood sexual abuse occurs more often in

23. Daly and Wilson, *Homicide,* p. 19.

24. Daly and Wilson, *Homicide,* p. 20.

25. Martin Daly and Margo Wilson, *The Truth about Cinderella: A Darwinian View of Parental Love* (London: Weidenfeld and Nicolson, 1998), p. 27.

26. Daly and Wilson, *Truth about Cinderella,* p. 28.

27. Robert Trivers, "Parental Investment and Sexual Selection," in *Sexual Selection and the Descent of Man 1871-1971,* ed. Bernard Campbell (Chicago: Aldine, 1972), p. 139.

28. Thomas Aquinas, *Summa Contra Gentiles* (London: Burns, Oates, Washbourne, 1971), vol. 3, part 2, pp. 114, 118.

fractured families — that is, households that are created as a result of divorce or separation. For instance, a massive long-term study of children in New Zealand found that 65.5% of the victims of molestation came from families that "experience[ed] at least one change of parents before age 15," compared to 33.5% of children who did not experience abuse. Similarly, in Great Britain, adults who suffered sexual abuse as children were more likely to have been brought up in some living arrangement other than with their natural father and mother. A review of 42 publications likewise observed that "the majority of children who were sexually abused . . . appeared to have come from single-parent or reconstituted families.'| Within fractured families, moreover, it is almost exclusively the female child who is vulnerable to abuse. More than 40 social science studies and papers conclude that a girl's risk of being sexually abused escalates after divorce or separation, yet the same is not true for boys.[29]

What is the import of these data about the relation of kinship and physical and sexual violence? It seems to be that, on average, the growth in family pluralism, rather than helping us escape from the violence of some intact marriages and families, has actually increased the prevalence of physical and sexual violence in modern societies.

But we must isolate at least one more cause of family violence — the psychological causes. This is a vast field of investigation, and I will make only a couple of simple observations. I have little doubt that human evolutionary history has endowed both males and females with the capacity for reactive violence. From a theological perspective, this is probably part of the goodness of God's created order. God has given us the instinctive capacity to defend ourselves when attacked, and when this inclination is properly directed by a principled *habitus*, it is both morally justifiable and a blessing. Evolutionary psychologists tell us that men may be hardwired to become jealous — sometimes insanely jealous — over the unfaithfulness of their wives. It is hypothesized that this is a leftover from our evolutionary past when males wanted to protect themselves from unknowingly raising other men's children.[30]

But there must be another psychological factor. Psychoanalysts, especially the followers of the American psychiatrist Heinz Kohut, claim that

---

29. R. Wilson, "Fractured Families, Fragile Children — The Sexual Vulnerability of Girls in the Aftermath of Divorce," *Child and Family Law Quarterly* 14, no. 1 (2002): 2.

30. Daly and Wilson, *Homicide,* pp. 193, 196.

much reactive violence is triggered by blows to our self-regard.[31] This opens up a cause of domestic violence that has great relevance for pastoral ministry. Much violence is fueled by the way people in family groups threaten each other, insult each other, and destroy one another's sense of selfhood and dignity. In addition to addressing the large-scale cultural, social-systemic, and marital-decline problems of modern societies, the churches must learn how to place family and marital communication on a new basis — one that solves conflicts with justice and without destroying self-regard and inflaming violent narcissistic rage. We need, in fact, a new communicative ethic that helps to implement the love ethic of equal regard in the concrete processes of family life — in the processes of pursuing goals, solving problems, and resolving conflicts.

Directions and Solutions

Addressing domestic violence in modern societies requires a complex work of culture. There is no single solution — no "magic bullet," as we often say in the United States. I want to go back over the four causes of domestic violence that I have just discussed and say more about how they can be addressed from the standpoint of the pastoral and public-policy strategies of the Christian churches and their various ministries.

I want to start with the last cause that I discussed. This was the so-called psychological cause — that combination of self-regard and reactive violence. I am not willing to call either self-regard or reactive violence sinful as such. On the other hand, we must not eliminate the element of sin that qualifies both our reactive violence and our self-regard. We are entitled by the goodness of creation to a healthy reactive protectiveness and a healthy self-regard. But human sin can corrupt and misdirect both of these natural and justifiable tendencies. This is one of the many places where Louis Janssens's distinction between moral and premoral goods is relevant. The natural self-regard that gives us a sense of self-cohesion and the natural reactive violence that protects us when threatened are *both premoral goods and not sinful in themselves*. But whether they are fully moral goods, in contrast to premoral goods, depends on their being guided by a love ethic of equal regard. Our natural self-regard and reactiveness can both be distorted by sin. Sin is precisely our universal tendency to secure

---

31. Heinz Kohut, *The Restoration of the Self* (New York: International Universities Press, 1977), p. 121.

ourselves against anxiety by excessive and morally unjustified uses of these natural goods of self-regard and reactive defensiveness.

Modern families need to learn a communicative ethic that is guided by the principle of equal regard and sustained by a profound sense of the grace of God. But what do I mean by a communicative ethic? I refer to new developments in the field of marriage education that are now gaining attention around the world. The old economic dependencies and authority structures that used to keep marriages and families together are collapsing in the modern world. Married couples and their children must now learn to stay together because they both love each other and can freely communicate with one another without sending each other into depression, defensiveness, and violent rage. The works of social scientists such as John Gottman, Howard Markman, Scott Stanley, David Olsen, and Harville Hendrix have isolated some of the basic rules of good marital, family, and parent-child communication. In many ways, their findings simply make more concrete the abstract love ethic of equal regard.

Good communication, especially around conflict, involves speaking for oneself without projecting thoughts into the mind of the other. It means listening carefully to the other, communicating to the other what one has heard them say, asking the other to validate your understanding of what the other is trying to communicate, and having the patience to endure this process until deeper shared understanding is achieved.[32] These principles can be made even more concrete. John Gottman tells us that men are especially inclined to become agitated when communicating about conflicts; hence, wives must learn to communicate with their husbands without unduly raising their defensive anxiety. Gottman also tells us that women become depressed because they often feel they cannot influence their husbands; this means, in turn, that men need to learn how to be open to influence and how to communicate this openness to their wives.[33]

It is my conviction that living these simple yet challenging rules of communication is actually a way to concretely implement the love ethic of equal regard. I also believe that this love ethic should be easier for Christians who come to their family relationships with the belief that one's spouse and offspring are children of God and for this reason deserve ulti-

---

32. H. Markman, S. Stanley, and S. L. Blumberg, *Fighting for Your Marriage: Positive Steps for Preventing Divorce and Preserving a Lasting Love* (San Francisco: Jossey-Bass, 1994).

33. John Gottman, *Why Marriages Succeed or Fail* (New York: Simon and Schuster, 1994), pp. 144-54.

mate respect. It also should be easier for Christians who enjoy the empowerment and calm of the grace of God, which give us patience to endure in the midst of difficult communications.

Marriage education in many ways already has been a part of Catholic marriage preparation, but some scholars think its excellent theological instruction should be supplemented by more emphasis on the ethics and skills of the communicative process. Furthermore, many experts believe that secular versions of education in this communicative ethic should become a universal aspect of the public education in all societies, long before young people actually become involved with each other romantically. This leads to the question of whether the churches should advocate marriage education in state-supported schools.

I will conclude by briefly, and I fear inadequately, pointing to ways the churches should address the other three causes of domestic violence that I discussed earlier. First, although authentic Christianity is not a major source of the kind of male dominance that leads to domestic violence, inauthentic Christianity may be a source. Hence, authentic Christianity must do everything possible to reclaim its basic impulse toward male humility and servanthood and critique those manifestations of male dominance and violence wherever they appear, both within and outside the churches.

Second, the Christian churches must resist and critique the forces of modernity that undermine family cohesion and that create the tensions that lead to domestic violence by both men and women, husbands and wives, fathers and mothers. Families probably need appropriate amounts of support from government and market in the form of tax breaks, flexible work hours, adequate vacation time, medical help, adequate child care, and flexible entry and exit from the workforce to match the rhythms of childbirth and child care. The churches should try to restrain the marketplace from unduly impinging on the lifeworld of family love and dependencies. Government supports are needed, as Catholic subsidiarity theory has so wisely argued, but they must be fine-tuned so that they do not themselves replace the natural parental investments and mutual dependencies required for family solidarity.

Third and finally, the churches must influence national law and legislatures to support disrupted families but do this without taking the route of giving a variety of informal living arrangements the moral and legal equivalence to marriage. Cohabiting couples may need legal mechanisms that will help them solve issues of violence and financial injustice, but this must not happen by making unintentional and nonpublic living arrangements equal to publicly witnessed and intentional marriage. One of the greatest contributions of the Roman Catholic Church to Western culture was the idea that the essence of marriage consisted of an intentional and mutual consent made in the present by the man and woman to take each other as husband and wife.[34] This Catholic contribution — this defining of valid marriage around the idea of consent — is something that this poor Protestant lecturer before you today never wants to relinquish. To lose marriage as an intentional institution marked by free consent will not solve any of the problems of families today, least of all the problem of domestic violence. I urge you to use your moral authority to retain in modern societies the essence of marriage built on free and publicly witnessed consent, partially in an effort to reduce domestic violence.

---

34. John Witte Jr., *From Sacrament to Contract: Marriage, Religion, and Law in the Western Tradition* (Louisville: Westminster John Knox, 1997), pp. 25-26, 32-35.

PART V

A Retrospective: Method in Practical Theology and the Family

The Relation of Practical Theology
to Theological Ethics (2005)

This chapter has two other incarnations. A much shorter form of it appeared as the appendix to the second edition of *From Culture Wars to Common Ground* (2000). This expanded version has been translated into German and will be published in a book on the relation of theological ethics to practical theology edited by the German theologians Michael Welker and Friedrich Schweitzer.*

This essay basically describes the practical-theological method used in the first edition of *From Culture Wars to Common Ground* (1997). When my colleagues and I wrote the first edition, we decided not to burden the book with abstract discussions about practical-theological method. We attempted simply to *do* good practical theology and not to *write about how to do it.* We often used among ourselves the analogy of the movie; we wanted to show the movie — let it unfold before the reader's eyes — rather than take the reader into the backroom where the retakes, editing, and soundwork were taking place.

Yet, it was obvious to many that *From Culture Wars to Common Ground* was highly informed by the practical-theological methodology outlined in *A Fundamental Practical Theology*. This essay, more than any other in this book, tries to make clear what that connection is all about. As I have pointed out in earlier chapters, the four steps of a fundamental practical theology and the five dimensions of theologically informed practical reason can all be found in *From Culture Wars to Common Ground* just as they can be found, to lesser degrees, in

*Michael Welker and Friedrich Schweitzer, eds., *Reconsidering the Boundaries between Theological Disciplines* (Münster: LIT, 2005), pp. 161-75.

Reweaving the Social Tapestry, Marriage and Modernization, and the chapters of this book. But the method and argument are complex; this essay may help make them more clear. In addition, this chapter tries to state once again why practical theology and theological ethics must be dialectically related into something like what I have frequently called a practical-theological ethics.

In this essay, I will develop further my view of the relation of practical theology to theological ethics. I will do this by illustrating how my views of this issue function to address a concrete practical issue — the problem of the worldwide transformation of families. Of course, the world as a whole is too large an arena to discuss. I will confine my remarks primarily to the United States on the assumption that the changes there have some continuities with those experienced in other countries. Nonetheless, the United States comes to these transformations out of a unique history. In my view, it is part of the task of both practical theology and theological ethics to account for how this history has influenced both family theory and family change in America.

I will develop my views by commenting on the implicit methodology of a recent book I co-authored entitled *From Culture Wars to Common Ground: Religion and the American Family Debate.*[1] It is the summary book of an eleven-book series published by the Religion, Culture, and Family Project located at the University of Chicago.[2] Although the subject matter of the book is the American debate over the *family,* it makes strong implicit claims about the nature of the disciplines of practical theology and theological ethics. It also addresses the relation of these two disciplines to the social sciences. These claims were not directly argued on the pages of the first edition of the book. We decided simply to enact our methodological commitments in the way we made our arguments rather than burden the reader with the technical matters that methodology entails. In this essay, I will try to make these commitments more visible, especially as they serve to illustrate a view of the relation of practical theology to theological ethics.

My claims go like this. When done rightly, good practical theology

1. Don Browning, Bonnie Miller-McLemore, Pamela Couture, Bernie Lyon, and Robert Franklin, *From Culture Wars to Common Ground: Religion and the American Family Debate* (Louisville: Westminster John Knox, 1997, 2000).

2. The Religion, Culture, and Family Project began in 1991 and has been funded by a series of grants from the Division of Religion of the Lilly Endowment, Inc.

and good theological ethics should look more alike than is generally the case. And, when done well, both should look more like good social science than is often thought to be appropriate. Let me be more specific. Practical theology in its various expressions is often thought to have responsibility for making good descriptions of the contexts of faithful Christian action and then offering good strategies of transformation in situations of Christian practice. I agree with this initial characterization of the obligations of practical theology. But I also have argued that practical theology must take more responsibility than it generally does for rendering critical judgments about *the norms* that should guide transformative practices. On the other hand, it is generally said that theological ethics has the task of articulating the norms of faith action; but I hold that it should also take more responsibility than it generally does for analyzing contexts of action and projecting strategies of transformation. I say this because of my conviction that the way ethical norms are formulated is necessarily affected by both the descriptions that precede them and the possible strategies that follow them. I argue for this strong relation between descriptive and normative thinking even though, as will become obvious below, I am not an advocate of what is generally called situation ethics.

If practical theology and theological ethics take their descriptive obligations seriously, not only will they look more like the social sciences but the social sciences will look more like forms of theology. Although we seldom ask the social sciences to take explicit responsibility for their implicit normative horizons, it is increasingly recognized that they cannot avoid normative commitments of some kind.[3] Hence, the difference, for instance, between theological ethics and the social sciences is whether they respectively choose to be implicit or explicit about their descriptions and norms; theological ethics chooses to be explicit about stating and defending its norms and implicit about its descriptions while the social sciences tend to be explicit about stating and defending their descriptions and implicit about their norms. Practical theology, when correctly pursued, should help mediate between these extremes by becoming explicit and critical about both its descriptions and its norms.

These views about the relation of practical theology, theological ethics, and the social sciences silently informed every page of *From Culture*

---

3. For works that inquire into the relation of ethics and the social sciences, see *Social Science As Moral Inquiry,* ed. Norma Haan, Robert Bellah, Paul Rabinow, and William Sullivan (New York: Columbia University Press, 1983); Alan Wolfe, *Whose Keeper? Social Science and Moral Obligation* (Berkeley: University of California Press, 1989).

Wars to Common Ground. In the preface of the first edition, we wrote that from one perspective our book could be understood as an "exercise in hermeneutic social science" similar to the method of the well-known *Habits of the Heart*. We also contended that our book has a far more "explicit argument for its normative religious and ethical" claims than does *Habits* From another perspective, we said that our book could be seen as a "project in practical theology." Because of our conviction that practical theology should take responsibility for critically defending its norms of action, we were in that statement already assuming an intimate relation between practical theology and theological ethics. These statements now obligate me to go further and attempt to answer more definitively the following questions: What is hermeneutic social science? What is practical theology? What is theological ethics? Why are they all, when rightly conceived, so similar yet still different? ·

In *From Culture Wars to Common Ground* we follow Hans-Georg Gadamer and the authors of *Habits of the Heart* in seeing all social science as seeking not just objective description and explanation but understanding as well. It is an understanding, however, as Gadamer argues, that resembles a conversation or dialogue. In fact, social science is from these perspectives a conversation or dialogue, as all attempts to understand anything must necessarily be.[4] The authors of *Habits* write in one of its footnotes, "Hans-Georg Gadamer has provided us with valuable guidance in our understanding of our work as always involving a dialogue with the tradition out of which we come."[5] By dialogue with tradition, they mean dialogue with some of the classics or basic monuments that provide the ideals and norms of a tradition. In *Habits* this dialogue with tradition was accomplished by describing and interpreting much of contemporary American life *in light of* the norms and ideals of two overlapping but distinguishable historic strands that shaped our democracy — the civic Republican tradition and the biblical covenantal tradition.[6] The central argument of *Habits* is that social science inevitably must locate itself within some historical tradition, and its descriptions and explanations of contemporary trends to some extent always must be influenced by the ideals informing that tradition. Social science, according to *Habits,* should ac-

---

4. Robert Bellah, Richard Madsen, William Sullivan, Ann Swidler, and Steven Tipton, *Habits of the Heart* (Berkeley: University of California Press, 1985), pp. 297-307; Hans-Georg Gadamer, *Truth and Method* (New York: Crossroad, 1982), pp. 330-33.

5. Bellah et al., *Habits of the Heart,* p. 330, n. 11.

6. Bellah et al., *Habits of the Heart,* pp. 28-31.

knowledge this truth and be more accountable for acknowledging its rootedness in tradition.

Gadamer develops and grounds these ideas in his monumental *Truth and Method*. He tells us that all dialogues or conversations have something of a circular character, but it is a circle that is not necessarily a vicious one.[7] The circle can be open, make progress, and actually deepen understanding. Viewed as a conversation, the process of understanding entails an exchange of questions and answers. Gadamer saw the purpose of the conversation as practical; its goal is to produce a working understanding between parties, to resolve conflicts, and to discover orientations to action.[8] The questions that we bring to any dialogue come out of our own history and all the histories before us that have shaped who we are. The history that has shaped us also affects the very way that we ask our questions; this history, and its implicit ideals, shape how we interpret the world before us and evaluate its tensions and conflicts. To even understand our own questions and our initial interpretation of what is happening in the situations surrounding us, we must deepen our understanding of the ideals that have colored what Gadamer called our "effective history."[9] To describe responsibly the social situations of today, we must also understand the history that has shaped these situations.

These insights inform my book *A Fundamental Practical Theology*.[10] This book in turn shaped much, but not all, of the methodological steps of *From Culture Wars to Common Ground. A Fundamental Practical Theology* converts Gadamer's hermeneutic circle into a comprehensive theological method that also has similarities with the social-science method that Robert Bellah and his colleagues describe. When Gadamer's hermeneutic circle is applied to theology, it turns all of theology into practical theology (what I have called a "fundamental practical theology"). In turn, it makes what we generally call practical theology — religious education, pastoral care, liturgies, and so on — into the culmination or last step of theology. According to this model, the steps or stages of fundamental practical theological reflection are (1) descriptive theology, (2) historical theology, (3) systematic theology and theological ethics, and (4) strategic practical theology.

Good theology, when viewed from the perspective of Gadamer's close association between understanding and praxis, should address problems

---

7. Gadamer, *Truth and Method,* pp. 235-40.
8. Gadamer, *Truth and Method,* p. 289.
9. Gadamer, *Truth and Method,* pp. 267-74.
10. Don Browning, *A Fundamental Practical Theology* (Minneapolis: Fortress, 1991).

and conflicts in contemporary social practices. It should try to describe these conflicts and, to some extent, explain what is producing them. All of this is part of *descriptive theology*. Because it should describe contemporary situations partially in light of the ideals and norms that shape present experience, theology should then go backward from the present into the past to determine whether it understands its ideals rightly and in their proper context. This task of interpretation and retrieval is the purpose of *historical theology*. Theology should then try to gain a more systematic or comprehensive understanding of these ideals or classics — ideals or classics that are generally conveyed in narratives and metaphors. Theology at this stage should also attempt to test these ideals in various ways. This is the task of what is often called *systematic theology* and its closely associated discipline of *theological ethics*. But when systematic theology and theological ethics are seen as part of a more inclusive fundamental practical theology, the original practical questions that first stimulated theological understanding organize and give direction to the inner, systematic moments of theology and ethics. Finally, the theologian (or theologians, if the task is collaborative) should return to the original situation with these ideals — now better understood and tested — to determine what light they can throw on the original context of action. Deeper interpretations of this situation should now be possible. And certainly, part of the test of these clarified ideals and norms should come from their capacity to order, heal, and nurture the persons and groups in the original situation of conflict and tension. This is the task of *strategic practical theology.*[11]

Descriptive Theology and Families

From Culture Wars to Common Ground is organized into four parts reflecting these four steps of a fundamental practical theology. Part I is titled "The Issues" and is aimed at accomplishing the tasks of descriptive theology. It describes from several perspectives the contemporary American debate and the situation of today's families. It asks the question, are there signs of increased family disruption in North American society, and, if so, how should they be understood from the perspective of Christian ideals and classics? This inquiry required, we believed, a "thick description" of the contemporary situation of families. We first listened at length to a number

---

11. See Browning, *A Fundamental Practical Theology,* pp. 47-56, for a more expanded discussion of these four movements or steps.

of real families — a technique used by *Habits* and employed by co-author Miller-McLemore in her work on motherhood.[12] The authors also tried to listen to each other, and we even revealed to our readers some of the tensions that we experienced as a team about interpreting family changes. This helped locate us in our unique histories and allowed our own individual voices and questions to shine forth; this is a procedure consistent with hermeneutic social science and now being used in the methods of practical theology exemplified by the writings of Miller-McLemore, Couture, Lyon, Franklin, and Browning.[13] As a more abstract part of the descriptive task, we also tried to set forth the demographic trends which help explain the rapid increase in divorce, fatherlessness, nonmarital births, and the decline in well-being of mothers and children that has gripped American life over the last four decades. These trends include the measurable rise of individualism in Western societies since the Enlightenment.[14] They also include the absorption of both men and women into the wage economy and the way this has drawn both sexes out of the home and away from children, and decreased the dependence of husband and wife on each other.[15] This descriptive task also meant showing how poverty and racism have interacted with individualism and market pressures to hurt families.[16] And finally, it involved describing the myriad new psychological stresses, most of which are produced by market pressures on working husbands and wives, that damage families and marriages.

In describing the factors contributing to family disruption, we wanted to accomplish something of the rhythm of understanding-explanation-understanding that philosopher Paul Ricoeur thinks so important for any descriptive and interpretive endeavor, be it in the area of social science, philosophy, or theology.[17] Our concern with causal factors

---

12. Bonnie Miller-McLemore, *Also a Mother: Work and Family as a Theological Dilemma* (Nashville: Abingdon, 1994).

13. See, for example, Pamela Couture, *Blessed Are the Poor: Women's Poverty, Family Policy, and Practical Theology* (Nashville: Abingdon, 1991); K. Brynolf Lyon, *Toward a Practical Theology of Aging* (Philadelphia: Fortress, 1985); Robert M. Franklin, *Another Day's Journey: Black Churches Confronting the American Crisis* (Minneapolis: Fortress, 1997).

14. Ron Lesthaeghe, "A Century of Demographic and Cultural Change in Western Europe: An Exploration of Underlying Dimensions," *Population and Development Review* 9, no. 3 (September 1983): 411-35.

15. Gary Becker, *The Economic Approach to Human Behavior* (Chicago: University of Chicago Press, 1976), pp. 169-250.

16. Browning et al., *From Culture Wars to Common Ground*, pp. 64-65.

17. Paul Ricoeur, *Hermeneutics and the Human Sciences* (Cambridge: Cambridge University Press, 1981), pp. 61-64.

contributed to the task of explanation. But the task of explanation is within this model a submoment of the wider concern to understand present family changes in light of the effective histories of the past. Hence, we contextualized these explanatory efforts by placing them within the larger narrative in which they occurred. In Chapter 4, written by Pamela Couture, a narrative history was set forth chronicling the diverse eighteenth- and nineteenth-century family traditions in the United States and how they interacted with modernizing trends to help create the more discrete demographic facts mentioned above. This entailed describing the covenantal model of the family associated with New England Puritanism. It involved describing the hierarchical model of family found in the southern Atlantic states, a model which also reflected, even in America, the English monarchy and its power over both church and family. It required telling the story of the influence on families of the largely Methodist-inspired revivals of the Second Great Revival (1813-38) and how they religiously sanctioned the divided gender spheres created by the industrial revolution.[18] Such religious and cultural histories are often ignored by social-science descriptions that use mainly economic models to explain transformations in family patterns. These historical narratives are crucial for understanding the larger struggles surrounding and stimulating social-systemic and economic trends.

Much of this narrative history was about how diverse expressions of American Christianity advanced different interpretations of the Western biblical and theological classics pertaining to family. Even today, the North American debate over the family is significantly shaped by these nineteenth-century interpretations of the ideals and norms of Jewish and Christian Scriptures and traditions. There is little doubt that most of these attempts to understand Jewish and Christian perspectives on family functioned to legitimate forms of patriarchy and divided spheres of public and private occupied by men and women. This raises the question, how should we *really* interpret Genesis, Jesus, Paul, Augustine, Aquinas, Luther, Calvin, and others on family? Did the nineteenth- and early-twentieth-century commentaries sometimes interpret these scriptural and historical texts inadequately? For instance, did they see a patriarchy in the texts that was not quite there or not there in the way that they thought it was?

18. May Ryan, *Cradle of the Middle Class: The Family in Oneida County, New York, 1790-1865* (Cambridge: Cambridge University Press, 1981); for our discussion of these historical periods, see *From Culture Wars to Common Ground*, pp. 74-84.

Families and Historical Theology

Part II is titled "Traditions," but it begins by addressing the questions about families developed in Part I and then takes them back into history as guides to historical retrieval. This section of the book is an exercise in historical theology. Even there, we gradually move backward in history from the near past to the distant past — from twentieth- and nineteenth-century American history to late medieval Roman Catholic and early Protestant sources (Aquinas, Roman Catholic canon law, and Luther). Then we went farther back to early Christian understandings of family as these developed within the Greco-Roman context of urban Mediterranean life. We carried our initial practical questions each step of the way as we moved back into history to understand, and sometimes to criticize, the key monuments, texts, and events that shaped Western and, finally, American ideas and ideals about family.

In Chapter 5, titled "Honor, Shame, and Equality in Early Christian Families," we advanced a different reading of biblical texts than has usually been put forth by either progressive or conservative interpreters. It is certainly different than almost all nineteenth-century American interpreters, who had so much to do with creating twentieth-century ideals of the traditional bread-earning father and domestic mother. Although early Christianity was still embedded in the patriarchy of antiquity, when interpreted against the background of Greco-Roman honor-shame codes and their celebration of male dominance and agency, the earliest strands of Christianity can be seen to have moved in the direction of what we called the equal-regard family and marriage.[19] In this view of families in the New Testament world, the headship and power of males should be seen as more properly associated with the civic family codes of the Greco-Roman world. The earliest pre-Pauline and Pauline forms of Christianity should be understood as in tension with these codes. In fact, it is more accurate to view these early Christian movements as transforming or even undermining antique patriarchy in the direction of more gender-egalitarian forms of marriage and family. We concluded that the theological task for our time is to extend this more properly Christian ethic of equal regard rather than carrying forward and wrongly legitimating the patriarchal family ethic associated with the cultural context of early Christianity rather than with more properly Christian impulses themselves.

---

19. Browning et al., *From Culture Wars to Common Ground,* pp. 141-47.

Families and Theological Ethics

Part III is titled "The Voices." It is primarily a dialogue between our emerging constructive position on family issues — what we call "critical familism" — and other contemporary voices in the family debate such as feminism, the therapeutic movement, conservative pro-family movements, and certain economic points of view. Critical familism is built on a love ethic of equal regard which I will explain more fully in later paragraphs. In developing these ideas, this section of the book also accomplishes some of the critical tasks of systematic theology and theological ethics. We try to state our position more systematically and develop core normative ideals more clearly. We deepen our understanding of the tradition and test it in light of other contemporary perspectives.

This section shows that *From Culture Wars to Common Ground* practices what David Tracy calls a "critical correlational" view of theology, in both its systematic and its ethical expressions. But notice, these more systematic and critical moments are located within the middle of a practical hermeneutical circle that begins and ends with questions coming from concrete situations. Or, to say it differently, these more systematic theological moments are surrounded and focused by the questions of a fundamental practical theology. Nonetheless, these more systematic moments of theology help us correlate our position, that is, find analogies and differences, with other competing interpretations of contemporary families. The correlational task also forces us to critically test our views in light of these alternatives and to give reasons in defense of our point of view.

Families and Strategic Practical Theology

Finally, Part IV is titled "Directions" and is an exercise in the fourth step of a fundamental practical theology — the step of strategic practical theology. Here we return to the contemporary American family situation and develop a more comprehensive practical theology for families that builds on the foregoing questions and investigations. This section also contains nearly a score of concrete recommendations for both the family life of churches and their efforts to influence public policy and the common good.

In this section, we develop more fully, with the help of psychoanalysis, a life-cycle theory of love as equal regard. This is an ethic we think is a useable guide to both Christian families and families in the wider society. An ethic of equal regard applies first of all to husband and wife, but it also applies to parents and children. To say this does not mean that adult parents grant equal decision-making power to their four- and five-year-old sons and daughters. But it does mean that parents should raise their children in such a way that they can become adults with the capacity to live by equal regard in relation with their parents, each other, and the wider community. A life-cycle theory of equal regard also holds that the meaning of this ethic shifts, even between husband and wife, as they find themselves at different points of the pilgrimage of life — the early years of education and career development, the years of childbirth and child-rearing, and the later years of ripe maturity and old age. The practical theology of *From Culture Wars to Common Ground* is also a public theology, as Kyle Pasewark and Garrett Paul grasped in their insightful interpretation of our family theory in *The Emphatic Christian Center.*[20]

The Role of Theological Ethics within a Fundamental Practical Theology

There is another strand of methodological steps that runs throughout *From Culture Wars to Common Ground.* This strand throws light on theological ethics and its crucial role within a more encompassing fundamental practical theology. It has to do with how practical theology invariably will require explicit theological-ethical arguments for which its practitioners should take responsibility. Because of this, the five dimensions of practical-moral reason developed in *A Fundamental Practical Theology* are also employed in this book on the family. What are these dimensions? *A Fundamental Practical Theology* argues that all moral thinking — whether secular or religious, Christian or non-Christian — contains five levels or dimensions: (1) a visional level generally conveyed through narrative and metaphor (often quite vague but still present in so-called secular moral thinking); (2) an obligational level guided by some implicit or explicit moral principle (neighbor love, the categorical imperative, or principles of utility); (3) a theory of premoral goods (goods that are satisfying but not directly moral, such as health, pleasure, or economic power); (4) some the-

---

20. Kyle Pasewark and Garrett Paul, *The Emphatic Christian Center* (Nashville: Abingdon, 1999). We also refer the interested reader to the recent book by Robert Kinast, *What Are They Saying about Theological Reflection?* (Mahwah, N.J.: Paulist, 2000). In this book, Kinast provides his own guide to the methodological relation between *A Fundamental Practical Theology* and *From Culture Wars to Common Ground.*

ory of the social, economic, and environmental pressures that constrain and limit our actions and wants; and, finally, (5) specific practices guided by very concrete but often changing rules.[21] Morality is thick, and to describe moral action requires description at all of these levels. It follows from this thickness that constructive ethical thinking is complex, and that the good thinker, or thinking community, should be making sound judgments at all of these different levels.

Where do these dimensions show up in *From Culture Wars to Common Ground?* Surprisingly, we Protestant authors concluded that the sophisticated family theory of Thomas Aquinas illustrated several of these dimensions. We amended Aquinas, but we also found a provocative model in his writings. Aquinas stood at the juncture between the accomplishments of Peter Lombard and the Catholic canonists and the later amendments of the Roman Catholic tradition in the Protestant Reformation. In fact, the first three of my five dimensions of ethical thinking — the visional, the obligational, and the premoral — are stunningly evident in Thomas Aquinas's explanation of and moral-theological argument for matrimony. Because of its clarity and relative adequacy, we use Aquinas as something of a model for our view of marriage and family and our understanding of love as equal regard.[22]

Here is the core of Aquinas's argument. First, I will discuss the level of premoral goods — dimension three of the five levels. Aquinas was perceptive in identifying some of the naturalistic goods that are satisfied by pair bonding between human male and female, such as the joint care of highly dependent human infants likely to be born of this bond, parental recognition and investment in the child by both father and mother (more difficult to achieve for the male), mutual helpfulness between male and female, and mutual sexual satisfaction (often spoken of negatively as avoiding lust or paying the marital debt, but nonetheless acknowledged).[23] Aquinas tells us that pair bonding between mother and father helps actualize these premoral goods. These goods and their actualization constitute a natural web of attractions, fulfillments, and reinforcements that are enjoyable to individual members of the couple as well as serviceable to the common good of the human race.

21. For an introduction to the five dimensions, see Browning, *A Fundamental Practical Theology,* pp. 139-70.

22. See *From Culture Wars to Common Ground,* pp. 107-24, for an interpretation of Aquinas where these three levels become evident.

23. See *From Culture Wars to Common Ground,* pp. 115-18, for Aquinas's discussion of these naturalistic conditions.

But these goods and their realization do not alone dictate the overall moral character of matrimonial bonding; they do not alone determine whether the bonding should be one of equal regard, of aristocratic rule by the husband, or perhaps even be polygynous. At the ethical or obligation level — level two — Aquinas argues that the bonding of husband and wife should be a matter of equity and friendship. This ethical principle is close to, but not identical with, our love ethic of equal regard. For Aquinas, a relation between husband and wife should be one of friendship because both female and male are made in the image of God, although, as we point out, Aquinas never fully moved beyond Aristotle's proportionate understanding of this friendship and equity. Yet his placing of the premoral good of matrimony within a more inclusive principle of moral obligation involving mutual friendship and equity is instructive for a critical grounding of matrimony and family as well as for a thick, multidimensional understanding of the love ethic of equal regard. Equal regard, when developed with Thomistic and Aristotelian resources, organizes a variety of premoral goods. On the other hand, when one views equal regard primarily within a Kantian framework, as the respected theological ethicist Gene Outka does, it tends to be limited to a thinner view of equal respect, omitting careful consideration of the premoral goods that equality shares and distributes.[24]

Finally, Aquinas places these two levels within an overarching theological narrative that helps illustrate the function and importance of the visional level of practical moral thinking. First, the biblical story about God's creation of the world gives him his understanding of the *imago Dei* in both male and female — the grounds for marriage as friendship and mutuality. The foundation of friendship in the doctrine of creation must be acknowledged even though, as I have hinted already, Aquinas believed the image of God was less perfectly manifest in women than in men. Second, his narrative of how the love of husband for wife should be modeled after the story of the unbreakable love of Christ for the church gave Thomas his argument for the permanence of marriage. My colleagues and I, in contrast to Aquinas, extended the Christ-church analogy and applied it to both husband and wife, an extension for which there are innerbiblical grounds. This distinguishes our view from most theologically

24. Gene Outka, *Agape: An Ethical Analysis* (New Haven: Yale University Press, 1972); see also his "Universal Love and Impartiality," in *The Love Commandments: Essays in Christian Ethics and Moral Philosophy,* ed. Edmund Santurri and William Werpehowski (Washington, D.C.: Georgetown University Press, 1992), pp. 1-92.

conservative perspectives that see this sacrificial love as primarily the responsibility of the husband; in our view, both husband and wife can and sometimes should play the christic role in marriage.[25] Furthermore, we use the Christ-church narrative and analogy to explain the role of the cross in marital love and not just to argue for the permanence or endurance of marriage. The sacrificial or self-giving love of the cross functions for us to revitalize and restore love as equal regard and mutuality. We follow Louis Janssens and several contemporary feminists in viewing sacrificial love (the meaning of the cross) not as an end in itself but as the second mile of enduring love sometimes needed to restore the core of love, that is, love as equal regard and mutuality.[26] The self-sacrificial moment of love, modeled after Christ's love for the church, is not in itself, in our view, an absolute impediment to divorce.

The point of this technical discussion is this: A full understanding of our love ethic of equal regard, as Aquinas developed it, exhibits the top three of the five dimensions of practical moral thinking: the level of premoral goods, the principled level of moral obligation (in our case, love as equal regard), and the narrative level that surrounds, gives meaning to, and actually informs the first two dimensions. The last two dimensions — social-ecological constraints and the concrete rules of marital practices — were constantly examined in both our descriptions of the contemporary situation and our historical work on the past. The importance of these last two dimensions of theological-ethical reasoning is often overlooked. Narratives, principles of obligation, and lists and hierarchies of relevant premoral goods are not enough for a thoroughly concrete ethic. Much of the debate in systematic theology and theological ethics remains at these more abstract levels. Productive work is often done by systematic theology and theological ethics at these levels — especially the narrative and principled levels. In choosing the adequacy of a neo-Thomistic formulation of equal regard, critically appropriating a list of premoral goods that marriage and family organize, and surrounding this inner-ethical core with a narrative about creation and the redemptive love of Christ, we are building on and profiting from debates at these abstract levels. But a fundamental practical theology (the full task of theology as a whole) should place these abstract refinements within a variety of concrete issues pertaining to cur-

25. Browning et al., *From Culture Wars to Common Ground,* p. 284.

26. See Louis Janssens's especially powerful formulation of the relation of mutual love to self-sacrificial love in his "Norms and Priorities of a Love Ethics," *Louvain Studies* 6 (1977): 207-38.

rent practices and constraints. This is what we did in our first moment of a fundamental practical theology — the moment of descriptive theology — when we tried to describe and explain both the practices *and* the cultural and social-systemic threats to contemporary families.

What is the point of both describing and normatively addressing the social and ecological constraints that shape families and the concrete rules that order their practices? The point is this: The social and ecological contexts surrounding marriage and family have drastically changed, and these changes have implications for the *concrete rules that should order the life of families.* As we saw above, changes in the situation of families are primarily due to the intensification of individualism as a cultural value and its interaction with the spread of modernization. One expression of these cultural and social-systemic forces is the fact that today both men and women have been drawn into ever deeper participation in the wage economy; this has developed partially out of the needs of the economic system and partially out of the drive to self-fulfillment by workers. Another expression of modernization has been the increasing spread of government into the lives of families through welfare and taxation. Habermas speaks of these two extensions of modernization through market and government bureaucracy as a colonization or "technizing of the life world."[27] The move of both men and women, husbands and wives, into the wage economy has weakened the mutual dependencies of marriage and family. The spread of government into the lives of families has offered troubled families needed assistance; but it has also provided alternative sources of help beyond spouse and other family members, thereby weakening patterns of dependency that hold families together. What do these two forms of modernization and their implications for the social-ecology of families mean for a love ethic of equal regard informed by the Christian narrative?

Allow me quickly to make some observations and also remind the reader that fuller amplifications of these points can be found in the pages of *From Culture Wars to Common Ground* as well as *A Fundamental Practical Theology.* First, a full implementation of a love ethic of equal regard demands at least that both men and women have the opportunity to participate to the extent of their desires and talents in both the public world of market and politics as well as the private world of housekeeping and child care. But to accomplish this requires changes in both the social system and the skills and competencies of couples. New emphases on marriage

---

27. Jürgen Habermas, *The Theory of Communicative Action,* vol. 2 (Boston: Beacon, 1987), p. 183.

education are required to help couples, long before marriage, learn the communication skills required to resolve the tensions of work and family life in modern societies.[28] Theologically, these communicative skills should be understood as competencies required to implement intersubjectively the love ethic of equal regard.

But the tensions between work and family cannot be left to be solved by the communicative competencies of individual couples. Both market and government must also help. One of the more popular ideas advanced in *From Culture Wars to Common Ground* is the concept of the sixty-hour workweek. This is the idea that a couple with children should not work in the wage economy more than a total of sixty hours between them. Research suggests that this arrangement is more satisfying than either full employment involving parents eighty to ninety hours between them a week in the wage economy or more traditional arrangements where one of the spouses, generally the husband, works forty to fifty hours each week outside of the home.[29] The sixty-hour week can be arranged thirty-thirty or twenty-forty as the couple's circumstances and talents permit. The sixty-hour week provides the stimulation of outside employment to both husband and wife. It also leaves more time for spouses to be with each other and for parents to be with their children. In this arrangement, husbands generally contribute more to housework and child care because they realize that their wives also work outside of the home. The sixty-hour workweek is something on which both market and government must cooperate in order to effect the social-systemic changes needed. There must be far more part-time jobs with benefits, more job sharing, more work at home. In order to actualize fully an ethic of equal regard, an analysis and change of the systems of modern society are required. A revised-correlational fundamental practical theology must engage both the world of religio-cultural ideas and norms and the world of productive and communicative social systems.

This needed change in the social systems of modern nations is one of many important factors that went into formulating the concept of critical familism. Critical familism is defined as the "theory, practice, and ecology" of a new family ideal, what we called the "committed, intact, equal-regard, public-private family."[30] *From Culture Wars to Common Ground* gave

---

28. Browning et al., *From Culture Wars to Common Ground*, pp. 202-18.

29. Jacqueline Olds, Richard Schwartz, Susan Eisen, William Betcher, and Anthony Van Niel, "Part-Time Employment and Marital Well-Being" (Belmont, Mass.: Department of Psychiatry, Harvard University, McLean Hospital, 1993).

30. For this summary statement, see Browning et al., *From Culture Wars to Common Ground*, p. 2.

a gentle boost to this religio-cultural ideal, but did so, we hope, with genuine concern for the welfare and dignity of all families. This is where social analysis comes into the picture once again. The forces disrupting families today are momentous. They cannot easily be changed, and even if change is possible (and we believe that it is) it will come slowly and unevenly. Both church and society must present their normative family visions in such a way as not to harm or disparage families that do not live up to these goals. Government should support families in their moments of need but not in ways that trap them into perpetual dependencies. Churches should reach out to all families as part of the church's mission to those in need. But they should do this without compromising their normative visions. There are inner-theological resources for achieving the delicate task of supporting all families yet holding forth normative visions of strong families and even Christian families. We developed the concept of "ironic-realism" derived from the Gospel of Mark.[31] We argued that the genius of authentic Christianity is its capacity to project commanding ideals and point toward perfection but also to admit that sin leads us to fall short of that which is expected. In the Sermon on the Mount, Jesus tells his disciples to "Be perfect, therefore, as your heavenly Father is perfect" (Matt. 5:48). On the other hand, when the rich young ruler called Jesus "Good Teacher," he replied, "Why do you call me good? No one is good but God alone" (Luke 18:18-19). There is an ironic relation between ideals and realities that runs throughout the teachings of Jesus and the writings of Paul. The tension and realism of this irony need to be applied fully to the emerging world situation of families, both within and outside of the church.

Concluding Words on Practical Theology, Theological Ethics, and the Social Sciences

Finally, near as our book is to the methodology of *Habits of the Heart*, it tries to be much more self-conscious about the obligations that hermeneutic social science should accept in arguing for, and not simply asserting, the normative horizon that it brings from the past. If hermeneutic social science accepted this responsibility, it would take a step toward

---

31. For an excellent discussion of ironic realism, see David Rhoads and Donald Michie, *Mark As Story: An Introduction to the Narrative of a Gospel* (Minneapolis: Fortress, 1982); for our use of ironic realism, see Browning et al., *From Culture Wars to Common Ground*, pp. 272-73.

moving into the arena of a hermeneutically oriented fundamental practical theology. The line between the social sciences and theology would still exist. Clearly, social sciences have the primarily obligation to refine our descriptions and explanations of social and psychological reality. But they can never do this fully without reference to ideals and ideas from the past; within the context of the West, this will inevitably lead, as Bellah has argued, to classics shaped by Jewish and Christian theology.[32] A fundamental practical theology can learn much from hermeneutic social science, but it is the task of theology to go beyond description and project commanding visions and norms informed by the Christian tradition yet critically tested for use in both church and society.

But within the practical hermeneutic interests of a fundamental practical theology, there is a great need for the more abstract systematic interests of theological ethics. These systematic interests will be pursued most relevantly when located within the overarching concerns of a fundamental practical theology. And, finally, the concrete actions of strategic practical theology will be most powerful when its original questions are informed by the more detailed inquiries of historical theology, systematic theology, and theological ethics. Strategic practical theology is tempted to short-circuit the full hermeneutic circle of a fundamental practical theology. But it must not. The complexity of the full task suggests that more and more, fundamental practical theology must be pursued as a cooperative interdisciplinary endeavor. Gradually universities and seminaries throughout the world must learn to train graduates in the collaborative efforts required by a fundamental practical theology. It is my conviction that only when this occurs can a genuine public theology be born and come to thrive.

32. Bellah et al., *Habits of the Heart,* pp. 28-32, 301.

Permissions and Acknowledgments

Each of the chapters in this volume had an earlier incarnation. I would like to thank the publishers below for their permission to reprint material from previously published sources:

Chapter 1, "Toward a Fundamental and Strategic Practical Theology," was originally published in *Shifting Boundaries: Contextual Approaches to the Structure of Theological Education,* ed. Barbara G. Wheeler and Edward Farley (Louisville: Westminster John Knox, 1991), pp. 295-328.

Chapter 2 was originally an address given at a meeting of ISERT (International Society for Empirical Research in Theology), University of Bielefeld, Germany, in April of 2004, and entitled, "Empirical Considerations in a Practical Theology of Families."

Chapter 3, "The Family Debate: A Middle Way," was first published in *The Christian Century* 110, no. 21 (July 14-21, 1993).

Chapter 4, "Is the Family a Conservative Issue?" was originally given as the Rerum Novarum Lecture, Catholic Archdiocese of Melbourne, Australia, on June 6, 1994.

Chapter 5, co-authored with Carol Browning, was first published as "Better Family Values," in *Christianity Today* 39, no. 2 (February 9, 1995): 29-32.

Chapter 6, "Children, Mothers, and Fathers in the Postmodern Family," appeared in *Pastoral Care and Social Conflict: Essays in Honor of Charles Gerkin,* ed. Pamela D. Couture and Rodney J. Hunter (Nashville: Abingdon, 1995), pp. 71-85.

Chapter 7, "Practical Theology and the American Family Debate," first appeared in the *International Journal of Practical Theology* 1 (1997): 136-60.

Chapter 8, "Altruism, Civic Virtue, and Religion," first appeared in *Seedbeds of Virtue: Sources of Competence, Character, and Citizenship,* ed. Mary Ann Glendon and David Blankenhorn (Lanham, Md.: Madison, 1995), pp. 105-29.

Chapter 9 was first published as "Biology, Ethics, and Narrative in Christian Family Theory," in *Promises to Keep: Decline and Renewal of Marriage in America,* ed. David Popenoe, Jean Bethke Elshtain, and David Blankenhorn (Lanham, Md.: Rowman and Littlefield, 1996), pp. 119-56.

Chapter 10, "The Dialectic of Archaeology and Teleology in Christian Marriage Symbolism," appeared first in *Currents in Theology and Mission* 28, nos. 3-4 (June-August 2001): 298-307.

Chapter 11, "Can Marriage Be Defined?" was originally published in *Word and World* 23, no. 1 (2003): 5-14.

Chapter 12, "The Task of Religious Institutions in Strengthening Families," was first circulated as a joint publication of the Religion, Culture and Family Project and the Communitarian Network, in August of 1998. That publication was adapted from Chapter 11 of *From Culture Wars to Common Ground,* by Don Browning, Bonnie Miller-McLemore, Pamela Couture, Bernie Lyon, and Robert Franklin (Louisville: Westminster John Knox, 1997).

Chapter 13 first appeared as "Critical Familism and the Reconstruction of Marriage," in *INTAMS Review* 9, no. 2 (2003): 216-27. That article was itself an extension of arguments and information found in chapter 1 and other parts of my *Marriage and Modernization* (Grand Rapids: Eerdmans, 2003).

Chapter 14 was originally published as "Egos without Selves: A Practical Theological Critique of the Family Theory of the Chicago School of Economics," in the *Annual of the Society of Christian Ethics* (Autumn 1994): 127-45.

Chapter 15, "Families and the Sixty-Hour Workweek: What It Means for Church, Society, and Persons," was first prepared for a lecture at Garrett-Evangelical Theological School in October of 2002.

Chapter 16 originally was published as "The Language of Health versus the Language of Religion: Competing Models of Marriage for the Twenty-First Century," in *Revitalizing the Institution of Marriage for the Twenty-First Century: An Agenda for Strengthening Marriage,* ed. Alan J. Hawkins, Lynn D. Wardle, and David Orgon Coolidge (Westport, Conn.: Praeger, 2002).

Chapter 17, "Critical Familism, Civil Society, and the Law," was presented at a conference on Family and Democracy at Hofstra Law School and was published in the *Hofstra Law Review* 32, no. 1 (Fall 2003): 313-29.

Chapter 18, "The Meaning of the Family in the Universal Declaration of Human Rights," was originally written as a plenary address for the Asian Pacific Dialogue on the Family conference held in October of 2004 and was earlier published in *The Family in the New Millennium*, ed. A. Scott Loveless and Thomas B. Holman (Westport, Conn.: Greenwood, 2006).

Chapter 19, "Adoption and the Moral Significance of Kin Altruism," was first published in *The Morality of Adoption: Social-Psychological, Theological, and Legal Perspectives,* ed. Timothy P. Jackson (Grand Rapids: Eerdmans, 2005), pp. 52-77.

Chapter 20, "Domestic Violence and the Ethic of Equal Regard," was originally prepared for a conference on domestic violence at the University of Leuven, Belgium, in February of 2005.

Chapter 21, "The Relation of Practical Theology to Theological Ethics," earlier appeared in *Reconsidering the Boundaries between Theological Disciplines,* ed. Michael Welker and Friedrich Schweitzer (Münster, Germany: LIT, 2005). A much shorter form of it appeared as the appendix to the second edition of *From Culture Wars to Common Ground: Religion and the American Family Debate,* which I co-authored with Bonnie Miller-McLemore, Pamela Couture, Bernie Lyon, and Robert Franklin (Louisville: Westminster John Knox, 2000).

Index

Adoption, ix, 193, 236, 347-50, 352, 355,
357-60, 362, 363, 365-73
Agape, 84, 96, 125, 170, 172, 186, 189,
190, 368, 371
Altruism, 44, 119-21, 131, 133, 134, 137,
138, 141, 143, 145, 154, 158, 161, 165,
189, 321, 330-39, 341-44, 347, 352-59,
361, 363, 365, 367, 368, 371, 372; kin
investment, 347-73
American (Family Debate), ix, 42, 51,
52, 63, 64, 70, 75, 76, 87, 103, 104, 111,
113, 115, 116, 121; family debate, 206,
284, 350, 392, 400
American Law Institute, 324
Aquinas, Thomas, ix, 37, 39, 44, 73, 87-
89, 121-27, 131, 135, 137, 139, 140, 141,
154, 155, 161-75, 180, 184-87, 189, 191,
194, 195, 197, 198-205, 210, 211, 215,
216n., 261, 278, 293-95, 301, 304, 305,
309, 317, 318, 334-38, 340, 341, 343,
352-54, 360, 361, 364, 367, 380, 382,
398, 399, 402-4
Aristotle, ix, 7, 8, 44, 88, 89, 106, 122,
131, 133, 135, 139-41, 155, 161, 164, 165,
176, 179, 180, 191, 198-200, 210-12, 214,
217, 258, 267, 278, 292, 301, 304-6, 309,
317, 331-35, 337, 343, 344, 353, 381, 382,
403
Augustine, 39, 123, 169, 197, 398

Becker, Gary, 39, 134, 263-70, 275-78,
280, 288, 300
Bellah, Robert, 33, 34, 39, 117, 146, 157,
268, 280, 290, 395, 408
Biology, vii, 73, 122, 123, 124, 137, 139,
140, 141, 154, 155, 157, 161, 173, 195,
198, 334, 337, 341, 366-68;
psychobiology, 154; sociobiology, 137,
143, 144, 157, 270, 342, 356
Brunner, Emil, 108, 125, 126, 339-41

Cahill, Lisa Sowle, 308, 336, 367, 368,
369, 370, 371, 372
Caritas, 97, 125, 170, 367
Catholic, Roman, 22, 46, 55, 61, 62, 70,
71, 73, 75, 85, 96, 97, 103, 105-7, 109-
12, 114, 120, 124-26, 140, 143, 161, 163,
173, 190, 211-13, 215, 216, 219, 225-30,
257, 259, 260, 271, 274, 275, 304, 305,
307, 316, 319, 321, 331, 334, 337-39, 341,
353, 354, 360, 361, 367-69, 371, 375,
378, 380, 382, 386, 387, 399, 402
Chicago School of Economics, 134,
263, 264, 266, 273, 288
Church, vii, viii, ix, 5, 6, 10, 13, 16-19,
22, 30, 32, 33, 36, 39, 41, 42, 44, 45, 51,
52, 55-60, 62-64, 68, 70-72, 74, 75, 77,
78, 80, 81, 83, 85, 87, 95, 97-100, 104-
7, 109, 123, 124, 126, 127, 133, 146-55,

161, 162, 169-71, 173, 184, 185, 187-91, 195, 197, 202, 203, 207-14, 217, 223, 224, 226-37, 241, 245, 257-62, 282-85, 294, 295, 314, 348-51, 354, 360, 361, 363, 369, 370, 380, 384, 386, 387, 398, 400, 403, 404, 407, 408

Civil Society, 40, 45, 46, 71, 131, 132, 133, 135, 136, 137, 139, 141, 143, 144, 145, 146, 147, 148, 150, 253, 210, 224, 226, 227, 228, 229, 235, 236, 239, 241, 254, 261, 265, 312, 313, 314, 316, 321, 322, 325, 326, 351, 358, 380

Co-habitation, Cohabitation, 38, 39, 55, 84, 104, 107, 209, 213, 244, 250-52, 257, 259-61, 271, 381

Covenant, 39, 41, 44, 86, 97, 103, 105, 106, 108, 207, 213, 215, 216, 240, 241, 252, 258, 262, 289, 316-20, 325, 339, 360-70, 394, 398

Critical Familism, vii, ix, 51, 61, 225, 226, 229, 230, 235, 237, 242, 243, 245, 254, 255, 286, 307, 312, 313, 314, 315, 316, 317, 319, 320, 321, 322, 323, 324, 325, 326, 327, 350, 351, 360, 365, 368, 371, 374, 400, 406

Cross, 45, 97, 125, 167, 187, 371, 376, 404

Divorce, 38-40, 53-55, 58, 59, 65, 66, 70, 76-79, 81, 84, 85, 90, 91, 93, 104, 105, 107, 109, 110, 112, 115, 118, 119, 134, 150, 156, 168, 169, 177, 178, 180, 187, 188, 193, 204, 209, 228, 229, 232-34, 240, 241, 250-54, 256, 258, 262, 268, 271, 273, 282, 299, 300, 312, 324, 325, 344, 348-50, 355, 381, 383, 397, 404

Dobson, James, 64, 79, 117

Doherty, William, 226, 233, 314

Eliade, Mircea, 171, 203

Engels, Frederick, 40, 92, 117, 289

Equal Regard, Equal-Regard, vii, ix, 44, 45, 51, 52, 57, 83-86, 95, 96-100, 125, 127-29, 131, 144, 150, 154-56, 175, 183, 188, 190-93, 206, 207, 217, 225, 227, 232, 233, 242, 255, 256, 262, 274, 275, 280-83, 297, 307-10, 313, 316, 317, 319, 320, 324, 325, 347, 350-52, 357, 359, 365, 371, 374-81, 384, 385, 387, 399-406

Eros, 368, 371

Evolutionary Psychology, 103, 120, 157, 195, 197, 199, 200, 204, 205, 294, 302, 306, 318, 335, 342-44, 353, 356, 367, 368, 382

Family, vii, viii, ix, x, xi, 4, 31, 32, 37-47, 51-60, 75-96, 98-100, 103-29, 131-35, 137-40, 142-45, 147-50, 152, 154-56, 158, 159, 161, 162, 165-67, 170, 173, 175-79, 181-83, 185-89, 192, 193, 197, 198, 200, 206, 210, 212-14, 216, 223-33, 235-39, 241-44, 246, 249, 250, 252-57, 262-66, 269-71, 273-77, 279, 281-85, 290, 295-97, 299, 300, 304, 306, 307, 310, 312-17, 319, 322-24, 326-31, 333-51, 354, 357-60, 363-65, 369, 371, 372, 374-76, 378, 380, 382-86, 392, 396-407; stepfamily, 204; as conservative issue, 61-74

Fathers, 44, 52, 54, 55, 57-59, 65, 66, 68, 73, 78, 79, 84, 86, 87, 90, 92, 109, 115, 116, 122, 140, 144, 157, 159, 164, 167, 168, 169, 173, 183, 186, 187, 199-202, 204, 206, 232, 235, 238-40, 245, 256, 257, 271, 272, 275, 279, 281, 282, 289, 295, 296, 307, 326, 333, 335, 338, 344, 349, 350, 377, 386

Frankena, William, 142, 316, 353

From Culture Wars to Common Ground (1997, 2000), ix, 42, 45n., 46n., 51, 61, 84, 202n., 206, 211n., 223, 225n., 245, 255, 256n., 262n., 283, 284, 288, 305n., 306, 307n., 309, 310, 313n., 318n., 323n., 335n., 350, 351n., 354, 357, 391, 392, 394-96, 397n., 398n., 399n., 400, 401, 404n., 405, 406

Fundamental Practical Theology (1991), vii, 3, 4, 6, 9, 11, 12, 14, 15, 18, 22, 26-29, 31-33, 35, 37, 147, 150, 154, 200, 280, 315, 391, 395, 396, 400, 401, 404-6, 408

Gadamer, Hans-Georg, vii, 3, 4, 5, 7, 8, 9, 11, 13, 14, 16, 20, 28, 33-35, 87, 136, 146, 247, 303, 317, 364, 394, 395

Giddens, Anthony, 39, 214

Good: moral, 301, 353, 354, 366, 372, 384; nonmoral goods, 29, 142, 268, 301; premoral, 116, 121, 125, 128, 200, 201, 208, 280, 297, 301, 304, 315, 316, 348, 353-55, 357, 359, 364, 365, 367, 372, 384, 401-4

Goode, William, 39, 249-53, 299

Habermas, Jürgen, viii, 4, 14, 21, 28, 29, 39, 40, 84, 93, 117, 129, 132, 133, 143, 248, 253, 265, 289, 315, 320, 322, 350, 357, 380, 405

Honor, and Shame, 43-45, 57, 72, 181-85, 187, 255, 256, 293-95, 309, 379, 380, 399

Human Rights, ix, 223, 246, 327-30, 337, 341, 342, 345, 346

Individualism, 21, 39, 42, 53, 56, 57, 65, 67, 76, 79, 91, 93, 95, 117, 118, 127-29, 157, 183, 205, 230, 252, 253, 266, 268, 269, 290, 298, 299, 358, 359, 397, 405

Janssens, Louis, ix, 85, 96, 127, 128, 142, 190, 191, 280, 281, 319, 351-53, 374-76, 378, 384, 404

Kant, Immanuel, 15, 45, 105, 128, 136, 141, 142, 144, 145, 217, 291, 292, 298, 314, 316, 319, 352, 362, 364, 375, 403

Kin Altruism. See Altruism: kin investment, 331, 370

Law, viii, ix, x, xi, 7, 18, 41, 46, 54-56, 59, 63, 72, 73, 103, 106, 107, 120, 126, 131, 137, 155, 167, 169, 173, 181, 188, 202, 208, 209, 211-18, 223, 224, 234, 240, 241, 253, 256, 257, 259-63, 265, 269-71, 273-75, 280-82, 288, 298, 300, 304, 306, 307, 312-14, 316, 318, 321-24, 326-31, 334, 336, 337, 339, 342, 343, 345, 346, 351, 360-62, 364, 365, 368, 370, 380, 386, 399

Leo XIII, 106, 211, 225, 305, 306, 337-39, 341, 353

Liberals, 61, 62, 64, 67, 69-71, 76-83, 105, 109, 110-12, 114, 117, 118, 151, 299

Locke, John, 211, 212, 214, 256, 305-7

Love, 39, 43-45, 78, 79, 85, 94-98, 100, 111, 112, 120, 122, 125, 127-29, 139, 140, 143, 149, 151, 152, 154, 164, 170-74, 180, 183-85, 187-89, 195, 196, 202, 203, 216-18, 234, 243, 256, 259, 266, 267, 275, 281, 286, 289, 291, 293-95, 297, 308, 309, 315, 320, 332, 333, 352, 358, 360-66, 368, 369, 371, 373, 376, 379, 386, 401, 403, 404; agape, 84, 96, 105, 125, 170, 172, 186, 187, 189, 190, 368, 371, 373, 375; caritas, 97 125, 170, 367; equal-regard, 44, 45, 57, 84, 85, 95-98, 100, 125, 127-29, 131, 155, 156, 188, 190-92, 217, 280, 282, 351, 352, 365, 371, 375, 376, 378, 380, 384, 385, 400, 402-6; eros, 368, 371

Luther, Martin, ix, 39, 96, 108, 125, 173-75, 184, 189, 212-16, 227, 257-59, 261, 282, 360, 361, 378, 380, 398, 399

Malik, Charles, 328, 329, 331, 333, 334, 336-38, 345

Marriage, vii, viii, ix, x, xi, 37-39, 41-47, 51-55, 58, 61, 65, 67, 72, 73, 75, 78, 79, 81, 84-86, 89, 93, 97, 103-12, 115-19, 121, 123, 125, 126, 129, 134, 154, 155, 157, 161, 162, 165, 167-76, 179, 182, 187-95, 197, 198, 200-202, 204, 206-19, 226-34, 236, 238-47, 249, 251-63, 266-68, 270, 271, 274, 275, 278-80, 282, 283, 285, 286, 289, 290, 293-95, 297-314, 316-29, 331, 333-44, 346, 347, 349, 350, 352, 355, 359-61, 364-69, 374, 375, 381, 383, 385-87, 397, 399, 402-6

Marriage and Modernization (2003), 42, 44n., 46, 84, 244, 245, 255n., 262n., 313n., 314n., 318n., 322n., 335n., 350, 351, 381, 391

McLanahan, Sara, 40, 77, 112, 113, 114, 116, 156n., 157n., 204, 300, 344n., 354, 355n.

Method in Practical Theology, 389-401

Midgley, Mary, 139, 140, 143, 163, 198n., 336, 353n., 356

Mill, John Stuart, 214, 278

Modernization, 46, 133, 244, 245, 246, 247, 248, 249, 251, 252, 253, 254, 257, 258, 261, 299, 312, 320, 347, 380, 381, 405

Mothers, 52-54, 58, 65-67, 69, 70, 75-77, 81, 82, 84, 86, 87, 90, 109, 115, 116, 119, 121, 144, 156, 157, 160, 174, 186, 187, 192, 202-4, 232, 238-40, 245, 250, 268, 269, 281, 289, 294, 295, 307, 324, 326, 327, 333, 335, 338, 343, 376, 377, 386, 397

Murray, Charles, 69, 81, 113

Mutuality, 79, 96-99, 112, 125, 128, 191, 193, 217, 266, 316, 350, 371, 376, 403, 404

Nachmanides, 37, 318, 333, 341

Niebuhr, Reinhold, 96, 107n., 376

Nygren, Anders, 96, 371, 376

Outka, Gene, 45, 84, 96, 127, 128, 352, 375, 376, 403

Ozment, Steven, 169n., 173n., 213n., 256, 282n.

Parents, 15, 40, 52-54, 58-60, 65, 66, 68-70, 73, 76, 77, 79, 82, 84, 86, 88-91, 93-95, 99, 104, 113, 114, 116, 120-23, 128, 134, 135, 138-40, 143, 144, 148, 156, 162, 164, 167, 180, 189, 193, 196, 198, 200, 204, 214, 218, 219, 225-27, 230, 232-34, 236-38, 240, 266, 267, 277, 285, 286, 300, 310, 319, 323, 325, 332-33, 335, 337-39, 342-44, 352-55, 357, 362, 363, 365-70, 372, 381, 383, 401, 406

Peters, Ted, 360-65, 369, 371

Plato, 88, 93, 133, 135, 139, 164, 165, 332, 339

Pope, Stephen, 140, 143, 163, 336, 354n.

Popenoe, David, 84, 89, 112, 113n., 116, 117, 122n., 157, 159, 161n., 171, 251-54, 272, 299n., 344n., 354

Posner, Richard, 39, 40n., 58, 86, 134, 137, 157, 161, 263-65, 267-81, 288, 300

Post, Stephen, 368-72

Practical Theology, vii, viii, ix, x, 5, 10, 6, 19, 25-27, 31-35, 38, 39, 44, 47, 85, 103-5, 109, 114, 132, 176, 223, 224, 263, 264, 288, 378, 391-95, 397, 400, 401; Fundamental, 3, 4, 6, 9, 11, 12, 17, 19, 22, 25-29, 31-33, 35, 37, 154, 347, 350, 391, 395, 396, 400, 401, 404-6, 408; Historical, 3, 4, 6, 9-11, 13, 17, 19-21, 23, 25, 26, 30, 31, 35, 36, 41, 154, 396, 399, 408; Systematic, 3, 4, 6, 9-11, 13, 14, 16-21, 23, 25-27, 29, 31, 35, 36, 41, 154, 176, 396, 400, 404, 408; Strategic, 4, 6, 9, 10, 13, 15-20, 29, 31, 35, 36, 41, 42, 46, 396, 400, 408

Premoral good. *See* Good: premoral

Religion, Culture, and Family Project, viii, ix, x, 4, 31, 38, 179, 263, 284, 285, 313, 350, 392

Research, vii, viii, ix, 4, 31, 32, 35, 36, 38, 40, 41, 43, 47, 64, 65, 66, 72, 76, 77, 82, 88, 110, 112, 113, 114, 134n., 168, 172, 182, 204, 223, 230, 234, 236, 237, 252, 272, 283, 285, 287, 297, 313, 316, 318, 321, 324, 325, 331, 354, 355, 377, 379, 380, 381, 406; critical, 3-47

Reweaving the Social Tapestry (2002), 42, 84, 245n., 262n., 286n., 287n., 313n., 323n., 350, 391

Ricoeur, Paul, viii, 4, 12, 13, 21, 33, 34-37, 120, 126, 127, 142, 161, 162, 172, 194-97, 203, 247, 292, 303, 351, 352, 365, 397

Sacrament, x, 39, 44, 73, 105, 106, 124, 154, 167-71, 173, 175, 197, 198, 201, 202, 207, 213-16, 257, 258, 260-62, 289, 295, 303, 318, 319, 335, 336, 339, 352, 370

Self-sacrifice, 96, 98, 99, 125, 127, 128, 145, 186-93, 266, 280, 376, 380

Shame, and Honor. *See* Honor, and Shame

Sixty-Hour Workweek, 45, 82, 232, 236-38, 283-87, 290, 293, 295, 296, 310, 312, 323, 325, 406

Society, vii, x, 16, 18, 22, 29, 31, 33, 35, 36, 40-43, 45, 46, 55, 57-60, 63, 68, 71, 82, 87, 89, 92, 94, 97, 105, 117, 119, 128, 131-33, 135-39, 141-48, 150, 151, 153, 161, 186, 207, 208, 209, 211, 214, 216, 218, 223, 235, 236, 239, 240-43, 245, 246, 250, 254, 255, 257, 259, 260, 261, 263, 265, 269-71, 273, 275, 279, 281, 283-88, 290, 291, 296, 297, 299, 302, 306, 310, 312-14, 316, 319-23, 325, 326, 328, 329, 331-34, 337, 339, 341, 342, 345, 347, 349, 351, 359, 358, 360, 363, 364, 369, 372, 376, 380, 382, 396, 400, 406, 408

Spheres of Creation, 108, 125

Stacey, Judith, 85, 86, 92, 95, 99, 150, 157, 161, 312

Subsidiarity, 106, 107, 109, 110, 225, 227, 229, 321, 331, 334, 337, 338, 386

Symbolism, 173, 175, 187, 194-98, 201-3, 339

Thatcher, Adrian, 244, 246, 247, 249, 254, 257-62

Tillich, Paul, 10-12, 349

Tracy, David, 11-13, 19, 20, 321n., 400

Universal Declaration of Human Rights, 327, 328n., 329n., 330, 341, 343, 345, 346

Van der Ven, Johannes, 5, 37n.

Violence, 65, 138, 183, 186, 210, 231, 234, 242, 332, 333, 344, 374-77, 379, 380, 382-84; domestic, 186, 374, 376-79, 381, 382, 384, 386, 387

Waters, Brent, 359, 360, 363, 366-69, 371, 372

Wilcox, Bradford, 314, 377, 380n.

Wilson, James Q., 52, 54, 58, 73, 161n., 273n., 356, 357

Wilson, Robin Fretwell, 344, 382, 383n.

Witte, John, x, 41, 55, 88n., 105n., 108, 207, 209n., 212-14n., 257n., 259n., 303n., 317n., 387n.

Wolfe, Alan, 40, 84, 117, 131-39, 141-46, 148, 251-54, 265, 266, 289, 320n., 393n.

Women, 42-46, 53, 54, 56, 57, 64, 68, 69, 72, 73, 79, 84, 85, 88-90, 92, 93, 96, 99, 100, 104, 107, 112, 115, 119, 124, 126-28, 139, 149, 150, 151, 156, 157, 166, 168, 171, 176-83, 186-89, 192, 194, 200-202, 204-7, 237, 240, 243, 245, 250, 251n., 253, 256, 257, 267, 268, 270, 271, 273-75, 282, 285, 288, 289, 293, 297, 300, 307, 309, 320, 323, 332, 351, 358, 370, 377-79, 385, 386, 397, 398, 403, 405

Work, and Family Issues, x, 286, 287